WARFARE, RITUAL, AND SYMBOL
IN BIBLICAL AND MODERN CONTEXTS

Society of Biblical Literature

Ancient Israel and Its Literature

Thomas C. Römer, General Editor

Editorial Board:
Suzanne Boorer
Mark G. Brett
Marc Brettler
Cynthia Edenburg
Victor H. Matthews
Gale A. Yee

Number 18

WARFARE, RITUAL, AND SYMBOL
IN BIBLICAL AND MODERN CONTEXTS

Edited by
Brad E. Kelle, Frank Ritchel Ames, and Jacob L. Wright

Society of Biblical Literature
Atlanta

Copyright © 2014 by the Society of Biblical Literature

All rights reserved. No part of this work may be reproduced or transmitted in any form or by any means, electronic or mechanical, including photocopying and recording, or by means of any information storage or retrieval system, except as may be expressly permitted by the 1976 Copyright Act or in writing from the publisher. Requests for permission should be addressed in writing to the Rights and Permissions Office, Society of Biblical Literature, 825 Houston Mill Road, Atlanta, GA 30329 USA.

Library of Congress Cataloging-in-Publication Data

Warfare, ritual, and symbol in biblical and modern contexts / edited by Brad Kelle, Frank R. Ames, and Jacob L. Wright.
    p. cm. — (Society of Biblical Literature ancient Israel and its literature ; 18)
Includes bibliographical references and index.
Summary: "Warfare, Ritual, and Symbol in Biblical and Modern Contexts is a collection of fifteen essays about rituals of war and their function. Comparative and interdisciplinary approaches are applied to texts in the Hebrew Bible, which are read in light of ancient Near Eastern literature, artifacts, and iconography and contemporary ritual and social theory. Introductory and concluding essays evaluate each contribution, locate contributions in the history of scholarship, and propose promising directions for further research. A majority of the essays were presented in 2010–2012 sessions of the SBL's Warfare in Ancient Israel Section"— Provided by publisher.
  ISBN 978-1-58983-958-8 (paper binding : alk. paper) — ISBN 978-1-58983-959-5 (electronic format) — ISBN 978-1-58983-960-1 (hardcover binding : alk. paper)
  1. War—Biblical teaching. 2. Bible. Old Testament—Criticism, interpretation, etc. 3. Middle Eastern literature—History and criticism. I. Kelle, Brad E., 1973–, editor. II. Ames, Frank Ritchel, editor. III. Wright, Jacob L., editor.
  BS1199.W2W37 2014
  221.8'355—dc23   2014002894

Printed on acid-free, recycled paper conforming to
ANSI/NISO Z39.48-1992 (R1997) and ISO 9706:1994
standards for paper permanence.

Contents

Abbreviations vii

Introduction
    Jacob L. Wright 1

Part 1: Social Determination of Rituals and Symbols

Theorizing Circumstantially Dependent Rites in and out of
    War Contexts
    Saul M. Olyan 15

Monumental Inscriptions and the Ritual Representation of War
    Nathaniel B. Levtow 25

Part 2: Rituals and Symbols of Escalation, Preparation, and Aggression

Joshua's Encounter with the Commander of Yhwh's Army (Josh
    5:13–15): Literary Construction or Reflection of a Royal Ritual?
    Thomas Römer 49

"A Sword for Yhwh and for Gideon!": The Representation
    of War in Judges 7:16–22
    Kelly J. Murphy 65

The Red-Stained Warrior in Ancient Israel
    Frank Ritchel Ames 83

"I Will Strike You Down and Cut off Your Head" (1 Sam 17:46):
Trash Talking, Derogatory Rhetoric, and Psychological
Warfare in Ancient Israel
David T. Lamb 111

"Some Trust in Horses": Horses as Symbols of Power in Rhetoric
and Reality
Deborah O'Daniel Cantrell 131

War Rituals in the Old Testament: Prophets, Kings, and the
Ritual Preparation for War
Rüdiger Schmitt 149

PART 3: RITUALS AND SYMBOLS OF PERPETUATION,
DE-ESCALATION, AND COMMEMORATION

Warfare Song as Warrior Ritual
Mark S. Smith 165

A Messy Business: Ritual Violence after the War
Susan Niditch 187

Postwar Rituals of Return and Reintegration
Brad E. Kelle 205

Does Yhwh Get His Hands Dirty? Reading Isaiah 63:1-6 in Light
of Depictions of Divine Postbattle Purification
Jason A. Riley 243

RESPONSE

Forging a Twenty-First-Century Approach to the Study of
Israelite Warfare
T. M. Lemos 271

Contributors 287
Index of Ancient Sources 289
Index of Modern Authors 301

Abbreviations

AB	Anchor Bible
ABD	*Anchor Bible Dictionary.* Edited by D. N. Freedman. 6 vols. New York: Doubleday, 1992.
ACCS	Ancient Christian Commentary on Scripture
ALASP	Abhandlungen zur Literatur Alt-Syren-Palästinas und Mesopotamiens
ANEP	*The Ancient Near East in Pictures Relating to the Old Testament.* Edited by J. B. Pritchard. Princeton: Princeton University Press, 1954.
ANET	*Ancient Near Eastern Texts Relating to the Old Testament.* Edited by J. B. Pritchard. 3rd ed. Princeton: Princeton University Press, 1969.
AOAT	Alter Orient und Altes Testament
AOTC	Apollos Old Testament Commentary
ArBib	The Aramaic Bible
AS	*Assyriological Studies*
ATD	Das Alte Testament Deutsch
BA	*Biblical Archaeologist*
BaM	*Baghdader Mitteilungen*
BASOR	*Bulletin of the American Schools of Oriental Research*
BBR	*Bulletin for Biblical Research*
BDB	Brown, F., S. R. Driver, and C. A. Briggs. *A Hebrew and English Lexicon of the Old Testament.* Oxford: Oxford University Press, 1907.
BETL	Bibliotheca ephemeridum theologicarum lovaniensium
BHS	*Biblia Hebraica Stuttgartensia.* Edited by K. Elliger and W. Rudolph. Stuttgart: Deutsche Bibelgesellschaft, 1983.
Bib	*Biblica*
BibInt	*Biblical Interpretation*
BibOr	Biblica et orientalia

BInS	Biblical Interpretation Series
BJS	Brown Judaic Studies
BKAT	Biblischer Kommentar, Altes Testament
BO	*Bibliotheca Orientalis*
BRev	*Bible Review*
BRS	The Biblical Resources Series
BWA(N)T	Beiträge zur Wissenschaft vom Alten (und Neuen) Testament
BZAW	Beihefte zur Zeitschrift für die alttestamentliche Wissenschaft
CAD	Oppenheim, A. Leo, et al., eds. *The Assyrian Dictionary of the Oriental Institute of the University of Chicago*. Chicago: The Oriental Institute, 1956–2010.
CAT	Commentaire de l'Ancien Testament
CBQ	*Catholic Biblical Quarterly*
CBR	*Currents in Biblical Research*
CHANE	Culture and History of the Ancient Near East
CKLS	Chuen King Lecture Series
COS	*The Context of Scripture*. Edited by W. W. Hallo. 3 vols. Leiden: Brill, 1997–2003.
CTH	Laroche, Emmanuel. *Catalogue des textes hittites*. Paris: Klincksieck, 1971
CTN	Cuneiform Texts from Nimrud
CTU	*The Cuneiform Alphabetic Texts from Ugarit, Ras Ibn Hani, and Other Places*. Edited by M. Dietrich, O. Loretz, and J. Sanmartín. Münster: Ugarit Verlag, 1995.
DJD	Discoveries in the Judean Desert
Dtr	Deuteronomistic
ER	*The Encyclopedia of Religion*. Edited by Mircea Eliade. 16 vols. New York: Collier Macmillan, 1987.
ERE	*Encyclopedia of Religion and Ethics*. Edited by J. Hastings. 13 vols. New York: Scribner, 1908–1927. Reprint, 7 vols., 1951.
ErIsr	*Eretz-Israel*
ESV	English Standard Version
ETCSL	Black, Jeremy, et al., *The Electronic Text Corpus of Sumerian Literature*. Oxford: University of Oxford, Faculty of Oriental Studies, 1998–2006.
FAT	Forschungen zum Alten Testament
FCB	Feminist Companion to the Bible

GKC	Gesenius, Friedrich W., E. Kautzsch, and A. E. Cowley. *Gesenius' Hebrew Grammar*. Oxford: Clarendon, 1980.
HALOT	Koehler, L., W. Baumgartner, and J. J. Stamm, *The Hebrew and Aramaic Lexicon of the Old Testament*. Translated and edited under the supervision of M. E. J. Richardson. 4 vols. Leiden: Brill, 1994–1999.
HAR	*Hebrew Annual Review*
HAT	Handbuch zum Alten Testament
HB	Hebrew Bible
HR	*History of Religions*
HSM	Harvard Semitic Monographs
HTKAT	Herders Theologischer Kommentar zum Alten Testament
HTR	*Harvard Theological Review*
HUCA	*Hebrew Union College Annual*
ICC	International Critical Commentary
IEJ	*Israel Exploration Journal*
Int	*Interpretation*
JAAR	*Journal of the American Academy of Religion*
JANES	*Journal of the Ancient Near Eastern Society*
JAOS	*Journal of the American Oriental Society*
JBL	*Journal of Biblical Literature*
JBQ	*Jewish Bible Quarterly*
JBS	Jerusalem Bible Studies
JCS	*Journal of Cuneiform Studies*
JHS	*Journal of Hellenic Studies*
JNES	*Journal of Near Eastern Studies*
JNSL	*Journal of Northwest Semitic Languages*
JR	*Journal of Religion*
JRitSt	*Journal of Ritual Studies*
JSOT	*Journal for the Study of the Old Testament*
JSOTSup	Journal for the Study of the Old Testament Supplement Series
JSS	*Journal of Semitic Studies*
KAI	*Kanaanäische und aramäische Inschriften*. H. Donner and W. Röllig. 2nd ed. Wiesbaden: Harrassowitz, 1966–1969.
KTU	*Die keilalphabetischen Texte aus Ugarit*. Edited by Manfred Dietrich, Oswald Loretz, and Joaquín Sanmartín. AOAT 24/1. Neukirchen-Vluyn, 1976. 2nd enlarged ed. of *KTU: The Cuneiform Alphabetic Texts from Ugarit, Ras Ibn Hani,*

	and Other Places. Edited by M. Dietrich, O. Loretz, and J. Sanmartín. Münster: Ugarit Verlag, 1995 (= *CTU*).
LÄ	*Lexicon der Ägyptologie*. Edited by W. Helck, E. Otto, and W. Westendorf. Wiesbaden: Harrassowitz, 1972.
LHBOTS	Library of Hebrew Bible/Old Testament Study
LUT	Luther
LXX	Septuagint
MdB	Le Monde de la Bible
MT	Masoretic Text
NAC	New American Commentary
NASB	New American Standard Bible
NCBC	New Cambridge Bible Commentary
NEA	*Near Eastern Archaeology*
NEchtB	Neue Echter Bibel
NIBCOT	New International Biblical Commentary on the Old Testament
NICOT	New International Commentary on the Old Testament
NIDOTTE	*New International Dictionary of Old Testament Theology and Exegesis*. Edited by Willem A. VanGemeren. 5 vols. Grand Rapids: Zondervan, 1997.
NIV	New International Version
NRSV	New Revised Standard Version
OBO	Orbis biblicus et orientalis
ÖBS	Österreichische biblische Studien
OBT	Overtures to Biblical Theology
Or	*Orientalia* (NS)
OTL	Old Testament Library
OtSt	*Oudtestamentische Studiën*
PEQ	*Palestine Exploration Quarterly*
Proof	*Prooftexts: A Journal of Jewish Literary History*
PTSD	Post-Traumatic Stress Disorder
QD	Quaestiones Disputate
RevExp	Review and Expositor
RGG⁴	*Religion in Geschichte und Gegenwart*. 4th ed. Edited by H. D. Betz, Don S. Browning, Bernd Janowski, and Eberhard Jüngel. 9 vols. Tübingen: Mohr Siebeck, 1998–2007.
RHR	*Revue de l'historie des religions*
RIMA	The Royal Inscriptions of Mesopotamia, Assyrian Periods
RIME	The Royal Inscriptions of Mesopotamia, Early Periods

RINAP	Royal Inscriptions of the Neo-Assyrian Period
SAA	State Archives of Assyria
SAAS	State Archives of Assyria Studies
SB	Standard Babylonian
SBLABS	Society of Biblical Literature Archaeology and Biblical Studies
SBLDS	Society of Biblical Literature Dissertation Series
SBLRBS	Society of Biblical Literature Resources for Biblical Studies
SBLSymS	Society of Biblical Literature Symposium Series
SBLWAW	Society of Biblical Literature Writings from the Ancient World
SBTS	Sources for Biblical and Theological Study
SBV	Standard Babylonian Version
SemeiaSt	Semeia Studies
SJOT	*Scandinavian Journal of the Old Testament*
STAR	Studies in Theology and Religion
SubBi	Subsidia Biblica
TDOT	Botterweck, G. Johannes, Helmer Ringgren, and Heinz-Josef Fabry. *Theological Dictionary of the Old Testament*. Translated by David E. Green. 15 vols. Grand Rapids: Eerdmans, 1974–2006.
TOTC	Tyndale Old Testament Commentaries
UF	*Ugarit-Forshungen*
VT	*Vetus Testamentum*
VTSup	Supplements to Vetus Testamentum
WBC	Word Biblical Commentary
WTJ	*Westminster Theological Journal*
WW	*Word and World*
ZA	*Zeitschrift für Assyriologie*
ZABR	*Zeitschrift für altorientalische und biblische Rechtgeschichte*
ZAW	*Zeitschrift für die alttestamentliche Wissenschaft*
ZDPV	*Zeitschrift des deutschen Palästina-Vereins*

Introduction

Jacob L. Wright

Warfare, Ritual, and Symbol in Biblical and Modern Contexts is a collection of twelve essays (and a response essay) about war-related rituals and symbols and their functions in textual, historical, and social contexts. Most of the essays feature comparative and interdisciplinary approaches applied to texts in the Hebrew Bible, which are read in light of ancient Near Eastern literature, artifacts, and iconography, as well as contemporary ritual and social theory. The editors hope this volume will make a timely contribution to a growing concentration on the ways social theory and ritual studies can contribute to the interpretation of biblical texts and ancient social realities, especially those related to warfare.

Because of the collection's interdisciplinary character—including essays that treat theoretical aspects of ritual and society as well as exegetical and historical matters—it will be of interest to a wide range of scholars whose research areas include archaeological, sociological, anthropological, ritual, and literary dimensions, especially in war-related texts and contexts. The mixture of theoretical examinations with particular historical and exegetical treatments will provide biblical scholars with new perspectives on Israelite warfare and its related rituals and symbols and will also be of interest to scholars working outside of biblical scholarship in fields related to military studies and social theory.[1]

---

1. This volume follows the interdisciplinary success of the most recent publication to come from the SBL Warfare in Ancient Israel Section. *Interpreting Exile: Displacement and Deportation in Biblical and Modern Contexts* (ed. Brad E. Kelle, Frank Ritchel Ames, and Jacob L. Wright; SBLAIL 10 [Atlanta: Society of Biblical Literature, 2011]) was recently selected as one of ten books on religion from 2011 for an award by the American Association of University Presses and was recommended for public and secondary school libraries. The award was in the category of works

Wars and warfare shaped the historical development and religious traditions of ancient Israel. They serve as leitmotifs in the narrative, poetic, and prophetic literatures of the Hebrew Bible. And they remain topics of interest and importance in biblical scholarship. Useful monographs and multiauthor works have been published on Israel's epic conflicts and historic battles, on its military tactics and strategic technologies, on its armies and heroic warriors, on comparative literature and ancient Near Eastern contexts, and on ideologies and ethics of war. But many questions remain, including questions about symbolism and rituals:

(1) What constitutes a symbol in war?
(2) What rituals were performed, and why?
(3) How did symbols and rituals function in and between wars and battles?
(4) What differing effects did they have on insiders and outsiders?
(5) In what ways did symbols and rituals function as instruments of war, the formation of states, and social reintegration?
(6) What role did they play in the production and use of texts?

The present volume is prompted by a collective interest to answer these and other questions pertaining to symbol and ritual as strategic elements in ancient Israelite warfare and as referents and components in the rhetoric of the Hebrew Bible. A majority of the essays were presented in 2010–12 sessions of the SBL Warfare in Ancient Israel Section. Both established and emerging scholars have contributed essays, which together showcase depth and breadth of the critical inquiry, along with the application of comparative and interdisciplinary approaches and social theory. The essays address questions about ritual behavior and symbolism in ancient Israelite warfare and related biblical texts and make six contributions to biblical scholarship in this area:

(1) They propose definitions of ritual and symbol for future warfare research.

"with a wide appeal and/or an expectation of lasting importance, [which] may also be of scholarly technical data on subjects of widespread, current interest."

(2) They set forth typologies of war-related rituals, their settings, and functions.
(3) They identify previously unrecognized rituals and symbolism in ancient Israelite warfare and related biblical texts.
(4) They compare emic and etic perspectives on the rites and symbols of war.
(5) They describe how symbolic acts and objects convey power, perpetuate violence, reintegrate combatants into communities, produce and are products of texts, and function as social agents and psychological weapons of war.
(6) They offer new insight into the provenance, structure, imagery, and interpretation of a variety of war-related texts in the Hebrew Bible.

The essays offer a further contribution as they approach the above topics. The articles extend the study of war-related rituals and symbols beyond the context of ancient Israel and the Hebrew Bible. Several explore connections between these elements and contemporary rituals and practices within modern militaries and societies. Others engage scholarship on rituals and symbols that appears in contemporary psychology, military studies, and clinical literature. The diverse perspectives, theoretical proposals, and specific case studies that emerge from these intersections provide new resources for biblical scholarship's ongoing consideration of the various dimensions and significance of warfare, ritual, and symbol, as well as the possible contributions such Israelite rituals and symbols might make to the study of modern realities related to warfare's execution and effects.

The essays fall along three coordinates: (1) Social Determination of Rituals and Symbols; (2) Rituals and Symbols of Escalation, Preparation, and Aggression; and (3) Rituals and Symbols of Perpetuation, De-escalation, and Commemoration.

The first group of essays explores how the meanings and functions of war-related rituals and symbols are textually, socially, and culturally determined in and by different contexts. Saul Olyan's opening piece examines a range of rites in biblical texts whose meaning depends on the circumstances depicted. These "circumstantially dependent rites" differ, on the one hand, from ritual actions that are injurious to a victim under any and all circumstances (for example, blinding; public genital exposure), and on the other hand, from ritual actions that always produce some kind of benefit to both agent and patient (for example, honorable burial of the dead;

clothing the naked). In contrast, the rites treated by Olyan can harm or humiliate an enemy, or they can create enmity or provoke military conflict—all depending upon circumstances. These include shaving and other forms of hair manipulation; disinterment and movement of the remains of the dead; the burning of corpses or bones; and circumcision. The question that guides Olyan's investigation is: What makes circumstantially dependent rites distinctive? The approach to the problem is exemplary in the care and precision with which its author treats all the evidence. The answers provided include identity of the agent, intent, and the potential role played by coercion. Circumstantially dependent rites can have either a winner and a loser or two beneficiaries. But the agent always profits in some way.

Nathaniel Levtow examines the ritual dimensions of Mesopotamian and biblical conquest "monuments." He discusses how Mesopotamian royal monumental victory inscriptions legitimize and perpetuate conquest and hegemony through their patterned inscriptions and ritual manipulation. Levtow calls attention to the ritual environments of monumental inscriptions and the ways they fulfill ritual roles in times of both war and peace. The ritual contexts of ancient Near Eastern monumental inscriptions are attested by three overlapping sets of evidence: (1) narrative accounts that depict monumental inscriptions engaged in ritual roles and settings; (2) ritual archaeological contexts in which monumental inscriptions have been excavated; and (3) monumental inscriptions that specify their ritual manipulation. For example, some of the earliest narratives of war, from the Early Dynastic Period in Mesopotamia, depict the ritual violation of boundary stones as a *casus belli*. Just as monumental inscriptions could be strategically erected and manipulated, they could also be removed and ritually violated. The archaeological evidence indicates that the stone monuments were erected near sanctuaries and city gates, as well as mountain passes—all ritually significant spaces. And in some cases there is evidence for the ritualized inscription and erection of the monuments.

In light of the available evidence, Levtow treats (1) the inscribed content of the monuments, (2) their social location, and (3) their social roles (namely, as the recipients of rituals and as the targets of attack). All the comparanda he collates elucidate both archaeological evidence from Israel (for example, the Tel Dan inscription) and biblical texts (for example, the Ebal traditions in Deuteronomy and Joshua). Levtow finally extends the discussion to cover weapons and "ritualized instruments of war." His wide-ranging conclusion will prove particularly useful to many who examine warfare in relation to ritual and symbol.

The second group of essays explores rituals and symbols that relate to the escalation, preparation, and aggression involved in the initiation and execution of war. Thomas Römer's contribution gives an unusually rich backdrop to the account of an exchange between the Commander of Yhwh's army and Joshua on the eve of the conquest (Josh 5:13–15). Römer begins by showing that this account is not, as assumed by many scholars, missing its conclusion. He suggests that the passage describes what Joshua sees in a vision, comparing the scene to a seventh-century B.C.E. account of Ashurbanipal's vision before his campaign against the Elamites in the official account of that campaign. This discussion provides a point of departure for a broad survey of related prebattle mantic rituals. By means of this survey, which is invaluable in its own right, Römer shows how the sword figures in the Joshua account in a similar manner to prebattle rituals in which kings receive a weapon from a deity.

Kelly Murphy's essay also treats this theme of the sword of Yhwh as a symbol of war's aggression, examining an excerpt from the Gideon account in the book of Judges. Although the featured battle in Judg 7 depicts no hand-to-hand combat between the Israelites and Midianites, it faithfully portrays some realities and practices of ancient warfare, while also adding various literary symbols and additions in order to address the book's larger concern with issues of power. Through an examination of the composition history of the text, in particular the now decontextualized "sword of Yhwh," the essay argues that the passage functions to transform the hesitant Gideon of Judg 6:1–7:15 back into the "mighty warrior" of the oldest Gideon traditions. Yet even while Gideon appears as a "mighty warrior," the final editors of the story make it explicit that it is the deity, though working with and through his human agent, who is ultimately responsible for the victory against the Midianites. Murphy's redactional analysis shows how the defeat of the Midianites is ultimately more symbolically than militarily significant. Israel's fighters are the underdogs, and, if they prevail, it is because the deity is with them, just as promised in the prebattle oracular ritual. The narrative downplays Gideon's military prowess for which he was likely celebrated through the ages (at least among some clans).

Frank Ames looks at the color red as a symbol for the status of warriors in the preparation for and execution of battle. Weapons, garments, and bodies of ancient Israelite warriors were reddened by the blood of the adversaries who had been wounded or slain in battle. Ancient Israelite warriors may also have stained their bodies red before engaging in battle.

Ames evaluates the evidence for body staining and explains its likely functions in the context of war. He considers at length modern theories, ancient Near Eastern contexts, as well as biblical and comparative texts. As Ames shows in his nuanced reading, when the red stain is actually blood, it serves as an "index," a sign that the warrior (both man and woman) has made a kill. When the stain is red dye, it serves as an "icon" representing blood, with its life-and-death valences. The observer should in both cases recognize the warrior's lethal, irresistible power. Aside from being used perhaps as a color to mark rank and belonging, the color indicated ruddiness and physical health, as well as offering the warrior a tactical advantage by intimidating the observer.

A common prebattle activity in various cultures is derogatory rhetoric and taunting speech. David Lamb shows how "trash talking," far from being an innovation of modern athletics, was a staple in ancient military contexts, the prerequisite *hors d'oeuvres*, to whet the appetite for battle. Examples of derogatory military rhetoric can be found in Egyptian sources being used by Thutmose III, Sethos I, and Ramesses II, and in the Hebrew Bible by Ahab, Elijah, Jezebel, Jehu, and David in his encounter with the Philistine giant. Lamb seeks to show how analysis of this type of psychological warfare in biblical literature elucidates some of the most colorful dialogue of the Hebrew Bible and provides an interpretive key to understanding the social dynamic behind these texts. Lamb's work draws on Geoffrey David Miller's categorizations of verbal feuding in the book of Judges, which include boasts, insults, parries, and responses to insults. Lamb situates his own research in a comparative context that includes both modern practices and evidence from the ancient world. This wider perspective draws attention to features and emphases in many biblical texts (the article focuses on narrative passages) that one might otherwise miss.

Deborah O'Daniel Cantrell's article looks at how horses figure as symbols of power in biblical literature. The warhorse was the ultimate symbol of power and destruction in the ancient world because of its effectiveness as a lethal weapon. Due to its unsurpassed speed, the horse was also the definitive symbol of freedom and deliverance. From a military perspective, trained warhorses were essential to the survival of Israel and Judah during the monarchic period. The essay explores the rhetoric of the Hebrew Bible prophets and poets who recognized the awe and reverence inspired by warhorses, but viewed them as a dangerous threat to their political and religious agendas. Cantrell draws on firsthand knowledge of horses and riding, and her contribution is informed by a remarkable wealth of information related to ancient warfare.

No military action in the ancient Near East could be undertaken without preceding ritual acts and omina. Rüdiger Schmitt's essay draws on comparative evidence to analyze biblical accounts of war oracles, execration rituals, and related preparatory symbolic actions by prophets. Schmitt provides a typology of the different kinds of rituals, their socio-religious setting, and their military and political functions. He treats the iconographic evidence from Iron Age Israelite and Judean seals and shows how they relate to the textual evidence.

Schmitt's treatment reveals how ritual strategies were regarded as critical to secure military success. Due to their literary character, the biblical narratives about interventions of men of god and prophets in military campaigns do not directly reflect, according to Schmitt, ritual interventions by prophets that can be used to reconstruct war rituals. The texts are not historical accounts of military campaigns and cannot be used for the reconstruction of preexilic war ideologies and related ritual practices. Nevertheless, Schmitt maintains that these stories do reflect how prophets and men of god participated in military campaigns. He draws two conclusions: (1) the ritual practices of war preparation, in particular prophetic consultations and execration rituals, did not differ in ancient Israel, Egypt, and Mesopotamia, and (2) these practices should be understood in the context of the closely related concepts of kingship and divinely authorized war in the ancient Near East.

The third group of essays explores the rituals and symbols related to perpetuation, de-escalation, and commemoration as war moves toward conclusion and becomes historical memory. Mark Smith researches early biblical poetry in this regard. By focusing on issues of dating, past scholarly discussions have failed to recognize a significant feature of early Israelite textual production beginning in the premonarchic period (Iron I), namely, that the texts focus to a great extent on war and warriors. Smith argues that warfare inspired the composition of several of these relatively early poems. Postbattle laments such as 2 Sam 1 may be understood as a ritualized behavior that served to create a community of shared mourners. The poem as a whole generated a communal identity for a "post-Saulide 'Israel.'" Smith speaks of David's lament as "a ritual instrument of public speech" that constitutes its audience as political subjects—that is, as "David's Israel."

According to Smith, the tradition of early heroic poetry was in no small way the domain of women, and it is arguable that a good deal of early Israelite heroic poetry should be situated in the context of oral women's song. Thanks to the work of Eunice Poethig, Carol Meyers, Sarit Paz, Susan Ackerman, and others, we have a number of excellent studies on the role of women in postbattle ritual. Smith cites the imaginative act represented by the poem of Judg 5. By means of the first-person voice, the author of that poem uses the figure of Deborah to dramatize postbattle victory. Deborah is the model of communal memory, one who commemorates a primordial, foundational conflict. Her example inspires the composer in the choice of poetic elements. With respect to ritual, Smith states that "while perhaps not ritualistic in a traditional religious sense, [the poem] is arguably a sort of political ritual that uses pieces of the past for its audience to participate in and thus to be literally in-formed." Judges 5 takes older (Iron I) pieces of a heroic, but "arguably insufficiently political, past" and "prepares its audiences for royal governance across tribal lines." Thus Smith implies that the poem does not hold up Yhwh as Israel's one, true king, as many would interpret its message.

Susan Niditch begins her piece on ritual violence after war with a reference to the psychoanalyst Jonathan Shay. After the cessation of combat, normal life is expected to resume. But this is not the case. Shay observes in his book *Achilles in Vietnam*[2] the many ways in which the traumatic experience of war makes itself felt in the lives of soldiers long after they have departed from the battlefield. Shay brings classical texts to bear on his research; Niditch shows how a number of biblical texts deal with the "loose ends" after the battle, reflecting concerns with reciprocity (implicit in vows), guilt, and group identity. Some of these texts relate to *events* following war, and others to dealings with human *captives* and captured *objects*. The biblical authors explore the options of dealing with these objects and captives, ranging from elimination to absorption.

One set of passages that Niditch discusses relates to war vows, vows gone awry, or tensions involving the interpretation of war vows (Josh 7, Judg 11, and 1 Sam 15). They point back to unresolved issues stemming from ritual actions that preceded and framed the fighting. In each case, acts of controlled sacrificial violence mark the exit from a particular war. To resolve the conflicts created by the vows, the actors resort to various forms of controlled ritual violence: the sacrifice of Jephthah's daughter; the

---

2. Jonathan Shay, *Achilles in Vietnam: Combat Trauma and the Undoing of Character* (New York: Scribner, 1995).

execution of Achan and Agag; the forcible taking of women for Benjamin. Another set of texts (Num 31:1–24; Deut 21:10–14) more overtly reflects an effort to transition from the violence of combat to the state of peace. But this transition too is achieved with violence. These texts reflect a conscious acknowledgment of the boundaries between wartime and peacetime. One might mention other texts that do the same, like 1 Kgs 2:5. But the texts discussed by Niditch do not simply acknowledge the boundary. They are concerned with the transition back to the normal conditions after war, and they seek this transition through symbolically charged ritual means, which include aspects of sacrifice, purification, and transformation.

Brad Kelle's essay shares the focus on postwar transitions for soldiers and communities. The essay's goal is to explore the possible indications of postwar rituals of return and reintegration within the Hebrew Bible. Kelle maps the Hebrew Bible texts that possibly present postwar rituals of return and reintegration and then considers them against the backdrop of other such rituals from the ancient Near East and elsewhere. In a subsequent, but more tentative and suggestive move, he concludes with an interdisciplinary engagement that explores some potential points of connection between these rituals and perspectives within contemporary warfare studies and psychology that may illuminate the symbolic functions of the rituals and why they take the shapes they do.

Kelle's essay is a model of the interdisciplinary approach to the study of war. It begins with two preliminary considerations. The first helpfully questions the preoccupation of past studies of war in the Bible with "holy war" or "Yhwh war." The second consideration relates to the nature of the evidence: what do we do when the biblical materials do not permit a comprehensive or even reliable picture of a phenomenon such as postwar rituals? The essay itself provides a very useful taxonomy of postbattle ritual activities, which include (1) purification of warriors, captives, and objects; (2) appropriation of booty; (3) construction of memorials and monuments; (4) celebration or procession; and (5) lament. It then concludes by engaging the emerging category of "moral injury" within psychology, military studies, and clinical literature in order to examine the possible symbolic functions of the biblical rituals, once again placing the subject within a thoroughly interdisciplinary context.

Jason Riley's essay directs a similar postwar ritual question to Israel's deity rather than Israel's warriors: "Does Yhwh get his hands dirty?" Did acts of killing or contact with blood defile the Israelite deity, as in the case of other ancient Near Eastern gods? Riley begins by cataloguing references of divine defilement and purification, with references to human defilement (in wartime) included in the footnotes. What he shows is that the Sumerian and Assyrian mythological examples parallel the acts of ritual purification described in royal inscriptions. Thus, the ancient Near Eastern deities were not impervious to impurity. Just as they could be defiled, they required purification, particularly after battle. Riley then asks whether there are comparable cases for Yhwh in the Hebrew Bible. The deity is often depicted as one who is actively involved in battle, with him as the subject of violent deeds. Riley focuses especially on Isa 63:1–6 and argues that this piece of poetry describes Yhwh returning from battle with garments soaked in blood. There is no reference to ritual purification in this text though, which raises the question: Does the passage suggest that Yhwh became ritually impure from his actions on the battlefield? To answer that question, Riley takes us on a detailed examination of two lines, with a significant payoff pointing toward an ancient Israelite conception that Yhwh could undergo war-related defilement and purification.

This preview should suffice to whet the reader's appetite for the many good things to be found in the following essays. As with any such collection, this volume offers a limited and necessarily incomplete treatment of war-related rituals and symbols. Even so, it successfully unites two significant trends in contemporary scholarship: (1) study of the realities and representations of war in ancient Israel and the Hebrew Bible, and (2) study of Israelite ritual and symbol, especially in dialogue with contemporary ritual theory. Still, the essays here constitute only an early move toward a comprehensive study of warfare, ritual, and symbol as they intersect in the biblical texts, making important contributions but also revealing often-unquestioned assumptions, overlooked dimensions, and possible new (or better) directions. In order to elucidate these elements and show how the essays might encourage further research, T. M. Lemos provides an evaluative and constructive response to the volume as a whole. Her concluding essay reflects attentively on some of the overarching themes, noteworthy findings, differing methodologies, as well as gaps in these articles. Most importantly, she gathers the essays' contributions and missing pieces in order to explore the possible form and content of a "twenty-first century approach" to the study of warfare. Whatever that form and content might be, perhaps this volume successfully makes the case that the future study of warfare in ancient Israel and the Hebrew Bible must include sustained attention to the multiple dimensions of ritual and symbol as they appear in various textual, historical, and social contexts.

Bibliography

Kelle, Brad E., Frank Ritchel Ames, and Jacob L. Wright, eds. *Interpreting Exile: Displacement and Deportation in Biblical and Modern Contexts*. Society of Biblical Literature Ancient Israel and Its Literature 10. Atlanta: Society of Biblical Literature, 2011.

Shay, Jonathan. *Achilles in Vietnam: Combat Trauma and the Undoing of Character.* New York: Scribner, 1995.

Part 1
Social Determination of Rituals and Symbols

Theorizing Circumstantially Dependent Rites in and out of War Contexts

Saul M. Olyan

In this essay I examine the wartime and nonwartime functions of a number of rites whose meaning is entirely dependent on circumstance. Such rites can be used by an agent to physically harm and/or humiliate an established foe or to create a new enemy and initiate war. But many texts suggest that they may also have beneficial functions for both the agents and those upon whom they act under certain circumstances, including in wartime. Such rites include shaving and other forms of hair manipulation; disinterment and the movement of the remains of the dead; the burning of corpses or bones; and circumcision. These circumstantially dependent rites contrast with other ritual acts that are injurious to a victim under any and all circumstances (for example, public stripping and genital exposure, blinding, or severing body parts of an enemy or offender; nonburial of the remains of the dead). They also differ from ritual action that always produces some kind of benefit to both agent and patient (for example, honorable burial of the dead; clothing the naked). What is it that makes circumstantially dependent rites distinct? In order to address this question, I examine the roles of intent, force, agency, and cultural norms in shaping circumstantially dependent ritual action.[1]

I begin with examples of noncircumstantially dependent rites. These are harmful or salutary under all circumstances, resulting in either physical and/or psychological injury (for example, shame) or in some kind of gain

---

[1]. This piece has been modified slightly (with permission) from the original published version. See Saul M. Olyan, "Theorizing Circumstantially Dependent Rites in and out of War Contexts," in *"The One Who Sows Bountifully": Essays in Honor of Stanley K. Stowers* (ed. Caroline Johnson Hodge et al.; BJS 356; Providence, R.I.: Brown Judaic Studies, 2013), 69–76.

(for example, honor) for the patient. (In each instance, the agent benefits, as I shall discuss.) Such noncircumstantially dependent rites are significant, as they provide a basis for establishing the distinctiveness of circumstantially dependent rites. My first example is the blinding of a defeated foe, in this case Zedekiah of Judah as narrated in 2 Kgs 25:7. Such blinding is one example of a wartime rite of punishment that is obviously never salutary for the patient. In this case, a defect (מום) that results in serious disability and, very likely, considerable shame, is imposed forcibly on the body of the victim. Although no explicit idioms of humiliation are used in this particular narrative, blindness imposed by an enemy is directly linked to reproach (חרפה) in 1 Sam 11:2. Furthermore, blindness is a divine curse in Deut 28:28-29, where it is associated with abandonment, helplessness, and victimization; these associations suggest shame indirectly, as other texts demonstrate.[2] Public stripping of a defeated enemy and his dependents is a second example of a rite that injures the victim without regard to circumstance, but in this case, the harm is exclusively psychological. In Isa 20:3-4, forced nudity is part of the experience of defeat and exile and is a source of humiliation for the victim.[3] Similarly, Lam 1:8 associates the exposure of the genitals of personified, defeated Jerusalem with her diminishment: "All who honored her deride her," // "For they have seen her nakedness." Nonburial of an enemy's corpse, an act that could result in mutilation by animals and birds, is a common *topos* in war narratives, as is the severing of body parts from a corpse—acts with which David threatens Goliath in 1 Sam 17:46. The public exhibition of an enemy's (often mutilated) corpse by hanging it on a tree or wall is another common motif in narratives of war, well illustrated by the Philistines' display of the stripped, headless corpse of Saul on the wall of Beth Shean (1 Sam 31:8-10). Other wartime rites that evidently shame an enemy under any and all circumstances include the tossing of a corpse (שלך, *hiphil*) in a public place instead of its honor-

---

2. Rejection by Yhwh is said to be shaming in Ps 53:6, as is defeat by and flight before an enemy in 2 Sam 19:4 (see also Jer 9:18; Ezek 7:18). Conversely, victory in battle confers honor to the victor (2 Kgs 14:10).

3. As indicated by the somewhat awkward ערות מצרים at the end of the verse, which is probably best rendered "[to the] shame of Egypt" in the context (see H. Niehr, "ערה 'ārâ," *TDOT* 11:346; NJPS; NRSV). See also Isa 47:3, regarding defeated Babylon: "Your nakedness (ערוה) will be revealed" // "Your reproach (חרפה) will be seen." This text ties shame and nakedness together directly, as does Lam 1:8 (see further below; all translations in this essay are my own).

able burial (for example, Josh 8:29; 10:27) and the placing of the foot on the neck of a defeated enemy (Josh 10:24). A number of narratives also associate rites of corpse mutilation, display by hanging, and corpse tossing with the punishment of offenders in nonwartime contexts (for example, 2 Sam 4:12; Jer 22:19 [with corpse-dragging, סחב]; see also Deut 21:22–23). Although explicit discussion of shame is not always present in the narratives, they typically construe such rites as having negative resonances of some kind (for example, the association of corpse display or blindness with divine curse, as in Deut 21:22–23 and 28:28–29). Furthermore, military defeat and abandonment by Yhwh are directly associated with humiliation in a number of other texts (for example, 2 Sam 19:4; Jer 9:18; Ezek 7:18; Ps 53:6), and rites such as the tossing or display of an enemy's corpse or his public stripping are typically coupled with the enemy's defeat.

In addition to ritual action that harms a patient under any and all circumstances, many rites consistently confer benefits on all participants. Appropriate burial and mourning of the dead are primary examples of such ritual acts. These honor the dead (2 Sam 10:3) and are expected of those having formal ties with them, such as family members and allies. In 2 Sam 2:5–6, such acts are said to be expressions of חסד, "covenant loyalty." These rites might even be undertaken by those who wish to establish a formal relationship with the dead and their survivors, as in 2 Sam 1:11–12, where David orders his men to mourn for Saul and defeated Israel even though officially they work for the enemy and are therefore expected to rejoice at the Philistine victory.[4] David in essence changes sides when he mourns, reaffiliating himself and his men with Israel and the Saulides. A second example of a rite that is always salutary is the clothing of the naked, mentioned as an ethical duty in texts such as Isa 58:7 and Ezek 18:7, 16.[5] Its opposite, the forced exposure of persons by stripping off their garments, is presented as a paradigmatic act of iniquity in Job 22:6. Just as coerced, public stripping and genital exposure is evidently shaming under all circumstances, clothing the naked is always understood to be salutary.

---

4. On the political dynamics of mourning and rejoicing, see Gary A. Anderson, *A Time to Mourn, a Time to Dance: The Expression of Grief and Joy in Israelite Religion* (University Park: Pennsylvania State University Press, 1991), 72–73, 93–95. On the political dynamics of mourning in 2 Sam 1 in particular, see Saul M. Olyan, *Biblical Mourning: Ritual and Social Dimensions* (Oxford: Oxford University Press, 2004), 53–54, 150–51.

5. See similarly Gen 9:23, by implication.

Similarly, honorable burial and the appropriate enactment of mourning rites may be contrasted with dishonoring ritual actions such as dragging and throwing the corpse, or leaving it exposed to the depredations of birds and wild beasts. The meanings of such acts are unmistakable as they have consistently positive or negative resonances.

Circumstantially dependent rites stand in contrast to the rites discussed above, whose meaning is not dependent on their context. I shall discuss four examples of such rites before considering what makes them distinct. Shaving and other forms of hair manipulation in ritual settings are my first example of a circumstantially dependent set of rites. These have no intrinsic meaning in the biblical context, though they may share in common the function of realizing and communicating status change of some kind (for example, the passage from pollution to purity or vice versa).[6] That shaving in a ritual setting can be humiliating and even result in war is illustrated by 2 Sam 10:1–5, where the Ammonites forcibly shave the beard hair of David's emissaries who have arrived in the Ammonite court to serve as comforters at the death of the Ammonite king.[7] This act, along with stripping and expulsion, are said to humiliate the embassy deeply and make the Ammonites, former allies, "odious" to David (נבאשו בדוד). Forced shaving of beard hair appears to be intended to mock the typical hair and beard manipulation often associated with mourning, whose agent is the mourner or comforter himself, not someone else acting coercively.

Contrast this scenario with the shaving of the female war captive's head in Deut 21:12. This is one of several rites she is to undertake in order to become the wife of her Israelite captor. (Along with her head shaving, she discards her "garment of captivity," cuts [?] her nails, and mourns her parents for a month while dwelling in the captor's house—all rites intended to terminate her previous identity [Deut 21:12–13].) Shaving in this instance functions to change status without any negative associations, as it does in other contexts as well. Just as shaving for one who is purifying himself from skin disease is a ritual component of his gradual purification in Lev 14:8, 9, the female prisoner's shaving helps to transform her from a foreign captive to the wife of an Israelite, a positive outcome in the writer's eyes.[8]

---

6. For the full argument, see Saul M. Olyan, "What Do Shaving Rites Accomplish and What Do They Signal in Biblical Ritual Contexts?" *JBL* 117 (1998): 611–22.

7. According to the MT, it is half the beard that is shaved.

8. Though the MT has the woman performing her own rites of transition (includ-

Other examples of ritual hair manipulation that lack negative associations are the Nazirite's shaving of his or her consecrated hair in order to complete the Nazirite vow (Num 6:18) and the Levites' shaving of their bodies to purify themselves for cultic service (Num 8:7).

Rites of disinterment and transportation of the remains of the dead are not infrequent occurrences in our narratives, including those of wartime. Such rites are represented as salutary or hostile, depending on the circumstances. A biblical example of disinterment and transportation of remains for a malevolent purpose is Jer 8:1–2, in which the author foretells the future exposure of the bones of the Judean elite after their removal from their tombs as a punishment for the worship of other gods. Though the bones were previously buried, they will not be reburied, and the text suggests their degradation by comparing them to dung on the surface of the ground. Nothing is said explicitly about the agent of this punishment of Judah's leaders, but an invading enemy in a time of war is a plausible candidate. A second, nonbiblical, wartime example of disinterment and transportation with a hostile intent is Ashurbanipal's description of his abuse of the tombs and remains of the kings of Elam. In this case, the bones of the former kings are said to be taken to Assyria in order to impose restlessness on their ghosts and deprive them of ancestral offerings (*kispu*) and libations of water.[9] Ashurbanipal's acts are very likely humiliating for the Elamites, as they do concrete harm both to Elamite tombs and to the ghosts of the dead Elamite kings.

In contrast to these examples, exhumation and movement of the remains of the dead could also be construed as salutary acts. According to 2 Sam 21:12–14, David has the bones of Saul and Jonathan disinterred and moved from Jabesh-Gilead to the Saulide ancestral tomb in Benjamin, presumably to curry favor with Saulides and other Benjaminites, as burial in the family tomb is the ideal, and it may well have been thought to have positive effects on how the dead fare in the afterlife. The impact of proper burial on the afterlife of the dead is attested in cuneiform texts, though

---

ing head shaving), the LXX reads second-person verbal forms, suggesting that the captor performs the rites of transformation. In either case, the rites have a positive outcome for the patient from the perspective of the text.

9. Rykle Borger, *Beiträge zum Inschriftenwerk Assurbanipals: Die Prismenklassen A, B, C = K, D, E, F, G, H, J und T sowie andere Inschriften* (Wiesbaden: Harrassowitz, 1996), 55 (Prism A vi 74–76 = F v 53–54).

explicit biblical evidence for it is lacking.[10] In any case, the narrative seems to be intended to portray David in a positive light in the wake of his acquiescence to the execution of several Saulides by the Gibeonites.[11] A second wartime example of beneficent disinterment and transportation concerns Merodach-Baladan, who is said to take along the disinterred remains of his ancestors as well as the images of his gods as he flees from Babylon before his enemy Sennacherib (according to Sennacherib's Nebi Yunus Slab Inscription). It seems likely that Merodach-Baladan sought to protect both the bones of his ancestors and the images of his gods from the kind of abuse meted out by Ashurbanipal in a later time.[12]

Burning the remains of the dead may be a salutary act or an act of hostility depending on the circumstances. Contrast Josiah's burning of the bones of the dead of Bethel on the Bethel temple's altar in order to pollute it (2 Kgs 23:16) with the Jabesh-Gileadites' burning of Saul's corpse and the corpses of his sons and the burial of their bones after the Jabeshites rescue their remains from the wall of Beth Shean (1 Sam 31:12). Both acts occur in settings of war; the movement of remains characterizes both narratives; and in both cases, the remains of the dead are burned. Yet the agent in one case is an invading enemy with hostile intent (Josiah) while the agents in the other instance are loyal subjects of a king who inconvenience themselves in order to provide an honorable burial for their ruler's remains and those of his sons. This act of the Jabeshites is explicitly associated with the appropriate mourning rite of fasting in 1 Sam 31:13 and—implicitly—with covenant loyalty (חסד) by David in a later scene in the narrative (2 Sam 2:5). In contrast, Josiah's actions clearly demonstrate malevolent intent, not only toward the Bethel sanctuary's altar but also toward the remains of the dead that are burned on it. In effect, Josiah not only destroys the Bethel sanctuary and pollutes the Bethel altar, but disinters and moves the remains of dead denizens of Bethel with the intent to cause harm, as suggested by his order not to disturb the tomb and bones of the favored man of god who prophesied against Bethel (2 Kgs 23:18). The nature of the harm is again elusive, given the limitations of the textual

---

10. On the desirability of burial in the family tomb, see Saul M. Olyan, "Some Neglected Aspects of Israelite Interment Ideology," *JBL* 124 (2005): 603–4, 607–11.

11. On salutary movement of the remains of the dead, see further ibid., 613.

12. See A. Kirk Grayson and Jamie Novotny, *The Royal Inscriptions of Sennacherib, King of Assyria (704–681 BC), Part 1* (RINAP 3/1; Winona Lake, Ind.: Eisenbrauns, 2012), 221 (text 34, lines 7–11).

evidence. It is, however, possible that the text assumes that the afterlife of those whose bones are disinterred and abused would be disturbed in one or more ways, and it probably envisions such acts as bringing shame on the surviving community.

Circumcision is my final example of a circumstantially dependent rite. In this case, the rite's effects are normally salutary in biblical contexts. In Gen 17, circumcision is a sign of the covenant between Yhwh and Abraham; in Exod 12:48, it functions to allow the uncircumcised resident alien male to "make the Passover"; and in Josh 5:9, circumcision during the wilderness wanderings removes (literally "rolls away") "the reproach (חרפה) of Egypt," a positive thing according to the writer, whatever the reproach might refer to. Thus, when interpreted in an Israelite context, circumcision has consistently positive associations: it removes shame; it grants admission to the cultic community; and it is a sign of Yhwh's covenant with Abraham. At the same time, the foreskin is stigmatized, associated with reproach (חרפה), stubbornness, exclusion, and profanation of holiness (for example, Gen 34:14; Deut 10:16; Jer 4:4; Isa 52:1; Ezek 44:7, 9). Yet in the war context of 1 Sam 18:27, David's removal of one hundred foreskins from the Philistine dead serves as a grotesque bride price that is intended as an act of hostility.[13] This is indicated by the fact that the Philistines are said not to practice circumcision as a cultural norm—they are often referred to as the "uncircumcised"—but their corpses have it imposed on them nonetheless; that the act parallels other forms of corpse mutilation quite closely (for example, cutting off the head or hands or feet) and would presumably have been construed as such by the Philistines of the narrative; and most revealing, that Saul's stated desire is to take vengeance (נקם) on his enemies through the act. In this instance, the cultural norms of the victim play a crucial role in shaping meaning. Though Saul's intent is to do his enemy harm, circumcision could not function effectively as a tool to achieve this end were it not for its alien status and likely negative resonances for Philistines.

What makes circumstantially dependent rites distinct? In each case, the rite itself tells us little or nothing when considered in isolation from its context. Shaving, the burning of bones or corpses, exhumation and transportation of the remains of the dead, and circumcision are rites

---

13. The MT reads 200; LXX[BL] and 2 Sam 3:14 read 100. On this, see P. Kyle McCarter Jr., *I Samuel: A New Translation with Introduction, Notes and Commentary* (AB 8; Garden City: Doubleday, 1980), 316.

whose meaning is not consistent or obvious but dependent upon considerations such as the identity and intent of the agent, the role played by coercion, and the cultural norms of participants. The agent performing the rite might be oneself or another person. Typically, rites performed by one on one's own body are salutary in some way (for example, shaving in order to achieve purification, as in Lev 14:8, 9, or to enter the mourning state).[14] In contrast, rites performed by an agent on a patient could have either beneficial or injurious effects on the patient, depending on the agent's identity as an established or newly minted friend or advocate, with beneficent intent, or as an enemy, with malevolent intent. The Jabeshites of 1 Sam 30 are loyal allies whose corpse burning is, like appropriate burial, construed as a salutary act; in contrast, Josiah is an enemy invader of Bethel whose bone burning is intended to cause harm both to the Bethel altar and the dead buried in Bethel's environs. David's disinterment, transportation, and reburial of the remains of Saul and Jonathan and his burial of the corpses of other Saulides position him as a new friend of Saulides and Benjaminites; in contrast, through their use of coerced shaving to abuse David's ambassadors, the Ammonites recast themselves as enemies of David. Unlike such circumstantially dependent rites, which could be performed by friend or foe, with beneficent or malevolent intent, rites that are always injurious to a patient are typically performed by an established or a new-found enemy (blinding; maltreatment of corpses; forced stripping and genital exposure), but never by a friend. Similarly, rites that are salutary to both agent and patient irrespective of circumstance are performed by an established or newfound friend or advocate.

Coercion can play an important role in determining the meaning of circumstantially dependent rites that it does not play with rites whose effects are always negatively or positively construed. Public exposure of the genitals is dishonoring whether it is coerced or not, because such nudity always has a negative resonance in biblical texts. David's self-diminish-

---

14. Though mourning has debasing dimensions, particularly when associated with petition of the deity or with national defeat or personal calamity, its enactment can have many salutary aspects that evidently outweigh whatever debasement might be suffered. Examples include the deity's positive response to the petitioner who has debased himself through embrace of mourning rites, or the establishment or perpetuation of social relationships that benefit the mourner. On this, see further Olyan, *Biblical Mourning*, 78–81, 90–94, 106–7.

ment in 2 Sam 6:16, 20 through (unintentional?) self-exposure while dancing before the ark is perceived no differently than the humiliation of David's forcibly exposed embassy in 2 Sam 10: in each case, dishonor is the result.[15] Yet contrast the forced shaving of the beards of David's emissaries to Ammon with the hair, beard, and eyebrow shaving of the person purifying himself from skin disease in Lev 14:9.[16] The coerced shaving of David's ambassadors contributes to their significant humiliation (2 Sam 10:4–5) while the shaving rites of the person purifying himself from skin disease are routine, have no evident associations with shame, and result in his cleansing and readmission to the community. These examples suggest that like an agent's intent, the presence or absence of coercion can be of primary importance in shaping the meaning of circumstantially dependent rites.

In addition to the identity and intent of the agent and the potential role played by coercion, cultural norms can play a part in determining the meaning of circumstantially dependent rites. Circumcision, usually constructed as an entirely salutary act in biblical texts, is clearly not so under the particular circumstances narrated in 1 Sam 18. Here, it is an act of hostility and vengeance given Philistine cultural norms and Saul's stated intent.

Though rites that are always injurious in some way have both a winner (the agent) and a loser (the victim), and rites that are always salutary have two beneficiaries (both agent and patient), circumstantially dependent rites can have either a winner and a loser or two beneficiaries. Interestingly, no matter what the type of rite or its circumstances, the agent always profits in some way. Examples of agents who gain something from their circumstantially dependent ritual actions include David, who in exhuming, transporting, and reburying Saul and Jonathan, and burying other Saulides, positions himself to appear as a friend of the House of Saul; Saul, who in calling for and receiving Philistine foreskins exacts vengeance on

---

15. Michal's sarcastic comment to David in 2 Sam 6:20 suggests that she finds his actions profoundly dishonoring. Note that Saul's self-exposure and helplessness in 1 Sam 19:24 are evidently intended to detract from his reputation. According to McCarter, in contrast to his portrayal in 1 Sam 10:10–12, Saul is "now more a victim of prophetic inspiration than a beneficiary of it; he participates in the prophesying as a sufferer, an invalid, and the ecstasy is for him a disease" (McCarter, *I Samuel*, 329; see also 331).

16. Verse 8 mentions that he shaves all of his hair; v. 9 is more specific.

his enemies through their humiliation and implicitly gains the honor of victory; and the Ammonites, who in shaming David's embassy and by extension, David himself, terminate their parity treaty with David, and presumably increase their honor at David's expense.

Bibliography

Anderson, Gary A. *A Time to Mourn, a Time to Dance: The Expression of Grief and Joy in Israelite Religion*. University Park: Pennsylvania State University Press, 1991.

Borger, Rykle. *Beiträge zum Inschriftenwerk Assurbanipals: Die Prismenklassen A, B, C = K, D, E, F, G, H, J und T sowie andere Inschriften*. Wiesbaden: Harrassowitz, 1996.

Botterweck, G. Johannes, Helmer Ringgren, and Heinz-Josef Fabry. *Theological Dictionary of the Old Testament*. Translated by David E. Green. 15 vols. Grand Rapids: Eerdmans, 1974–2006.

Grayson, A. Kirk, and Jamie Novotny. *The Royal Inscriptions of Sennacherib, King of Assyria (704–681 BC), Part 1*. RINAP 3/1. Winona Lake, Ind.: Eisenbrauns, 2012.

McCarter, P. Kyle, Jr. *I Samuel: A New Translation with Introduction, Notes and Commentary*. AB 8. Garden City: Doubleday, 1980.

Olyan, Saul M. *Biblical Mourning: Ritual and Social Dimensions*. Oxford: Oxford University Press, 2004.

———. "Some Neglected Aspects of Israelite Interment Ideology." *JBL* 124 (2005): 601–16.

———. "Theorizing Circumstantially Dependent Rites in and out of War Contexts." Pages 69–76 in *"The One Who Sows Bountifully": Essays in Honor of Stanley K. Stowers*. Edited by Caroline Johnson Hodge, Saul M. Olyan, Daniel Ullucci, and Emma Wasserman. BJS 356. Providence, R.I.: Brown Judaic Studies, 2013.

———. "What Do Shaving Rites Accomplish and What Do They Signal in Biblical Ritual Contexts?" *JBL* 117 (1998): 611–22.

Monumental Inscriptions and the Ritual Representation of War*

Nathaniel B. Levtow

1. Introduction

The tapestry of war narratives spanning the Pentateuch and Deuteronomistic History invokes ritualized memorial traditions dating back to the earliest extant monumental inscriptions and narrative iconography in the ancient Near East. These Israelite narratives trace paths of victory through waters and wilderness, over hills and mountaintops, with ritual conquest motifs unfolding along the way as Yhwh and Israel vanquish other gods and peoples and claim hegemony over newly acquired territory.[1] The winding Deuteronomistic narrative of warfare, divine kingship, and state formation alludes to its own ritual memorialization, moreover, through prescribed invocations and rites performed in central sanctuaries after Israelite victories. This includes ceremonial invocations of the path Yhwh cleared for Israel from Mesopotamia to Egypt to Canaan (Exod 19:3–6; Deut 6:20–25; 26:5–10; Josh 24:2–13) as well as instructions for the Israelites to install inscribed stelae beside a sacrificial altar upon their victorious

---

* I thank Brad E. Kelle, Frank Ritchel Ames, and Jacob L. Wright for their invitation to contribute to this volume and for their editorial assistance. I thank also Saul M. Olyan for providing helpful comments on this paper, the final draft of which was completed with support from a National Endowment for the Humanities Summer Stipend (2013). Any views, findings, conclusions, or recommendations expressed in this publication do not necessarily reflect those of the National Endowment for the Humanities.

1. On ritual conquest motifs, see Frank M. Cross, *Canaanite Myth and Hebrew Epic: Essays in the History of the Religion of Israel* (Cambridge: Harvard University Press, 1973), 91–144.

entry into lands west of the Jordan river (Deut 27:1-8; 11: 29-32; Josh 8:30-35; 24:25-27).

The ritual installation of triumphal monuments along routes of conquest through the Levant is a widely attested practice most commonly associated with Neo-Assyrian imperial expansion in the West. Innumerable Mesopotamian royal inscriptions include accounts of territorial conquests by named kings and their divine patrons. Such accounts were often inscribed on monumental stelae publicly displayed in conquered lands in a variety of settings ranging from central sanctuaries and city gates to remote mountain passes. These inscriptions commonly follow annalistic battle narratives with equally formulaic descriptions of postbattle social orders and then conclude with prohibitions against their violation and prescriptions for their own ritual maintenance. The purpose of this paper is to identify the ritual roles of such victory monuments within the strategic environment of ancient Near Eastern warfare and to reexamine comparable traditions in the Hebrew Bible.[2] I will argue that ancient Near

---

2. By "victory monuments" I refer to publicly displayed ancient Near Eastern royal monuments inscribed with accounts of the conquests of named kings. Such triumphal stelae may also be classified as "memorial" or "commemorative" and are included among the broader class of ancient Near Eastern royal monumental inscriptions that strategically display the names and deeds of the rulers who commissioned them. There is much fluidity across functional and descriptive categories of ancient Near Eastern royal monuments and their classification is debated. So-called "votive" (or "dedicatory") inscriptions, "commemorative" (or "memorial") inscriptions, and "building" inscriptions can all designate royal monuments inscribed with the names and pious and heroic deeds of rulers. Ancient monumental inscription practices blend such categories and defy modern attempts at their rigid classification. See Sandra L. Richter, *The Deuteronomistic History and the Name Theology:* lᵉšakkēn šᵉmô šām *in the Bible and the Ancient Near East* (BZAW 318; Berlin: de Gruyter, 2002), 130-47, esp. 136 n. 32; idem, "The Place of the Name in Deuteronomy," *VT* 57 (2007): 344 and n. 4; William W. Hallo, "The Royal Inscriptions of UR: A Typology," *HUCA* 33 (1962): 1-43; Joel Drinkard, "The Literary Genre of the Mesha' Inscription," in *Studies in the Mesha Inscription and Moab* (ed. J. Andrew Dearman; SBLABS 2; Atlanta: Scholars Press, 1989), 131-54; Alan R. Millard, "The Practice of Writing in Ancient Israel," *BA* 35 (1972): 99; Govert van Driel, "On 'Standard' and 'Triumphal' Inscriptions," in *Symbolae Biblicae et Mesopotamicae Francisco Mario Theodoro de Liagre Böhl Dedicatae* (ed. M. A. Beek; Leiden: Brill, 1973), 99-106. On biblical and ancient Near Eastern conquest accounts, see K. Lawson Younger Jr., *Ancient Conquest Accounts: A Study in Ancient Near Eastern and Biblical History Writing* (JSOTSup 98; Sheffield: Sheffield Academic Press, 1990).

Eastern victory monuments signified the ritualization of warfare on two complementary levels: on one level, conquest and hegemony were orchestrated into strategically patterned textual and iconographic representations on publically displayed stone monuments; on a second level, these monumental representations of war were themselves ritually engaged in strategic social settings.[3] This doubly ritualized orchestration of war and its aftermath—in which patterned victories and resultant social formations were inscribed upon ritually deployed monuments—served to legitimize and perpetuate the presence and power of victorious gods and kings in their native and conquered lands. In these respects, the strategic installation and manipulation of victory monuments illuminates socially productive ritual dimensions to the prosecution and representation of war in the Hebrew Bible and the ancient Near East.

2. The Ritual Environments of Monumental Inscriptions in the Ancient Near East

The ritual contexts of ancient Near Eastern monumental inscriptions are attested by three overlapping sets of evidence: (1) narrative accounts that depict monumental inscriptions engaged in ritual roles and settings; (2) ritual archaeological contexts in which monumental inscriptions have been excavated; and (3) monumental inscriptions that specify their ritual

---

3. By "ritualization" I refer to the "production of ritual acts"—that is, the production of special, strategic ways of acting that "structure and nuance an environment" (Catherine Bell, *Ritual Theory, Ritual Practice* [NewYork: Oxford University Press, 1992], 140). Such acts are "strategic" in that they legitimate themselves and the environments they structure. A ritual environment of this sort, writes Bell, is "constructed and reconstructed by the actions of social agents within it" and "provides an experience of the objective reality of the embodied subjective schemes that have created it" (ibid.). Royal victory monuments, I argue, can embody and create social realities in this way because they both represent and configure the social environments in which they are installed. They depict hegemonic and hierarchical social orders, they are installed in strategic places (e.g. royal sanctuary cellas and mountain passes), and they require special interactions (e.g. public readings aloud, anointings with oil, and sacrifices) with powerful social agents (e.g. priests, kings, and scribes). The "textual medium" (a monumental inscription) thus achieves social agency through the "ritual medium" (interactions with people) and this strategic interaction between agents (human and artifactual) can durably affect the social world. See Catherine Bell, "Ritualization of Texts and Textualization of Ritual in the Codification of Taoist Liturgy," *HR* 27 (1988): 390–92. On the agency of artifacts, see n. 43 below.

manipulation. This range of evidence reveals the ritual roles and contexts of monumental inscriptions in times of both war and peace. During wartime, they were strategically installed and manipulated by victorious peoples and strategically removed and violated by formerly vanquished peoples. During peacetime, they remained installed in sanctuary settings and retained active roles as textual and iconographic representations of conquest and hegemony.

2.1. Narrative Accounts Depicting Monumental Inscriptions in Ritual Roles and Settings

Royal monumental victory inscriptions played central roles in the prosecution and representation of warfare throughout the ancient Near East for millennia. These roles are depicted in Early Dynastic narrative inscriptions including the Stele of the Vultures, which textually and iconographically represents a mid-third millennium B.C.E. border conflict between the southern Mesopotamian states of Lagash and Umma.[4] This stele's inscription, which stands at the very beginning of the public monumental narrative tradition, describes how Eanatum of Lagash defeated the ruler of Umma and installed inscribed boundary stones marking the disputed border between these two states:

> Eanatum, the man of just commands, measured off the boundary [from Umma], left (some land) under the control of Umma and erected a monument on that spot.... [He] defeated Umma.... Eanatum destroyed the foreign lands [for the god Ningirsu]; Eanatum restored to the god Ningirsu's control [his] beloved [field], the Gu'eden.[5]

---

4. RIME 1, 125–40 (9.3.1); Jerrold S. Cooper, *Reconstructing History from Ancient Inscriptions: The Lagash-Umma Border Conflict* (Sources from the Ancient Near East 2/1; Malibu: Undena, 1983), 45–48 (no. 2); idem, *Sumerian and Akkadian Royal Inscriptions, Volume 1: Presargonic Inscriptions* (New Haven: American Oriental Society, 1986), 33–39 (La 3.1); Irene J. Winter, "After the Battle Is Over: The Stele of the Vultures and the Beginning of Historical Narrative in the Ancient Near East," in *On Art in the Ancient Near East*, Volume 2: *From the Third Millennium B.C.E.* (ed. Irene J. Winter; CHANE 34.2; Leiden: Brill, 2010), 3–51. The conflict was over a tract of agricultural and grazing lands (the Gu'eden) and associated water rights along the border between Lagash and Umma (Winter, "After the Battle," 30–31).

5. RIME 1, 131–32 (9.3.1: x.12–xii.4); Winter, "After the Battle," 30–31.

Following its relatively succinct battle account, this stele's extant inscription is then structured around a series of six oaths in which the ruler of Umma swears upon "the great battle nets" of six deities not to violate the territory of Lagash or to remove or destroy the boundary stelae placed in the disputed borderlands (the "Gu'eden"). A contemporary inscription associated with Eanatum's nephew Enmetana recounts how the ruler of Umma violated these oaths, marched upon Lagash, and removed and destroyed the inscribed boundary stones:

> The god Enlil, king of the lands, father of the gods, by his firm command demarcated the border for the gods Ningirsu and Shara. Mesilim, king of Kish, at the command of the god Ishtaran surveyed the field and erected stelae there. (But) Ush, ruler of Umma, acted arrogantly—he ripped out (or smashed) those stelae and marched on the steppe of Lagash. The god Ningirsu, warrior of Enlil, at Enlil's just command, did battle with Umma. At Enlil's command, he cast the great battle net upon it.[6]

These earliest narratives of war represent the installation and violation of stone boundary monuments as pivotal engagements with physical representations of the divine will and human social contracts inscribed upon them.[7] Their removal and destruction is represented not as collateral damage of cross-border military campaigns but as a ritual violation and focus of the conflict itself, its cause and consequence. As Irene Winter notes, the longest sequence inscribed on the Stele of the Vultures is occupied not with the battle itself but with the formulaic series of oaths and rituals in which the leader of Umma swears not to violate boundary stelae installed after the battle.[8] These oaths negotiate territorial hegemony by orchestrating human interactions with stone monuments.[9] Moreover,

---

6. RIME 1, 195 (9.5.1: i.1–29); Cooper, *Reconstructing History*, 49–50 (no. 6); Christopher Woods, "Mutilation of Image and Text in Early Sumerian Sources," in *Iconoclasm and Text Destruction in the Ancient Near East and Beyond* (ed. Natalie N. May; Oriental Institute Seminars 8; Chicago: The Oriental Institute of the University of Chicago, 2012), 34. Woods (ibid.) writes that "the stelae were tangible embodiments of the agreement that was arbitrated by a third party, Mesilim, King of Kish."
7. Ibid., 34.
8. Winter, "After the Battle," 21.
9. Zainab Bahrani writes in this respect of "conceptions of violence and power that were inseparable from conceptions of the body and its control; and the processes and rituals of war that these formulations of the body and power made possible" (*Rituals of War: The Body and Violence in Mesopotamia* [New York: Zone Books, 2008], 15).

not only does the Stele of the Vultures orient its inscription around strategic human engagements with boundary stelae, but this Sumerian monument was itself ritually engaged in strategic social settings. It was most likely installed in the temple of Ningirsu at Girsu, and this ritual placement of the monument would have provided a strategic environment in which to engage its agency as a physical representation of Lagash's hegemony over disputed borderlands with Umma.[10] The social agency of the Stele of the Vultures is, furthermore, textually invoked toward the end of its extant inscription:

> "The stele, its name is not a man's name; it is: 'the god Ningirsu, Lord, Crown of Lumma, is the life of the Pirig-eden canal.' The stele of the Gu'eden—beloved field of Ningirsu (which) Eanatum for Ningirsu returned to his (the god's) hand—he (Eanatum) erected it."[11]

Evidence for the ritual agency of royal monumental victory inscriptions thus dates back to the Early Dynastic period in which Sumerian statuary

---

For modern rationalists, the ritualized instrumentalization of warfare in the ancient Near East finds a distant echo in von Clausewitz's description of war as "violence that arms itself with the inventions of art and science" (Carl von Clausewitz, *On War* [trans. J. J. Graham; Harmondsworth: Penguin, 1968], 101) (cited in Bahrani, *Rituals of War*, 9).

10. Winter, "After the Battle," 27. The Stele of the Vultures refers to the disputed Gu'eden as "the beloved field of the god Ningirsu," which may indicate its designation as land holdings belonging to the temple of Ningirsu at Girsu, a satellite city of Lagash (ibid., 29–30). See RIME 1: 132 (9.3.1: xii 21–xiii 2): "Eanatum erected (this) [monument] in the lofty temple." On the deposition of boundary stones (*kudurrus*) in sanctuaries, see Kathryn E. Slanski, *The Babylonian Entitlement narûs* (kudurrus): *A Study in Their Form and Function* (ASOR Books 9; Boston: ASOR, 2003), 61.

11. Winter, "After the Battle," 27; RIME 1, 140 (9.3.1: rev. x. 23–xi.32). Winter emphasizes that the Stele of the Vultures is dedicated to, named after, and erected for the god Ningirsu, that the majority of its fragments were found near a temple to Ningirsu in a sacred precinct of the city Girsu, and that its obverse is "carved with a monumental figure of Ningirsu as the icon of victory over Umma" ("After the Battle," 27–28). The figure may possibly depict Eanatum; Winter notes "the distribution of five of the six excavated fragments on or around Tell 'K' at Girsu, a low mound within the city on which the main temple to Ningirsu was situated" (ibid.; see also RIME 1, 126). This suggests for Winter that the stele originally stood "as both testimony and votive in the god's sanctuary," and that the stele "was not merely intended as a commemorative monument; it was rather meant to be a living testimonial witness to the historicity of the events and the legitimacy of the legal terms … it recorded" ("After the Battle," 28).

and stelae were assigned divine determinatives, given names, inscribed in the first person (as if they spoke), and received sacrifices.[12] The agency of monumental Sumerian inscriptions is likewise invoked in Gudean and Old Akkadian royal statuary inscriptions including that of a Sargonic ruler (perhaps Naram-Sin) who claims that he "fashioned an image of himself, a golden eternal statue (depicting) his might and the battles in which he had been victorious."[13] As Joan Goodnick Westenholz notes, "these public monuments contained both historical narratives of military conquests and iconic depictions of royal might."[14] Moreover, the agency of such monumental Sumerian representations of conquest was engaged not only by the social groups responsible for their original production and installation but also by Elamite rulers who abducted and usurped them approximately one thousand years later.[15] The ritual foundations of these monumental victory inscription traditions were thus laid in the mid-third millennium B.C.E. and continued to develop over the following millennia in the ancient Near East.

---

12. Woods writes that "the inviolability of monuments of this type is demonstrated by the fact that they were often deified—the Sumerian term, na-ru2-a, capable of taking the divine determinative—with the monuments themselves being revered, receiving offerings, possessing temples and temple personnel" ("Mutilation of Image and Text," 34).

13. Joan G. Westenholz, "*Damnatio Memoriae*: Destruction of Name and Destruction of Person in Third-Millennium Mesopotamia," in May, *Iconoclasm and Text Destruction*, 95–96, citing RIME 2, 160 (1.4.1001: 4–12).

14. Ibid., 95; see also Winter, "After the Battle," 27–28. Westenholz ("*Damnatio Memoriae*," 96) cites Irene Winter's salient observations concerning the ritual dynamics of UR III royal statuary, including the strategic "introduction of the ruler into, and the appropriation of, ritual space hitherto belonging to the god" (Irene J. Winter, "'Idols of the King': Royal Images as Recipients of Ritual Action in Ancient Mesopotamia," *JRitSt* 6 [1992]: 34). "What may be particular to the Mesopotamian situation is the power vested in the image of the ruler, the alam-lugal, as it takes its place in ... ritual contexts," Winter writes. "Identified by likeness, inscription, and name *as* the ruler ... ritually consecrated to *be* the ruler, the image plays upon representation and manifestation ... The nature of the ritually empowered royal image is such that it brings signifier (the statue) and signified (the ruler) together" [emphasis original] (ibid.).

15. On the Elamite abduction of Mesopotamian monuments to Susa, see Nathaniel B. Levtow, "Text Destruction and Iconoclasm in the Hebrew Bible and the Ancient Near East," in May, *Iconoclasm and Text Destruction*, 320 n. 32, with references noted there.

2.2. Archaeological Evidence for the Ritual Environments of Monumental Victory Inscriptions

Narrative accounts inscribed on the earliest Mesopotamian victory stelae indicate how warfare stimulated the production of and strategic interaction with stone monuments that textually, iconographically, and ritually represented divine and human identities and relationships. The agency such objects exercised in war contexts was similarly exercised in times of peace in so far as these monuments remained installed and engaged in strategic locations. As noted above, the Stele of the Vultures was most likely installed in the temple of Ningirsu in the sacred quarter of Girsu, and stone boundary monuments of the sort depicted in its inscription continued to be installed in second and first millennium B.C.E. Babylonian sanctuaries.[16] Second and first millennium B.C.E. Assyrian monumental victory inscriptions were likewise set up in ritual environments, including the stele of Adad-nirari III (ca. 810–783 B.C.E.) set up beside a sanctuary altar at Tell al Rimah and the Great Monolith of Ashurnasirpal II (883–859 B.C.E.) that stood by the entrance to Ninurta's temple at Nimrud.[17] Although comparatively fewer in number, extant Northwest Semitic royal monumental inscriptions were likewise installed and engaged in ritual settings in city gates and sanctuaries.[18]

Much textual and archaeological evidence thus reveals how ancient Near Eastern social groups engaged victory monuments in sanctuary settings as ritual embodiments of royal and divine hegemony and how these objects were therefore strategically targeted in wartime. Numerous Southern Mesopotamian monuments were usurped and abducted to Susa by the Elamite king Shutruk-Nahhunte (ca. 1185–1155 B.C.E.), as noted above, whereas the stele of Adad-Nirari III was strategically erased but left standing beside the altar in its sanctuary at Tell al Rimah.[19] The ritual installa-

---

16. See n. 10 above.

17. Tell al Rimah: RIMA 3, 209–12 (A.0.104.7); Great Monolith: RIMA 2, 237–54 (A.0.101.17).

18. For examples, see Levtow, "Text Destruction and Iconoclasm," 318–19 n. 29. See also the discussion of the Tel Dan inscription below and cf. Seymour Gitin, Trude Dothan, and Joseph Naveh, "A Royal Dedicatory Inscription from Ekron," *IEJ* 47 (1997): 1–16.

19. On Susa artifacts, see n. 15 above; on the Tell al Rimah stele, see Stephanie Page, "A Stela of Adad-nirari III and Nergal-ereš from Tell al Rimah," *Iraq* 30/2 (1968): 139–53.

tion and manipulation of such monuments made manifest their semantic content in the social world; their abduction, violation, alteration, and destruction signified the annihilation or reconfiguration of that content and the social identities and formations it represented.

2.3 VICTORY MONUMENTS THAT SPECIFY THEIR RITUAL MANIPULATION

The social agency of ancient Near Eastern victory monuments is further attested by self-referential ritual prescriptions and prohibitions inscribed upon them. Mesopotamian and Levantine monumental inscriptions frequently conclude their accounts of military and political domination with curses that specify how they are not to be displaced from their original setting or physically violated in any way, and these same inscriptions often mandate the performance of attendant sacrificial and anointing rites.[20] A victory monument of Tiglath-pileser III (744–727 B.C.E.) first celebrates how this Neo-Assyrian king "personally conquered all of the lands from sunrise to sunset," then delineates the resultant Assyrian hegemonic order, and finally narrates its own installation and ritual maintenance:

> I had a stele made in the vicinity of the mountains. I depicted on it (symbols of) the great gods, my lords, (and) I fashioned my royal image on it. I inscribed on it the mighty deeds of (the god) Ashur, my lord, and [my] personal achievements (that) I accomplished again and again throughout (all of) the lands … May a future ruler read aloud (this inscription), wash it with water, anoint (it) with oil, (and) make an offering.[21]

The ritual installation and maintenance of such Assyrian victory monuments is narratively depicted in the following inscription of Tiglath-pileser I (1114–1076 B.C.E.):

---

20. See Richter, *Deuteronomistic History and the Name Theology*, 134–35.
21. Hayim Tadmor and Shigeo Yamada, *The Royal Inscriptions of Tiglath-Pileser III (744–727 BC) and Shalmaneser V (726–722 BC), Kings of Assyria* (Winona Lake: Eisenbrauns, 2011), 86–87 (no. 35: ii 18–24, iii 31–36, iii 6'–10'). On reading aloud, see Seth L. Sanders, *The Invention of Hebrew* (Traditions; Urbana: University of Illinois Press, 2009), 147, 224 n. 18. For similar accounts of the installation of Assyrian victory stelae cf. RIMA 3, 209 (A.0.104.6: 21–22) (Adad-nirari III); and the Dadusha Stele (Bahija Khalil Ismaïl and Antoine Cavigneaux, "Dādušas Siegesstele IM 95200 aus Ešnunna: Die Inschrift," *BaM* 34 [2003]: 149–51 [xii–xv]).

I wrote on my monumental and clay inscriptions my heroic victories, my successful battles, (and) the suppression of the enemies (and) foes of the god Ashur which the gods Anu and Adad granted me. I deposited (them) in the temple of Anu and Adad, the great gods, my lords, forever. In addition, (concerning) the monumental inscriptions of Shamshi-Adad (III) my forefather I anointed (them) with oil, made sacrifices, (and) returned them to their places.[22]

3. Ritualized Victory Monuments, Treaty Tablets, and Weaponry in Ancient Israel

Evidence for the installation and manipulation of ancient Near Eastern triumphal monuments, such as the narrative and ritual inscriptions and archaeological contexts discussed above, has parallels in Israelite literary and archaeological contexts as well. Sandra Richter has documented significant continuities between Hebrew idioms associated with Deuteronomistic "name theology" traditions and Akkadian idioms associated with name-emplacement practices in Mesopotamian royal monumental inscription traditions.[23] Richter identifies the Deuteronomistic phrases *šakkēn šēm* and *śîm šēm* as adaptations of the Akkadian *šuma šakānu*, which signifies the practice of rulers engraving their personal names upon votive and triumphal monuments to claim ownership of the monuments and the sites in which they are installed and hegemony over the peoples and territories identified in their inscribed content. Richter argues on this basis that Deuteronomistic references to Yhwh "placing his name" are to be "associated in some manner with an inscribed monument or newly claimed territory or both."[24] In particular, Richter links these Deuteronomistic name-emplacement idioms to the installation of inscribed stelae beside an altar at the early Israelite central sanctuary on Mount Ebal (Deut 27:1–8; 11: 29–32; Josh 8:30–35).

Richter marshals convincing evidence in support of this argument for Deuteronomistic employment of Mesopotamian royal monumental inscription name-emplacement traditions, and I wish to build upon Rich-

---

22. RIMA 2, 30 (A.O.87.1: viii 39–49). This text then concludes with instructions for future princes to ritually refurbish the inscriptions of Tiglath-pileser I (viii 50–62) and with curses against those who violate them (viii 63–88).

23. Richter, *Deuteronomistic History and the Name Theology;* idem, "Place of the Name."

24. Richter, "Place of the Name," 344.

ter's thesis by focusing on the ritual environments in which such monuments were engaged.²⁵ As Richter notes, these Deuteronomistic traditions do not only represent clear extensions of Mesopotamian traditions in which rulers' names are "placed" (that is, inscribed) upon public monuments; they also extend another aspect of those same Mesopotamian traditions in which such monumental inscriptions are themselves "placed" in ritual environments.²⁶ This doubly ritualized emplacement of monumental inscriptions indicates not only how rulers claimed ownership of votive objects, buildings, cities, and territories and hegemony over subject peoples; it also indicates how such monuments came to ritually embody royal and divine presence and power. For just as ancient Near Eastern

---

25. Richter rejects the so-called "name theology" interpretive tradition in modern scholarship that identifies biblical idioms such as *lĕšakkēn šĕmô šām* as evidence of a Deuteronomistic theological innovation toward a more transcendent conception of divine presence. According to Richter, this modern interpretive tradition incorrectly posits a D "demythologization" program in which anthropomorphic depictions of Yhwh preserved in early Pentateuchal sources (J/E) are replaced by more abstract depictions of Yhwh "causing his name to dwell" in the temple as a "hypostasis." See Richter, *Deuteronomistic History and the Name Theology*, 7–39, where she argues that this interpretation is based on an outmoded theory of "nominal realism," which she defines as "the supposed perception on the part of the ancient Semite that the name of an item or person, as a symbol of the thing or person named, was in fact real, having consubstantial existence with the name bearer" (ibid., 15). Richter rightly resists such evolutionary models of the development of Israelite religion and convincingly identifies such biblical name-emplacement idioms as borrowings from Mesopotamian monumental inscription traditions in which personal names are inscribed upon royal monuments to establish ownership of and claim hegemony over objects, buildings, lands, and peoples. My focus here falls not on *conceptions* of royal and divine presence but on *interactions* with their ritual representations. In this respect, my argument diverges somewhat from Richter's in that I claim the ritual installation and manipulation of monumental inscriptions establishes not only ownership and hegemony but also a strategic space for human interactions with their referent kings, gods, and social orders. I here concur with Woods, who notes with respect to Sumerian monuments discussed above that "abstract notions of the divine were equated, in a very real sense, with their concrete man-made embodiments" ("Mutilation of Image and Text," 36), and with Winter, "Idols of the King," 34 (on which see n. 14 above). On recent critiques of Richter's argument, see Michael Hundley, "To Be or Not to Be: A Reexamination of Name Language in Deuteronomy and the Deuteronomistic History," *VT* 59 (2009): 533–55; see also Victor A. Hurrowitz, review of Sandra L. Richter, *Deuteronomistic History and the Name Theology*, *JHS* 5 (2004–2005): 595–96.

26. Richter, "Place of the Name," 358–61.

iconodules ritually interacted with cult statues and aniconic stelae as embodiments of their divine referents, so too could the ritual installation and manipulation of monumental inscriptions serve to ritually embody their textual and iconographic referents and content.[27] Mesopotamian and Levantine monumental inscriptions were often engraved with corollary iconography and commonly occupied cultic positions identical to those of cult statues. In Northwest Semitic cultural spheres, such engraved and inscribed monumental stelae could effectively serve the same role as aniconic "standing stones" (*maṣṣēbōt*) as recipients of ritual action.[28]

Richter notes how the opening pericope of the Deuteronomic code recalls the widespread practice of violating ancient Near Eastern monumental inscriptions and cultic iconography through their displacement and destruction and through the effacement and usurpation of personal names inscribed upon them (Deut 12:1–5).[29] Evidence for such practices has been identified in Israelite archaeological contexts at Tel Dan, where fragments of a ninth century B.C.E. Aramean victory stele were excavated from eighth century B.C.E. ritualized city gate precincts.[30] Excavators of the fragments argue that this monument to Aramean hegemony was symbolically smashed by Israelites because it served as a "reminder of the former weakness of their kingdom."[31] In light of the ritualized monumental inscription traditions discussed above and of the ritual environment of the city gate area in which the Tel Dan inscription was found, this monumental representation of war would have served not simply as a "reminder" but as an interactive physical manifestation of Aramean conquests in—and

---

27. On ritual iconic embodiment, see Nathaniel B. Levtow, *Images of Others: Iconic Politics in Ancient Israel* (Biblical and Judaic Studies from the University of California, San Diego 11; Winona Lake: Eisenbrauns, 2008).

28. See Richter, "Place of the Name," 347, 360–61.

29. Ibid., 345–6; Richter, *Deuteronomistic History and the Name Theology*, 209–10. See also Jacob L. Wright, "Remember Nehemiah: 1 Esdras and the *Damnatio Memoriae Nehemiae*," in *Was 1 Esdras First? An Investigation into the Priority and Nature of 1 Esdras* (ed. Lisbeth S. Fried; SBLAIL 7; Atlanta: Society of Biblical Literature, 2011), 145–63; and Levtow, "Text Destruction and Iconoclasm," 334–5, which lacks discussion of these studies.

30. On the archaeological context of the Tel Dan inscription, see Avraham Biran and Joseph Naveh, "An Aramaic Stele Fragment from Tel Dan," *IEJ* 43 (1993): 81–98; idem, "The Tel Dan Inscription: A New Fragment," *IEJ* 45 (1995): 1–18.

31. Biran and Naveh, "The Tel Dan Inscription," 9. Rachel Ben-Dov, personal communication.

hegemony over—disputed borderlands with Israel. The content and "biography" of the Tel Dan inscription in these respects recalls the hegemonic claims over disputed borderlands between Lagash and Umma and the subsequent violation of boundary stones depicted in the Early Dynastic monumental inscriptions of Eanatum and Enmetana.

Although I have focused on royal monumental victory inscriptions as a special class of ritualized artifacts, a range of other manufactured objects occupied similar ritual roles in ancient Near Eastern war contexts. The Ebal traditions discussed by Richter represent covenant rituals in which treaty tablets were installed beside altars in sanctuaries following military victories. Such treaty tablets resemble victory monuments in both their inscribed content and their ritual emplacement. Treaty tablets were often inscribed with patterned recollections (or anticipations) of warfare together with formulaically inscribed specifications of the vassal status of imperial subjects and the status of allies. When installed and engaged in sanctuary settings, their patterned representations of past battles and resultant social orders formalized and legitimized a suzerain's hegemonic claims and associated treaty stipulations. This is exhibited not only by Deuteronomistic traditions associated with the Ebal sanctuary but also by Neo-Assyrian treaty inscriptions such as the Succession Treaties of Esarhaddon (excavated in sanctuary settings at both Nimrud and Tell Tayinat), and by the Aramaic treaty stelae of Sefire.[32] Elements of such ritualized treaty installations are evident also in Israelite ark traditions that place legislative tablets in the cella of the Jerusalem sanctuary (1 Kgs 8:6–9). As Victor Hurowitz observed, these "tablets of testimony" are inscribed in the first person as if the suzerain were "speaking out of the rock" ("I am Yhwh"), similar to the Mesopotamian monumental inscriptions noted above and to a number of Northwest Semitic royal triumphal stelae as well ("I am Mesha," "I am Zakur," "I am Azatiwada," "I am Kilamuwa").[33]

---

32. On Tell Tayinat, see Bernard M. Levinson, "Esarhaddon's Succession Treaty as the Source for the Canon Formula in Deuteronomy 13:1," *JAOS* 130 (2010): 340; on Nimrud, see JoAnn Scurlock, "Getting Smashed at the Victory Celebration, or What Happened to Esarhaddon's so-called Vassal Treaties and Why," in May, *Iconoclasm and Text Destruction*, 175–86; on Sefire (*KAI* 222), see Levtow, "Text Destruction and Iconoclasm," 318–19 n. 29.

33. Yhwh "speaking out of the rock": Victor A. Hurowitz, "What Can Go Wrong with an Idol?" in May, *Iconoclasm and Text Destruction*, 299. Mesha: *KAI* 181; Zakur: *KAI* 202; Azatiwada: *KAI* 26; Kilamuwa: *KAI* 24. For a hyperbolic Neo-Assyrian example of this phenomenon, see the Great Monolith, which supplements its lengthy

Emplaced within the ark, these Israelite tablets became ritually engaged focal sites of the divine suzerain's presence and legislation. The ark-throne complex itself represents an iconic focus of Yhwh's interactive agency at centralized Israelite temple cults in Shilo (1 Sam 3) and Jerusalem (2 Kgs 19:14–16). It likewise features prominently as a heroic protagonist in Israelite war narratives (1 Sam 4:1–7:2; compare Josh 6) and is "called by the name of Yhwh of hosts enthroned upon the cherubim" (2 Sam 6:2) similar to the way personal names and divine determinatives are assigned to Mesopotamian royal monuments.[34]

The sacred emplacement and strategic engagement of ancient Near Eastern political artifacts—including triumphal stelae, treaty tablets and law codes—is thus attested across East and West Semitic cultural spheres. Much like cult images, these manufactured objects served as focal recipients of cult in ways that made manifest in the social world the identities and relationships inscribed and engraved upon them. Publicly displayed monumental artifacts of this sort represented and legitimized conquest and hegemony through their traditionally patterned inscriptions and iconography and through prescribed human interactions with their materiality and agency.

The ritual agency of inanimate representations of warfare and political domination was not limited to victory monuments, law codes, and treaties. As Seth Sanders notes, the weapons made for Baal by Kothar-wa-Hasis are activated through imperative incantations such that they, not Baal, become agents of divine conquest in Ugaritic conflict myth.[35] Archaeological comparanda for such literary motifs of weaponized agency might include inscribed arrowheads and axeheads that identify the names of war-

---

and vivid conquest narrative with the following claims in the voice of Ashurnasirpal II: "I am king, I am lord, I am praiseworthy, I am exalted, I am important, I am magnificent, I am foremost, I am a hero, I am a warrior, I am a lion, and I am virile" (RIMA 2, 239–40 [A.0.101.17: 33–36]).

34. On textual variants of 2 Sam 6:2, see however P. Kyle McCarter Jr., *I Samuel* (AB 8a; Garden City: Doubleday, 1980), 163. Note also 1 Kgs 7:2, where sanctuary pillars are assigned personal names (Boaz and Yachin), on which see Carol L. Meyers, "Jachin and Boaz in Religious and Political Perspective," *CBQ* 45/2 (1983): 167–78. Cf. Gen 28:18–22, where a stone is anointed with oil and the site in which it is installed is assigned a name, and Gen 33:20, where an altar is assigned a divine name.

35. Sanders writes of how Kothar-wa-Hasis "creates two magic weapons that are also incantations," such that "the sentences themselves ... smash into Baal's opponent" (*Invention of Hebrew*, 51).

riors with the materiality of their weaponry, as if the two act as one body. Such artifacts claim more than ownership in that they represent named warriors who pierce enemy bodies and can literally "kill with words."[36] A corollary to such agency ascribed to personally named weaponry may be found in the sword of Goliath which, as Mark S. Smith notes, was placed behind an ephod in the sanctuary of Nob (concerning this weapon David claims "there is none like it" [1 Sam 21:9]); although Goliath's armor was taken to David's tent rather than to the Nob sanctuary (1 Sam 17:54), the installation of armor in sanctuary settings is likewise attested when Saul's armor is placed in the Philistine temple of Astarte (1 Sam 31:10).[37] Evidence for ritualized instruments of war extends back to Early Dynastic inscriptions such as the Stele of the Vultures, in which the ruler of Umma swears upon "battle nets" of major deities to respect the boundary stones installed by Eanatum in Ningirsu's "beloved field." A ritualized fluidity between animate and inanimate instruments of war is further attested in Assyrian royal inscriptions that refer to living kings as artifactual weapons, as when Ashurnasirpal II indentifies himself in the first person on the Great Monolith as a "merciless weapon."[38] The social agency ascribed to politically strategic artifacts in war contexts is likewise evident in their ritual burial, which further signifies how inanimate objects were ritually imbued with social agency—in various states of activation or dormancy—in ways that directly affected human beings before, during, and after the wars waged around them.[39]

4. Conclusion: Ritual Warfare and the Agency of Its Representation

The prosecution of war in the ancient Near East may be described as the orchestration of strategic violence in ritualized social environments. War-

---

36. See ibid., 106–7.
37. Mark S. Smith, "Warrior Culture in Early Israel," paper presented at the Albright Institute of Archaeological Research, Jerusalem, February 24, 2011. See also Smith's essay in the present volume.
38. RIMA 2: 239–40 (A.0.101.17: 38–9).
39. On the ritual burial of artifacts in sites unassociated with human burials, see Nathaniel B. Levtow, "Artifact Burial in the Ancient Near East," in *The One Who Sows Bountifully: Essays in Honor of Stanley K. Stowers* (ed. Caroline J. Hodge et al.; BJS 356; Providence, R.I.: Brown Judaic Studies, 2013), 141–51.

fare was in this respect not dissimilar to sacrificial temple cult, as a special theater of operations in which prescribed patterns of practice were performed by controlled social hierarchies and understood to determine the form and fate of societies. As in sacrificial temple cult, ritual roles were assigned across multiple arenas of ancient Near Eastern warfare. Humans naturally engaged the gods most closely in spheres of activity where successful conduct—the effective performance of alimentary sacrifice or the successful prosecution of war—meant life or death for individuals and social groups.

Biblical authors routinely foreground causal links between sacrificial cult and warfare. Successful conduct in war depended on successful conduct in cult. This is attested by the successful sacrifice of Mesha's firstborn son (2 Kgs 3:27), by the disastrous sacrificial errors committed by the Elide priesthood at Shiloh (1 Sam 2:12-17), and by Saul's unlawful sacrifice at Gilgal (1 Sam 13:9-14). On the largest of biblical scales, these inseparable correlations between ritual and warfare are evident in the catastrophic political consequences of the cultic errors committed by the people and kings of Israel and Judah (2 Kgs 17 and 24, respectively).[40] These interwoven dynamics of warfare and ritual are embedded in Israelite battle narratives. The Jericho conquest narrative is in this respect so formulaically structured that it appears to be modeled more closely upon ritually prescriptive texts delineating priestly conduct for burnt offerings than upon traditional military historiography (Josh 6). The ritually patterned textualization of warfare evident in such biblical narratives recalls the formulaic

---

40. I have focused on foreign conflicts and imperial contexts, yet it should be noted that the ritualization of warfare and the animation of its instruments obtained in civil war contexts as well. In this respect, ancient Israel's paradigmatic moment of internal conflict is projected onto a ritually symbolic setting in which Moses forces his own people to drink the watered ashes of the molten calf they formed (Exod 32:20). This ritual ordeal subversively achieves a unification of divine and human subjects and objects within an iconic cultic framework, inverting divine embodiment by ritually incorporating "the enemy within" (I thank Mark S. Smith for this insight into the golden calf episode as a ritual incorporation of civil war). The ritual representation of civil covenantal violations may find an archaeologically attested corollary in the ceremonial destruction of Esarhaddon's succession treaties at Nimrud. These treaties represent the disloyalty of vassals as a form of civil disobedience, albeit within an imperial framework of Assyrian domination. Their destruction during the conquest of Kalhu ritually inverted that hegemonic social order within the heart of the Assyrian palace-temple complex. See n. 32 above.

war annals inscribed on Mesopotamian royal monuments, just as Deuteronomistic name-emplacement formulas recall (following Richter) those same ritualized Mesopotamian monumental traditions.[41]

The operative principle of ancient Near Eastern temple cult was the proper maintenance of divine presence in local sites, made manifest through the construction of sanctuaries and the installation and manipulation of divine images and related cultic accoutrements. Through their production and ritual deployment, these crafted products became objects and subjects of rites. These material foci of cult were textually, iconographically, and ritually imbued with the divine and royal identities they represented and the social groups structured around their cults. Hierarchies of status and power were likewise structured through patterned military practices oriented around the local presence and power of gods and kings. Ancient Near Eastern warfare thus involved the production, deployment, violation, and destruction of inanimate objects ritually imbued with the presence and power of divine patrons and their earthly regents. In theaters of war, acts of strategic violence engaged not only human bodies but also—and more importantly for the ancients—a range of such manufactured objects that represented conquest and hegemony and that occupied central roles in cultic settings. These ritualized representations of theopolitical power attracted military engagement and became primary targets in attacks upon temples, palaces, and cities. Ancient Near Eastern iconographic and textual battle narratives often focus more on the function and fate of such artifacts than on the humans who fought amidst them.[42]

Warfare may thus be described as a sphere of ritual activity through which ancient Near Eastern cultures imbued inanimate objects with agency and engaged those objects in strategic social settings. In support of this argument I have highlighted the ritually productive dynamics of warfare in the creation of a class of artifacts—victory monuments—that were understood to have, as Irene Winter notes, "the same agency as

---

41. On Assyrian war annals, see Richter, *Deuteronomistic History and the Name Theology*, 133–34. On the narrative dynamics of Assyrian palace reliefs, see Irene J. Winter, "Royal Rhetoric and the Development of Historical Narrative in Neo-Assyrian Reliefs," in *On Art in the Ancient Near East, Volume 1: Of the First Millennium B.C.E.* (ed. Irene J. Winter; CHANE 34.1; Leiden: Brill, 2010), 3–70. On the interplay between ritualization and textualization, see Bell, *Ritual Theory*, 118–42; idem, "Ritualization of Texts," 366–92.

42. See, for example, the Stele of the Vultures and the Ark Narrative (1 Sam 4:1–7:2).

living beings."⁴³ I have also noted how these ritual dynamics extended beyond the cultic contexts of triumphal monuments to other ritualized artifacts of war such as treaty tablets, weapons, and armor. These objects were treated like human beings and gods because they exercised agency in the strategic settings in which they were deployed. In their ritualized social locations, through patterned human engagements, they exercised force upon people as affective embodiments of gods, kings, and social relationships. As such they were uniquely qualified to win central roles in theaters of war, where the performance of strategic, controlled violence targeted vulnerable enemy formations. Warfare and its representation were in this respect embedded in the ritualized social fabric of the ancient Near East. The practice of warfare tore and rewove that fabric but remained of a piece with it. Engagements with ritualized objects thereby became focal theaters of battle in ancient Near Eastern representations of warfare, while clashes between warriors were often relegated to the background as less adeptly configured instruments for the orchestration of controlled violence.

Victory stelae stood as socially productive sites for the convergence of cult and conflict in the ancient Near East. They still stand as testimonies to the degree to which ancient warfare was ritualized in both its prosecution and its monumental representation. Their patterned blends of past conquests and present social orders were mutually reinforced through their self-prescribed maintenance rites for the future. These multiply ritualized representations of war choreographed conquest and hegemony in strategically embedded and socially durable ways that directly influenced the development of the biblical text. Deuteronomistic conquest narratives likewise promote ritually orchestrated representations of war, the canonization of which solidified their strategic emplacement as firmly as stone monuments set up in sanctuaries. By recalling and prescribing its own ceremonial invocation and installation, biblical historiography perpetually embedded itself in new social environments.⁴⁴ True victory thus came

---

43. Winter describes "agency" as "the affective or instrumental force exerted by a source of energy or action upon a recipient," which could be "exercised not only by individuals, but also by social institutions and material objects" ("Agency Marked, Agency Ascribed: The Affective Object in Ancient Mesopotamia," in Winter, *On Art in the Ancient Near East,* 2:308). On cognitive theories of agency, see Levtow, "Artifact Burial," n. 18.

44. The biblical text thereby invokes its own agency through the ritualized con-

long after the battles, when their scriptural representation transformed fleeting conquests into an enduring monument to an idealized social order for future generations.

BIBLIOGRAPHY

Bahrani, Zainab. *Rituals of War: The Body and Violence in Mesopotamia.* New York: Zone Books, 2008.
Bell, Catherine. *Ritual Theory, Ritual Practice.* New York: Oxford University Press, 1992.
———. "Ritualization of Texts and Textualization of Ritual in the Codification of Taoist Liturgy." *HR* 27 (1988): 366–92.
Biran, Avraham and Joseph Naveh. "An Aramaic Stele Fragment from Tel Dan." *IEJ* 43 (1993): 81–98.
———. "The Tel Dan Inscription: A New Fragment." *IEJ* 45 (1995): 1–18.
Clausewitz, Carl von. *On War.* Translated by J. J. Graham. Harmondsworth: Penguin, 1968.
Cooper, Jerrold S. *Reconstructing History from Ancient Inscriptions: The Lagash-Umma Border Conflict.* Sources from the Ancient Near East 2/1. Malibu: Undena, 1983.
———. *Sumerian and Akkadian Royal Inscriptions, Volume 1: Presargonic Inscriptions.* New Haven: American Oriental Society, 1986.
Cross, Frank Moore. *Canaanite Myth and Hebrew Epic: Essays in the History of the Religion of Israel.* Cambridge: Harvard University Press, 1973.
Driel, G. van. "On 'Standard' and 'Triumphal' Inscriptions." Pages 99–106 in *Symbolae Biblicae et Mesopotamicae Francisco Mario Theodoro de Liagre Böhl Dedicatae.* Edited by M. A. Beek. Leiden: Brill, 1973.
Drinkard, Joel. "The Literary Genre of the Mesha' Inscription." Pages 131–54 in *Studies in the Mesha Inscription and Moab.* Edited by J. Andrew Dearman. SBLABS 2. Atlanta: Scholars Press, 1989.
Gitin, Seymour, Trude Dothan, and Joseph Naveh. "A Royal Dedicatory Inscription from Ekron." *IEJ* 47 (1997): 1–16.
Hallo, William W. "The Royal Inscriptions of UR: A Typology." *HUCA* 33 (1962): 1–43.

---

vergence of its semantic content and performative iconicity, on which see James W. Watts, "The Three Dimensions of Scripture," *Postscripts* 2 (2006): 135–59.

Hundley, Michael. "To Be or Not to Be: A Reexamination of Name Language in Deuteronomy and the Deuteronomistic History." *VT* 59 (2009): 533–55.

Hurrowitz, Victor A. Review of Sandra L. Richter, *Deuteronomistic History and the Name Theology*. *JHS* 5 (2004–2005): 595–96.

———. "What Can Go Wrong with an Idol?" Pages 259–310 in *Iconoclasm and Text Destruction in the Ancient Near East and Beyond*. Edited by Natalie N. May. Oriental Institute Seminars 8. Chicago: The Oriental Institute of the University of Chicago, 2012.

Ismaïl, Bahija Khalil, and Antoine Cavigneaux. "Dādušas Siegesstele IM 95200 aus Ešnunna. Die Inschrift." *BaM* 34 (2003): 129–56.

Levinson, Bernard M. "Esarhaddon's Succession Treaty as the Source for the Canon Formula in Deuteronomy 13:1." *JAOS* 130 (2010): 337–47.

Levtow, Nathaniel B. "Artifact Burial in the Ancient Near East." Pages 141–51 in *The One Who Sows Bountifully: Essays in Honor of Stanley K. Stowers*. Edited by Caroline J. Hodge, Saul M. Olyan, Daniel Ullucci, and Emma Wasserman. BJS 356. Providence, R.I.: Brown Judaic Studies, 2013.

———. *Images of Others: Iconic Politics in Ancient Israel*. Biblical and Judaic Studies from the University of California, San Diego 11. Winona Lake, Ind.: Eisenbrauns, 2008.

———. "Text Destruction and Iconoclasm in the Hebrew Bible and the Ancient Near East." Pages 311–62 in *Iconoclasm and Text Destruction in the Ancient Near East and Beyond*. Edited by Natalie N. May. Oriental Institute Seminars 8. Chicago: The Oriental Institute of the University of Chicago, 2012.

McCarter, P. Kyle, Jr. *I Samuel*. AB 8a. Garden City: Doubleday, 1980.

Meyers, Carol L. "Jachin and Boaz in Religious and Political Perspective." *CBQ* 45 (1983): 167–78.

Millard, Alan R. "The Practice of Writing in Ancient Israel." *BA* 35 (1972): 98–111.

Page, Stephanie. "A Stela of Adad-nirari III and Nergal-ereš from Tell al Rimah." *Iraq* 30/2 (1968): 139–53.

Richter, Sandra L. *The Deuteronomistic History and the Name Theology: lešakkēn šemô šām in the Bible and the Ancient Near East*. BZAW 318. Berlin: de Gruyter, 2002.

———. "The Place of the Name in Deuteronomy." *VT* 57 (2007): 342–66.

Sanders, Seth L. *The Invention of Hebrew*. Traditions. Urbana: University of Illinois Press, 2009.

Scurlock, JoAnn. "Getting Smashed at the Victory Celebration, or What Happened to Esarhaddon's So-Called Vassal Treaties and Why." Pages 175–86 in *Iconoclasm and Text Destruction in the Ancient Near East and Beyond*. Edited by Natalie N. May. Oriental Institute Seminars 8. Chicago: The Oriental Institute of the University of Chicago, 2012.

Slanski, Kathryn E. *The Babylonian Entitlement narûs* (kudurrus)*: A Study in Their Form and Function*. ASOR Books 9. Boston: ASOR, 2003.

Smith, Mark S. "Warrior Culture in Early Israel." Paper presented at the Albright Institute of Archaeological Research, Jerusalem, February 24, 2011.

Tadmor, Hayim, and Shigeo Yamada. *The Royal Inscriptions of Tiglath-Pileser III (744–727 BC) and Shalmaneser V (726–722 BC), Kings of Assyria*. Winona Lake, Ind.: Eisenbrauns, 2011.

Watts, James W. "The Three Dimensions of Scripture." *Postscripts* 2 (2006): 135–59.

Westenholz, Joan G. "*Damnatio Memoriae*: Destruction of Name and Destruction of Person in Third-Millennium Mesopotamia." Pages 89–122 in *Iconoclasm and Text Destruction in the Ancient Near East and Beyond*. Edited by Natalie N. May. Oriental Institute Seminars 8. Chicago: The Oriental Institute of the University of Chicago, 2012.

Winter, Irene J. "After the Battle Is Over: The Stele of the Vultures and the Beginning of Historical Narrative in the Ancient Near East." Pages 3–51 in *On Art in the Ancient Near East, Volume 2: From the Third Millennium B.C.E.* Edited by Irene J. Winter. CHANE 34.2. Leiden: Brill, 2010.

———. "Agency Marked, Agency Ascribed: The Affective Object in Ancient Mesopotamia." Pages 307–32 in *On Art in the Ancient Near East, Volume 2: From the Third Millennium B.C.E.* Edited by Irene J. Winter. CHANE 34.2. Leiden: Brill, 2010.

———. "'Idols of the King': Royal Images as Recipients of Ritual Action in Ancient Mesopotamia." *JRitSt* 6 (1992): 14–42.

———. "Royal Rhetoric and the Development of Historical Narrative in Neo-Assyrian Reliefs." Pages 3–70 in *On Art in the Ancient Near East, Volume 1: Of the First Millennium B.C.E.* Edited by Irene J. Winter. CHANE 34.1. Leiden: Brill, 2010.

Woods, Christopher. "Mutilation of Image and Text in Early Sumerian Sources." Pages 33–56 in *Iconoclasm and Text Destruction in the Ancient Near East and Beyond*. Edited by Natalie N. May. Oriental

Institute Seminars 8. Chicago: The Oriental Institute of the University of Chicago, 2012.

Wright, Jacob L. "Remember Nehemiah: 1 Esdras and the *Damnatio Memoriae Nehemiae*." Pages 145–63 in *Was 1 Esdras First? An Investigation into the Priority and Nature of 1 Esdras*. Edited by Lisbeth S. Fried. SBLAIL 7. Atlanta: Society of Biblical Literature, 2011.

Younger, K. Lawson, Jr. *Ancient Conquest Accounts: A Study in Ancient Near Eastern and Biblical History Writing*. JSOTSup 98. Sheffield: Sheffield Academic Press, 1990.

PART 2
RITUALS AND SYMBOLS OF
ESCALATION, PREPARATION, AND AGGRESSION

Joshua's Encounter with the Commander of Yhwh's Army (Josh 5:13–15): Literary Construction or Reflection of a Royal Ritual?

Thomas Römer

1. Introduction:
The Book of Joshua and Assyrian Warfare Propaganda

It has often been observed that Assyrians were masters in warfare and also in warfare propaganda, using texts and images to their advantage. Within the biblical text of 2 Kgs 18–20, which combines different accounts of the aborted siege of Jerusalem in 701 B.C.E., a passage recalls how high officers of the Assyrian army were sent by the king to Jerusalem. In front of the wall of the city one of these officers utters a speech (in the Judean language!), inviting the inhabitants of the city to surrender and to accept the Assyrian king as their friend:

> Then the Rabshakeh stood and called out in a loud voice in the language of Judah, "Hear the word of the great king, the king of Assyria! ... Do not let Hezekiah make you rely on Yhwh by saying, Yhwh will surely deliver us, and this city will not be given into the hand of the king of Assyria. ... Make your peace with me and come out to me; then every one of you will eat from your own vine and your own fig tree, and drink water from your own cistern.... Has any of the gods of the nations ever delivered its land out of the hand of the king of Assyria? ... Who among all the gods of the countries have delivered their countries out of my hand, that Yhwh should deliver Jerusalem out of my hand?" (2 Kgs 18:28–35)

This scene is probably not just an invention of the author of the biblical narrative. It is likely based on a concrete ritual of propaganda that would take place during the siege of a city. A relief from the palace of Sargon II[1] illustrates the attack on the city of Pazashi, otherwise unknown. It can be identified with the city of Panzish, since the inscription locates it in the land of Manna in front of the pass leading to the land of Zikirtu[2]. A battering ram, which approaches the city, figures in the representation of the siege of the city. In the turret one can distinguish a man apparently holding an open scroll from which he is reading. This may indeed be a propaganda text written in the language of the besieged city inviting the population to surrender. This psychological warfare, which is still used somewhat differently in modern wars (for example, distribution of pamphlets encouraging desertion in the Persian Gulf War), is part of a broader Assyrian agenda of "rituals" that aim at demonstrating the superiority of the Assyrian king, his gods and his army.

This demonstration can also be made by oracles given to the king before the campaign, by royal inscriptions or by letters to the gods. In the Hebrew Bible, the book of Joshua resembles this kind of warfare propaganda and may also be warfare rituals. As shown especially by K. Lawson Younger and John Van Seters,[3] the book of Joshua contains an important number of parallels to Neo-Assyrian and other warfare accounts and ideology. In Josh 10:8, Yhwh delivers an oracle for Joshua at the cusp of a decisive battle: "Fear not, for I have handed them over to you; not one of them shall stand before you" (see also Josh 1:3–6; 11:6). This oracle very closely parallels numerous oracles given to Esarhaddon by prophets of the goddess Ishtar, assuring him of future victory, as in the following example (SAA 9 1.1): "Esarhaddon, king of the lands, fear not ... I am Ishtar of Arbela, I will flay your enemies and deliver them up to you. I am Ishtar of Arbela. I go before you and behind you".[4] There is also an interesting parallel between a "Letter to the God" written on behalf of Sargon II and an episode from Josh 10:10–11. Sargon's "Letter" relates the victory of the Assyr-

---

1. An image of this relief can be found in Yigael Yadin, *The Art of Warfare in Biblical Lands in the Light of Archaeological Study,* (New York: McGraw-Hill, 1963), 320.

2. I owe this information to Lionel Marti, CNRS, Paris.

3. K. Lawson Younger Jr., *Ancient Conquest Accounts: A Study in Ancient Near Eastern and Biblical History Writing* (JSOTSup 98; Sheffield: JSOT Press, 1990); John Van Seters, "Joshua's Campaign of Canaan and Near Eastern Historiography," *SJOT* 2 (1990): 1–12.

4. Quoted from Martti Nissinen, *Prophets and Prophecy in the Ancient Near East* (SBLWAW 12; Atlanta: Society of Biblical Literature, 2003), 102.

ian army thanks to an intervention of the storm god Adad. The Assyrian and the biblical texts relate a great slaughter of enemies on the descent or ascent of a mountain, and then both episodes are followed by divine military intervention: "The rest of the people, who had fled to save their lives … Adad, the violent, the son of Anu, the valiant, uttered his loud cry against them; and with flood cloud and stones of heaven, he totally annihilated the remainder."[5] In a similar way, Josh 10:11 reports: "As they fled before Israel, while they were going down the slope of Beth-Horon, Yhwh threw down huge stones from heaven on them as far as Azekah, and they died; there were more who died because of the hailstones than the Israelites killed with the sword." Other examples could be added in order to show how deeply the first part of the book of Joshua is influenced by ancient Near Eastern and especially Neo-Assyrian warfare ideology. The question one may ask at this stage is whether these parallels are purely literary imitations or whether they also reflect concrete rituals of warfare.

The Assyrian divine oracles forecasting the king's victory against his enemies are delivered by male or female prophets who are mostly associated with the sanctuary of Ishtar. In the book of Joshua, Yhwh speaks directly to Joshua without any intermediary. This phenomenon may be understood as a literary transformation of a concrete practice that is attested elsewhere in the Hebrew Bible, as for instance in 1 Kgs 22:6: "Go up; Yhwh will give it (Ramoth-Gilead) into the hand of the king"; or in Jer 27:17–20, where a negative oracle is given to the king by the prophet Jeremiah. The direct communication between Yhwh and Joshua is therefore based on a prophetic oracular practice, but this oracular practice has been altered either to show that Joshua is indeed as much a prophet as he is a military leader or in order to present him as a second Moses who has the privilege of a direct communication with Yhwh.

The book of Joshua must therefore be understood primarily as a literary and ideological construction in which the invention of the conquest of the land serves the theological agenda of the Deuteronomists.[6] On the

---

5. Younger, *Ancient Conquest Accounts*, 210.
6. See Nadav Na'aman, "The 'Conquest of Canaan' in the Book of Joshua and in History," in *From Nomadism to Monarchy: Archaeological and Historical Aspects of Early Israel* (ed. Israel Finkelstein and Nadav Na'aman; Jerusalem: Israel Exploration Society; Washington, D.C.: Biblical Archaeological Society, 1994), 218–81; and Erhard Blum, "Überlegungen zur Kompositionsgeschichte des Josuabuches," in *The Book of Joshua* (ed. Ed Noort; BETL 250; Leuven: Peeters, 2012), 137–57.

other hand, by including motifs and symbols from ancient Near Eastern warfare discourses, some texts may also allow to uncover reflections of older practices and rituals, beyond their actual function. This point can be illustrated with a short and enigmatic text: Joshua's encounter with the chief of Yhwh's army.

2. Joshua 5:13–15 in Its Present Literary Context

Joshua 5, as it now stands, insures the transition from the crossing of the Jordan in Josh 3:1–5:1 to the divine destruction of Jericho in Josh 6. One can distinguish three units that at first glance appear quite unrelated: the circumcision of the second generation born in the wilderness by Joshua at Gilgal (5:2–9); the first celebration of the Passover in Gilgal combined with the cessation of the manna (5:10–12); and, finally, Joshua's encounter with the chief of Yhwh's army (5:13–15[7]):

> When Joshua was in Jericho,[8] he looked up, and saw: and behold a man standing over against him, his sword drawn in his hand. Joshua went to him and said to him: are you for us or for our adversaries? He said: No, I am the chief of Yhwh's army. Now I have come. Joshua fell on his face to the earth. [He bowed down][9] and said to him: What does my lord say to his servant? The chief of Yhwh's army said to Joshua: Take off your sandal from your foot. Indeed, the place where you are standing is holy. [And Joshua did so.][10]

---

7. For questions of textual criticism, see Klaus Bieberstein, *Josua-Jordan-Jericho: Archäologie, Geschichte und Theologie der Landnahmeerzählungen Josua 1–6* (OBO 143; Fribourg: Universitätsverlag; Göttingen: Vandenhoeck & Ruprecht, 1995), 226–29; and Blažej Štrba, *Take Off Your Sandals from Your Feet! An Exegetical Study of Josh 5, 13–15* (ÖBS 32; Frankfurt am Main: Lang, 2008), 81–91.

8. בִּירִיחוֹ is often translated "by Jericho" or "next to Jericho" because it does not seem logical that Joshua finds himself already in Jericho. As we will see, one should maintain the grammatical meaning and translate "in Jericho."

9. וַיִּשְׁתָּ֫חוּ is missing in LXX. The verb may have been added in order to emphasize Joshua's "pious" behavior.

10. The final notice of accomplishment is lacking in LXX; it may be a later addition in order to underline Joshua's obedience.

This episode has often been considered to be somewhat out of place, a fragment of an older conquest account, or an etiological narrative legitimizing the existence of a sanctuary next to Jericho.[11]

On the literary level, the text is not so "out of order" as many commentators claim. There is no doubt that verse 15 seeks to establish a parallel between Joshua and Moses:

שַׁל־נַעַלְךָ מֵעַל רַגְלֶךָ כִּי הַמָּקוֹם אֲשֶׁר אַתָּה עֹמֵד עָלָיו קֹדֶשׁ הוּא
Take off your sandal from your foot. Indeed, the place where you are standing is holy. (Josh 5:15)

שַׁל־נְעָלֶיךָ מֵעַל רַגְלֶיךָ כִּי הַמָּקוֹם אֲשֶׁר אַתָּה עוֹמֵד עָלָיו אַדְמַת־קֹדֶשׁ הוּא
Take off your sandals from your feet. Indeed, the place where you are standing is holy ground. (Exod 3:5)

It is not clear which text depends on the other, but it is clear that through these verses Joshua appears as a new Moses. Interestingly the whole chapter of Josh 5 points back almost in a concentric way to the beginning of the Moses story:[12]

A Divine revelation to Moses (Exod 3)
 B Passover (Exod 12:1–28)
  C Circumcision for the Passover (Exod 12:43–50; see also 4:24–26)
   D Crossing of the Sea (Exod 14)
    Sinai and wilderness
   D' Crossing of the Jordan (Josh 3–4)
  C' Circumcision before the Passover (Josh 5:2–9)
 B' Passover (Josh 5:10–12)
A' Divine revelation to Joshua (Josh 5:13–15)

It is possible that the episodes relating the circumcision and the Passover are post-Dtr texts, which could belong to a "Hexateuchal redaction."[13] In

---

11. See, for instance, Martin Noth, *Das Buch Josua* (HAT I/7; Tübingen: Mohr, 1953), 23.

12. See also Bieberstein, *Josua-Jordan-Jericho*, 418.

13. For the theory of a competion between a Hexateuch and a Pentateuchal redaction see Eckhart Otto, *Das Deuteronomium im Pentateuch und Hexateuch: Studien zur Literaturgeschichte von Pentateuch und Hexateuch im Lichte des Deuterono-*

this context the apparition of the divine warrior in Josh 5:13 can be understood as accomplishing the promise made in Exod 23:20: "I am going to send an angel in front of you, to guard you on the way and to bring you to the place that I have prepared." Its aim is to connect the book of Joshua as narrowly as possible to the foregoing Pentateuch and thus to *de facto* create a Hexateuch. To that purpose, the redactors also make use of an older tradition, which includes the apparition of a divine warrior.

In the Hebrew Bible, this motif has parallels in Num 22:31 (see v. 23) and 1 Chr 21:16.

Num 22:31: וַיַּרְא אֶת־מַלְאַךְ יהוה נִצָּב בַּדֶּרֶךְ וְחַרְבּוֹ שְׁלֻפָה בְּיָדוֹ
1 Chr 21:16: וַיַּרְא אֶת־מַלְאַךְ יהוה עֹמֵד ... וְחַרְבּוֹ שְׁלוּפָה בְּיָדוֹ
Josh 5:13: וַיַּרְא וְהִנֵּה־אִישׁ עֹמֵד לְנֶגְדּוֹ וְחַרְבּוֹ שְׁלוּפָה בְּיָדוֹ

All three texts concur in the description of the drawn sword; whereas Numbers and Chronicles use the term מַלְאַךְ יְהוָה, the author of Josh 5:13 uses the more neutral אִישׁ because the identity of the mysterious person will be revealed later. It is therefore plausible that, in the Hebrew Bible, Josh 5:13–14 is the oldest of the three texts.

In its present context this episode can well be related to the foregoing stories. The exclamation of Yhwh's commander-in-chief, "Now I have come," can be read as a response to the circumcision and the Passover. Now that the people, who in fact constitute Joshua's army, have accomplished both rituals, the conquest, which the previous generation was unable to accomplish (Num 13–14), can start. There may also be a reference to the theophany in the circumcision episode in Josh 5:2–9.[14] The use of אַנְשֵׁי הַמִּלְחָמָה in 5:4 prepares the military vision of Joshua and the expression חַרְבוֹת צֻרִים ("flint knives") in 5:2–3 describing the tool of the circumcision (see צוּר in Exod 4:24–26) may allude to the importance of the sword in 5:13. However, despite these links to the preceding episodes, in its present form, Josh 5:13–15 remains an awkward text.

---

miumsrahmen (FAT 30; Tübingen: Mohr Siebeck, 2000) and Thomas C. Römer and Marc Z. Brettler, "Deuteronomy 34 and the Case for a Persian Hexateuch," *JBL* 119 (2000): 401–19.

14. Erhard Blum, "Beschneidung und Passa in Kanaan. Beobachtungen und Mutmaßungen zu Jos 5" in *Freiheit und Recht: Festschrift für Frank Crüsemann zum 65. Geburtstag* (ed. Christof Hardmeier, Rainer Kessler and Andreas Ruwe; Gütersloh: Chr. Kaiser/Gütersloher Verlagshaus, 2003), 292–322, 309–10.

As already mentioned, the order of the divine commander-in-chief for Joshua to take off his sandals and Joshua's execution of this order do not make much sense, if it were not for the fact that they establish a parallel between Joshua and Moses. One may therefore assume that verse 15 did not constitute the original ending of the encounter.[15] The continuation to 5:14 must be found elsewhere.

3. Joshua 5:13–15 in Its Original Literary Context

In his commentary on Joshua, Richard Nelson suggests that the original ending of Josh 5:13–15 was "cut out as offensive for theological sensibilities."[16] There is, however, an easier solution, namely to consider Josh 6:2 and following as the continuation of Joshua's encounter in 5:13–15. Indeed, it has sometimes been suspected that 6:1 is a later insertion which aims to emphasize that the city was totally shut up and could therefore be attacked (Deut 20:11–12 stipulates that when a city "opens" [פתח] itself, it shall not be destroyed);[17]

> He said: No, I am the chief of Yhwh's army. Now I have come. Joshua fell on his face to the earth. [He bowed down] and said to him: What does my lord say to his servant? (5:14)
>
> Yhwh said to Joshua; See I have given into your hand Jericho, [along with its king and his soldiers]. (6:2)[18]

---

15. See also Cuthbert A. Simpson, *The Early Traditions of Israel: A Critical Analysis of the Pre-Deuteronomic Narrative of the Hexateuch* (Oxford: Basil Blackwell, 1948), 287–88. See similarly Volkmar Fritz, *Das Buch Josua* (HAT I/7; Tübingen: Mohr, 1994), 63.

16. Richard D. Nelson, *Joshua: A Commentary* (OTL; Louisville: Westminster John Knox, 1997), 82.

17. Edmond Jacob, "Une théophanie mystérieuse: Josué 5, 13–15," in *Ce Dieu qui vient: Etudes sur l'Ancien et le Nouveau Testament offertes au Professeur Bernard Renaud à l'occasion de son soixante-cinquième anniversaire* (ed. Raymond Kuntzmann; LeDiv 159; Paris: Cerf, 1995), 131–35; Jacques Briend, "Les sources de l'histoire deutéronomique: Recherches sur Jos1–12" in *Israël construit son histoire: L'historiographie deutéronomiste à la lumière des recherches récentes* (ed. Albert de Pury, Thomas Römer and Jean-Daniel Macchi; MdB 34; Genève: Labor et Fides, 1996), 343–74, 353.

18. The king and the soldiers do not play a major role in the following story. The king of Jericho appears however in Josh 2. They may either reflect an older account of the conquest of Jericho, or constitute later additions.

It is not unusual that a text switches from the "chief of Yhwh's army" to Yhwh himself; such passages are frequent in the Hebrew Bible (see for instance Exod 3:2-4 or Judg 6:12-14). If we accept this reconstruction of the original narrative, we are also able to understand why the episode opens with a statement indicating that Joshua is in Jericho. The "in" would then indicate that the context of the encounter is that of a vision. This theory can be strengthened by a comparison with an Assyrian text, the report of Assurbanipal's campaign against Elam. This campaign is preceded by a vision in which a prophet sees the goddess Ishtar armed and standing in front of the king telling him that she will fight for him in his war against the Elamites:

> Ištar heard my desperate sighs and said to me: "Fear not!" She made my heart confident, saying: "Because of the prayer you said with your hand lifted up, your eyes being filled with tears, I have compassion with you." The very same night as I implored her, a visionary (šabrû) lay down and had a dream. When he woke up, he reported to me the nocturnal vision shown to him by Ištar: "Ištar who dwells in Arbela entered, having quivers hanging from her right and left and holding a bow in her hand. She had drawn a sharp-pointed sword, ready for battle. You stood before her and she spoke to you like a mother who gave birth to you. Ištar, the highest of the gods, called you and gave you the following order: 'You are prepared for war, and I am ready to carry out my plans.' You said to her: 'Wherever you go, I will go with you!' But the Lady of Ladies answered you: 'You stay here in your place ... until I go accomplish that task.'"[19]

This Assyrian document from the seventh century B.C.E. contains several parallels to Josh 5: the king who prepares for war receives through a vision of a seer an oracle of victory given by the goddess Ishtar, who appears with a drawn sword and ready to engage in battle. This very much resembles the depiction of the commander of Yhwh's army. Joshua's bowing down precedes the divine announcement of the handing over of Jericho and matches Assurbanipal's prayer which precedes the vision of the specialist who then sees Ishtar apparently already standing in the battlefield. It is, therefore, quite plausible to argue that the author of Josh 5:13-14 has taken over such an account, which may, however, itself also reflect the ritual of preparation for a king before waging war. The Assyrian text suggests the existence of a practice where a specialist is put in a condition to have a vision in which

---

19. Quoted from Nissinen, *Prophets and Prophecy*, 147-48.

a divine warrior appears and promises divine assistance for the coming battle. The description of the drawn sword and the imminence of the battle are very similar in both texts. We should therefore take our investigation one step further and ask whether the motif of the drawn sword has any relation to a warfare ritual.

4. Joshua 5:13–15 and the Question of a Ritual Background

It has become clear that the military nuance of the theophany introduces the following conquest stories and gives Joshua a royal status. Is the emphasis on the drawn sword of the divine warrior proper only to ancient Near Eastern iconography of the warrior god, or can we also detect behind this motif the recollection of a royal ritual? Othmar Keel has pointed out Egyptian texts and images reflecting the idea that a deity hands his weapons over to the king in order to guarantee his victory against his enemies.[20] An inscription from Karnak relates a dream of Merenptah, which comes quite close to Josh 5:13–15. He sees in his dream something "like a statue of Ptah," who speaks to the king and gives him his sword in order to strengthen his heart: "Then his majesty saw in a dream as if a statue of Ptah were standing before Pharaoh.... He spoke to him: 'Take thou (it),' while he extended to him the sword, 'and banish thou the fearful heart from thee.'"[21] The handing over of divine arms to the Pharaoh is apparently a common iconographic motif. A stele from Beth-Shean shows Ramses II stretching out his right hand in order to receive the divine sword from Amon-Re. The inscription reads: "I am giving thee the victory.... I am giving you the boundaries as far as you desirest.... Accept for yourself a sword against all foreign countries."[22] In the so-called Israel stele there is a double picture of Merenptah receiving a sword from Amon-Re. In this inscription, Amon-Re tells him: "Take for yourself your sword for valour, in every foreign country."[23] A similar scenario occurs for Ramses III in

---

20. Othmar Keel, *Wirkmächtige Siegeszeichen im Alten Testament: ikonographische Studien zu Jos 8,12–26; Ex 17,8–13; 2 Kön 13,4–19 und I Kön 22,11* (OBO 5; Fribourg: Universitätsverlag; Göttingen: Vandenhoeck & Ruprecht, 1974), 82–88.

21. James Henry Breasted, *Ancient Records of Egypt: Historical Documents From the Earliest Times to the Persian Conquest* (New York: Russell & Russell, 1962), 245 §582.

22. J. Černý, "Stela of Ramesses II from Beisan," *ErIsr* 5 (1958): 75*–82*, 76.

23. Kenneth A. Kitchen, *Ramesside Inscriptions: Historical and Biographical: 4, Merenptah and the Late 19th Dynasty* (Oxford: Blackwell, 1969), IV/1, 10.

Medinet Habu: Ramses III receives a divine sword and in the next scene he is on a chair and a prince is holding the sword for him. This motif of the handing over of a sword given by a god is probably more than a literary and iconographical motif and may correspond to a ritual, in which, perhaps after a vision or a dream incubation, a sword is given to the king by a priest or another cultic person.

The theme of divine weapons given to the king is also attested in the Levant. Jean-Marie Durand has published letters relating to the storm god Addu of Aleppo, the "prototype of the Babylonian Marduk."[24] These documents report that when the king of Mari was enthroned, Addu sent to the king of Mari the weapons with which he had defeated the Sea. A letter written perhaps by the governor of Terqa (A.1858) informs Zimri-Lim that Addu's armaments have arrived from Aleppo and that he has placed them in the temple of Dagan while waiting for further instructions of the king.[25] Another letter (A.1858) provides further information: a prophet received the following oracle from Addu: "I have given the whole land to Yahdun-Lin [the father of Zimri-Lim], and because of my arms, no rival arose for him in battle." Later, in the same letter Addu also addresses an oracle to the present king Zimri-Lin: "I have brought you to the throne of your father and I have given you the arms with which I fought against the Sea. I have anointed you with the oil of my invincibility and no one could stand in front of you."[26] As Jean-Marie Durand rightly points out, these letters must reflect a royal ritual in which a king, either on the day of his enthronement or before waging a war, receives divine arms meant to confirm divine assistance and establish the king's superiority. A similar case can be detected in the inscription of Yahdun-Lim, in which he claims: "Dagan proclaimed my kingship, gave me the powerful weapon that fells the kings, my enemies."[27]

The so-called Broken Obelisk from the eleventh century B.C.E. may also refer to the handing over of a divine weapon, even if the interpretation is much discussed. On the picture a divine hand emerging from the

---

24. Jean-Marie Durand, *Le culte d'Addu d'Alep et l'affaire d'Alahthum* (Florilegium Marianum VII; Paris: Société pour l'étude du Proche-Orient Ancien, 2002), 1.

25. Ibid., 14–15.

26. Ibid., 134–37.

27. Quoted after Lluís Feliu, *The God Dagan in Bonze Age Syria* (CHANE 9; Leiden: Brill, 2003), 158. I thank Jack Sasson for pointing out this text to me.

winged disk in heaven is handing over a bow[28] to the Assyrian king, often identified with Aššur-bel-ka. The text, which apparently is a compilation from at least two different sources, opens with an introduction in which it is stated that the king acts with the support of the god Aššur (?). This could be related to a gift of divine arms to a king, but even if this evidence is not as clear as the foregoing ones there are enough extrabiblical indications that support the existence of a ritual during which the king was invested with divine arms.

Going back to the Hebrew Bible, such a handing over is also attested in Ezek 30:22–26. This passage, which is part of a larger oracle against Egypt in 30:20–26, is probably a reworking of the older oracle found in v. 20–21:[29]

> Therefore thus says the Lord Yhwh: I am against Pharaoh king of Egypt, and will break his arms, [both the strong arm and the one that was broken][30]; and I will make *the sword* fall from his hand.... I will strengthen the arms of the king of Babylon, and put *my sword* in his hand; but I will break the arms of Pharaoh, and he will groan before him with the groans of one mortally wounded. I will strengthen the arms of the king of Babylon, but the arms of Pharaoh shall fall. And they shall know that I am Yhwh, when I put my sword into the hand of the king of Babylon. He shall stretch it out against the land of Egypt, and I will scatter the Egyptians among the nations and disperse them throughout the countries. Then they shall know that I am Yhwh.

The broken arms of Pharaoh are opposed to the strong arms of the Babylonian king and the sword of Pharaoh, which—if we relate this oracle to the Egyptian texts and images discussed above—was given to him by the gods of Egypt is opposed to Yhwh's sword, which Yhwh will now give to the king of Babylon. This oracle clearly presupposes the idea of handing over a divine weapon to a king, but here the king is a foreign king, who becomes, like Cyrus in Second Isaiah, the tool of Yhwh's military intervention in favor of his people. Ezekiel 30 may, therefore, also present an appropriation of a royal ritual.

---

28. See, for instance, Tallay Ornan, "Who Is Holding the Lead Rope? The Relief of the Broken Obelisk," *Iraq* 69 (2007): 59–72, 60.

29. See, for instance, Walter Zimmerli, *Ezechiel* (BKAT 13/1-2; Neukirchen-Vluyn: Neukirchener, 1969), 740–46.

30. This precision is added because the older oracle only spoke of one arm of Pharaoh that Yhwh announces to break.

In the light of these parallels we may indeed imagine that the short encounter of Joshua with the chief of Yhwh's army is composed with the practice of such a ritual in mind. Interestingly, in the conquest of Ai, Joshua is equipped with a sword. In 8:18 Yhwh says to him: "'Stretch out the sword that is in your hand toward Ai (נְטֵה בַּכִּידוֹן אֲשֶׁר־בְּיָדְךָ אֶל־הָעַי), for I will give it into your hand.' And Joshua stretched out the sword that was in his hand toward the city." If we compare this passage with Josh 5:13–15, we find that the sword has now wandered from the divine commander to the earthly commander. As in 5:15, Joshua immediately obeys the divine order. Joshua's sword appears again in 8:26 in the final comment on Israel's victory: "Joshua did not draw back his hand, with which he stretched out the sword, until he had utterly destroyed all the inhabitants of Ai." In Josh 8, however the author uses the rarer word כִּידוֹן instead of חרב. This may be explained by the fact that Josh 8 is an older story written without knowledge of the scene of Josh 5:13–15.[31] The word חרב associated with Joshua appears in Josh 10:28 ("Joshua took Makkedah on that day, and struck it and its king with the edge of the sword") and similarly in 10:32, 27, 39, etc., and in Josh 11:10 ("Joshua took Hazor, and struck its king down with the sword"; compare also 11:12). Since the texts never explain how Joshua got his sword, the best hypothesis might indeed be to imagine that he received the divine sword after the encounter related in Josh 5:13–15.

5. Summary

The book of Joshua appropriates several concepts and ideologies of Neo-Assyrian and other ancient Near Eastern warfare propaganda. Joshua's encounter with the commander of Yhwh's army can be related to Assyrian oracles in which the king receives the promise of divine assistance before the battle. In its present context, the scene follows the circumcision of the second wilderness generation and the celebration of the first Passover in the land. The divine warrior appears, therefore, after the accomplishment of rituals that highlight Israel's status as Yhwh's people. Originally, however, Josh 5:13–15 was conceived as the opening of the conquest story that begins in 6:2. In a vision Joshua sees the divine commander with a sword,

---

31. Keel (*Wirkmächtige Siegeszeichen*, 86–87) thinks that Josh 5:13–15 had originally כִּידוֹן, which later had been changed into חרב.

and through this commander, Yhwh ensures Joshua that he has given Jericho into his hands.

The importance of the sword can be related to iconographic and textual documents from Egypt, Mari and Assyria where a king receives divine weapons before battle or at the moment of his enthronement. This motif probably reflects a concrete ritual in which a divine sword or bow (or other weapons) were given to the king by a priest or another cultic person. Since Joshua, who is depicted as a royal figure, often appears after 5:13–15 with a sword, we can speculate that this sword was given to him by the divine messenger. The literary legitimization of Joshua may, therefore, be based on a royal ritual known to the author of 5:13–15. The theme of a god-given sword is not limited to the ancient Near East. Perseus receives a sword from Zeus to kill Medusa; in Japanese mythology the magical sword Kusanagi was given to the emperor by a goddess; and one may also think of King Arthur and so on. In this respect Josh 5:13–15 participates in an almost archetypical topic of royal legitimization.

Bibliography

Bieberstein, Klaus. *Josua-Jordan-Jericho: Archäologie, Geschichte und Theologie der Landnahmeerzählungen Josua 1–6*. OBO 143. Fribourg: Universitätsverlag; Göttingen: Vandenhoeck & Ruprecht, 1995.

Blum, Erhard. "Beschneidung und Passa in Kanaan: Beobachtungen und Mutmaßungen zu Jos 5." Pages 291–322 in *Freiheit und Recht: Festschrift für Frank Crüsemann zum 65. Geburtstag*. Edited by Christof Hardmeier, Rainer Kessler, and Andreas Ruwe. Gütersloh: Chr.Kaiser/Gütersloher Verlagshaus, 2003.

———. "Überlegungen zur Kompositionsgeschichte des Josuabuches." Pages 137–57 in *The Book of Joshua*. Edited by Ed Noort. BETL 250. Leuven: Peeters, 2012.

Breasted, James Henry. *Ancient Records of Egypt: Historical Documents From the Earliest Times to the Persian Conquest*. New York: Russell & Russell, 1962.

Briend, Jacques. "Les sources de l'histoire deutéronomique. Recherches sur Jos 1–12." Pages 343–74 in *Israël construit son histoire: L'historiographie deutéronomiste à la lumière des recherches récentes*. Edited by Albert de Pury, Thomas Römer, and Jean-Daniel Macchi. MdB 34. Genève: Labor et Fides, 1996.

Černý, J. "Stela of Ramesses II from Beisan." *ErIsr* 5 (1958): 75–82.

Durand, Jean-Marie. *Le culte d'Addu d'Alep et l'affaire d'Alahthum*. Florilegium Marianum VII. Paris: Société pour l'étude du Proche-Orient Ancien, 2002.

Feliu, Lluís. *The God Dagan in Bonze Age Syria*. CHANE 19. Leiden: Brill, 2003.

Fritz, Volkmar. *Das Buch Josua*. HAT I/7. Tübingen: Mohr, 1994.

Jacob, Edmond. "Une théophanie mystérieuse: Josué 5, 13–15." Pages 131–35 in *Ce Dieu qui vient: Etudes sur l'Ancien et le Nouveau Testament offertes au Professeur Bernard Renaud à l'occasion de son soixante-cinquième anniversaire*. Edited by Raymond Kuntzmann. LeDiv 159. Paris: Cerf, 1995.

Keel, Othmar. *Wirkmächtige Siegeszeichen im Alten Testament: ikonographische Studien zu Jos 8,12–26; Ex 17,8–13; 2 Kön 13,4–19 und I Kön 22,11*. OBO 5. Fribourg: Universitätsverlag; Göttingen: Vandenhoeck & Ruprecht, 1974.

Kitchen, Kenneth A. *Ramesside Inscriptions: Historical and Biographical. 4, Merenptah and the Late 19th Dynasty*. Oxford: Blackwell, 1969.

Na'aman, Nadav. "The 'Conquest of Canaan' in the Book of Joshua and in History." Pages 218–81 in *From Nomadism to Monarchy: Archaeological and Historical Aspects of Early Israel*. Edited by Israel Finkelstein and Nadav Na'aman. Jerusalem: Israel Exploration Society; Washington, D.C.: Biblical Archaeological Society, 1994.

Nelson, Richard D. *Joshua: A Commentary*. OTL. Louisville: Westminster John Knox, 1997.

Nissinen, Martti. *Prophets and Prophecy in the Ancient Near East*. SBLWAW 12. Atlanta: Society of Biblical Literature, 2003.

Noth, Martin. *Das Buch Josua*. HAT I/7. Tübingen: Mohr, 1953.

Ornan, Tallay. "Who Is Holding the Lead Rope? The Relief of the Broken Obelisk." *Iraq* 69 (2007): 59–72.

Otto, Eckhart. *Das Deuteronomium im Pentateuch und Hexateuch: Studien zur Literaturgeschichte von Pentateuch und Hexateuch im Lichte des Deuteronomiumsrahmen*. FAT 30. Tübingen: Mohr Siebeck, 2000.

Römer, Thomas C., and Marc Z. Brettler. "Deuteronomy 34 and the Case for a Persian Hexateuch." *JBL* 119 (2000): 401–19.

Simpson, Cuthbert A. *The Early Traditions of Israel: A Critical Analysis of the Pre-Deuteronomic Narrative of the Hexateuch*. Oxford: Basil Blackwell, 1948.

Štrba, Blažej. *Take Off Your Sandals from Your Feet! An Exegetical Study of Josh 5, 13–15*. ÖBS 32. Frankfurt am Main: Lang, 2008.

Van Seters, John. "Joshua's Campaign of Canaan and Near Eastern Historiography." *SJOT* 2 (1990): 1–12.

Yadin, Yigael. *The Art of Warfare in Biblical Lands In the Light of Archaeological Study.* 2 vols. New York: McGraw-Hill, 1963.

Younger, K. Lawson, Jr. *Ancient Conquest Accounts: A Study in Ancient Near Eastern and Biblical History Writing.* JSOTSup 98. Sheffield: JSOT Press, 1990.

Zimmerli, Walter. *Ezechiel.* BKAT 13/1–2. Neukirchen-Vluyn: Neukirchener, 1969.

"A Sword for Yhwh and for Gideon!":
The Representation of War in Judges 7:16–22

Kelly J. Murphy

1. Introduction

Stories of swords enclose the book of Judges. As the book opens, Judah "[fights] against Jerusalem ... [putting] it to the sword and [setting] the city on fire" (1:8). At the end of the book, Judg 21 records how Israel commands that the 12,000 soldiers "put the inhabitants of Jabesh-gilead to the sword, including the women and the little ones" (21:10). In between, conflicts dominate and stories of swords punctuate the book: Ehud makes for himself a "cubit-length" sword, carrying it into Eglon's palace and thrusting it into his belly (3:16, 21–22), while "all of the army of Sisera" falls by the sword in Barak and Deborah's victory (4:16). Within the story of Gideon, found in Judg 6–8, sword appears four times (7:14, 20, 22; 8:20; compare 9:54), most notably in the war cry uttered by Gideon and his men, *ḥereb layhwh ûləgidəôn*, "A sword for Yhwh and for Gideon!" (7:20). Judges is at once about conflict, about how later writers and editors of the biblical material remembered the emergence and formation of early Israel and its leaders, and about what these later writers and editors perceived as the power behind the sword, namely, Yhwh. In many ways, Judg 6–8 is this story in miniature.

Moreover, the Gideon story in Judg 6–8 is a rich source for studying one way in which the Hebrew Bible depicts both war rituals and symbolism in the premonarchic period—from prebattle rituals to the battles themselves.[1] The scene in Judg 7:16–22 depicts the first of two battles

---

1. Jean Louis Ska writes of plot and battle depiction in the biblical texts, "The modern reader feels frustrated by the lack of interest in 'happenings.' For instance, the Bible almost never narrates the details of a battle. The emphasis seems to lie else-

between Gideon's army of three hundred men and the Midianite enemy who, according to the final form of the text, had descended into Israel as "thick as locusts" and as innumerable as their camels (6:5).[2] Despite the fact that the deity initially charges Gideon to "deliver Israel from the hand of Midian" in 6:14, the actual battle with the Midianites is not begun until forty-one verses later, in 7:16. Judges 6 features stories of Gideon's repeated tests to ensure that Yhwh is indeed "with him" (6:11–24), Gideon's renaming scene (6:25–32), a scene in which Yhwh's spirit "clothes" (*lbš**) Gideon and Gideon calls out the local tribes to do battle (6:33–35), and the infamous fleece scene that reiterates that the deity will go into battle with Gideon (6:36–40). Judges 7 continues with a divine injunction to reduce Gideon's sizeable army through a strange water test (7:1–8) and an oneiric account in which Gideon overhears the prediction of his forthcoming victory from the mouth of the enemy (7:9–15).[3] Finally, Judg 7:16–22 details the long-awaited battle. By the time the initial battle begins in 7:16, it is, as Victor Matthews notes, "almost an afterthought."[4]

Yet while the final form of Judg 6–8 largely focuses on the relationship between the divinely appointed hero Gideon and the deity, the original sto-

---

where. Events are often at the service of a certain 'display' of truth, of the revelation of a certain aspect of God" (*"Our Fathers Have Told Us": Introduction to the Analysis of Hebrew Narratives* [Rome: Editrice Pontificio Instituto Biblico, 2000], 18). Though this is frequently the case, here in Judg 7:16–22 the narrative gives an unusual amount of detail about what happens not only immediately preceding the battle, but also in the battle plan and attack itself.

2. The material in 6:1–6 is most likely a later addition to the text and was likely not known (at least in its entirety) to the author of the original war story found in 7:16–21. For various redactional theories, see Walter Groß, *Richter* (HThKAT; Freiburg: Herder, 2009), 367–69, 388–89; Susan Niditch, *Judges: A Commentary* (OTL; Louisville: Westminster John Knox, 2008), 89; Alberto Soggin, *Judges: A Commentary* (OTL; Philadelphia: Westminster, 1981), 109–13. A second battle—and probably the earliest stratum of the Gideon material—is found in 8:4–21.

3. Overall, Judg 6:11–24, 25–32, 36–40; 7:1–8, 9–15 comprise the expanded final form of the Gideon story and feature a "divine assurance" motif in which Gideon, not quite the "mighty warrior" the angel names him but rather embodying his status as the "least in his family," repeatedly asks for signs and assurances from the deity that he will be victorious. These additions largely reflect later redactors' unease with the earlier stories of an independent warrior (and set the stage for the critique of both the leadership of the judges overall and kingship in particular; see 8:22–35).

4. Victor H. Matthews, *Judges and Ruth* (NCBC; Cambridge: Cambridge University Press, 2004), 93.

ries about Gideon seem to have mainly focused on war stories, and many scholars argue that some of this original material can be found in 7:16–21 and 8:4–21.[5] Numerous signs in the text indicate that this original material paints Gideon as a fearless leader, a ruthless warrior, a clever tactician—a genuine *gibbôr ḥayil*, the "mighty warrior" that the divine messenger claims him to be in 6:12.[6] The irony is that while the final form of the text has very little to do with that original *gibbôr ḥayil*, whose presence is seen only fleetingly in Judg 6–8 (cf. 7:16–21; 8:4–21), Gideon is most often remembered for being a warrior (if not necessarily a particularly brave one). Repeatedly the Gideon of the battlefield appears outside of the Bible: he is the focus of A. Malamat's article "The War of Gideon and Midian: A Military Approach," in which Malamat argues, "modern military science fully justifies [Gideon's] plan and its postulates as they are revealed in the Biblical account."[7] John Laffin's *Links of Leadership: Thirty Centuries of Military Command* begins with a chapter entitled "Gideon Started It," in which he outlines fourteen principles put into effect by Gideon and emulated, according to Laffin, by countless leaders after him.[8] One principle includes "Choose the most suitable weapons for the action in hand."[9] More recently an episode of *Veggie Tales*, featuring Larry the Cucumber as Gideon, depicts Larry/Gideon defeating the Midianites with horns, flashlights, and an army reduced to six carrots and six peas (they carry no

---

5. For instance, Groß argues that 7:16–22 may be part of a pre-Deuteronomistic Gideon narrative, part of which might be an older story that cannot now be reconstructed, writing, "7:16–22 sind literarisch einheitlich und Bestandteil der vordtr Gideon-Erzählung. Mit hoher Wahrscheinlichkeit wurde eine altere Erzahlung verwendet und zugleich so eingeschmolzen, dass sie nicht mehr rekonstruiert und erst recht nicht mehr literarkritisch herausoperiert werden kann" (*Richter*, 383). Of 8:4–21 he notes that 8:4, 7b, 10–12, 18bR* may be part of a pre-Deuteronomistic story that now incorporates the revenge story also found scattered throughout 8:4–21 (ibid., 386).

6. Out of all of the heroes in Judges, it is only Gideon and Jephthah who are named *gibbôrim*. As Gregory Mobley notes, "Etymologically, with its doubled middle consonant, *gibbôr*, is an intensive form of *geber*, 'man.'" In other words, as Mobley says, a *gibbôr* is "masculinity squared" (*The Empty Men: The Heroic Tradition of Ancient Israel* [New York: Doubleday, 2005], 35).

7. A. Malamat, "The War of Gideon and Midian: A Military Approach," *PEQ* 85 (1953): 62.

8. John Laffin, *Links of Leadership: Thirty Centuries of Military Command* (New York: Abelard-Schuman, 1970), 17–26.

9. Ibid., 19.

swords!).¹⁰ In short, later readers and interpreters often remember Gideon as both warrior and clever tactician, even if the final form of the text has altered Gideon's straightforward depiction as *gibbôr ḥayil*.

In the following pages, I will examine how the Gideon narrative, especially in Judg 7:16–22, appears to faithfully portray some realities and practices of ancient Israelite warfare, while also examining how various redactional expansions have modified the text.¹¹ Specifically, the focus will be on how the weapons that Gideon's men carry into battle have been expanded from an earlier story, turning the clever tactics of Gideon the *gibbôr ḥayil* into a comedic battle account that, together with the addition of verse 22 and the symbolic role of the sword in the final form of the narrative, emphasizes the power of Yhwh.

2. Traditional Elements of War in Judges 7:16–22

In the final form of the narrative, the battle unfolds accordingly: Judg 7:16 explains that Gideon divides the remaining three hundred men who are with him into three companies of an unspecified number (7:16). He outfits them with horns and empty jars, with torches hidden inside the jars (7:16). In 7:17–18 he commands them, "Look at me, and do the same; when I come to the outskirts of the camp, do as I do. When I blow the horn, I and all who are with me, then you also blow the horns around the whole camp, and shout, 'For Yhwh and for Gideon!'" Judges 7:19 explains how Gideon's men approach the camp at night, and then the one hundred men with Gideon blow the horns and smash the jars in their hands. Next, all three companies blow their horns, hold up the torches that were concealed in the jars, and shout, "A sword for Yhwh and for Gideon!" (7:20). Gideon's men then remain in place around the camp, while inside the camp the Midianites run, cry out, and flee to an unspecified location (7:21). A

---

10. "Gideon Tuba Warrior: A Lesson in Trusting God," *Veggie Tales* (New York: Sony Music Entertainment, 2006).

11. A previous version of this paper was presented in the SBL Warfare in Ancient Israel Section at the SBL Annual Meeting (San Francisco, November 2011). That paper was a revised version of part of a chapter from my dissertation, "Mapping Gideon: An Exploration of Judges 6–8" (Ph.D. diss., Emory University, 2011). I thank Mark S. Smith for reading an earlier draft of this paper and am grateful for his thoughts on synergy. Additionally, I am grateful to Jacob L. Wright, who also read various drafts and helped in countless ways.

third (and final) blowing of all three hundred of the horns occurs, at which point Yhwh "set every man's sword against his fellow" in the Midianite camp and the Midianites again flee, this time (presumably) toward the Jordan (7:22). This sets the stage for Gideon to cross the Jordan and pursue the Midianite kings as found in the abbreviated battle account scattered throughout 8:4–21.

In the final account, no hand-to-hand combat occurs. Instead, the series of events adds up to an attack strategy centered on psychological warfare.[12] The narrative depicts Gideon and his men using trickery to route the enemy: a surprise attack under cover of darkness, dividing the small Israelite forces into groups to surround the enemy camp and give the impression of a much larger force, and the sounds of loud cries, breaking jars, and the blowing of horns to scare the enemy awake. Verses 16–21 recount the actions of the Israelite soldiers, never once mentioning the deity apart from the battle cry. The result of these tactics creates pandemonium in the Midianite camp: while all of Gideon's men stand in their places around the camp, in 7:21 the Midianite camp runs, cries out,[13] and flees.[14] Swords do not clash, the deity does not intervene, and the battle is over without ever having really begun. Judges 7:22 belatedly introduces Yhwh onto the battlefield after the enemy soldiers have already fled and seemingly after the "battle" is finished.

Though clearly the text has been rewritten and theologically updated, a number of elements in Judg 7:16–22 seem to reflect real battle practices from the ancient Near East.[15] The division of the troops into three companies is a traditional stratagem that appears with some frequency throughout the biblical corpus.[16] Within the book of Judges itself, such a threefold division occurs in Judg 9, where Abimelech divides his troops into three companies (9:43). Outside of Judges, the book of Samuel records the use

---

12. Daniel Isaac Block, *Judges, Ruth* (NAC 6; Nashville: Broadman & Holman, 1999), 283.

13. The subject of the verb—whether Israelite or Midianite—is difficult to ascertain. The *hiphil* form of the verb is usually found as a sort of war cry, which would make more sense if attributed to Gideon's men. See Soggin, *Judges*, 144.

14. The MT contains both a *ketiv* (*wayānîsû*) and a *qere* (*wayānôsû*) reading. The qere reading makes more sense here (Block, *Judges, Ruth*, 283).

15. As Mobley writes, "The narrative of Gideon preserves the most complete series of martial rituals, a full catalogue of Holy War, of any single biblical narrative" (*The Empty Men*, 152).

16. Cf. Block, *Judges, Ruth*, 281–82; Groß, *Richter*, 441; Soggin, *Judges*, 143.

of a similar strategy on more than one occasion, both by Israelites (1 Sam 11:11; 2 Sam 18:2) and by their enemies (1 Sam 13:17–18). Earlier in the Gideon story, Gideon had amassed a large army composed of Israelite men from various tribes—32,000 soldiers according to 7:3. Yet the original Gideon narrative probably only knew three hundred men; the additions reflect a later updating to make the story about "all Israel" rather than a local tribal affair.[17] Thus, a redactor added the scene in 7:1–8 to explain how Gideon goes from having a large number of troops to only three hundred before the battle. In this way, the three hundred men with Gideon, though small in number, will stand against the Midianites in the ensuing verses, reinforcing the idea that even the small, underdog army can prevail against a larger enemy—especially if they have the deity on their side.[18] While the three hundred men likely remain from an original story about Gideon and his small band of warriors, and also reflect traditional battle stratagem, the number becomes symbolic in Judg 7. Three hundred is the number of men ordained by the deity to go into battle with Gideon, through which the deity will illustrate that he, and not Gideon or the Israelites alone, will deliver Midian into their hands (see 7:2, 4, 7).

Additionally, the presence of the horns (Hebrew *šôpār*) is not surprising in a text about conflict and battle. Repeatedly in the biblical texts the *šôpār* serves as the sound to battle or as announcing conflict. In Judg 3:27, Ehud called the Israelites to fight against the Moabites by sounding the *šôpār*, and in 6:34 Gideon uses the *šôpār* to call out the local tribes to battle.[19] That the sound of a *šôpār* might cause fear is evident from Exod 19:16, where the blast of the *šôpār* is so loud that "all the people trembled." In these respects, the Gideon narrative falls well within the larger category of biblical war stories, drawing upon what appear to be standard battle tactics (at least as depicted literarily in biblical texts).

---

17. See especially Judg 6:33–35. These verses shift the focus from Gideon's own Abiezerites to the larger tribe of Manasseh and several other tribes as well (6:34–35). Additionally, the Midianite enemy forces have increased, too, and now also include the Amalekites and "people of the East" (6:33). In the main section of Judg 8 (vv. 4–21), the focus will return to Gideon and his small band of men, while the end of the Gideon narrative in 8:22–35 returns to the "Israelites" overall. See Mobley, *The Empty Men*, 137; Soggin, *Judges*, 139.

18. Jacob L. Wright, in a conversation with the author, August 2010; Also Mobley, *The Empty Men*, 137–42.

19. Also, e.g., Josh 6:4–20; 1 Sam 13:3; 2 Sam 2:28; 2 Chr 13:12, 14; Jer 4:19; Amos 2:2; 3:6; Zeph 1:16.

Moreover, beyond the apparently traditional tactics, 7:16–22 also utilizes themes common to various war-centered narratives within the Hebrew Bible, including the prevalent extrabiblical and biblical motif that the battle belongs to the deity, who is the root of the people's success.[20] Repeatedly throughout the book of Judges—and in the Gideon narrative in particular—the Hebrew *yād*, "hand," is repeated.[21] As Yairah Amit notes, in the world of Judges, hands symbolize power.[22] The text clearly emphasizes that it is through Yhwh that the Midianites will be delivered into Gideon's hand—that whatever power Gideon holds in his hands, it comes from the deity (compare 7:7, 9, 14–15). Such a portrayal of Yhwh reflects the widespread ancient Near Eastern idea that the gods might command a king or leader to go into battle and/or that the gods might accompany armies into battle. Thus, the gods were ultimately credited for any victory.[23] Just as Yhwh promised to give the Midianites into Gideon's hand, the god Dagan promised to deliver Zimri-Lim's enemies into his power—literally, "to fill (into) the hand of" Zimri-Lim.[24] Additionally, the gods promised Esarhaddon that they would "march with [him]" into battle after granting him an oracle encouraging him to go to war, while the Moabite king Mesha attributed his victories to the god Chemosh, who "caused me to triumph over all of my adversaries."[25] In short, both via the use of traditional tactics and through its adaptation of common war themes from both biblical and extrabiblical texts, the Gideon war narrative found in 7:16–22 closely aligns with some known practices and beliefs about warfare from the ancient world.

---

20. E.g., Exod 23:27; Deut 7:23; Josh 10:10, 11; 24:7; Judg 4:15; 1 Sam 5:11; 7:10; 14:15, 20. Also the frequent discussions of the divine warriors throughout Sa-Moon Kang, *Divine War in the Old Testament and in the Ancient Near East* (BZAW 177; Berlin: de Gruyter, 1989).

21. See 1:2, 4, 6–7, 35; 2:14–16, 18, 23; 3:4, 8, 10, 15, 21, 28, 30; 4:2, 7, 9, 14, 21, 24; 5:26; 6:1–2, 9, 21, 36–37; 7:2, 6–9, 11, 14–16, 19–20; 8:3, 6–7, 15, 22, 34; 9:16–17, 24, 29, 33, 48; 10:7, 12; 11:21, 26, 30, 32; 12:2–3; 13:1, 5, 23; 14:6; 15:12–15, 17–18; 16:18, 23–24, 26; 17:3, 5, 12; 18:10, 19; 19:27; 20:16, 28.

22. Yaira Amit, *The Book of Judges: The Art of Editing* (BInS 38; Leiden: Brill, 1999), 265.

23. *ANET*, 281.

24. *ANET*, 623.

25. *ANET*, 289, 320.

3. Textual Growth in Judges 7:16–22

Yet even a cursory analysis of 7:16–22 reveals contradictory details that suggest diachronic growth in the text—and therefore that whatever original narrative might be behind the story, it is not an accurate portrayal of "real" warfare. Rather, the existing text seems to include a hodgepodge of elements meant to elicit other associations. Tensions in the narrative include the number of "weapons" taken into the battle by Gideon's men and their precise function, as well as whether the text credits Gideon and his men for the victorious outcome or if the victory comes directly from divine intervention. All of these inconsistencies make the final form of the text, to borrow from George Moore, "redundant and confused."[26]

One of the principle issues of confusion in Judg 7:16–22 is the number of weapons wielded by Gideon's three hundred men as they approach the enemy camp. Judges 7:16 records: "he divided the three hundred men into three companies, and put *horns* into the hands of all of them, and *empty jars*, with *torches* inside the jars" (emphasis added). Additionally, in 7:20, the soldiers cry out "A sword for Yhwh and for Gideon," despite the fact that nowhere else in the battle account do the Israelites wield swords. Commentators and interpreters have long been aware of how complicated this makes the text, beginning at least as far back as Gregory the Great, who noted of Gideon and his men, "They go therefore to battle with trumpets, with lamps and with pitchers. This, as we have said, was an unusual order of battle."[27] Wellhausen explains, "The weapons with which the nocturnal attack of the 300 is made are torches, pitchers, and trumpets; the men have not a hand left to hold swords (vii. 20); and the hostile army has accordingly to do itself the work of its own destruction (vii. 22)."[28] Or, per Soggin, "to sound a trumpet holding a torch in the other hand, and alternating between blowing the horns and uttering [a] war-cry is a complex operation at the best of times."[29] Horns, empty jars, and torches—even without the swords from verse 20—are more than an ordinary soldier

---

26. George F. Moore, *A Critical and Exegetical Commentary on Judges* (ICC; Edinburgh: T&T Clark, 1989), 207.

27. John R. Franke and Thomas C. Oden, *Joshua, Judges, Ruth, 1–2 Samuel* (ACCS; Downers Grove, Ill.: InterVarsity Press, 2005), 131–32.

28. Julius Wellhausen, *Prolegomena to the History of Israel* (Atlanta: Scholars Press, 1994), 244.

29. Soggin, *Judges*, 145–46.

could effectively carry (and much less use) in battle. The overabundance of weaponry—and the decidedly unweapon-like nature of some of the weapons—suggests that the text is best read diachronically and symbolically rather than solely mined for historical facts about warfare and weaponry.

Judges 7:17–18 appears to reflect one of the earliest lines of the text, where Gideon's instruction to his men lacks any mention of the jars or torches from 7:16: "Look at me, and do the same; when I come to the outskirts of the camp, do as I do. When I blow the horn, I and all who are with me, then you also blow the horns around the whole camp, and shout, 'For Yhwh and for Gideon!'" Notably, the horns are the only instrument mentioned in Gideon's initial instructions in 7:18. In fact, throughout the pericope, only the five-fold mention of the horns is consistent about their purpose: the horns are to be blown (verses 16, 18, 19, 20, 22). All of these clues suggest that the horns were original to the story, while the jars and torches may be later additions.[30] As is often observed, the use of the horns in the final form of the Gideon narrative recalls the story of Joshua and Jericho, where Joshua conquers the city of Jericho with horns and no real battle (Josh 6:4–5).[31] In both stories, the armies use horns, shouting, and encircling the enemy camp—and not hand-to-hand combat. However, the Gideon narrative lacks any divine instructions, unlike the account in Joshua (see Josh 6:2–3). While Gideon appears to be working at the behest of and synergistically with Yhwh, there is no suggestion that Yhwh dictates to Gideon *how* to defeat the Midianites, something that is clearly outlined

---

30. Soggin explains the puzzle of vv.16–23 by identifying a two-phase development in the narrative: there was an initial story about the war strategy employed by Gideon and his men in which torches were hidden in the jars which were later broken outside the enemy camp at night. This, in combination with the war cry, resulted in the confusion and flight of the enemy. The second phase involved updating the narrative to include the appropriate theological elements: a later (Deuteronomistic?) editor added the horns to produce a scene not unlike the narrative about Jericho (cf. Josh 6:1) and Yhwh receives credit for the victory via the insertion of v. 22 (Soggin, *Judges*, 146). Moore attributes the proliferation of weapons not to editorial expansion but to a combination of sources: horns derive from *E*, the jars and torches from *J* (Moore, *A Critical and Exegetical Commentary*, 207–8). While he is certainly wrong about the presence of either *J* or *E* sources in Judges, he may be correct in noting that there are different versions of the story behind the variant details.

31. E.g., Manfred Görg, *Josua* (NEchtB 30; Würzburg: Echter, 1991), 28; Niditch, *Judges*, 98; Soggin, *Judges*, 146.

for Joshua in the Jericho account.[32] Rather, the earliest portions of the narrative suggest that the battle plan comes from Gideon, a clever tactician.[33]

In addition to the horns, the final form of the text also has Gideon's men carrying "jars" into battle. The Hebrew for "jar" in Judg 7 is *kād*, a word that occurs in only a few other places in the Hebrew Bible. Normally, *kād* refers to a pitcher used to store either water (Gen 24:14; 1 Kgs 18:34) or flour (1 Kgs 17:12)—and it never occurs elsewhere in the context of war. Based on the usage of *kād* throughout the biblical texts, James Kelso suggests that these vessels would have been large and designed for carrying water (compare Gen 24:14 1 Kgs 18:34)—and so hardly battleworthy.[34] The narrative mentions the jars only in verses 16, 19, and 20; they are absent from Gideon's initial command in verse 18.[35] In verse 16, the jars conceal hidden torches, while verse 19 does not mention torches, but only that the men sound the horns and smash the jars, perhaps indicating that the original function of the jars in the narrative was to create a startling noise outside the enemy camp.[36] The combination of sounding horns and smashing jars would thus produce a powerful occurrence of sonic warfare.[37] Verse 20 again mentions the jars alongside the

---

32. That Gideon can be understood as working with Yhwh is not a new observation; see Block, *Judges, Ruth*, 282; Matthews, *Judges*, 93. On the question of revelation regarding the battle plan, Barry G. Webb notes, "The strategy that Gideon employs in the attack is not a revealed one as far as we can tell from the details of the narrative, but one devised by Gideon himself. The only thing that has been revealed to him, by the overheard conversation in the Midianite camp, is the nervousness of the enemy" (*The Book of Judges* [NICOT; Grand Rapids: Eerdmans, 2012], 247).

33. Groß, *Richter*, 464; Jacob L. Wright, personal communication.

34. James L. Kelso, *The Ceramic Vocabulary of the Old Testament* (New Haven: American Schools of Oriental Research, 1948), 19; Mark S. Smith cites Kelso and notes that Baal drinks from a *kd* in his feast in CAT 1.3 I, where "the vessel's size is emphasized (cf. Deut 32:20; Ps 91:7; CS 267–69)," later adding that "Baal's feast … translates superlative drinking in the form of number of vessels into a single divine vessel capable of handling a comparable quantity of wine" (*The Ugaritic Baal Cycle: Volume II* [Leiden: Brill, 2009], 111). The image of *kd* in the feast described in the Baal cycle, along with Kelso's discussion of *kād* in the biblical texts, again suggests that the "jars" Gideon's men carried into battle were very large—highlighting the comedic nature of their battle gear.

35. See Uwe Becker, *Richterzeit und Königtum: Redaktionsgeschichtliche Studien zum Richterbuch* (Berlin: de Gruyter, 1990), 167.

36. See ibid., 171.

37. For a discussion of sonic warfare and the battle of Jericho, see Jacob L. Wright,

torches, but it is unclear in this verse whether the jars originally covered the torches the soldiers carried in their left hands. Uwe Becker's conclusion seems best: the original function of the jars in the narrative was not to conceal lit torches, but rather to produce noise.[38] The decidedly unweapon-like nature of the jars, their absence in Gideon's instructions in verses 17–18, and the fact that throughout 7:16–22 the exact function of the jars is inconsistent, suggests perhaps that the presence of "jars" in the battle account is the result of a later redactional expansion. The hidden torches also seem to be a later addition or a variant detail from some other version of the story, now found only in verses 16 and 20. In short, in the final form of the text, Gideon's men appear not only to carry a comedic proliferation of weaponry into battle—but also, if Kelso is correct, then even the very jars they carry into battle would have been comically large.

Verse 20a appears to recognize the problem posed by the abundance of weapons and so attempts to clarify, explaining how the soldiers managed to wield concurrently horns, jars, and torches: "So the three companies blew the horns and broke the jars, holding in their left hands the torches, and in their right hands the horns to blow."[39] By explaining that the jars hid the torches, the original function of the jars—to make noise when broken and thus add to the clamor outside the enemy camp—changes.[40] It is possible that the addition of "with torches inside the jars" from the end of verse 16b is from the same hand as verse 20, while the beginning of verse 19b contains the original function: the empty jars were broken to create clamor.[41] Though the original story of surprise attack by night, sonic warfare, and surrounding the camp to make the small army appear larger all suggest carefully worked out tactics, the final presentation of the

---

"Warfare and Wanton Destruction: A Reexamination of Deuteronomy 20:19–20 in Relation to Ancient Siegecraft," *JBL* 127 (2008): 431. Wright notes, "Although the term is used here tongue-in-cheek, sonic and ultrasonic warfare (USW), which employs sound-pressure and -power, represents a heavily researched area in modern military technology and is already employed by many armies in both their lethal and nonlethal arsenals. Additional biblical examples are found in Judg 7:18–22; 2 Chr 13:15; 20:21–23" (ibid., 431 n. 30).

38. Becker, *Richterzeit und Königtum*, 171.

39. Soggin, *Judges*, 144–45; for more on the addition of v. 20, see Becker, *Richterzeit und Königtum*, 171–72.

40. Becker, *Richterzeit und Königtum*, 171.

41. See ibid., 171–72. Alternatively, see Mobley, *The Empty Men*, 161.

battle after the redactional expansions is strange and comedic, necessitating the apparently redactional explanation found in verse 20.

Next, in verse 20b, Gideon's men repeat the battle cry from verse 18b, "For Yhwh and for Gideon," but here Gideon and his men add the word *ḥereb*, "sword," to the beginning of the battle cry, producing "A sword for Yhwh and for Gideon." According to von Rad, a battle in a biblical "holy war" traditionally opened with a battle cry, an example of which he finds preserved in 7:20.[42] Thus, this twice-uttered war cry (verses 18, 20) gives the battle account yet another realistic stamp. Yet the narrative does not otherwise record that Gideon's men carried swords; in fact, the narrative depicts only the Midianites as sword-wielding in verse 22. Thus, the battle cry "A *ḥereb* for Yhwh and for Gideon!" is a surprising addition. To solve this, *BHS* suggests replacing "horns to blow (*haššôpārôt*)" in the first half of verse 20 with "the sword (*haḥereb*)" so that the complete verse would instead read, "So the three companies blew the horns and broke the jars, holding in their left hands the torches, and in their right hand the sword, and they cried, 'A sword for Yhwh and for Gideon!'" However, no textual witness supports the deletion of the horns in favor of *ḥereb*.[43] Moore suggests that the addition of "sword" in verse 20 is a gloss by a redactor, with "For Yhwh and for Gideon!" being the original form of the battle cry.[44] Yet already in 7:14—perhaps part of the oldest Gideon story—the text mentions Gideon's sword, suggesting that perhaps a remnant of an older story has now been decontextualized in the theologically updated battle account found in 7:16–22.[45]

4. "A Sword for Yhwh and for Gideon!"

Whether the battle cry is original to the story or not, both instances—"for Yhwh and for Gideon" in verse 18 and "a sword for Yhwh and for Gideon" in verse 20—have caused Gideon's character nothing but grief through-

---

42. Gerhard von Rad, *Holy War in Ancient Israel* (trans. Marva J. Dawn; Grand Rapids: Eerdmans 1991), 48. He points readers to Josh 6:5; 1 Sam 17:20, 52, as well as an "extremely spiritualized form" of this element in 2 Chr 20:21–22.
43. Soggin, *Judges*, 143–44.
44. Moore, *A Critical and Exegetical Commentary*, 210.
45. On Judg 7:9–15 containing parts of the oldest Gideon narrative, see Groß, *Richter*, 381, 389, 437–440; on the sword as perhaps leftover from an older story, see ibid., 441–42.

out the history of interpretation. Two examples: Tammi Schneider notes that by including his name in the battle cry, "Already the deity's fears were actualized; Gideon took partial responsibility for the victory even before it was accomplished."[46] Similarly, Dennis Olson writes, "Gideon had earlier felt that he was nothing (6:15) and the Lord was everything (7:15). But now in this shout Gideon claims a piece of spotlight along with God."[47] For these—and other—final form readings, the addition of Gideon in the battle cry shifts the focus from Yhwh to Gideon and becomes an act of hubris on Gideon's part. Yet placed within the larger context of Judg 6–7—and the larger ancient Near Eastern belief that gods accompanied their chosen leaders into battle—it seems possible to understand the battle cry as a natural extension of Yhwh's election of Gideon as leader and his promise to "be with him" from 6:16.[48] Clothed with Yhwh's spirit in 6:34, Gideon now works synergistically with the deity, as expressed in the battle cry "For Yhwh and for Gideon!"

In short, the battle cry recognizes that the battle belongs to Yhwh, who works with and through the hand of his human agent. In fact, the scene in 7:9–15, which now stands at the end of a series of scenes in which Gideon asks for divine signs and assurances, aligns with other ancient Near Eastern texts that depict an omen-seeking ritual by a king or leader before they go into battle; through this omen ritual the king or leader is reassured that the deity both sanctions the battle and will be with him.[49] In Judg 7:9, the deity commands Gideon to "Get up and attack, for I have given the Midianites into your hand." Building on the idea found in the final form of the text that Gideon needed numerous signs before he would act, the deity now provides one final omen: Gideon is to go down to the Midianite camp where he "shall hear what they say, and afterward [his] hands shall be strengthened to attack the camp" (7:10). Here the text clearly sanctions a battle led by Gideon—it is his divinely assigned duty as *gibbôr*. Gideon goes down and overhears one of the enemy men telling a dream to his

---

46. Tammi J. Schneider, *Judges* (Berit Olam; Collegeville, Minn.: Liturgical, 2000), 115; see Block, *Judges, Ruth*, 282.

47. Dennis Olson, "Judges," in *The New Interpreter's Bible: Volume 2* (Nashville: Abingdon, 1998), 803.

48. For a discussion of the *Mitsein* idea in Egypt and Mesopotamia, see Kang, *Divine War*, 102.

49. For a discussion of omens before battle across the ancient Near East, see Kang, *Divine War*, 42–45, 56–65, 70–80, 98–101, 215–19.

comrade, describing how he saw "a cake of barley bread [tumble] into the camp of Midian," striking a tent that then collapses (7:13). The second Midianite guard interprets the dream, "This is no other than the sword of Gideon son of Joash, a man of Israel; into his hand God has given Midian and all the army" (7:14). Gideon's sword, the enemy soldiers rightly recognize, is the deity's sword. Thus, when Gideon and his men cry out in 7:20, "A sword for Yhwh and for Gideon," the battle cry extends the idea that Yhwh and Gideon work synergistically to defeat the enemy—as predicted in the prebattle omen account found in 7:9–15. The sword in verse 20 is a realization of Yhwh's power over the Midianites with his human agent—not an expression of Gideon's overconfidence or his hubris in battle.[50] Verse 21 then appears to conclude the story: "every man stood in his place all around the camp, and all the men in camp ran; they cried out and fled." Gideon's attack strategy works—and the Midianite enemy flee without any hand-to-hand combat taking place.

In 7:16–21, the text appears to preserve elements of Gideon as *gibbôr ḥayil*, even if the original story is now hidden under the comedic expansion of the weaponry his soldiers carry with them into the so-called battle. Yet then Judg 7:22 recounts, "When they blew the three hundred horns, Yhwh set every man's sword against his fellow and against all the army; and the army fled as far as Beth-shittah toward Zererah, as far as the border of Abel-meholah, by Tabbath"—despite the fact that the enemy had already fled in verse 21. The difference between verses 16–21 and verse 22 is one of the agent; in verse 22, it is *only* Yhwh who "set every man's sword against his fellow and against all the army." The deity alone, and not Gideon working with the deity, thus becomes responsible for the destruction of the enemy camp—even if this is seemingly unnecessary in light of verse 21. In short, verse 22 serves as a theological corrective to a story that otherwise highlights Gideon's status as capable, independent *gibbôr ḥayil*, who acknowledges the deity in his war cries, but who otherwise effectively works alone.[51] Verse 22, as Wellhausen notes of the Gideon story overall, "cast[s] the man into the shade behind the Deity."[52]

Most importantly, 7:22 presents an ironic twist to the presence of the sword in the battle cry in verse 20: Yhwh is so powerful that he can

---

50. For other understandings of the sword, see Block, *Judges, Ruth*, 282; Groß, *Richter*, 442; Matthews, *Judges*, 93; Webb, *The Book of Judges*, 248–49.

51. See Soggin, *Judges*, 145.

52. Wellhausen, *Prolegomena*, 243.

cause the Midianites to die by their own swords.[53] In the end, Gideon and his men do not need the swords mentioned in the battle cry. In the final form of the Gideon narrative, the sword becomes symbolically important. Othmar Keel writes, "Many rites and symbols visualize the participation of divine powers in the legitimation, execution, and success of war."[54] Repeatedly, swords in both the broader biblical and extrabiblical evidence serve, per Keel, as "powerful symbols of victory."[55] Frequently, the biblical authors place a sword in the hands of a human, who then fights for the deity. As Keel notes, "the motif of the divinity who holds out or presents a sword of victory to a commander is widespread." [56] He cites as examples the angelic commander in Josh 5:13–15, Joshua's divine sword in Josh 8:18–26, and Judas' golden sword in 2 Macc 15:15, which all come from the deity but are wielded by human agents, symbolizing divine power and victory.[57] In the story of Judg 7, the deity never gives a sword to Gideon—but nevertheless the enemy rightly recognizes in the prebattle omen ritual that the battle will be won by the Israelites because of Gideon's god: "This is no other than the sword of Gideon son of Joash, a man of Israel; into his hand God has given Midian and all the army" (7:14).[58] If the war cry "A sword for Yhwh and for Gideon!" is in fact part of the oldest story, later writers and editors carefully decontextualized it not only through the comedic proliferation of weapons, but also through the addition of verse 22.[59] In case there is any confusion over the power behind Gideon's sword, Yhwh's divine intervention in the last verse of the battle scene clarifies that it is the deity who finally wins the battle. Gideon's sword—from both 7:14 and 7:20—is intricately linked to Yhwh's power, and Yhwh even controls the swords of the foreign enemy army. The power behind the sword clearly belongs to Yhwh.

---

53. Block, *Judges, Ruth*, 282.
54. Othmar Keel, "Powerful Symbols of Victory: The Parts Stay the Same, the Actors Change," *JNSL* 25 (1999): 205.
55. Ibid.
56. Ibid., 213–14.
57. Ibid.
58. See Matthews, *Judges*, 93.
59. For a different understanding of the history of vv. 16–22, especially v. 22, see Becker, *Richterzeit und Königtum*, 170–72.

5. Conclusions

In the final form of the narrative, the soldiers both blow the horns and shout war slogans, while also breaking jars containing lit torches inside them and simultaneously holding the horns. From a literary perspective, the use of such "weapons" underscores the difference between Gideon's men and the Midianites already set up at the beginning of the narrative: this is a battle between the underdogs (Israel) and their militarily and numerically superior (Midianite) opponents. In the final form of the narrative, the weapons become symbolic—the Israelites will win a battle even when they enter into it without proper weaponry. They will win armed only with horns, jars, and torches—and without actually fighting. The combination of seemingly "real" warfare elements alongside war-related symbols functions to make 7:16–22 the turning point in the Gideon narrative, transforming the anxious, hesitant Gideon of the final narrative back into the "mighty warrior" that he originally was. Per Judg 7:20, Gideon carries a sword—for Yhwh and for himself. In its final form, the narrative in Judg 7:16–22 makes explicit, primarily through war-related symbols, that the deity—and not Gideon or any human actors—is *ultimately* responsible for the victory against the Midianites.

In the end, the defeat of the Midianites becomes more symbolically than militarily significant: the underdogs prevail and the deity is with them, just as he promised Gideon in 6:16 (see also 6:36–40; 7:1–8; 7:9–15). The final narrative downplays Gideon's military prowess by adding various outfitting elements that turn an originally brilliant military strategy into a comedic account of a battle, where the only swords belong to the enemy and they use the swords to kill one another. Gideon, so anxious and fearful until 7:15b in the final form of Judg 6–8, becomes fearless in this account while the numerically superior enemy comically flees from a band of three hundred unarmed soldiers. If the battle narrative in 7:16–22 does not necessarily reflect entirely the warfare practices of premonarchic Israel, the final form of the Gideon narrative does serve as an essential pan-Israelite myth, stressing concerns that reflect much later Israelite society. Is Yhwh really "with" the Israelites? Will Yhwh be victorious against the enemy? The presence of *ḥereb* functions as a powerful symbol of Yhwh's power and victory, while verse 22 provides a theological corrective to an earlier literary stratum of the narrative. Such a theological corrective is in tune with the later updating of the Gideon narrative, which sought to impose the divine on an otherwise largely mundane literary tradition.

Bibliography

Amit, Yaira. *The Book of Judges: The Art of Editing*. Translated by J. Chipman. BInS 38. Leiden: Brill, 1999.
Becker, Uwe. *Richterzeit und Königtum: Redaktionsgeschichtliche Studien zum Richterbuch*. BZAW 192. Berlin: de Gruyter, 1990.
Block, Daniel Isaac. *Judges, Ruth*. NAC 6. Nashville: Broadman & Holman, 1999.
Franke, John R., and Thomas C. Oden. *Joshua, Judges, Ruth, 1–2 Samuel*. ACCS. Downers Grove, Ill.: InterVarsity Press, 2005.
"Gideon Tuba Warrior: A Lesson in Trusting God." *Veggie Tales*. New York: Sony Music Entertainment, 2006.
Görg, Manfred. *Josua*. NEchtB 30. Würzburg: Echter, 1991.
Groß, Walter. *Richter*. HThKAT. Freiburg: Herder, 2009.
Kang, Sa-Moon. *Divine War in the Old Testament and in the Ancient Near East*. BZAW 177. Berlin: de Gruyter, 1989.
Keel, Othmar. "Powerful Symbols of Victory: The Parts Stay the Same, the Actors Change." *JNSL* 25 (1999): 205–40.
Kelso, James L. *The Ceramic Vocabulary of the Old Testament*. New Haven: American Schools of Oriental Research, 1948.
Laffin, John. *Links of Leadership: Thirty Centuries of Military Command*. New York: Abelard-Schuman, 1970.
Malamat, A. "The War of Gideon and Midian: A Military Approach." *PEQ* 85 (1953): 61–75.
Matthews, Victor H. *Judges and Ruth*. NCBC. Cambridge: Cambridge University Press, 2004.
Mobley, Gregory. *The Empty Men: The Heroic Tradition of Ancient Israel*. New York: Doubleday, 2005.
Moore, George F. *A Critical and Exegetical Commentary on Judges*. ICC. Edinburgh: T&T Clark, 1989.
Niditch, Susan. *Judges: A Commentary*. OTL. Louisville: Westminster John Knox, 2008.
Olson, Dennis. "Judges" in volume 2 of *The New Interpreter's Bible*. Edited by Thomas B. Dozeman, R. E. Clements, Peter D. Quinn-Miscall, Robert B. Coote, Dennis L. Olson, Kathleen A. R. Farmer, and Bruce C. Birch. Nashville: Abingdon, 1998.
Rad, Gerhard von. *Holy War in Ancient Israel*. Translated by Marva J. Dawn. Grand Rapids: Eerdmans, 1991.

Schneider, Tammi J. *Judges*. Berit Olam. Collegeville, Minn.: Liturgical, 2000.
Ska, Jean Louis. *"Our Fathers Have Told Us": Introduction to the Analysis of Hebrew Narratives*. Rome: Editrice Pontificio Instituto Biblico, 2000.
Smith, Mark S. *The Ugaritic Baal Cycle: Volume II*. Leiden: Brill, 2009.
Soggin, J. Alberto. *Judges: A Commentary*. OTL. Philadelphia: Westminster, 1981.
Webb, Barry G. *The Book of Judges*. NICOT. Grand Rapids: Eerdmans, 2012.
Wellhausen, Julius. *Prolegomena to the History of Israel*. Atlanta: Scholars, 1994.
Wright, Jacob L. "Warfare and Wanton Destruction: A Reexamination of Deuteronomy 20:19–20 in Relation to Ancient Siegecraft." *JBL* 127 (2008): 423–58.

The Red-Stained Warrior in Ancient Israel

Frank Ritchel Ames

In and around ancient Israel, the bodies, clothing, and armaments of warriors were at times stained red—a display of color that is both evocative and horrific.[1] References to red-stained warriors are found in the Hebrew Bible in 1 Sam 16–17; 1 Kgs 2; Isa 63; Ezek 23; Nah 2; Zech 9; Song 5; Lam 4; and in ancient Near Eastern texts such as the First Soldiers Oath, Aqhatu Legend, and Kirta Epic, among others. This essay first presents the textual evidence for warrior staining as literary trope and ritual behavior and then discusses its use as sign and symbol in the context of warfare in ancient Israel. The fundamental question addressed is, How did the red stain function? In proposing an answer, I have applied methods from contemporary biblical criticism and have incorporated perspectives from the social and biological sciences, including cognitive linguistics, which itself is an interdisciplinary method relevant to understanding how symbols work. It is assumed that symbols are embodied and situated—perhaps to greater degrees than typically acknowledged. The theoretical framework

---

1. In the Hebrew Bible, אדם, the principal term for the color red, represents hues ranging from light red to dark brown (Athalya Brenner, *Colour Terms in the Old Testament* [JSOTSup 21; Sheffield: JSOT Press, 1982], 80). Because אדם is the principal chromatic term for the color, "its references are less restricted and much more given to manipulation and flexible usage than a comparable term in a language where the colour field as a whole is better developed" (ibid.). Brenner correlates color terms in biblical Hebrew with Berlin and Kay's universal stages of color term evolution (Brent Berlin and Paul Kay, *Basic Color Terms: Their Universality and Evolution* [Berkeley: University of California Press, 1969], 56). For criticism of Berlin and Kay's theory, see John Cage, *Color and Meaning: Art, Science, and Symbolism* (Berkeley: University of California Press, 2000), 102–20; and Don Dedrick, *Naming the Rainbow: Colour Language, Colour Science, and Culture* (Synthese Library 274; Dordrecht, The Netherlands: Kluwer Academic, 1998).

that cognitive linguistics contributes is described in the second part of the essay. The first part explores the textual evidence.[2]

1. Textual Evidence of Red-stained Warriors

Isaiah 63:1–6 portrays Yhwh returning from battle clothed in red robes, and the text characterizes the divine warrior as a victorious avenger who singlehandedly defeats the enemies of Israel—in this instance, adversarial Edom. In the poetic dialogue of the text, a sentry in Zion (compare 62:6) sees a person clothed in red-stained garments returning from Edom and asks the person to self-identify and to explain the origin of the red stain:

Question: "Who is this that comes from Edom,
from Bozrah in garments stained crimson?[3]
Who is this so splendidly robed,
marching in his great might?"

Answer: "It is I, announcing vindication,
mighty to save."

Question: "Why are your robes red,
and your garments like theirs who tread the wine press?"

Answer: "I have trodden the wine press alone,
and from the peoples no one was with me;
I trod them in my anger
and trampled them in my wrath;
their juice spattered on my garments,
and stained all my robes.
For the day of vengeance was in my heart,
and the year for my redeeming work had come.

---

2. The ideas developed here are adapted from a paper entitled "Ancient Israelite Warfare and the Stained Body," which I presented to the Warfare in Ancient Israel section at the Society of Biblical Literature Annual Meeting, San Francisco. November 19, 2011.

3. Based on context, it is likely that the problematic word חמוץ in Isa 63:1 means "bright red" (*HALOT*, 327), though the preferred reading of the text might well be חמור, from the root חמר, "to be red," an emendation discussed in Julian Morgenstern, "Further Light from the Book of Isaiah upon the Catastrophe of 485 B.C.," *HUCA* 37 (1966): 15.

> I looked, but there was no helper;
> I stared, but there was no one to sustain me;
> so my own arm brought me victory,
> and my wrath sustained me.
> I trampled down peoples in my anger,
> I crushed them in my wrath,
> and I poured out their lifeblood on the earth."
> (Isa 63:1–6 NRSV)

It is Yhwh who answers the two questions, and the reader learns that Yhwh is returning from battle wearing robes that are spattered and stained red with the blood of an enemy who has been trodden under foot and crushed like grapes, having incurred the unrestrained press of divine wrath. The divine warrior is characterized as powerful ("mighty"; v. 1) and victorious ("I poured out their lifeblood on the earth"; v. 6), and as a furious combatant who needs no assistance in overcoming an opponent. The independent power of the warrior is emphasized by the use of the boastful phrases, "I have trodden … alone" and "no one was with me" in verse 3; and "no helper," "no one to sustain me," and "my own arm" in verse 5; and by the repeated use of first-person pronouns in verses 3–6. Isaiah portrays Yhwh as a mighty, ruddy warrior, and the ability and visual appearance of the warrior are intertwined. The question-and-answer schema exhibits a parallel (a-b//a'-b') but asymmetrical structure, with the first exchange presenting a brief summary (v. 1) and the second an expansion describing Yhwh's identity and acts (vv. 2–3). The second exchange expresses an idea that is essentially the same as the first: the warrior overcame the opponent and is powerful. Political power is emphasized in a subtle way, for the impression given in the first exchange is that royalty approaches.[4] An interplay between the similar sounding words *Edom* (אדום; v. 1) and *red* (אדם; v. 2; compare Gen 25:25), however, links the name of the nation to the evidence of its defeat, and directs attention to the violence that has adorned the approaching person. The red stain is blood, and the stained outfit identifies a triumphant warrior who possesses irresistible, lethal strength.[5]

---

4. Matthew J. Lynch, "Zion's Warrior and the Nations: Isaiah 59:15b–63:6 in Isaiah's Zion Traditions," *CBQ* 70 (2008): 256.

5. Clothing stained red from blood is also mentioned in Isa 9:1–7, which anticipates an end of war and a time of peace. In the text, Zion rejoices over the defeat of its enemies and in the destruction of the instruments of violent oppression, including the

Similar imagery is employed in Zech 9:15, which associates Yhwh's empowerment of the people of Zion for battle with the blood of slain opponents that is consumed and flows into the mouths and over the bodies of the Israelite warriors: "They shall devour and tread down the slingers; they shall drink their blood like wine, and be full like a bowl, drenched like the corners of the altar."[6] The text offers solace and hope of deliverance for a downtrodden people, yet the gore horrifies. Readers are told that the Israelites will devour their enemies and in the process will be covered with blood. Zechariah's human warriors, like Isaiah's divine warrior, will be stained red.

In the vision report of Nahum, red attire adorns the warriors who attack and defeat Nineveh:

> The shields of his warriors are red;
> > his soldiers are clothed in crimson
> The metal on the chariots flashes
> > on the day when he musters them;
> > the chargers prance.
> The chariots race madly through the streets,
> > they rush to and fro through the squares;
> their appearance is like torches,
> > they dart like lightning. (Nah 2:3–4 NRSV [Heb. 2:4–5])

Nahum's description of the army and its furious attack is "fear-evoking,"[7] but past, present, and future perspectives meld in the prophet's words, as do metaphorical and literal elements, and the reader meets difficult-to-resolve textual issues and ambiguities. Caution and tentativeness must attend interpretive conclusions, but it is clear that Nahum envisions a swift strike by red-stained warriors driving horse-drawn chariots.[8] The warriors

---

footwear and uniforms of the warriors: "For all the boots of the trampling warriors and all the garments rolled in blood shall be burned as fuel for the fire" (v. 5 NRSV).

6. On the interpretive difficulties presented by Zech 9:15, see Susan Niditch, "Good Blood, Bad Blood: Multivocality, Metonymy, and Meditation in Zechariah 9," *VT* 61 (2011): 641–45.

7. J. Daryl Charles, "Plundering the Lion's Den—A Portrait of Divine Fury (Nahum 2:3–11)," *Grace Theological Journal* 10 (1989): 190.

8. Red horses are mentioned in Zech 1:8 and 6:2, and it is possible that Zechariah's horses were stained or draped in red in the tradition of the red-stained warrior. David L. Petersen, however, argues convincingly that Zechariah envisions only the natural hues of horses, not colors that symbolize the blood of war, the dawning of a new era,

are ruddy in appearance, but the red (אדם) and crimson (תלע) seen on their shields and clothing invite a variety of plausible explanations. The crimson could be reflections of sunlight (compare the parallel line in verse 3b, "the metal on the chariots flashes," and a similar phenomenon described in 1 Macc 6:39). The reddish hues could be incidentally related to the oil used to treat leather shields (compare 2 Sam 1:21; Isa 21:5). The red, of course, could be the blood of adversaries being slain in the battle (compare Isa 63:1–6).[9] Each of these interpretations is reasonable, but another merits consideration: the bodies, clothing, and equipment of the warriors had been ritually stained. In the text, the red shields and crimson clothing are present at the beginning of the day of battle—"on the day when [the commander] musters them" (v. 3b)—not just after the conflagration. They are taken *into* as well as *out of* the battle. The stains, of course, could be blood stains that remain from a previous battle. Ancient warriors engaging an enemy in hand-to-hand combat would become bloody as well as muddy, with their equipment and garb stained and discolored. It is also possible that the warriors carried shields, wore tunics, and had saddle blankets or chariot coverings that had been dyed red in preparation for battle, perhaps with red ochre or some other pigment, perhaps with human or animal blood.[10] The presence of the stain early in the sequence of the envisioned events gives weight to this interpretation. Marvin A. Sweeney draws the same conclusion and argues that it is "more likely" that Nahum's warriors "have reddened themselves as a means to terrify and undermine the morale of the defending soldiers who will imagine their own blood splattered all over the attacking troops."[11] Whereas Isaiah's red-stained warrior is returning from battle, Nahum's red-stained warriors are entering the fray, with the stain applied in preparation for battle.

---

the cosmic regions of heaven, earth, and sea, or the continents of Asia, Europe, and Africa—interpretations that have been proposed by other biblical scholars (David L. Petersen, *Haggai and Zechariah 1–8: A Commentary* [OTL; Philadelphia: Westminster, 1984], 141–43). Petersen's interpretation does not dispute that the horses are symbolic, only that the individual colors are symbols; rather, they are natural, common colors that provide a measure of verisimilitude (ibid., 141).

9. Mark Allen Hahlen, "The Background and Use of Equine Imagery in Zechariah," *Stone-Campbell Journal* 3 (2000): 243–60.

10. See Kevin J. Cathcart, *Nahum in the Light of Northwest Semitic* (BibOr 26; Rome: Biblical Institute Press, 1973), 86–89.

11. Marvin A. Sweeney, "Nahum," in *The Twelve Prophets* (Berit Olam; Collegeville, Minn.: Liturgical Press, 2000), 2:438.

Ezekiel 23:11–27 mentions red warriors in the allegorical personification of unfaithful Judah as Oholibah, who "lusted after the Assyrians, governors and commanders, warriors clothed in full armor" (v. 12). Oholibah's misdirected desire is aroused by the sight of

> male figures carved on the wall, images of the Chaldeans portrayed in vermilion, with belts around their waists, with flowing turbans on their heads, all of them looking like officers—a picture of Babylonians whose native land was Chaldea. (vv. 14–15 NRSV).

The warriors in the carving are red or, as the NRSV translates שָׁשַׁר, "vermilion," bright red (v. 14).[12] An artist's decision to use the color red in a given painting may be artful, incidental, or arbitrary, but in this case it is helpful to keep in mind that the author behind the allegory is also the artist behind the painting, and in the world imagined by Ezekiel, warriors are vermilion, powerful, and arousing. The multivalent nature of a symbol is at work in Ezekiel's use of red, for the color has sexual and military associations.[13]

Similar associations are at play in the Song of Songs, which refers to the ruddy warrior in the opening line of Shulammite's description of her lover:

> My beloved is all radiant and ruddy,
>   distinguished among ten thousand. (5:10 NRSV)

The adjectives "radiant and ruddy" characterize Shulammite's lover as handsome and as a warrior, an interpretation consistent with Carol Meyers's observation that the Song is laden with military imagery.[14] For instance, Shulammite's lover draws upon military imagery when he compares her to "a mare among Pharaoh's chariots" (1:9), a tower decorated with the "shields of warriors" (4:4), and "an army with banners" (6:4). Her lover's palanquin, moreover, is escorted by columns of warriors:

> Around it are sixty mighty men
>   of the mighty men of Israel,

---

12. The term שָׁשַׁר is used in the Hebrew Bible only here and in Jer 22:14.

13. Cynthia R. Chapman, "Sculpted Warriors: Sexuality and the Sacred in the Depiction of Warfare in the Assyrian Palace Reliefs and in Ezekiel 23:14–17," in *The Aesthetics of Violence in the Prophets* (ed. J. M. O'Brien and C. Franke; LHBOTS 517; New York: T&T Clark, 2010), 1–17.

14. Carol Meyers, "Gender Imagery in the Song of Songs," *HAR* 10 (1987): 209–23.

>   all equipped with swords
>   and expert in war,
>   each with his sword at his thigh
>   because of alarms by night (3:7–8 NRSV).

In 5:10 the phrase "radiant and ruddy" is juxtaposed to "ten thousand," a parallel that bears a military connotation.[15] Thus, the handsome man in the Song is characterized as a military man, and perhaps as a member of a renowned class of warriors, each "distinguished among ten thousand" (v. 10).

The term "ruddy" is also applied to David, one of Israel's renowned warriors and perhaps the most famous, who in 1 Sam 16–17 is characterized as the divinely favored successor of King Saul. In the story of Samuel's anointing of David above his brothers—all of whom are presumed to be more suitable candidates—much is made of David's appearance.

> Jesse made seven of his sons pass before Samuel, and Samuel said to Jesse, "The LORD has not chosen any of these." Samuel said to Jesse, "Are all your sons here?" And he said, "There remains yet the youngest, but he is keeping the sheep." And Samuel said to Jesse, "Send and bring him; for we will not sit down until he comes here." He sent and brought him in. Now he was ruddy, and had beautiful eyes, and was handsome. The LORD said, "Rise and anoint him; for this is the one." Then Samuel took the horn of oil, and anointed him in the presence of his brothers; and the spirit of the LORD came mightily upon David from that day forward. (1 Sam 16:10–13b NRSV)

In the narrative that immediately follows the anointing, David is summoned to play the lyre to ease a torment brought upon Saul by "an evil spirit from God," and the narrative mentions David's prowess as musician, warrior, and speaker, and his favored status. He is described as "skillful in playing, a man of valor, a warrior, prudent in speech, and a man of good presence; and the LORD is with him" (v. 18b), and so he becomes Saul's armor-bearer. The familiar account of David and Goliath or, better, David and Saul, immediately follows (17:1–58), and in the account David proves to be the better match for Goliath, if not in physical stature, then in a

---

15. The Song draws imagery from warfare and from other domains, including architecture (3:4; 7:8; 8:8–11), astronomy (6:10), dance (6:13), diplomacy (8:11), geography (6:4; 7:8), and mythology (3:8).

brazen, faith-induced courage. David, as the story goes, cannot manage the weight and bulkiness of Saul's bronze helmet and coat of mail, nor his heavy sword, and eschews these for a staff, sling, and "five smooth stones" (17:38–40). The narrative reports that the Philistine in response disdained David, because David was "only a youth, ruddy and handsome in appearance" (v. 42). The appearance of this under-equipped and ostensibly unworthy challenger insulted the Philistine, who bellowed, "Am I a dog, that you come to me with sticks?" (v. 43). David's age and appearance infuriated the seasoned and perhaps more scarred opponent. David, who did not fit the profile of a mighty warrior or worthy opponent, was, nonetheless, the color of one.[16]

A staining of belt and sandals with the "blood of war" is mentioned in the Court History of David (2 Sam 9–20 and 1 Kgs 1–2), the concluding segment of which reports the succession of Solomon, who is advised to settle family scores and remove political opponents. According to 1 Kgs 2:5–6, David advises Solomon to put Joab to death for murdering Abner and Amasa.[17] Joab had offended David by "retaliating in time of peace for blood that had been shed in war, and putting the blood of war on the belt around his waist, and on the sandals on his feet" (v. 5b).[18] The clause וישם דמי־מלחמה בשלם ויתן דמי מלחמה בחגרתו אשר במתניו ובנעלו אשר ברגליו can be read either as a figure of speech related to peacetime retaliation for lives lost during war or as a report of a ritual act.[19] The meaning of the ritual is not clear, but the narrative characterizes the act as inappropriate during a time of peace. The staining of the belt and sandals, one may infer, would have been appropriate during wartime. Other images of warriors reddening feet with blood are found in Pss 58:10 and 68:22–23.

Lamentations 4:7–9 describes the plight of a specific class of Judeans after the fall of Jerusalem:

---

16. The ruddiness described in 1 Sam 16–17 and in Lam 4 is more likely natural skin tone, but this observation does not invalidate the association between red coloration and military role.

17. James W. Flanagan, "Court History or Succession Document? A Study of 2 Samuel 9–20 and 1 Kings 1–2," *JBL* 91 (1972): 172–81.

18. The staining of footwear is observed in other cultures. For instance, Bannock warriors, encountered by migrants along the Oregon Trail, stained moccasin insteps red to show that they had stepped in the blood of a slain enemy, a symbol of prowess in battle (Sally Zanjani, *Sara Winnemucca* [Lincoln: University of Nebraska Press, 2001], 146).

19. Vladimír Kubáč, "Blut im Gürtel und in Sandalen," *VT* 31 (1981): 225–26.

Her princes were purer than snow,
 whiter than milk;
their bodies were more ruddy than coral,
 their hair like sapphire.
Now their visage is blacker than soot;
 they are not recognized in the streets.
Their skin has shriveled on their bones;
 it has become as dry as wood.
Happier were those pierced by the sword
 than those pierced by hunger,
whose life drains away, deprived
 of the produce of the field (NRSV).

The NRSV translators identified this group of survivors in Jerusalem as "her princes" (v. 7a), but it has been proposed that the word נזיריה be read נעריה, "her warriors," the reading adopted here.[20] Before the devastation of the city, the bodies of these warriors were "more ruddy than coral" (v. 7b). Afterward, they became increasingly emaciated from lack of food (vv. 8–9). Although the passage describes a loss of health, the ruddiness mentioned is not solely an indicator of physical wellbeing; in context, it characterizes previously healthy warriors, who would have been happier dying by the sword than by hunger (v. 9). Nonetheless, in this text, the ruddiness (אדמו, v. 7b) most likely refers to natural skin color.

The Middle Hittite First Soldiers' Oath provides extrabiblical evidence for the staining of the body.[21] The Oath contains a series of curses levied against conscripts who in some way might prove disloyal to the king of Hatti or, in the press of battle, might be tempted to desert the war band and escape the dangers of the fray. Each curse in the series begins with a ritual that serves up an object lesson. The diviner places an object in the hand of the warrior or on the ground, then describes or destroys the object, and petitions the oath deities to harm in the same manner the warrior who abandons duty. The last curse in the tablet (§16), though itself not about the practice of staining, provides a useful example of the literary pattern

---

20. See *BHS apparatus criticus* and Gideon R. Kotzé, "A Text-Critical Analysis of the Lamentations Manuscripts from Qumran" (Th.D. diss., University of Stellenbosch, 2011), 151–56. On the use of נער as a designation for warrior, see *HALOT*, 707; cf. Judg 9:54; 1 Sam 14:1; 21:3–5; Isa 13:18; and Neh 4:10.

21. "The First Soldiers' Oath (1.66)," translated by Billie Jean Collins (*COS* 1.66:164–67).

repeated throughout the list: the ritual leader ignites and extinguishes a fire before the warriors and says, "As this burning fire was extinguished, who[ever] breaks these oaths, let these oath deities seize him, and also may his life, his youth, (and) his prosperity in future—together with his wives and his sons—be extinguished in the same way."[22] The preceding curse, §15, which does refer to staining, follows the pattern, though in a more complicated way: the ritual leader presents the warrior with a red pelt and says, "Just as they make this red pelt blood colored and from it the bl[oo]d color does not leach out, in the same way may the oath deities seize you and may it (i.e., the blood color) not leave you."[23] The troops taking the oath, it appears, received a red pelt or had bodies reddened by ritual, with the intention that the warrior's commitment and the crimson stain would endure.

The concluding section of the poetic Aqhatu narrative (*CTU* 1.19 iv 28–61) provides a compelling example of warrior body staining.[24] The conclusion recounts how Pugatu avenges the death of Aqhatu, her brother, by assassinating Yatpanu, who had killed him. The final lines of the tablet are not extant, but the trajectory of the narrative suggests that Pugatu succeeds and kills Yatpanu. To prepare herself, Pugatu bathes and reddens her body (lines 41–43), outfits and arms herself (lines 44–45), then conceals the stain, uniform, and weapons beneath a woman's cloak that disguises the role she is assuming and masks her violent intent (line 46).[25] The evidentiary text reads,

> [A shellfish she brought] from the sea,
>   she bathed and [reddened herself],[26]
>   she reddened herself with the sea snail,
> whose [army][27] occupies a field in the sea.

---

22. Ibid., 167.

23. Ibid.

24. "Aqhat" (Simon B. Parker, *Ugaritic Narrative Poetry* [SBLWAW 9; Atlanta: Scholars Press, 1997], 76–78).

25. Observations about the Aqhatu Legend in this paragraph are adapted from Frank Ritchel Ames, "Women and War in the Hebrew Bible" (Ph.D. diss., University of Denver and Iliff School of Theology, 1998), 68–70.

26. Restoring lines 41–42 to *trtḥ[ṣ].w[ta]dm* based on formulaic use of "bathe and redden" (cf. *CTU* 1.14 ii 9 and iii 52) and parallel *tidm* in the line (Parker, "Aqhat," 77).

27. Restoring *alp* to the gap in line 43, *d[alp].šd.zuh.bym*, and translating "whose [army]" rather than "whose [source]" (*contra* ibid.).

> Underneath she donned the garb of a warrior,
>> she put a [dagger] in her sheath,
>> a sword she put in her [scabbard],
> and over these she donned the garb of a woman.

Pugatu transforms herself into a warrior by washing and staining her body, donning the clothing of a warrior, and arming herself with a dagger and/or sword—practical and symbolic acts that betray murderous purposes. In the course of her preparations, she stained herself red (lines 41–42).[28] She is, quite literally, dressed to kill, for she wears (but conceals) battle gear.[29] The significance of her attire is patent, and, for her plan to succeed, Pugatu must disguise herself, and she does so with a woman's cloak. By covering "the garb of a warrior" with "the garb of a woman," Pugatu conceals her weapons and her violent plan, allowing her to gain access to an unsuspecting victim. Her skin, attire, and weapons would signal an attack, but the outer, woman's attire conceals the threat and belies peace and safety in her presence. In lines 43–46 corresponding references to types of clothing ("warrior's" and "woman's") and layering ("underneath" and "over") dress up the quatrain and, in a striking intersection of form and meaning, surround the references to weapons ("dagger" and "sword"). The literary and strategic guise works. Pugatu arrives at Yatpanu's tent, is mistaken for a "hireling"—either a maidservant, wine steward, or a consort (lines 50–52)—and gains access to Yatpanu. In the layered attires and roles of maidservant-warrior, Pugatu pours Yatpanu's wine, then pours out his life (lines 52–end).

The red-stained warrior also makes an appearance in the epic of Kirta, who pines for a spouse, children, and an enduring dynasty (*CTU* 1.14 i 7–37).[30] To achieve this objective and guided by a vision of his father, Illu,

---

28. Although this reference to staining has been widely interpreted as an application of purple dye extracted from sea snails (following J. C. de Moor, "Murices in Ugaritic Mythology," *Or* 37 [1968]: 212–15), the established interpretation is not certain. Dennis Pardee notes, the text's depiction of the sea snail and its habitat range is unusual; purple dye is associated with royalty; and "rouged" is a translation of the Ugaritic term *'dm*, "red," rather than *'iqn'u* or *pḥm* ("The Aqhatu Legend [1.103]," translated by Dennis Pardee [*COS* 1.103:356 n. 130]).

29. Meindert Dijkstra and J. C. de Moor, "Problematic Passages in the Legend of Aqhatu," *UF* 7 (1976): 199, 212.

30. "Kirta" (translated by Edward L. Greenstein in Parker, *Ugaritic Narrative Poetry*, 9–48).

Kirta plans a campaign against the city of Udmu, where he will take a bride (ii 6–iii 32). In the vision, Kirta learns that the campaign requires the sacrifice of lamb, bird, wine, and honey, a stockpiling of food for Kirta's own city and army (ii 12–34), and ritual staining:

> Wash yourself, and rouge yourself too,
> wash your hands to the elbow,
> [Your fin]gers as far as the shoulder. (ii 9–11)[31]

In addition, Kirta is advised to prosecute the war with a large army that even includes mercenaries hired by widows, as well as only sons, the lame and blind, and newlyweds (ii 41–50; compare iv 21–28)—groups customarily exempt from military service. Kirta obeys Illu's instructions, including those about ritual staining, and before the campaign, reddens himself (1.15 ii 21–iii 30).[32] Though prepared for a large-scale, lengthy seige, Kirta attacks only outlying towns and does not harm the city, Udmu, again following the instructions that had been given. In accordance with the vision, Kirta conquers by a display of force and secures the spouse and offspring he desired (iii 20–25). The ruddy warrior takes a bride: a motif also found in the Hebrew Bible (for example, Song 3:6–11; Ps 45).

2. Red Stain as Sign and Symbol in Warfare

Biblical and other ancient Near Eastern texts provide prima facie evidence that the bodies, clothing, and weapons of warriors were reddened—a recognizable literary trope that reflects material culture and social practice in various ancient Near Eastern communities. Details are few but provocative. Some texts attribute the reddening to the detritus of battle, the blood from wounded opponents (Isa 63:1–6); in other texts red stain was applied before engaging the enemy and was part of a preparatory ritual (First Soldiers' Oath §15; Aqhatu 1.19 iv 46–61; Kirta 1.14 ii 9–26); and in others, the ruddy complexion seems a natural and attractive hue of the warrior's skin (1 Sam 17:42; Song 5:10).[33] Whether natural, inciden-

---

31. Ibid., 14.
32. Ibid., 18.
33. Anat's bloodbath is an example of a post-battle ritual (*KTU* 1.3 ii 13–14), about which see John B. Geyer, "Blood and the Nations in Ritual and Myth," *VT* 57 (2007): 1–20.

tal, or intentional, red coloration—unlike a conditioned body, protective clothing, camouflage, or weaponry—would not have strengthened, protected, or empowered a warrior *directly*.[34] Rather, the coloration is a sign that, when observed with other visual and situational clues, identified a person as a warrior.[35] This is patent in the story of Pugatu who concealed red skin and warrior's garb under a woman's cloak to mask her maleficent intent and potential; Pugatu needed to wear a disguise to draw near to her victim (Aqhatu 1.19 iv 51–61). Except for Isaiah's vision of Yhwh returning from battle, which employs a question-and-answer schema as a rhetorical strategy (Isa 63:1–6), the story of Pugatu and other texts that portray reddened warriors do not interpret the stain or include explanatory glosses for the reader. The evidentiary texts envision a reader who would recognize the sign.

The red stain, however, is not merely a sign. It is also a symbol—something that is inherently ambiguous but, through human perception and social construction, evokes relatively predictable aggregates of meaning, emotion, and action.[36] The symbol is a prompt—a stimulus that

---

34. Patrizia Calefato, *The Clothed Body* (trans. Lisa Adams; Dress, Body, Culture; New York: Berg, 2004), 15.

35. For example, ancient Israelite warriors could be identified from a מד, "soldier's garment" (2 Sam 20:8), or כלי גבר, "battle gear" (Deut 22:5). Interpreting כלי גבר as battle gear rather than "man's apparel" (NRSV) was proposed by Cyrus H. Gordon ("A Note on the Tenth Commandment," *JAAR* 31 [1963]: 208–209) and finds precedent in the Talmud (*b. Nazir 59a*) and *Tg. Onkelos* (see B. Grossfeld's translation in *The Targum Onqelos to Deuteronomy* [ArBib 9; Wilmington: Michael Glazier, 1988], 64: "A woman should not wear a man's *armament*"). The verse is situated in a chiasm that spans Deut 19:1–22:8 and is the structural counterpart of the warfare laws of 20:1–18 (Ames, "Women and War," 49–99). Deuteronomy 19:1–22:8 applies the prohibition of murder (5:17) to various life-and-death situations, including warfare (Stephen A. Kaufman, "The Structure of the Deuteronomic Law," *Maarav* 1/2 [1978/1979]: 105–58).

36. Definitions of *symbol* abound; many are useful, and some highly influential. Victor Turner, for instance defined a symbol as "a thing regarded by general consent as naturally typifying or representing or recalling something by possession of analogous qualities or by association in fact or thought" (*The Forest of Symbols: Aspects of Ndembu Ritual* [Ithaca: Cornell University Press, 1967], 19). Understandably, I offer a new definition with a degree of trepidation. As Northrop Frye confessed, "The word 'symbol' is a term of such Protean elusiveness that my instinct, as a practical literary critic, has always been to avoid it as much as possible" (Northrop Frye, "The Symbol as a Medium of Exchange," in *The Secular Scripture and Other Writings on*

elicits complex responses—and, to greater and lesser degrees, responses among members of a social group can be observed, correlated, and anticipated, though their most interesting functions may be latent rather than manifest.[37] Symbols do not have precise meanings; rather, they bear rich meanings, for symbolism condenses and multiplies associations.[38] Condensation and multivocality are, to borrow a phrase from David I. Kertzer, "virtues of ambiguity."[39]

My understanding of symbolism is grounded in cognitive theory,[40] and the analysis that follows, which is interdisciplinary in nature, draws key insights from cognitive-based studies of signed languages, primarily Sarah F. Taub's *Language from the Body: Iconicity and Metaphor in American Sign Language*. Taub concluded,

> Language, in any modality, is motivated—it draws on structures and associations in the language user's conceptual system. Iconicity, a feature of all languages, is based on our ability to associate sensory images

---

Critical Theory, 1976–1991 [ed. Joseph Adamson and Jean Wilson; Collected Works of Northrop Frye 18; Toronto: University of Toronto Press, 2006], 327). Definition, of course, cannot be avoided. Signs and symbols both represent things, but the difference "is a matter of degree, depending on the density of different and disparate meanings that [the symbol] connotes, on the intensity of feelings that it evokes, and on its action-impelling properties" (Abner Cohen, *Two-dimensional Man: An Essay on the Anthropology of Power and Symbolism in Complex Society* [Berkeley: University of California Press, 1974], 24). Turner also refers to symbols as "triggers of social action" ("Symbolic Studies," *Annual Review of Anthropology* 4 [1975]: 155).

37. A distinction that, according to Robert K. Merton, "was devised to preclude the inadvertent confusion, often found in the sociological literature, between conscious *motivations* for social behavior and its *objective consequences*" (*Social Theory and Social Structure* [enlarged ed.; New York: The Free Press, 1968], 115).

38. David I. Kertzer, *Ritual, Politics, and Power* (New Haven: Yale University Press, 1988), 11.

39. Ibid., 69.

40. See George Lakoff, "Cognitive Linguistics Versus Generative Linguistics: How Commitments Influence Results," *Language & Communication* 11 (1991): 53–62. Contrast the cognitive approach of Stefan Thomas Gries, "Introduction" in *Corpora in Cognitive Linguistics: Corpus-Based Approaches to Syntax and Lexis* (ed. Stefan Th. Gries and Anatol Stefanowitsch; Trends in Linguistics, Studies and Monographs 172; Berlin: de Gruyter, 2006), 1–18, to the generative approach of Noam Chomsky, *Aspects of the Theory of Syntax* (Cambridge: MIT Press, 1965). For a complete introduction, see William Croft and D. Alan Cruse, *Cognitive Linguistics* (Cambridge Textbooks in Linguistics; Cambridge: Cambridge University Press, 2004).

with concepts, simplify those images, and create analogues of them using the resources of the language, all the while preserving the essential structure of the original image. Conceptual metaphor, another feature of all languages, creates associations between abstract and concrete conceptual domains. Although all languages have metaphor and iconicity, signed languages excel at putting the two together to create a vast range of iconic and metaphorical/iconic words, inflections, and syntactic structures. To give a real description and explanation of these phenomena, we must adopt a theory of linguistics that can also draw on the complexities of conceptual structure; we must not separate off semantics from syntax and phonology but must integrate them together in one linguistic representation. In short, we must adopt the cognitive linguistics point of view.[41]

Two assumptions that ground cognitive linguistics are especially relevant to the analysis of the red-stained warrior: "conceptual representation is the outcome of the nature of the bodies humans have and how they interact with the sociophysical world ... [and] meaning, as it emerges from language use, is a function of the activation of conceptual knowledge structures as guided by context."[42] In short, symbols are embodied and situated. With this theoretical framework in mind, I turn to the question: How did red stain on the warrior's body function in the context of war? An answer can be inferred from the form, deployment, experience, and perception of the symbol.[43]

---

41. Sarah F. Taub, *Language from the Body: Iconicity and Metaphor in American Sign Language* (Cambridge: Cambridge University Press, 2001), 231. Taub adds, "The field of linguistics owes a great debt to the world's Deaf communities for creating and sharing language in the signed modality. Signed languages are vital to our progress in figuring out the human language capacity, because their iconicity is too strong and pervasive and multifaceted to ignore. Truly taking signed languages seriously will cause a revolution in spoken-language linguistics: a new direction for all of us language scholars as we enter the third millennium" (ibid.). See, e.g., Karen Emmorey, *Language, Cognition, and the Brain: Insights from Sign Language Research* (London: Lawrence Erlbaum, 2002).

42. Vyvyan Evans, "Cognitive Linguistics," in *The Routledge Pragmatics Encyclopedia* (ed. Louise Cummings; New York: Routledge, 2010), 47. Evans also states that "language is the outcome of general properties of cognition," and "grammar is conceptual in nature" (ibid.).

43. Victor Turner infers the meaning of a symbol from (1) interpretations given by indigenous informants, (2) the use to which the symbol is put, and (3) the context in which the symbol is used, including the varied uses of the symbol within the culture.

(1) *Form* and its relation to function are a consideration in the analysis, for a sign can resemble its semiotic object. Charles S. Peirce recognized levels of abstraction and so classified signs as icons, indexes, or symbols: an *icon* resembles its object; an *index* is an effect of the object, and the relationship between a *symbol* and its object is solely conventional and arbitrary.[44] However, semblances as well as social constructions matter. Empirical studies of signed languages show that the meanings of some hand gestures are fairly transparent and can be guessed correctly by nonsigning, nonnative observers.[45] Language is conventional, but seeing certain signs is almost like seeing their referents due to the marked iconicity of the signs. However, as Taub points out, "Iconicity is not an objective relationship between image and referent; rather, it is a relationship between our mental models of image and referent. These models are partially motivated by our embodied experiences common to all humans and partially by our experiences in particular cultures and societies."[46] Iconicity is "dependent on our natural *and* cultural conceptual associations" [italics mine].[47] In the analysis of color symbolism, iconicity has implications. As Philip P. Arnold points out, "There are no set universal characteristics of color symbolism just as there are no completely cultural-specific meanings of color."[48] Color symbolism tends to be motivated, for it "emerges from

---

Turner labels these the exegetical, operational, and positional meanings (Turner, *The Forest of Symbols*, 50–52). I also look to Turner's three sources for inferring meaning, but I employ a different set of rubrics that place strong emphasis on the relationship between form and function, natural and cultural associations, stimulus and response (i.e., on the complex nature of bio-psycho-social perception).

44. Floyd Merrell, "Charles Sanders Peirce's Concept of the Sign," in *The Routledge Companion to Semiotics and Linguistics* (ed. Paul Cobley; London: Routledge, 2001), 31.

45. Taub (*Language from the Body*, 19) cites Emanuela Cameracanna et al., "How Visual Spatial-Temporal Metaphors of Speech Become Visible in Sign," in *Perspectives on Sign Language Structure: Papers from the Fifth International Symposium on Sign Language Research, Vol. 1* (ed. Inger Ahlgren, Brita Bergman, and Mary Brennan; Durham: International Sign Linguistics Association, 1994), 55–68. See also Pamela Perniss, Robin L. Thompson, and Gabriella Vigliocco, "Iconicity as a General Property of Language: Evidence from Spoken and Signed Languages," *Frontiers in Psychology* 1/227 (2010): 1–15.

46. Taub, *Language from the Body*, 19–20.

47. Ibid., 20.

48. Philip P. Arnold, "Colors," *ER* 3:1860.

the immediate material experience of human beings."[49] Blood is red, and red resembles blood, and blood is associated with common human experiences of life and death. An episode in the account of Jehoram's campaign against Moab displays the associative chain:

> When they rose early in the morning, and the sun shone upon the water, the Moabites saw the water opposite them as red as blood. They said, "This is blood; the kings must have fought together, and killed one another. Now then, Moab, to the spoil!" (2 Kgs 3:22–23 NRSV)

The Moabite warriors saw water that looked red, concluded that the water was blood, and inferred that the opposing forces were fighting and killing one another: red stands for blood which stands for death. Red, blood, and death are associated in some of the evidentiary texts that have been discussed. Red on the robes of Isaiah's divine warrior represents the blood of slain Edomites (Isa 63:6). Nahum's reddened warriors slaughtered the inhabitants of the "City of bloodshed" (Nah 3:1). Joab dabbed the blood of his victims on his belt and shoes (1 Kgs 2:5–6). The stained pelt of the First Soldiers' Oath is blood colored (§15). The resemblance of sign to signified is not to be discounted, neither is it to be oversimplified. In some texts, the stain is an icon that represents blood; in others, it is an index because the stain is blood and provides evidence that opponents were slain; in more than a few texts, the stain is a symbol (using Peirce's narrow definition of the term) that represents an abstract concept such as hegemony.

(2) *Deployment* refers to the strategic positioning of resources—a term often applied to the movement of military personnel and equipment into the theater of war. The use of the rubric is particularly apropos in an analysis of the red-stained warrior. The symbol is deployed with the warrior who could be observed in the war camp, on the battlefield, and upon returning home. For Isaiah's sentry, the sight of an unrecognized person coming toward the city in crimson garments evoked unease and prompted urgent questions related to the person's identity and intent (Isa 63:1–3). The unrecognized person could be a foe advancing to fight or a friend returning from battle. The stain that adorned the shields, clothes, and chariots of the warriors who raced through Nineveh was deployed as an element of the assault (Nah 2:3–4). Goliath confronted David's ruddy appearance on the battlefield (1 Sam 17:42–43). Pugatu reddened her body

---

49. Ibid.

and otherwise armed herself before engaging her adversary (*CTU* 1.19 iv 41–45).

(3) The *experience* of the sign for the warrior and the opponent would not have been the same; body art is experienced differently by wearers and observers. For the warrior wearing the stain, the experience would be primarily tactile and indirectly visual. The warrior would feel the application of the stain on the skin and would have been aware of the texture of the clothing and the weight of arms and armor, but the warrior would only see the stain partially on his or her extremities or indirectly on other warriors. The opponent, on the other hand, would see the stain directly in its entirety and could not avoid looking at the stain when engaging the advancing warrior or army. The sight and effect of the red stain, unless intentionally concealed, would have been unavoidable.

(4) *Perception* is the recognition and interpretation of sensory stimuli, and the dynamics of the process are biological, psychological, and sociological.[50] Icons, indexes, and symbols are bio-psycho-social stimuli that prompt both conscious responses and unconscious reactions, and the effects of exposure to the color red are best regarded as multidimensional. Responses to symbols are conditioned, and meanings are socially constructed, but neurophysiology plays a role. One need only consider the implications of red-green color vision deficiencies for the recognition and interpretation of color-dependent symbols in contemporary society, and inherited color defects are "extremely common."[51] The body engages a sociophysical world and perceives.

Edmund Leach observed that red has associations that cross multiple cultures and concluded: "Certainly it is very common to find that *red* is treated as a sign of *danger*, which may be derived from red = blood. But *red* is also quite often associated with *joy* which might come from red = blood = life."[52] Red ochre has been used widely as pigment, and when mixed with

---

50. Paul Rookes and Jane Willson, *Perception: Theory, Development, and Organisation* (Routledge Modular Psychology; London: Routledge, 2000), 1.

51. Maureen Neitz and Jay Neitz, "Color Vision Defects," in *Ocular Disease: Mechanisms and Management* (ed. Leonard A. Levin and Daniel M. Albert; Philadelphia: Saunders, 2010), 479. The prevalence of red-green color deficiencies in the United States and western Europe is estimated to be 1 in 12 among males and 1 in 230 among females (ibid.).

52. Edmund Leach, *Culture and Communication: The Logic by which Symbols Are Connected* (Themes in the Social Sciences; New York: Cambridge University Press, 1976), 57–58.

water "may closely resemble the appearance of blood spilled by human activities."[53] Human stores of red ochre have been dated to 250,000 years ago, and archaeologists generally accept that "the earliest use of ochre was for proto-symbolic body decoration."[54] Ernst E. Wreschner, after reviewing the distribution of red ochre in numerous prehistoric burial sites, concluded that making tools and collecting ochre are "meaningful regularities in human evolution."[55] The widespread association of red ochre with blood, death, and life, he dubbed a Neanderthal innovation that cannot be explained by enculturation and diffusion alone.[56] Wreschner concluded that red became "a synonym for blood and life, for danger and death," because biological evolution framed social construction.[57]

The neurophysiological effects of exposure to red have been tested in various ways. Andrew J. Elliot and Markus A. Maier hypothesized that exposure to the color red prompts avoidance behaviors; in short, seeing red signals danger and prompts flight—an oversimplification that admits many exceptions, but the conclusion is supported by studies of human and primate responses.[58] Elliot and Maier acknowledge that the meanings associated with colors are socially constructed, but they add this important caveat:

> These learned associations may be bolstered by or even derived from an evolutionarily ingrained predisposition across species to interpret red as a signal of danger in competitive contexts. For example, in primates, red on the chest or face (due to a testosterone surge) signals the high status,

---

53. Nicole Boivin, "From Veneration to Exploitation: Human Engagement with the Mineral World," in *Soils, Stones and Symbols: Cultural Perceptions of the Mineral World* (ed. Nicole Boivin and Mary Ann Owoc; New York: Routledge, 2004), 16. In the same volume, also see Paul S. C. Taçon, "Ochre, Clay, Stone and Art: The Symbolic Importance of Minerals as Life-Force among Aboriginal Peoples of Northern and Central Australia," 31–42.

54. Piotr Sadowski, *From Interaction to Symbol: A Systems View of the Evolution of Signs and Communication* (Iconicity in Language and Literature 8; Amsterdam: John Benjamins, 2009), 104.

55. Ernst E. Wreschner, "Red Ochre and Human Evolution: A Case for Discussion," *Current Anthropology* 21 (1980): 631.

56. Ibid. See also Wil Roebroeks et al., "Use of Red Ochre by Early Neandertals," *Proceedings of the National Academy of Sciences* 109 (2012): 1889–94.

57. Wreschner, "Red Ochre and Human Evolution," 633.

58. Andrew J. Elliot and Markus A. Maier, "Color and Psychological Functioning," *Current Directions in Psychological Science* 16 (2007): 250–54.

and thus danger, of an opponent. ... Thus, through both specific and general associative processes that may themselves emerge from biologically based proclivities, red carries the meaning of failure in achievement contexts, warning that a dangerous possibility is at hand. This warning signal is posited to produce avoidance-based motivation that primarily has negative implications for achievement outcomes.[59]

Exposure to the color red correlates with changes in heart rate variability, cognitive performance, motor strength, and performance attainment and can provoke seizures in individuals who have some forms of epilepsy.[60] Red uniforms also affect the outcomes of sports competitions.[61] Andrei Ilie (in a coauthored study) proposed that "increased redness during aggressive interaction may act as a signal of relative dominance in humans," and the researchers concluded that red "may trigger a powerful psychological distractor signal in human aggressive competition."[62]

---

59. Ibid., 251. The primate research to which Elliot and Maier refer is discussed in J. M. Setchell and E. J. Wickings, "Dominance, Status Signals, and Coloration in Male Mandrills (*Mandrillus Sphinx*)," *Ethology* 111 (2005): 25–30.

60. Andrew J. Elliot et al., "A Subtle Threat Cue, Heart Rate Variability, and Cognitive Performance," *Psychophysiology* 48 (2001): 1340–45; Andrew J. Elliot et al.,"Color and Psychological Functioning: The Effect of Red on Performance Attainment," *Journal of Experimental Psychology: General* 136 (2007): 154–68; Vincent Payen et al., "Viewing Red Prior to a Strength Test Inhibits Motor Output," *Neuroscience Letters* 495 (2011): 44–48; Brian P. Meier et al., "Color in Context: Psychological Context Moderates the Influence of Red on Approach- and Avoidance-Motivated Behavior," *PLoS One* 7 (2012): 1–5; Robert S. Fischer, et al., "Photic- and Pattern-induced Seizures: A Review for the Epilepsy Foundation of America Working Group," *Epilepsia* 46 (2005): 1433.

61. Russell A. Hill and Robert A. Barton, "Red Enhances Human Performance in Contests," *Nature* 435 (2005): 293. Norbert Hagemann, Bernd Strauss, and Jan Leißing ("When the Referee Sees Red," *Psychological Science* 19 [2008]: 769–71) attribute the competitive advantage reported by Hill and Barton to the effect of the color red on the referee and not the opponent: "We propose that the perception of colors triggers a psychological effect in referees that can lead to bias in evaluating identical performances" (769). See also S. Ioan, M. Sandulache, and S. Avramescu, "Red is a Distracter for Men in Competition," *Evolution and Human Behavior* 28 (2007): 285–93.

62. Andrei Ilie et al., "Better to Be Red than Blue in Virtual Competition," *Cyber-Psychology & Behavior* 11 (2008): 377.

3. Conclusions

The portrayal of warriors in the evidentiary texts suggests that the bodies, clothing, and weapons of warriors in and around ancient Israel were at times stained red. When the stain is actually blood, it is an index, the effect of a cause, and the sign suggests that the warrior has killed an opponent in battle. When the stain is red dye, it is an icon that represents blood, with blood's complex life-and-death associations. Whether icon or index, the stain, I propose, is also an abstract symbol that bears an aggregate of meanings from which the observer will likely infer that the warrior possesses lethal, irresistible power.

How did red stain function? First, red stain identified the warrior. Whether natural or artificial, incidental or intentional, the stain, in combination with other material, behavioral, and contextual clues, prompted the observer to regard the ruddy man or woman a person of war. Isaiah's vision of Yhwh returning from Edom in bloodied robes and the Aqhatu legend's account of Pugatu concealing her weapons, war attire, and stained body, presuppose that the color red marked a warrior. Some of the warriors in the evidentiary texts are officers, but it is not clear whether red stain signified a particular rank or status, or if distinctive patterns of stain were used to differentiate tribes, clans, or families. Point of view, of course, matters in the perception of identity. The adorned body is "context-dependent," subject to "undercoding," and "understood and appreciated by different social strata".[63] Thus, the warrior is not simply a warrior but is a situated warrior whose appearance evokes contextualized identifications. Based on allegiances, the inhabitants of a city would perceive the stained warrior to be a warrior-deliverer or a warrior-destroyer. Ruddiness was an indicator of physical health and would make the warrior handsome and attractive to the opposite sex. Fellow warriors would consider the stained warrior an ally and would see a reflection of themselves. Applying and observing the stain would also affect the perception of the warrior, who embraced as well as expressed an identity.

Second, red stain afforded the warrior a tactical advantage. Blood, which the red stain represents, was "perceived as being simultaneously pure and impure, attractive and repulsive, sacred and profane; it is at

---

63. Fred Davis, *Fashion, Culture, and Identity* (Chicago: University of Chicago Press, 1992), 8.

once a life-giving substance and a symbol of death."[64] However, point of view again matters.[65] I propose that the stain emboldened the wearer and intimidated the observer. In ancient Israel, blood was equated with life (Deut 12:23) and was believed to possess apotropaic properties. Applications of blood ostensibly saved the lives of a nonconforming Moses (Exod 4:24–26), members of Hebrew households in Egypt (Exod 12:7), and the leaders of the Hebrews who had fled Egypt (Exod 24:8–11).[66] These traditions are part of the aggregate of meaning of the symbol, though not exhausting its meaning. Staining skin, clothing, and weapons red perhaps cleansed and consecrated the warrior, but these functions, though important, seem incidental in the context of warfare, for they are neither strategic nor tactical.[67] But the stain was deployed in warfare and did serve a tactical function. The red stain symbolized life for the dowsed warrior and death for the confronted opponent, who in the stain saw the horrific symbol of the warrior's lethal, irresistible power. For the warrior, the stain symbolized protection and life; for the opponent, defeat and death. The red stain emboldened the warrior and intimidated the opponent, who, seeing red, experienced its subtle but real bio-psycho-social effects. In ancient Israelite warfare, the red stain granted a tactical advantage over the opponent.

Bibliography

Ames, Frank Ritchel. "Women and War in the Hebrew Bible." Ph.D. diss., University of Denver and Iliff School of Theology, 1998.

---

64. Jean-Paul Roux, "Blood," *ER* 2:985.
65. Dennis J. McCarthy demonstrates that blood is symbolic in and beyond ancient Israel ("Symbolism of Blood and Sacrifice," *JBL* 88 [1969]: 166–76; and "Further Notes on the Symbolism of Blood and Sacrifice," *JBL* 92 [1973]: 205–10), but I am not convinced that blood symbolizes life in Israel and death among other people groups. William K. Gilders criticizes and attributes McCarthy's conclusion about blood to "the assumption that it can have but one meaning in each cultural context" (*Blood Ritual in the Hebrew Bible: Meaning and Power* [Baltimore: The Johns Hopkins University Press, 2004], 4).
66. S. David Sperling, "Blood," *ABD* 1:761–63.
67. According to Raymond Firth, the identification of incidental associations is critical in the analysis of symbols (*Symbols: Public and Private* [Ithaca: Cornell University Press, 1973], 27). To do this, I have tried to focus on the deployment of symbols to achieve military objectives.

Arnold, Philip P. "Colors." Pages 1860–62 in vol. 3 of *The Encyclopedia of Religion*. Edited by M. Eliade. 16 vols. New York: Macmillan, 1987.
Berlin, Brent and Paul Kay. *Basic Color Terms: Their Universality and Evolution*. Berkeley: University of California Press, 1969.
Boivin, Nicole. "From Veneration to Exploitation: Human Engagement with the Mineral World." Pages 1–29 in *Soils, Stones and Symbols: Cultural Perceptions of the Mineral World*. Edited by Nicole Boivin and Mary Ann Owoc. New York: Routledge, 2004.
Brenner, Athalya. *Colour Terms in the Old Testament*. JSOTSup 21. Sheffield: JSOT Press, 1982.
Cage, John. *Color and Meaning: Art, Science, and Symbolism*. Berkeley: University of California Press, 2000.
Calefato, Patrizia. *The Clothed Body*. Translated by Lisa Adams. Dress, Body, Culture. New York: Berg, 2004.
Cameracanna, Emanuela, Serena Corazza, Elena Pizzuto, and Virginia Volterra. "How Visual Spatial-Temporal Metaphors of Speech Become Visible in Sign." Pages 55–68 in *Perspectives on Sign Language Structure: Papers from the Fifth International Symposium on Sign Language Research, Vol. 1*. Edited by Inger Ahlgren, Brita Bergman, and Mary Brennan. Durham: International Sign Linguistics Association, 1994.
Cathcart, Kevin J. *Nahum in the Light of Northwest Semitic*. BibOr 26. Rome: Biblical Institute Press, 1973.
Chapman, Cynthia R. "Sculpted Warriors: Sexuality and the Sacred in the Depiction of Warfare in the Assyrian Palace Reliefs and in Ezekiel 23:14–17." Pages 1–17 in *The Aesthetics of Violence in the Prophets*. Edited by J. M. O'Brien and C. Franke. LHBOTS 517. New York: T&T Clark, 2010.
Charles, J. Daryl. "Plundering the Lion's Den—A Portrait of Divine Fury (Nahum 2:3–11)." *Grace Theological Journal* 10 (1989): 183–201.
Chomsky, Noam. *Aspects of the Theory of Syntax*. Cambridge: MIT Press, 1965.
Cohen, Abner. *Two-dimensional Man: An Essay on the Anthropology of Power and Symbolism in Complex Society*. Berkeley: University of California Press, 1974.
Croft, William and D. Alan Cruse. *Cognitive Linguistics*. Cambridge Textbooks in Linguistics. Cambridge: Cambridge University Press, 2004.
Davis, Fred. *Fashion, Culture, and Identity*. Chicago: University of Chicago Press, 1992.

Dedrick, Don. *Naming the Rainbow: Colour Language, Colour Science, and Culture.* Synthese Library 274. Dordrecht, The Netherlands: Kluwer Academic, 1998.

Dijkstra, Meindert and J. C. de Moor. "Problematic Passages in the Legend of Aqhatu." *UF* 7 (1976): 171–218.

Elliot, Andrew J. and Markus A. Maier. "Color and Psychological Functioning." *Current Directions in Psychological Science* 16 (2007): 250–54.

Elliot, Andrew J., Markus A. Maier, A. C. Moller, R. Friedman, and J. Meinhardt. "Color and Psychological Functioning: The Effect of Red on Performance Attainment." *Journal of Experimental Psychology: General* 136 (2007): 154–68.

Elliot, Andrew J., Vincent Payen, Jeanick Brisswalter, François Cury, and Julian F. Thayer. "A Subtle Threat Cue, Heart Rate Variability, and Cognitive Performance." *Psychophysiology* 48 (2001): 1340–45.

Emmorey, Karen. *Language, Cognition, and the Brain: Insights from Sign Language Research.* London: Lawrence Erlbaum, 2002.

Evans, Vyvyan. "Cognitive Linguistics." Pages 46–50 in *The Routledge Pragmatics Encyclopedia.* Edited by Louise Cummings. New York: Routledge, 2010.

Flanagan, James W. "Court History or Succession Document? A Study of 2 Samuel 9–20 and 1 Kings 1–2." *JBL* 91 (1972): 172–81.

Firth, Raymond. *Symbols: Public and Private.* Ithaca: Cornell University Press, 1973.

Fischer, Robert S., Graham Harding, Giuseppe Erba, Gregory L. Barkley, and Arnold Wilkins. "Photic- and Pattern-induced Seizures: A Review for the Epilepsy Foundation of America Working Group." *Epilepsia* 46 (2005): 1426–41.

Frye, Northrop. "The Symbol as a Medium of Exchange." Pages 327–41 in *The Secular Scripture and Other Writings on Critical Theory, 1976–1991.* Edited by Joseph Adamson and Jean Wilson. Collected Works of Northrop Frye 18. Toronto: University of Toronto Press, 2006.

Geyer, John B. "Blood and the Nations in Ritual and Myth." *VT* 57 (2007): 1–20.

Gilders, William K. *Blood Ritual in the Hebrew Bible: Meaning and Power.* Baltimore: The Johns Hopkins University Press, 2004.

Gordon, Cyrus H. "A Note on the Tenth Commandment." *JAAR* 31 (1963): 208–9.

Gries, Stefan Thomas. "Introduction." Pages 1–18 in *Corpora in Cognitive Linguistics: Corpus-Based Approaches to Syntax and Lexis.* Edited by Stefan Th. Gries and Anatol Stefanowitsch. Trends in Linguistics. Studies and Monographs 172. Berlin: de Gruyter, 2006.

Grossfeld, Bernard. *The Targum Onqelos to Deuteronomy: Translated, with Apparatus, and Notes*. ArBib 9. Wilmington, Del.: Michael Glazier, 1988.

Hagemann, Norbert, Bernd Strauss, and Jan Leißing, "When the Referee Sees Red." *Psychological Science* 19 (2008): 769–71.

Hahlen, Mark Allen. "The Background and Use of Equine Imagery in Zechariah." *Stone-Campbell Journal* 3 (2000): 243–60.

Hill, Russell A. and Robert A. Barton. "Red Enhances Human Performance in Contests." *Nature* 435 (2005): 293.

Ilie, Andrei, Silvia Ioan, Leon Zagrean, and Mihai Moldovan. "Better to Be Red than Blue in Virtual Competition." *CyberPsychology & Behavior* 11 (2008): 375–77.

Ioan, S., M. Sandulache, and S. Avramescu. "Red is a Distracter for Men in Competition." *Evolution and Human Behavior* 28 (2007): 285–93.

Kaufman, Stephen A. "The Structure of the Deuteronomic Law." *Maarav* 1/2 (1978/79): 105–58.

Kertzer, David I. *Ritual, Politics, and Power*. New Haven: Yale University Press, 1988.

Kotzé, Gideon R. "A Text-Critical Analysis of the Lamentations Manuscripts from Qumran." Th.D. diss., University of Stellenbosch, 2011.

Kubač, Vladimír. "Blut im Gürtel und in Sandalen." *VT* 31 (1981): 225–26.

Lakoff, George. "Cognitive Linguistics Versus Generative Linguistics: How Commitments Influence Results." *Language & Communication* 11 (1991): 53–62.

Leach, Edmund. *Culture and Communication: The Logic by Which Symbols Are Connected*. Themes in the Social Sciences. New York: Cambridge University Press, 1976.

Lynch, Matthew J. "Zion's Warrior and the Nations: Isaiah 59:15b–63:6 in Isaiah's Zion Traditions." *CBQ* 70 (2008): 244–63.

McCarthy, Dennis J. "Further Notes on the Symbolism of Blood and Sacrifice." *JBL* 92 (1973): 205–10.

———. "Symbolism of Blood and Sacrifice." *JBL* 88 (1969): 166–76.

Meier, Brian P., Paul R. D'Agostino, Andrew J. Elliot, Markus A. Maier, and Benjamin M. Wilkowski. "Color in Context: Psychological Context Moderates the Influence of Red on Approach- and Avoidance-Motivated Behavior." *PLoS One* 7 (2012): 1–5.

Merrell, Floyd. "Charles Sanders Peirce's Concept of the Sign." Pages 28–39 in *The Routledge Companion to Semiotics and Linguistics*. Edited by Paul Cobley. London: Routledge, 2001.

Merton, Robert K. *Social Theory and Social Structure*. Enlarged ed. New York: The Free Press, 1968.

Meyers, Carol. "Gender Imagery in the Song of Songs." *HAR* 10 (1987): 209–23.

Moor, Johannes C. de. "Murices in Ugaritic Mythology." *Or* 37 (1968): 212–15.

Morgenstern, Julian. "Further Light from the Book of Isaiah upon the Catastrophe of 485 B.C." *HUCA* 37 (1966): 1–28.

Neitz, Maureen and Jay Neitz. "Color Vision Defects." Pages 478–85 in *Ocular Disease: Mechanisms and Management*. Edited by Leonard A. Levin and Daniel M. Albert. Philadelphia: Saunders, 2010.

Niditch, Susan. "Good Blood, Bad Blood: Multivocality, Metonymy, and Meditation in Zechariah 9." *VT* 61 (2011): 639–45.

Parker, Simon B., ed. *Ugaritic Narrative Poetry*. SBLWAW 9. Atlanta: Scholars Press, 1997.

Payen, Vincent, Andrew J. Elliot, Stephen A. Coombes, Aïna Chalabaev, Jeanick Brisswalter, François Cury. "Viewing Red Prior to a Strength Test Inhibits Motor Output." *Neuroscience Letters* 495 (2011): 44–48.

Perniss, Pamela, Robin L. Thompson, and Gabriella Vigliocco. "Iconicity as a General Property of Language: Evidence from Spoken and Signed Languages." *Frontiers in Psychology* 1/227 (2010): 1–15.

Petersen, David L. *Haggai and Zechariah 1–8: A Commentary*. OTL. Philadelphia: Westminster, 1984.

Roebroeks, Wil, Mark J. Sier, Trine Kellberg Nielsen, Dimitri De Loecker, Josep Maria Parés, Charles E. S. Arps, and Herman J. Mücher. "Use of Red Ochre by Early Neandertals." *Proceedings of the National Academy of Sciences* 109 (2012): 1889–94.

Rookes, Paul and Jane Willson. *Perception: Theory, Development, and Organisation*. Routledge Modular Psychology. London: Routledge, 2000.

Roux, Jean-Paul. "Blood." Pages 985–87 in vol. 2 of *The Encyclopedia of Religion*. Edited by M. Eliade. 16 vols. New York: Macmillan, 1987.

Sadowski, Piotr. *From Interaction to Symbol: A Systems View of the Evolution of Signs and Communication*. Iconicity in Language and Literature 8. Amsterdam: John Benjamins, 2009.

Setchell, J. M. and E. J. Wickings. "Dominance, Status Signals, and Coloration in Male Mandrills (*Mandrillus Sphinx*)." *Ethology* 111 (2005): 25–30.

Sperling, David S. "Blood." Pages 761–63 in vol. 1 of *The Anchor Bible Dictionary*. Edited by D. N. Freedman. 6 vols. New York: Doubleday, 1992.

Sweeney, Marvin A. "Nahum." Pages 415–50 in *The Twelve Prophets*. 2 vols. Berit Olam. Collegeville: Liturgical, 2000.

Taçon, Paul S. C. "Ochre, Clay, Stone and Art: The Symbolic Importance of Minerals as Life-Force among Aboriginal Peoples of Northern and Central Australia." Pages 31–42 in *Soils, Stones and Symbols: Cultural Perceptions of the Mineral World*. Edited by Nicole Boivin and Mary Ann Owoc. New York: Routledge, 2004.

Taub, Sarah F. *Language from the Body: Iconicity and Metaphor in American Sign Language*. Cambridge: Cambridge University Press, 2001.

Turner, Victor. *The Forest of Symbols: Aspects of Ndembu Ritual*. Ithaca: Cornell University Press, 1967.

———. "Symbolic Studies." *Annual Review of Anthropology* 4 (1975): 145–61.

Wreschner, Ernst E. "Red Ochre and Human Evolution: A Case for Discussion [with Comments by Ralph Bolton, Karl W. Butzer, Henri Delporte, Alexander Häusler, Albert Heinrich, Anita Jacobson-Widding, Tadeusz Malinowski, Claude Masset, Sheryl F. Miller, Avraham Ronen, Ralph Solecki, Peter H. Stephenson, Lynn L. Thomas, and Heinrich Zollinger]." *Current Anthropology* 21 (1980): 631–44.

Zanjani, Sally. *Sara Winnemucca*. Lincoln: University of Nebraska Press, 2001.

"I Will Strike You Down and Cut off Your Head" (1 Sam 17:46): Trash Talking, Derogatory Rhetoric, and Psychological Warfare in Ancient Israel

David T. Lamb

1. Introduction

"Scorn and defiance; slight regard, contempt, and anything that may not misbecome the mighty sender, doth he prize you at. Thus says my King": this is Shakespeare's version of the taunt uttered by the Duke of Exeter, messenger of Henry V, to Charles VI of France.[1] Exeter's words are more dramatic, but perhaps not as entertaining, as the taunt, "Your mother is a hamster and your father reeks of elder-berry," spoken by John Cleese in Monty Python's *The Holy Grail*.[2]

Trash talking, far from being an innovation of modern athletics, literature, or film, was a staple course in ancient military contexts, the prerequisite *hors d'oeuvres*, to whet the appetite for battle. Examples of derogatory military rhetoric can be found in Egyptian sources by Thutmose III, Sethos I, and Ramesses II; in Assyrian sources by Sargon II and Sennacherib; and in the Hebrew Bible by David, Ahab, Elijah, Jezebel, Jehu, Ben-hadad, Jehoash, the Rabshakeh, and even Yhwh himself. An analysis of this aspect of psychological warfare in biblical literature will elucidate some of the most colorful dialogue of the Hebrew Bible and provides an interpretive key in understanding the social dynamic behind these texts.

---

1. Act 2, scene 4.
2. *Monty Python and the Holy Grail*, directed by Terry Gilliam and Terry Jones (Michael White Productions, 1975).

2. Insults, Boasts, and Predictions

Trash talking was often used in military contexts as a means of psychological warfare, and it could involve three components: (1) insults that ridicule an enemy, (2) boasts that exalt the speaker, their country, or their gods; and (3) predictions of victory by the speaker over the opponent. Each of the three components contributes to the rhetorical impact of the speech. Although one might assume that the speaker's purpose is to intimidate the enemy,[3] trash talking is not always heard by the object of the taunt, and one purpose in military contexts is to motivate and inspire the speaker's compatriots. Examples of trash talking examined here will include both speech addressed directly to an opponent and words spoken about an opponent. As with athletes today, comments not made directly to an opponent often still reach their ears. Since confidence is crucial for an army to achieve victory, if verbal assaults succeed at instilling fear in an opponent and courage in one's own troops, the battle is half-won before any blood is spilt. The most effective way to counter the intimidating effects of derogatory rhetoric is to reciprocate in kind, as will be seen in the interaction between David and the Philistine giant.

3. Trash-Talk Research

Nothing has been written specifically about trash talking in the Hebrew Bible, but Margaret R. Eaton's article on "flyting" (verbal dueling) in the Hebrew Bible perhaps comes closest.[4] While Eaton discusses relevant examples, she unfortunately offers little analysis into the dynamics of taunt speech, and her discussion of the "David and Goliath" narrative is limited to a few verses (1 Sam 17:41–47). However, as this examination will show, taunt speech dominates the entire narrative.

The most insightful works related to the topic of biblical trash talking are Geoffrey David Miller's two examinations of verbal feuding in the book of Judges.[5] He offers a theory of verbal feuding and identifies four types:

---

3. See David G. LoConto and Tori J. Roth, "Mead and the Art of Trash Talking: I Got Your Gesture Right Here," *Sociological Spectrum* 25 (2005): 223–24.

4. Margaret R. Eaton, "Some Instances of Flyting in the Hebrew Bible," *JSOT* 61 (1994): 3–14.

5. Geoffrey David Miller, "Verbal Feud in the Hebrew Bible: Judges 3:12–30 and 19–21," *JNES* 55 (1996): 105–17; and idem, "A Riposte Form in the Song of Deborah,"

boasts, insults, parries (responses to boasts), and ripostes (responses to insults). However, his concern for extended conflicts (feuds) rather than short-term conflicts (duels) makes the analysis less directly relevant to the contexts examined here.

For discussions of insulting in ancient Greek culture, see Jan N. Bremmer,[6] or in Iraqi Arabic, see Sadok Masliyah,[7] whose article is particularly relevant as it includes significant interaction with the Hebrew Bible and specifically analyzes the use of animals in insults. The animal used most frequently in these insults, the dog, is the focus of D. Winton Thomas's classic work.[8]

Recent sociological studies discuss the patterns and impact of trash talking in contemporary sports.[9] One of the issues currently debated in sociological journals is the appropriateness of trash talking in sports. Herbert D. Simons argues that trash talking is a normal aspect of athletic competition and therefore should not be prohibited.[10] Nicholas Dixon, however, believes that trash talking in sports is inexcusable and that attempts to defend it are "disingenuous."[11] Surprisingly, Dixon appears to be unaware of Simon's article which presumably would have provided a foil for his arguments. While modern sociological studies debate its appropriateness, within the ancient Near East and the Hebrew Bible trash talking was not only accepted as normal, but was also seen to be a divinely inspired activity.

---

in *Gender and Law in the Hebrew Bible and the Ancient Near East* (ed. V. H. Matthews, B. M. Levinson; and T. S. Frymer-Kensky; JSOTSup 262; Sheffield: Sheffield Academic Press, 1998), 113–27.

6. Jan N. Bremmer, "Verbal Insulting in Ancient Greek Culture," *Acta Antiqua Academiae Scientiarum Hungaricae* 40 (2001): 61–72.

7. Sadok Masliyah, "Curses and Insults in Iraqi Arabic," *JSS* 46 (2001): 267–308.

8. D. Winton Thomas, "*Kelebh* 'Dog': Its Origin and Some Usages of It in the Old Testament," *VT* 10 (1960): 410–27.

9. For a helpful sociological discussion of the rationale and rules of trash talking in modern athletics, see LoConto and Roth, "Trash Talking," 215–30.

10. Herbert D. Simons, "Race and Penalized Sports Behaviors," *International Review for the Sociology of Sport* 38 (2003): 5–22.

11. Nicholas Dixon, "Trash Talking, Respect for Opponents and Good Competition," *Sport, Ethics and Philosophy* 1 (2007): 96–106.

4. Bulls and Birds, Falcons and Foxes: Trash Talking in the Ancient Near East

Before examining taunt speech in the Hebrew Bible, it will be helpful to discuss examples in ancient Near Eastern literature in order to understand the role it served in military contexts more broadly. According to the Babylonians, trash talking goes back to the time of creation. Before their duel in the *Enuma Elish*, Tiamat and Marduk exchanged taunts and insults. As Marduk approaches Tiamat, she is described as "framing savage defiance in her lips" (*ANET*, 66; *COS* 1:397). In response to her threats, Marduk exclaims, "Against the gods, my fathers, thou hast confirmed thy wickedness.... Stand up thou, that I and thou meet in single combat" (*ANET*, 67; *COS* 1:398). Tiamat then became "like one possessed; she took leave of her senses" and cried out in fury as their cosmic battle ensued (*ANET*, 67; *COS* 1:398). It thus appears trash talking was divinely initiated.

Eaton discusses an example of flyting from the Egyptian narrative of Sinuhe.[12] Sinuhe is challenged to a duel by a hero from Retenu who informs Sinuhe that he would be shamed and plundered. During the battle, Sinuhe dodges arrows and declares, "I shot him, my arrow sticking in his neck. He screamed; he fell on his nose. I slew him with his axe. I raised my war cry over his back, while every Asiatic shouted" (*COS* 1:79).

Ancient royal inscriptions from Egypt and Assyria functioned as a type of trash talking by publicly exalting previous military victories in a hyperbolic tone in order to intimidate potential opponents who might read them or hear of them. Thutmose III repeatedly describes his opponent as a "feeble enemy" (*COS* 2:7, 9, 11, 12, 16). One inscription describes Thutmose in the exaggerated tone that is typical of taunt speech: "He is a king who fights alone, without a multitude to back him up. He is more effective than a myriad of numerous armies. ... No one can touch him. ... He is a stout-hearted bull" (*COS* 2:14–15).

Sargon II describes how the noise of his weapons or the sound of his approaching army causes his enemies to flee in fear (*COS* 2:296–297; 300).[13] Sennacherib describes the effect of his approach on Merodach-

---

12. Eaton, "Flyting in the Hebrew Bible," 4.
13. Sargon's inscription here parallels the biblical story of the four lepers who discover that the besieging Arameans have fled because Yhwh caused them to hear a great army so that they thought the Hittites and the Egyptians were approaching (2 Kgs 7:6–7).

Baladan of Babylon: "And he, doer of evil, saw the advance of my campaign from afar. Fear fell upon him and he abandoned all his forces and fled to Guzummani" (*COS* 2:301). Sennacherib also boasts about the effect that the siege of Jerusalem had upon Hezekiah: "He himself, I locked up in Jerusalem, his royal city, like a bird in a cage" and therefore Hezekiah was "overwhelmed by the awesome splendor of [Sennacherib's] lordship" (*COS* 2:303; I discuss the 2 Kings version of this campaign below).

Other ancient Near Eastern royal inscriptions include specific examples of taunt speech. The First Beth-Shan Stela describes an incident where the exploits of Sethos I cause the chiefs of his enemies to "go back on all the boast of their mouths" (*COS* 2:25). In another inscription, Sethos speaks about the 'Apiru who have arisen, "Who [do they] think they are, these despicable Asiatics? ... They shall find out about him whom they did not know–[the ruler val]iant like a falcon *and* a strong bull widestriding and sharp-horned ... to hack up the [entire] land of Dja[hy]!" (*COS* 2:28). Another inscription describes how the enemies of Sethos fear him, "dread of him is in their hearts ... as they forget (even how) to draw the bow, spending the day in the caves, hidden away like foxes (*COS* 2:31).

In the victory stele of King Piye of Egypt, after he hears about the lack of success of his army against his enemy, he rages like a "panther" and declares, "I shall go north myself. I shall tear down his works. I shall make him abandon fighting forever" (*COS* 2:45). Sama'gamni, a leader of the Hatallu tribal confederation brags about an upcoming campaign, "We will seize his cities of the steppe; and we will cut down their fruit trees" (*COS* 2:279.4c).

In an inscription narrating the battle at Qadesh against Muwatallis II of Hatti, Ramesses II taunts his own troops, presumably to exhort them to greater exploits, "How cowardly are your hearts!" (*COS* 2:36). Later in the inscription, he tells his shield-bearer, "I shall go into them like the pounce of a falcon, killing, slaughtering, felling to the ground. What are these effeminate weaklings to you, for millions of whom I care nothing" (*COS* 2:36). Bergmann discusses similar examples from ancient Near Eastern and Hebrew Bible sources that refer to defeated warriors condescendingly as females.[14]

---

14. The majority of Bergmann's examples come from prophetic literature. See Claudia Bergmann, "We Have Seen the Enemy, and He is Only a 'She': The Portrayal of Warriors as Women," *CBQ* 69 (2007): 651–72.

The presence of trash talking in the midst of a duel within the *Iliad* has led numerous scholars to discuss parallels between the narratives of the David and Goliath and that of Hector and Achilles.[15] Hector proclaims to Achilles that he will strip off his glorious armor and return his corpse to the Achaians.[16] Achilles replies that Hector will pay for all the deaths of his companions (*Il.* 22.249–272). Later, in the midst of their battle, Achilles informs Hector that "the dogs and birds will rend you—blood and bone" (*Il.* 22.416). Based on these parallels, Azzan Yadin argues that the David-Goliath narrative was intentionally Hellenized in the spirit of the *Iliad* in the sixth century.[17] However, the presence of similar ancient Near Eastern parallels elsewhere undermines Yadin's theory. Threats involving scavengers consuming human corpses are found in numerous other Deuteronomistic History contexts (see the discussion of David and the Philistine below), and Esarhaddon's vassal treaties include curses that describe how the flesh of those who break the agreement are meant to be fed upon by eagles, vultures, dogs, and pigs (*ANET*, 538).

The most striking point of similarity among these ancient Near Eastern examples is how zoomorphic language is used rhetorically. The speaker uses powerful, predatory animals (panthers, falcons, and strong bulls) to describe his own actions and behavior. These creatures epitomize aggressive, dominant behavior. Frequent references to them in association with the speaker would therefore be utilized to intimidate even battle-hardened warriors. Since the current Pharaoh was thought to be an incarnation of the falcon-god Horus, references to a falcon by Sethos and Ramesses would remind the inscription readers of the rulers' divine nature.

Conversely, the speaker compares his enemy to smaller animals of prey. In particular these animals are situated in contexts emphasizing their weakness (a hiding fox or a caged bird for Hezekiah), thus communicating that the opponent is vulnerable and certain to be defeated by their dominant opponent.

---

15. For example, see Roland de Vaux, "Single Combat in the Old Testament," in *The Bible and the Ancient Near East* (Garden City: Doubleday, 1971), 122–35; Eaton, "Flyting in the Hebrew Bible," 5; Azzan Yadin, "Goliath's Armor and Israelite Collective Memory," *VT* 54 (2004): 389.

16. A similar taunting exchange occurs between Paris and Menelaus (see de Vaux, "Single Combat," 128).

17. Azzan Yadin, "Goliath's Armor and Israelite Collective Memory," *VT* 54 (2004): 373–95.

Finally, after the inevitable conquest, the corpses of the opponents are going to be consumed in a gruesome manner by dogs and birds. The impact of imagining your own body as carrion, being gnawed upon by scavengers could terrify even the most experienced warriors facing an imminent battle. Similar zoomorphic language is also frequently used in narratives of Hebrew Bible trash talking.

These numerous examples of taunts, boasts, insults, and curses suggest that trash talking was pervasive in ancient Near Eastern military contexts. Through the use of derogatory rhetoric and exaggerated claims ancient Near Eastern leaders waged psychological warfare before and after the actual bloodshed occurred to intimidate opponents and encourage allies. If they were successful at inspiring fear in their foes and courage among their friends, military victory would have been a likely outcome.

5. Flailing Flesh and Smoldering Stumps:
Trash Talking in the Hebrew Bible

The Hebrew Bible includes numerous incidents which could be categorized as trash talking. While taunt speech in the Psalms (e.g., Ps 108:8–9) or in prophetic literature (e.g., Isa 14:3–23) could also be examined in this discussion, it is difficult to determine the narrative contexts for these poetic texts and whether or not they were actually spoken.[18] Therefore, I will focus here on narrative contexts.

I will discuss three concentrations of trash talking: (1) Elijah, Jezebel, and Jehu; (2) the Rabshekeh, Hezekiah, and Yhwh; and (3) David and the Philistine giant. However, before looking at these concentrations, I will briefly examine various examples of taunt speech scattered throughout Hebrew narratives.

Not surprisingly, texts in the Pentateuch focus on Israel's conflicts with Egypt during the Exodus and with Canaanites as they approach the promised land. The Song of Moses (a postvictory extended taunt-celebration song)[19] narrates the pre-Red Sea boasts of the Egyptians, how they foolishly predicted that they would pursue the fleeing Israelites, overtake

---

18. For discussions of rhetorical features of prophetic taunts, see Jeff S. Anderson, "The Metonymical Curse as Propaganda in the Book of Jeremiah," *BBR* 8 (1998): 1–13; and Ze'ev Weisman, *Political Satire in the Bible* (Atlanta: Scholars Press, 1998), 73–81.

19. See also the Song of Deborah (Judg 5).

them, destroy them, and divide the spoil (Exod 15:9).[20] In an attempt to encourage the despondent Israelites after the troubling report of the twelve spies, Caleb declares to them that the Canaanites will be "bread for us; their protection is removed from them" (Num 14:9). Balaam delivers an oracle directly to the Moabite king, Balak, prophesying his defeat by Israel's God: "God who brings [Israel] out of Egypt, is like the horns of a wild ox for him, he shall devour the nations that are his foes and break their bones.... He crouched, he lay down like a lion, and like a lioness, who will rouse him?" (Num 24:8–9 NRSV).

In the book of Judges when the people of Succoth refuse to give provisions to his starving soldiers Gideon declares to them, "I will flail your flesh with the thorns of the wilderness and with briers" and after finishing off the Midianite captains, he fulfills his vow against Succoth (Judg 8:7, 16). After he defeated a thousand Philistines, Samson composes a taunt poem to adulate over his victory: "With the jawbone of a donkey, I have slain a thousand men" (Judg 15:16 NRSV).

Texts from the books of Samuel and Kings include trash talking in a variety of contexts. Three of the taunt speeches were unsuccessful at achieving their intended goal: To avoid a fight, Abner warns Asahel, "Turn away from following me; why should I strike you to the ground?" but Asahel ignored the warning only to be killed just as Abner predicted (2 Sam 2:22). To avoid capture, the people of Jerusalem taunt David by telling him that even the blind and the lame could keep him from entering the city (2 Sam 5:6) but their politically incorrect (at least to our postmodern ears) taunt does little to dissuade David who easily takes the stronghold of Zion. To intimidate the people, a giant of Gath taunts Israel, but Jonathan, son of David's brother Shimei, quickly dispatches him (2 Sam 21:21).

Trash talking occurs in wisdom contexts involving rulers who speak in a proverb and a parable. After Ben-hadad of Aram threatens to obliterate Samaria and turn it into dust, Ahab retorts proverbially, "One who puts on armor should not brag like one who takes it off" (1 Kgs 20:10–11). Amaziah of Judah issues a taunt and a challenge to fight with Jehoash of Israel, and Jehoash's parable, which may sound diplomatic, is rather insult-

---

20. See also my discussion of this song in "Compassion and Wrath as Motivations for Divine Warfare," in *Holy War in the Bible: Christian Morality and an Old Testament Problem* (ed. H. Thomas, J. Evans, and P. Copan; Downers Grove, Ill.: InterVarsity Press, 2013), 138–39.

ing: Jehoash portrays himself as a wild beast and a strong cedar but portrays Amaziah as a thistle to be trampled upon (2 Kgs 14:8–10).[21]

Taunt speech also appears in contexts involving prophets even though some of the language is more typically associated with adolescent male humor. Larry G. Herr argues convincingly that the dialogue between Micaiah and Zedekiah (1 Kgs 22:19–25) is essentially a scatological exchange of insults, as the two prophets each speak of passing "wind" (*rûaḥ*) back and forth.[22] When Elisha encounters a gang of actual adolescents they mock him by chanting, "Go up, you baldhead! Go up, you baldhead!" and the prophet responds with a curse—not recorded in the text—that presumably prompted the two she-bears to instantly appear and attack the lads (2 Kgs 2:23–24).[23]

Moving from the Former to the Latter Prophets, the prophet Isaiah delivers a message of encouragement from Yhwh to Ahaz of Judah which insults the two rulers who are threatening him from the north, Rezin of Aram and Pekah of Israel: "Do not let your heart be faint because of these two smoldering stumps of firebrands" (Isa 7:4).[24] Finally, in the book of Nehemiah, when Sanballat mocks Nehemiah, the Jews, and their wall, "That stone wall they are building—any fox going upon it would break it down" (Neh 3:35 [ET 4:3]), Nehemiah responds in kind with an imprecatory prayer that God would "turn their taunt back on their own heads, and give them over as plunder in a land of captivity" (Neh 3:36 [ET 4:4]).

6. CANINE CONSUMPTION: ELIJAH, JEZEBEL, JEHU, AND OTHERS

The first concentration of taunt speech to be examined here involves prophets (Elijah, Elisha's prophetic apprentice), rulers (Jezebel, Ahab, Jehu) and

---

21. Donald J. Wiseman also argues that Amaziah's comments are not simply an invitation to meet, but rather are a taunt and a challenge to fight (D. J. Wiseman, *1 and 2 Kings* [TOTC 9; Downers Grove, Ill.: InterVarsity Press, 1993], 245).

22. Larry G. Herr, "Polysemy of Rûah in 1 Kings 22:19–25," in *To Understand the Scriptures: Essays in Honor of William H. Shea* (ed. David Merling; Berrien Springs, Mich.: Institute of Archaeology at Andrews University, 1997), 29–31.

23. See also my discussion of this text in *God Behaving Badly: Is the God of the Old Testament Angry, Sexist and Racist?* (Downers Grove, Ill.: InterVarsity Press, 2011), 95–98.

24. While this text obviously appears in prophetic literature, I have included it in this discussion because the narrative context makes it clear that Isaiah's words were meant to be spoken to Ahaz (Isa 7:3–4).

even Yhwh.²⁵ On Mount Carmel Elijah mocks the prophets of Ahab and Jezebel, suggesting that Baal's silence is due to the fact that he is presently urinating and defecating (1 Kgs 18:27). While most English translations have Elijah describing Baal as meditating or wandering, Rendsberg persuasively argues for the scatological interpretation of Elijah's remarks.²⁶ After Elijah slaughters the prophets, Queen Jezebel vows to kill him in retaliation (1 Kgs 19:1–2).²⁷ Despite his recent dramatic victory on Mount Carmel, her trash talking effectively instills fear in the prophet, prompting him to flee (1 Kgs 19:3).

Eventually Elijah recovers sufficiently from his fear of Jezebel's threat so that, in response to the stoning of Naboth, he is able to deliver a message from Yhwh to Ahab and Jezebel describing how dogs and birds will devour the corpses of the king and queen and their family (1 Kgs 21:19–24). Elisha's prophetic apprentice repeats another version of this divine curse to Jehu at his anointing, particularly emphasizing the canine consumption of Jezebel's remains (2 Kgs 9:10). Jehu enters into the fray with some extreme trash talking, telling Jehoram immediately before killing him that his mother Jezebel is both a sorceress and a whore (2 Kgs 9:22). LoConto and Roth observe that among contemporary trash talkers the type of sexual harassment that Jehu utters against Jehoram's mother is typically considered "out of bounds."²⁸ In her final taunt, Jezebel calls Jehu, "Zimri" (2 Kgs 9:31), a curious title that takes on an insulting tone when one recalls that Zimri was not only killed by Jezebel's father-in-law, Omri, but was also the shortest reigning ruler of Israel and Judah (only seven days; 1 Kgs 16:15).²⁹ The narrative provides a graphic fulfillment of these predictions as Jezebel is ejected from her tower window by her loyal

---

25. I discuss Elijah's conflict with Ahab and Jezebel in "'A Prophet Instead of You': Elijah, Elisha and Prophetic Succession," in *Prophecy and the Prophets in Ancient Israel: Proceedings from the Oxford Old Testament Seminar* (ed. J. Day; LHBOTS 531; New York: T&T Clark, 2010), 172–87. I discuss Jehu's violent accession and his interaction with Jezebel in my *Righteous Jehu and his Evil Heirs: The Deuteronomist's Negative Perspective on Dynastic Succession* (Oxford Theological Monographs; Oxford: Oxford University Press, 2007), 85–102.

26. Gary A. Rendsburg, "The Mock of Baal of 1 Kings 18:27," *CBQ* 50 (1988): 414–17.

27. David makes a similar vow to his men about Nabal after his lack of hospitality (1 Sam 25:22).

28. LoConto and Roth, "Trash Talking," 225.

29. Zimri, like Jehu, was a general who killed his king (1 Kgs 16:15).

eunuchs, her blood splatters on the wall, the horses trample on her carcass, the dogs consume her remains and then deposit her final form as excrement in the fields (2 Kgs 9:33–37). Not surprisingly, these verses do not regularly appear on inspirational posters.

7. Eating Dung and Drinking Urine: The Rabshakeh, Hezekiah, and Yhwh

The second concentration of trash talking involves the Rabshakeh of Assyria (an official of Sennacherib), Hezekiah, Isaiah and Yhwh.[30] The Rabshakeh begins by insulting Egypt, "that broken reed of a staff" (2 Kgs 18:21). He then taunts Hezekiah that even if Assyria were to give Israel two thousand horses, they could not find riders, and if they were able, they still could not defeat even the most pathetic Assyrian captain (2 Kgs 18:23–24). Finally, he tells all the Israelites that they are doomed to eat their own dung and drink their own urine (2 Kgs 18:27). In both his initial message to Isaiah and in his later prayer to Yhwh, Hezekiah focuses on how the Rabshakeh's words "mock the living God" (2 Kgs 18:4, 16). Isaiah's second response involves a message for Hezekiah from Yhwh that addresses Sennacherib in the second person and begins with Yhwh's offense at being mocked and reviled (2 Kgs 19:22–23). Yhwh eventually responds with some divine trash talking toward Sennacherib: "Because you have raged against me and your arrogance has come to my ears, I will put my hook in your nose and my bit in your mouth; I will turn you back on the way by which you came (2 Kgs 19:28). While the text provides no record of the Assyrian monarch hearing the divine taunt, it does mention the divine slaughter of 185,000 Assyrian soldiers and the regicide committed by Sennacherib's sons against their father, which led to the succession of Esarhaddon (2 Kgs 19:35–37).

8. Lions, Bears, and Dogs: David and the Philistine

Perhaps the most dramatic example of concentrated taunt speech is found in the narrative of David and the Philistine giant in 1 Sam 17. While this narrative presents numerous textual problems, this discussion will remain

---

30. Danna Nolan Fewell ("Sennacherib's Defeat: Words at War in 2 Kings 18:13–19:37," *JSOT* 34 [1986]: 79–90) argues that this narrative is best perceived as a verbal duel between Yhwh and Sennacherib.

focused on the taunting aspects within the dialogue.³¹ I will simply refer to David's opponent as "the Philistine" since the text of 1 Sam 17 calls him "Goliath" by name only twice (vv. 4 and 23), but refers to him as "the Philistine" twenty-one times (e.g., 17:10, 11, 16, 23, 26).

While 1 Sam 17 is perhaps the best example of trash talking in the Hebrew Bible, most commentators skim over the taunts in the text. Simon J. De Vries's analysis of David's victory over the Philistine involves text, form, and redaction critical approaches, but has little room for examining the role that taunt language plays in the narrative.³² Despite a focus on honor and shame in the David narratives, Gary Stansell barely mentions David's triumph over Goliath and makes no reference to their taunt dialogue which presumably would have been directly relevant to his thesis.³³ Yadin connects the David and Goliath narrative to the Greek epic tradition, specifically *The Illiad*, but focuses more on armor than speech.³⁴ Gregory T. K. Wong's examination of the rhetoric of 1 Sam 17 focuses exclusively on armament.³⁵

In 1 Sam 17, the taunting begins as the Philistine shouts out a taunting challenge to the nation and their king, "Today I defy (*ḥārap*) the ranks of Israel! Give me a man that we may fight together" (v. 10 NRSV). While BDB defines *ḥārap* as "reproach" or "taunt," most English translations (e.g., ESV, NRSV, NIV, NASB) and commentators (e.g., McCarter, Klein, Firth) tone down the taunt rhetoric by translating the word in verse 10 simply as "defy" and make it appear that the giant is merely issuing a challenge to duel.³⁶

---

31. On the discrepancy between the MT and the LXX (Vaticanus), see Dominique Barthélemy and David. W. Gooding, *The Story of David and Goliath, Textual and Literary Criticism: Papers of a Joint Research Venture* (OBO 73; Fribourg: Éditions Universitaires, 1986); the LXX (Vaticanus) omits 1 Sam 17:12–31, 55–18:5. On tensions concerning the portrayal of David in 1 Sam 16–17, and tensions concerning the identity of the person who killed Goliath, see the various commentators; in 1 Sam 17:49 David killed Goliath; in 2 Sam 21:19 Elhanan killed Goliath; and in 1 Chr 20:5 Elhanan killed Lahmi, brother of Goliath.

32. Simon J. De Vries, "David's Victory over the Philistine as Saga and as Legend," *JBL* 92 (1973): 23–36.

33. Gary Stansell, "Honor and Shame in the David Narratives," *Semeia* 68 (1994), 56.

34. Yadin, "Goliath's Armor," 373–95.

35. Gregory T. K.Wong, "A Farewell to Arms: Goliath's Death as Rhetoric against Faith in Arms," *BBR* 23 (2013): 43–55.

36. P. Kyle McCarter, *I Samuel* (AB 8; Garden City: Doubleday, 1980), 284; Ralph

A challenge does not necessarily imply insult. Hans Wilhelm Hertzberg perceives no insult in the initial challenge, arguing that the insult only emerges later in the narrative.[37] However, the word *ḥārap* in this context clearly implies taunting.[38] Appropriately, Robert Alter translates *ḥārap* in verse 10 as "insulted" ("I am the one who has insulted the Israelite lines this day!"), and Mark K. George renders it as "shame" ("Today I shame the ranks of Israel").[39] Several German translations also give *ḥārap* a stronger derogatory flavor with "hohngesprochen" (LUT, "treat with scorn") or "verhöhne" (EIN, ELB: "jeer"). David and the men of Israel certainly perceive the Philistine's initial words as an insult and repeatedly refer to it as a reproach that needs to be overcome (vv. 25–26, 36, 45). By ignoring or downplaying the initial taunt of the Philistine, these scholars have missed a crucial aspect of this narrative. Taunting is arguably the major theme of the entire narrative.

The giant's taunting of Israel is not limited to his first speech but it continues throughout the narrative. He "took his stand" morning and evening for forty days (v. 16). While most commentators completely ignore or barely mention this verse (e.g., Alter, Baldwin, Gordon, Hertzberg, McCarter),[40] Klein makes the reasonable assumption that the Philistine did not simply stand before Israel, but actually repeated his initial comments for forty consecutive days.[41] According to the text the Israelites were already "dismayed and greatly afraid" after his initial speech (v. 11), so a barrage of perhaps eighty repetitions of similar trash talking could have

---

W. Klein, *1 Samuel* (WBC 10; Waco: Word, 1983), 169; David G. Firth, *1 and 2 Samuel* (AOTC 8; Downers Grove, Ill.: InterVarsity Press, 2009), 190.

37. Hans Wilhelm Hertzberg, *1 and II Samuel: A Commentary* (trans J. S. Bowden; OTL; Philadelphia: Westminster, 1964), 149.

38. Mark K. George ("Constructing Identity in 1 Samuel 17," *BibInt* 7 [1999], 398) notes that Goliath's challenge is more than just a challenge; it is an insult to the honor of Israel.

39. Robert Alter, *The David Story: A Translation with Commentary of 1 and 2 Samuel* (New York: Norton, 1999), 102; George, "Constructing Identity," 398–99. The NASB renders *ḥārap* as "taunt" or "taunted" in 1 Sam 17:26, 36, and 45.

40. See Alter, *The David Story*, 103; Joyce G. Baldwin, *1 and 2 Samuel: An Introduction and Commentary* (TOTC 8; Downers Grove, Ill.: InterVarsity Press, 1988), 126; Robert P. Gordon, *I and II Samuel: A Commentary* (Library of Biblical Interpretation; Exeter, U.K.: Paternoster, 1986), 155; Hertzberg, *I and II Samuel*, 149–50; McCarter, *I Samuel*, 293–98.

41. Klein, *1 Samuel*, 177.

been psychologically devastating. In verse 23, the text makes it explicit that the Philistine repeated his words from before, and this time David heard it. The giant's taunts have the same effect on the Israelites that they did previously: flight and fear (v. 24).

Interestingly, David's very first words in the Hebrew Bible include an insult targeting the Philistine.[42] He asks, "What shall be done for the man who kills this Philistine and takes away the reproach from Israel? For who is this uncircumcised Philistine, that he should taunt the armies of the living God?" (v. 26).[43] If one agrees with Alter's premise that the first words spoken by an individual in the narrative are meant to define their character, then, interestingly, trash talking would characterize David.[44] David's question focuses on the shame the Philistine's initial words brought upon Israel ("reproach," "taunt"), as well as the death he deserves.

Twice in the narrative David refers to the giant derogatively as "this uncircumcised Philistine" (vv. 26 and 36). The term "uncircumcised" *ārēl* is used eight times in the Deuteronomistic History, seven of them in a context of derision specifically targeting Philistines (Judg 14:3; 15:18; 1 Sam 14:6; 17:26, 36; 31:4; 2 Sam 1:20). While David's insult is not heard by the giant, derogatory rhetoric is used to not only to intimidate opponents, but also to empower allies. Presumably, within the narrative David's mock was meant to empower the Israelites after the Philistine's previous diatribes left them demoralized (1 Sam 17:11).

Before the Philistine has an opportunity to taunt David, his brother and his king insult him first. After overhearing David's question, Eliab denigrates not only his occupation as a shepherd but also his level of responsibility: "those few sheep" (v. 28). Alter is unusual among commentators for emphasizing the contemptuous nature of Eliab's remarks to his younger brother.[45] While Saul's comments do not appear as harsh as Eliab's, nonetheless, he ridicules David's lack of ability, experience, and age

---

42. David does not speak during his anointing (1 Sam 16:1–13).

43. In a discussion of insult formulas, George W. Coats ("Self-Abasement and Insult Formulas," *JBL* 89 [1970], 19) examines the parallel between David's question here ("Who is this uncircumcised Philistine…?") and the one spoken by Rib-Addi in Amarna letter 72 ("What is Abdi-Ašuirta, the servant, the dog, that he should take the land of the king to himself?").

44. Alter does not focus on the taunting aspect of David's speech here, but on David's concern for personal profit (Alter, *The David Story*, 105).

45. Ibid.

(v. 33), themes that are echoed in the Philistine's mocking of David before their battle (vv. 42–43).

In an interesting trash-talking twist, David takes his brother's shepherding insult and transforms it into a boast, using unexpected zoomorphic terms to describe the Philistine. He compares the Philistine to a lion and a bear, animals that are typically used as self-descriptors to intimidate foes. David, however, has already killed such beasts while serving as a lowly shepherd, so he declares he will do the same to "this uncircumcised Philistine" (vv. 34–37).

The trash talking reaches its climax when David and the Philistine finally meet. When the Philistine giant sees David, he despises David's youthfulness, and says to David: "Am I a dog, that you come at me with sticks?" (1 Sam 17:43). He then curses David by his gods and says, "Come to me, and I will give your flesh to the birds of the air and to the wild animals of the field" (1 Sam 17:44). The Philistine takes offense at David's size, age, and appearance. Like David, he uses an unexpected zoomorphic term for himself, but his use of "dog" in a rhetorical question (with an implied negative answer) sets up his taunt of David's choice of a "stick" as a weapon in contrast to his own "weaver's beam"-like spear (1 Sam 17:7). The Philistine's trash talking concludes with a graphic description of Davidic carrion.

David's response to Goliath ends the trash-talking session:

> This day the LORD will deliver you into my hand, and I will strike you down and cut off your head. And I will give the dead bodies of the host of the Philistines this day to the birds of the air and to the wild beasts of the earth, that all the earth may know that there is a God in Israel. (1 Sam 17:46))

While David's taunt begins and ends theologically, the middle includes bold predictions of the decapitation that he will accomplish and of the carrion consumption that will follow his deed. David's language echoes that of his adversary, although he expands the scavengers' diet to include the corpse of not just his opponent but of those of the entire Philistine army. David's theological retort to the Philistine's divine curse confidently attributes his perhaps unexpected but definitely imminent victory to God.[46]

---

46. See David G. Firth, "That the World May Know: Narrative Poetics in I Samuel

The narrative concludes with a fulfillment notice about the Philistine's decapitation but makes no mention of scavengers (vv. 51–54).

Scholarly discussions that limit the taunting to verses 42–47 miss an important theme that permeates the chapter. While the physical fighting is limited to two verses (vv. 48–49), the verbal feuding—the taunting, boasting, and insulting—dominates the entire narrative. The narrative includes multiple rounds of trash talking, much of it prior to the climatic exchange between David and the giant. The Philistine begins by shouting insults to the Israelite army (v. 10), and then repeats these over the course of forty days (vv. 16 and 23). The Israelites respond with fear (vv. 11 and 24) until David finally replies in kind with a taunt targeting the Philistine (v. 26), which is responded to by Eliab and Saul with insults emphasizing David's lack of experience (vv. 28, 33). David counters by boasting that his shepherding experiences have prepared him perfectly for slaughtering this "bear" of a man (vv. 34–36). When they finally meet face-to-face to trade barbs about canine carrion and decapitation, their rhetorical skills have had a sufficient warm-up. While the compositional history of the David-Philistine narrative was undoubtedly complex, trash talking brings an element of unity to this problematic text.

9. Biomorphic and Zoomorphic, Scatological and Theological

While perhaps not expected in sacred Scripture, trash talking is a frequent feature of the literature of both the Hebrew Bible and the ancient Near Eastern. Psychological warfare through the medium of trash talking was apparently a major feature of ancient conflict. To be effective, the derogatory rhetoric needed to be dramatic, intimidating, and even shocking. The graphic imagery and colorful terminology of these taunt speeches not only provide insights into the military strategy of these heroic individuals, but also entertain readers with vivid portrayals of ancient warriors attempting to instill courage and fear among their friends and foes.

Three concluding observations, therefore, need to be made about the graphic nature of the language of biblical trash talking. First, it is both biomorphic and zoomorphic. The participants in the contestants are described using terminology from the natural world, both as plants (e.g.,

---

16–17," in *Text and Task: Scripture and Mission* (ed. M. Parsons; Bletchley, U.K.: Paternoster, 2005), 20–32.

cedar, thistle, stumps, sticks) and as animals (wild ox, beast, lion, fox, bird, dog, and so on). As a largely agrarian society, ancient people were less isolated from the natural world than we are today, and so they were more familiar with the threats nature can bring. A claim to be lionesque in the field of battle would be more intimidating in an age where gruesome lion attacks were not uncommon.

Second, biblical trash talking is scatological. The speakers would describe not only themselves and their opponents, but also certain animals as being engaged in scatological activities: passing wind, drinking urine, being eaten, eating dung, making dung, and becoming dung. While familiar to everyone on a daily basis, these activities would not have been considered appropriate topics for public speech. Listeners would be shocked, not only that the subject of scatology was broached in such a blatant manner, but also that their deaths would be envisioned in such an appalling manner. The rhetorical impact of using scatological language could have been devastating.

Third, biblical trash talking is surprisingly theological. In addition to being used to intimidate enemies and motivate allies, trash talking is also used to exalt Yhwh since military conflicts were understood as taking place on both a human and a divine level. But Yhwh is not only honored by it, he also initiates it. While Dixon viewed trash talking in sports negatively, the Hebrew Bible clearly perceives it positively through this association with Yhwh. Through the medium of his prophets (Balaam, Elijah, Micaiah, Elisha's apprentice, and Isaiah), the text portrays Yhwh as a trash talker. Yes, Israel's enemies talk trash, but so do the heroes of the narrative, and even Israel's God.

Bibliography

Alter, Robert. *The David Story: A Translation with Commentary of 1 and 2 Samuel.* New York: Norton, 1999.
Anderson, Jeff S. "The Metonymical Curse as Propaganda in the Book of Jeremiah." *BBR* 8 (1998): 1–13.
Baldwin, Joyce G. *1 and 2 Samuel: An Introduction and Commentary.* TOTC 8. Downers Grove, Ill.: InterVarsity Press, 1988.
Barthélemy, Dominique, and David. W. Gooding. *The Story of David and Goliath, Textual and Literary Criticism: Papers of a Joint Research Venture.* OBO 73. Fribourg: Éditions Universitaires, 1986.

Bergmann, Claudia. "We Have Seen the Enemy, and He Is Only a 'She': The Portrayal of Warriors as Women." *CBQ* 69 (2007): 651-72.

Bremmer, Jan N. "Verbal Insulting in Ancient Greek Culture." *Acta Antiqua Academiae Scientiarum Hungaricae* 40 (2001): 61-72.

Coats, George W. "Self-Abasement and Insult Formulas." *JBL* 89 (1970): 14-26.

De Vries, Simon J. "David's Victory over the Philistine as Saga and as Legend." *JBL* 92 (1973): 23-36.

Dixon, Nicholas. "Trash Talking, Respect for Opponents and Good Competition." *Sport, Ethics and Philosophy* 1 (2007): 96-106.

Eaton, Margaret R. "Some Instances of Flyting in the Hebrew Bible." *JSOT* 61 (1994): 3-14.

Fewell, Danna Nolan. "Sennacherib's Defeat: Words at War in 2 Kings 18:13-19:37." *JSOT* 34 (1986): 79-90.

Firth, David G. *1 and 2 Samuel*. AOTC 8. Downers Grove, Ill.: InterVarsity Press, 2009.

———. "That the World May Know: Narrative Poetics in I Samuel 16-17." Pages 20-32 in *Text and Task: Scripture and Mission*. Edited by in Michael Parsons. Bletchley, U.K.: Paternoster, 2005.

George, Mark K. "Constructing Identity in 1 Samuel 17." *BibInt* 7 (1999): 389-412.

Gordon, Robert P. *I and II Samuel: A Commentary*. Library of Biblical Interpretation. Exeter, U.K.: Paternoster, 1986.

Herr, Larry G. "Polysemy of Rûah in 1 Kings 22:19-25." Pages 29-31 in *To Understand the Scriptures: Essays in Honor of William H. Shea*. Edited by David Merling. Berrien Springs, Mich.: Institute of Archaeology at Andrews University, 1997.

Hertzberg, Hans Wilhelm. *1 and II Samuel: A Commentary*. OTL. Translated by J. S. Bowden. Philadelphia: Westminster, 1964.

Hyman, Ronald T. "The Rabshakeh's Speech (II Kg 18-25): A Study of Rhetorical Intimidation." *JBQ* 23 (1995): 213-20.

Klein, Ralph W. *1 Samuel*. WBC 10. Waco, Tex.: Word, 1983.

Lamb, David T. "Compassion and Wrath as Motivations for Divine Warfare." Pages 133-52 in *Holy War in the Bible: Christian Morality and an Old Testament Problem*. Edited by Heath Thomas, Jeremy Evans and Paul Copan. Downers Grove, Ill.: InterVarsity Press, 2013.

———. *God Behaving Badly: Is the God of the Old Testament Angry, Sexist and Racist?* Downers Grove, Ill.: InterVarsity Press, 2011.

———. "'A Prophet Instead of You': Elijah, Elisha and Prophetic Succession." Pages 172–87 in *Prophecy and the Prophets in Ancient Israel: Proceedings from the Oxford Old Testament Seminar*. Edited by John Day. LHBOTS 531. New York: T&T Clark, 2010.

———. *Righteous Jehu and his Evil Heirs: The Deuteronomist's Negative Perspective on Dynastic Succession*. Oxford Theological Monographs. Oxford: Oxford University Press, 2007.

LoConto, David G., and Tori J. Roth. "Mead and the Art of Trash Talking: I Got Your Gesture Right Here." *Sociological Spectrum* 25 (2005): 215–30.

Masliyah, Sadok. "Curses and Insults in Iraqi Arabic." *JSS* 46 (2001): 267–308.

McCarter, P. Kyle. *I Samuel*. AB 8. Garden City: Doubleday, 1980.

Miller, Geoffrey David. "Attitudes toward Dogs in Ancient Israel." *JSOT* 32 (2008): 487–500.

———. "A Riposte Form in the Song of Deborah." Pages 113–27 in *Gender and Law in the Hebrew Bible and the Ancient Near East*. Edited by Victor H. Matthews, Bernard M. Levinson, and Tikva S. Frymer-Kensky. JSOTSup 262. Sheffield: Sheffield Academic Press, 1998.

———. "Verbal Feud in the Hebrew Bible: Judges 3:12–30 and 19–21." *JNES* 55 (1996): 105–17.

Monty Python and the Holy Grail. Directed by Terry Gilliam and Terry Jones. Michael White Productions, 1975.

Niditch, Susan. *War in the Hebrew Bible: A Study in the Ethics of Violence*. New York: Oxford University Press, 1993: 90–105.

Rendsburg, Gary A. "The Mock of Baal of 1 Kings 18:27." *CBQ* 50 (1988): 414–17.

Rudman, Dominic. "Is the Rabshakeh also among the Prophets? A Rhetorical Study of 2 Kings XVIII 17–35." *VT* 50 (2000): 100–110.

Simons, Herbert D. "Race and Penalized Sports Behaviors." *International Review for the Sociology of Sport* 38 (2003): 5–22.

Stansell, Gary. "Honor and Shame in the David Narratives." *Semeia* 68 (1994): 55–79.

Vaux, Roland de. "Single Combat in the Old Testament." Pages 122–35 in *The Bible and the Ancient Near East*. Translated by Damian McHugh. Garden City: Doubleday, 1971.

Weisman, Ze'ev. *Political Satire in the Bible*. SemeiaSt 32. Atlanta: Scholars Press, 1998.

Winton Thomas, D. "*Kelebh* 'Dog': Its Origin and Some Usages of It in the Old Testament." *VT* 10 (1960): 410–27.

Wiseman, Donald J. *1 and 2 Kings*. TOTC 9. Downers Grove, Ill.: InterVarsity Press, 1993.

Wong, Gregory T. K. "A Farewell to Arms: Goliath's Death as Rhetoric against Faith in Arms." *BBR* 23 (2013): 43–55.

Yadin, Azzan. "Goliath's Armor and Israelite Collective Memory." *VT* 54 (2004): 373–95.

"Some Trust in Horses":
Horses as Symbols of Power in Rhetoric and Reality

Deborah O'Daniel Cantrell

Warhorses were the most lethal weapon known in the ancient world. Such was the raw power of the horse in time past, as today. They choose not to kill us every time we ride them. Weighing over a thousand pounds with a mounted warrior, trained warhorses easily knocked the enemy to the ground and trampled them to death with their sharp hooves, slicing and crushing vital organs. The warrior assisted by pinning the victim to the ground with his spear. Death was painful, but swift. Warhorses vanquished enemies on the battlefield immediately. Pharaohs, kings, and poets immortalized their reliability as killing machines, faithful defenders, and lifesavers.[1] The warhorse became the ultimate symbol of power in literature, art, and reality.

Paradoxically, horses were also esteemed as agents of rescue because they provided the only certain means of escape from an advancing army. With their ability to reach speeds of nearly 40 mph, they could outrun the foot soldiers and distance the rider from the range of deadly arrows. The ancient Hebrews knew firsthand that horses were the difference between

---

1. For example, Ramses II (1279–1213 B.C.E.; henceforth all dates are B.C.E.) prominently featured his chariot horses in monumental palace reliefs with glorifying inscriptions such as, "I crushed a million countries by myself on Victory-in-Thebes, Mut-is-content, my great horses; it was they whom I found supporting me, when I alone fought many lands. They shall henceforth be fed in my presence, whenever I reside in my palace" (Miriam Lichtheim, "The Kadesh Battle Inscriptions of Ramses II," *Ancient Egyptian Literature: A Book of Readings* [3 vols.; Berkeley: University of California Press, 1973–80], 2:70).

life and death on the battlefield.[2] Horses provided immediate deliverance on the battlefield, as recounted by the narrow escape of Ben-hadad, king of Aram, retreating on horseback from Ahab's forces during the Aramean invasion of Israel (1 Kgs 20:20).

Hebrew poetry extolled the beauty, death-defying bravery, and dominance of the warhorse, intoxicated by its own killing power, as it charged into the chaos of battle. The book of Job gives this description: "He paws with force, he runs with vigor, charging into battle. He scoffs at fear; he cannot be frightened; he does not recoil from the sword"[3] (Job 39:21–22). The nature of the warhorse was idealized as one of God's most awesome creations.[4] It is not surprising that the officers and warriors who rode them and commanded chariots were also revered in the cultural milieu: "and she lusted after her lovers, the Assyrians—warriors … all of them handsome young men and mounted horsemen" (Ezek 23:6).

The "horsemen of Israel" were so famous among the citizenry that the prophet Elisha had visions of them commanding chariots of fire as they came to transport Elijah to heaven[5] (2 Kgs 6:17). In fact, the Israelite chariotry, at least 50 chariots, guarding Samaria during the Assyrian conquest in 720 were so respected that they were left intact as an "elite" *kisir sharruti* regiment of the Assyrian home guard.[6] As recorded on the Nimrud Prism, Sargon II (722–705) claims to have conscripted two hundred Samarian chariots for his royal contingent, although his Annals and the Display Inscription mention fifty chariots.[7] Even so, it is quite probable that the

---

2. Deborah O. Cantrell, *The Horsemen of Israel: Horses and Chariotry in Monarchic Israel (Ninth-Eighth Centuries* B.C.E.*)* (History, Archaeology, and Culture of the Levant 1; Winona Lake: Eisenbrauns, 2011), 35–41, 62–63.

3. For an analysis of the Job 39 warhorse as symbolic of chaos, inner-violence, and undeserved suffering, see David Odell, "Images of Violence in the Horse in Job 29:18–25," *Proof* 13 (1993): 163–73.

4. Other ancient texts acknowledge the high status of the warhorse: for example, the seventh-century Assyrian fable, "The Ox and the Horse," in which the two creatures debate which of them is the bravest, strongest, and most beneficial to society (Wilfred G. Lambert, *Babylonian Wisdom Literature* [Oxford: Clarendon, 1960; repr., Winona Lake, Ind.: Eisenbrauns, 1996], 175–83).

5. Martinus A. Beek, "The Meaning of the Expression 'The Chariots and the Horsemen of Israel' (II Kings ii 12)," *OtSt* 17 (1972): 1–10.

6. Nigel Tallis, "Ancient Near Eastern Warfare," in *The Ancient World at War* (ed. Philip de Souza; New York: Thames & Hudson, 2008), 64.

7. Stephanie Dalley, "Foreign Chariotry and Cavalry in the Armies of Tiglath-

impressive reputation of the "horsemen of Israel" was further enhanced by this event, and their proficiency, therefore, remained in the collective memory of the citizenry.

Often warhorses, as the ultimate symbol of death and destruction, became icons in the geopolitical diatribes of the prophets who were frequently at odds with the rulers and their military advisers.[8] Their universal allure and almost mystical supremacy in battle resulted in elevating warhorses symbolically and, in the varied expressions of the Hebrew prophets, caused the ordinary populace to place unwarranted trust in the power of the military to save them from danger. The prophets inveighed against the notion that horses, as inspired symbols of military might, were superior to a basic trust in the God of Israel. This cautionary missive was eloquently expressed in Isa 31:1: "Woe to those who go down to Egypt for help, who rely on horses, who trust in the multitude of their chariots and in the great strength of their horsemen, but do not look to the Holy One of Israel, or seek help from the Lord." Zechariah's postexilic oracle against the enemies of Jerusalem also reiterates the theme of divine omnipotence: "'On that day I will strike every horse with panic and its rider with madness,' declares the Lord" (Zech 12:4).

Political rhetoric similar to that of the prophets is also reflected in the Psalms: "Some trust in chariots and some in horses, but we trust in the name of the Lord our God" (Ps 20:7); "A horse is a vain hope for deliverance; despite all its great strength it cannot save" (Ps 33:17); and "At your rebuke, O God of Jacob, both horse and chariot lie still" (Ps 76:6). The people considered the power of the horse both awe-inspiring and frightening. Although venerated in the public imagination, the prophets manipulated images of warhorses symbolically as weapons of destruction and terror, often in support of their own, divinely revealed, political agendas.[9]

---

pileser III and Sargon II," *Iraq* 47 (1985): 31–48. Bob Becking, *The Fall of Samaria: A Historical and Archaeological Study* (Leiden: Brill, 1992), 41–42. For the West Semitic names appearing as officers in the Assyrian Horse Lists, see Stephanie Dalley and John N. Postgate, *The Tablets from Fort Shalmaneser* (CTN 3; London: British School of Archaeology in Iraq, 1984), 173.

    8. Douglas A. Knight, *Law, Power, and Justice in Ancient Israel* (Louisville: Westminster John Knox, 2011), 77.

    9. Norman K. Gottwald, *The Politics of Ancient Israel* (Louisville: Westminster John Knox, 2001), 234–35.

In fact, death by trampling under the sharp, flint hooves of warhorses was feared and dreaded as one of the most violent and disgraceful ways to die in the ancient world.[10] The account of the ignoble death of Queen Mother Jezebel at Jezreel, the cavalry headquarters of the Northern Kingdom, emphasized regime change and marked the end of the militaristic Omrides.[11] The usurper, Jehu, publically executed Jezebel by trampling her under the horses' hooves of his chariot forces (2 Kgs 9:33). Subsequently, death by trampling became a literary motif used by numerous prophets to symbolize their predictions of imminent doom and disaster. From Isaiah in the late eighth-century context: "you were left lying unburied, *like a trampled corpse* [in] the clothing of the slain, gashed by the sword" (Isa 14:19, emphasis added). Later from Ezekiel, Tyre is warned about the approaching army of Nebuchadnezzar: "His horses will be so many that they will cover you with dust. Your walls will tremble at the noise of the war horses, wagons and chariots when he enters your gates. ... *The hoofs of his horses will trample* all your streets" (Ezek 26:11, emphasis added).

The Iron Age populace, familiar with the realities of warfare, understood that, in fact, horses' hooves may have killed more enemies than arrows on the battlefield. Arrows and spears tended to wound and incapacitate, resulting in immediate death only if they happened to hit an artery or pierce the heart. When the Israelite king Joram was wounded in battle with the Arameans, he recovered from his wounds at Jezreel; later, while fleeing in his chariot, Jehu's arrow pierced his heart (2 Kgs 9:15, 24). The detailed description of this immediate death suggests that it was a rare occurrence. By contrast, King Ahab reportedly received an arrow wound during battle, but was propped in his chariot, slowly bleeding to death for the entire day, finally dying at sunset (1 Kgs 22:34–35). Death from puncture wounds typically occurred days later from infection—as portrayed in the biblical accounts of two of Judah's kings: Ahaziah, who was wounded in his chariot by Jehu but died later at Megiddo[12] (2 Kgs 9:27), and Josiah,

---

10. Cantrell, *Horsemen of Israel*, 27–31.

11. Brad E. Kelle, *Ancient Israel at War 853–586 bc* (Essential Histories 67; Oxford: Osprey, 2007), 29–33.

12. However, the Tel Dan inscription contradicts this account and claims that the Aramean king—probably Hazael—killed Ahaziah. See Megan Bishop Moore and Brad E. Kelle, *Biblical History and Israel's Past: The Changing Study of the Bible and History* (Grand Rapids: Eerdmans, 2011), 277–78.

who was badly wounded in battle at Megiddo, but died after he returned to Jerusalem (2 Chr 35:23–24).

Spears and swords had to be used with precision to kill instantly; they had to hit the target between the armor openings, something that the chaos of the battlefield usually prevented.[13] However the stomping action of the horse, bruising and puncturing organs with its four sharp hooves by repeatedly stepping into the stomach and on other sensitive areas, killed the enemy within minutes, if not seconds.[14] Ancient battle armor was helpful in deflecting arrows but virtually useless against the half-ton weight of a horse. Obviously, any serious consideration of ancient battlefield tactics must include an assessment of the killing power and potential for lethal damage inflicted by the horses, as well as the prevalent fear that such could happen.

The threat of being trampled to death was perhaps the fundamental reason that the convention of chariot warfare reigned over mounted combat as the preferred method of warfare for nearly a thousand years.[15] As a practical matter, it was substantially more difficult to pull a warrior from a chariot and throw him to the ground than to simply knock him off a horse's back. The chariot warrior benefited from three major advantages: the protection offered by the leather or metal chariot siding; the possibility of intertwining his feet securely in the leather lattice-woven bottom of the chariot; and the ability to fight with both hands while the charioteer handled the horses. By comparison, a mounted rider had to control his horse, shield himself, and manipulate his weapon simultaneously, in addition to being an accomplished rider.[16] Either way, whoever

---

13. Richard A. Gabriel and Karen S. Metz, *From Sumer to Rome: The Military Capabilities of Ancient Armies* (Contributions in Military Studies 108; Westport, Conn.: Greenwood, 1991), 93.

14. Personal communication with Timothy J. Hinton, M.D. Internist, Assistant Professor of Medicine, Vanderbilt University; Board Certified in Internal Medicine by American Board of Internal Medicine, 2005.

15. Cantrell, *Horsemen of Israel,* 136–41. For the contribution of advances in bitting, saddlery, and riding skill on warfare conventions, see Robert Drews, *Early Riders: The Beginnings of Mounted Warfare in Asia and Europe* (New York: Routledge, 2004), 65–95. For a discussion of how the various units of the Neo-Assyrian chariotry may have functioned during battle, see Fabrice de Backer, "Some Basic Tactics of Neo-Assyrian Warfare," *UF* 39 (2008): 69–116, and Backer, "Evolution of War Chariot Tactics in the Ancient Near East," *UF* 41 (2010): 29–46.

16. For a discussion of the military effects of horseback riding and chariots as

was unfortunate enough to be prostrate on the ground under the hooves of warhorses, whether they were harnessed as a chariot team or only one horse with a mounted warrior, was in imminent danger of being trampled to death. Also, even if the downed warrior was successful in regaining his footing, a chariot warrior could escape the battle by simply jumping aboard the chariot, whereas the cavalryman had the difficulty of catching his horse and trying to remount from the ground in the chaos of battle.[17]

Of course, this is not to suggest that all warhorses were trained to kill; certainly some trampling was accidental, and warfare conventions changed over time as riding skill and weaponry advanced.[18] However, there is historical reference to the Persians teaching their cavalry horses to trample fallen soldiers by practicing on dummy corpses filled with straw, and it is entirely possible that this practice, or a similar one, was also a part of equine training for earlier armies.[19] The Hebrew Bible certainly reflects memories of the terrors associated with the killing force of warhorses. Isaiah described the aggressiveness of the invading Assyrian enemy in a late eighth-century setting: "Their arrows are sharp, all their bows are strung; their *horses' hoofs seem like flint*, their chariot wheels like a whirlwind" (Isa 5:28, emphasis added). From Nahum, a seventh-century battle scene is depicted against Nineveh: "The crack of the whips, the clatter of wheels, galloping horses and jolting chariots! Charging cavalry, flashing swords and glittering spears! Many casualties, piles of dead, bodies without number, people stumbling over corpses" (Nah 3:2–3). In a sixth-century context, the prophet Habakkuk described the Babylonian cavalry: "Their horses are swifter than leopards, fiercer than wolves at dusk. Their cavalry gallops headlong; their horsemen come from afar. They fly like a vulture

---

"engines of war," see David W. Anthony, *The Horse, The Wheel, and Language* (Princeton: Princeton University Press, 2007), 222–24, 397–405.

17. Various ground-to-horse mounting procedures were a regular part of training for Greek cavalry. See Ann Hyland, *The Horse in the Ancient World* (Westport, Conn.: Praeger, 2003), 138.

18. For the fascinating chronicle of how the Comanche's superior riding skills and alacrity for mounted combat stymied the Texas Rangers and thwarted the progress of settlement in the American West for more than half a century, see S. C. Gwynne, *Empire of the Summer Moon* (New York: Scribner, 2010), 28–35, 73–88, 132–48.

19. Aelian, *On Animals* 16.25. A battle inscription of Ramses III (1187–1156) reads: "The horses were quivering in every part of their bodies, prepared to *crush the foreign countries under their hoofs*" (J. A. Wilson, trans., "The War against the Peoples of the Sea," *ANET*, 26, emphasis added).

swooping to devour; they all come bent on violence" (Hab 1:8). Clearly, the general perception of the lethal danger of warhorses was acknowledged and widespread during the Iron Age.

The Hebrew prophets warned against relying on military might as a solution to the immediate problem of an invading enemy. Isaiah, Hosea, Micah, and Amos cautioned their audiences that their reliance for deliverance should be placed on God, not on the seemingly limitless power of horses. As expressed in Isa 30:15: "In repentance and rest is your salvation, in quietness and trust is your strength but you would have none of it. You said, 'No, we will flee on horses.' Therefore you will flee! You said, 'We will ride off on swift horses.' Therefore your pursuers will be swift." Hosea, a contemporary of Isaiah, also sounded the warning: "Assyria cannot save us, we will not mount warhorses" (Hos 14:3). The underlying belief in the context of both passages is that the army with the fastest, fittest horses would win, and that escape from the enemy would require access to swift horses.

The biblical prophets also were united thematically in the belief that, even though both Israel and Judah had huge equine resources, God was supreme and could subdue the most advanced military weaponry. For example, Micah warned Judah: " 'In that day,' declares the Lord, 'I will destroy your horses from among you and demolish your chariots' " (Mic 5:10), and Amos says similarly: " 'I killed your young men with the sword, along with your captured horses,' ... declares the Lord" (Amos 4:10). Their threats that God would destroy the horses symbolically represented the downfall of the nation of Judah, as had been the fate of Israel earlier when the Assyrians invaded.

Israel in the late eighth century was not a tranquil place. Israel was the battleground for the invading Assyrian army, led by their aggressive, battle-seasoned kings, Tiglath-pileser III (745–727), Shalmaneser V (727–722), and Sargon II (721–705). Assyria had the most powerful army in the world at that time, primarily because of its highly effective chariotry and horsemen.[20] To combat the mighty armies of its neighbors, as early as the ninth century Israel developed an extensive chariotry force and the infrastructure to support it.[21] At the Battle of Qarqar in 853, King

---

20. Stephanie Dalley, "Ancient Mesopotamian Military Organization," in *Civilizations of the Ancient Near East* (ed. Jack M. Sasson; New York: Simon & Schuster Macmillan, 1995), 413–22.

21. Baruch Halpern, "Centre and Sentry: Megiddo's Role in Transit, Administra-

Ahab of Israel led the largest chariot contingent, some two thousand strong, to fight the Assyrians.[22]

The Tel Dan Stele fragment (about 841) proclaims the Aramean victories against Israel and Judah and claims that "thousands of chariots and thousands of horsemen" were involved in the battles.[23] Horses continued to be key weaponry in the armies of Israel and Judah for the next hundred years. In the late eighth century, Isaiah described the land as "full of horses" with "no end to their chariots" (Isa 2:7) and decried against Judah, "Your choicest valleys are full of chariots and horsemen are posted at the city gates" (Isa 22:7).

The Isaiah reference to horses *posted at the city gates* is especially illuminating. Archaeological excavations reveal that by the late eighth century, Israel and Judah had developed an extensive defensive network of walled cities with chambered gates at their entrances to expedite the hitching and unhitching of chariot horses. These six and four chambered gates are found at Dan, Hazor, Bethsaida, Jezreel, Megiddo, Gezer, Ashdod, Lachish, Beer-sheba, and other sites, as well as various key locations in Moab.[24] Armies or messengers could travel between these strategically located fortresses conveniently without overtiring the horses. It was possible to travel from Dan to Beer-sheba, the entire length of Israel and Judah, via chariot or on horseback in one day by changing horses as necessary at these locations. The chambered gates served as convenient stalls to harness and attend to the physical needs of horses, thereby expediting travel, as well as supporting the rapid deployment of chariotry units for defensive purposes.[25]

Jezreel has been identified as the location of the military headquarters and cavalry depot for the Northern Kingdom during the reign of the Omrides.[26] Its proximity to the large Ein Jezreel spring, its panoramic

---

tion and Trade," in *Megiddo III: The 1992-1996 Seasons* (ed. I. Finkelstein, D. Ussishkin, and B. Halpern; 2 vols.; Jerusalem: Tel Aviv University Press, 2000), 2:535-77.

22. Anson F. Rainey and R. Steven Notley, *The Sacred Bridge* (Jerusalem: Carta, 2006), 200. See also Shigeo Yamada, *The Construction of the Assyrian Empire: A Historical Study of the Inscriptions of Shalmaneser III (859-824 b.c.) Relating to His Campaigns to the West* (CHANE 3; Boston: Brill, 2000), 156-63.

23. William M. Schniedewind, "Tel Dan Stela: New Light on Aramaic and Jehu's Revolt," *BASOR* 302 (1996): 75-90.

24. Cantrell, *Horsemen of Israel*, 76-86, Fig 4.1 at 77.

25. Ibid., 76-86.

26. David Ussishkin, "Excavations at Tel Jezreel 1992-1993: Second Preliminary Report," *Levant* 26 (1994): 1-48. See also Norma Franklin, "Jezreel: Before and after

view of the Jezreel Valley, and strategic position on the Via Maris trade route and key military highway made it the ideal location.[27] Jezreel could easily have been the mustering location for Ahab's forces in the Battle of Qarqar in 853. The chambered gates at Jezreel faced south toward the capital city, Samaria. Jezreel provided protection for Samaria, because an invading army first had to pass by the Jezreel military compound. In addition, Jezreel was strategically situated as a point of departure for troops battling in Transjordan and Aram.[28] It is to Jezreel that the Israelite kings returned after battles against Ramoth Gilead (2 Kgs 8:28; 9:15–16). Also, as mentioned above, Jehu ordered the execution of Jezebel by trampling at Jezreel.[29]

The largest and most sophisticated chariot training center in the ancient world was located at Megiddo, situated on the main trading routes connecting Egypt, Syria, Phoenicia, and Mesopotamia.[30] Perhaps built by Jeroboam II in the mid eighth century to support his invasions into the north, Megiddo provided permanent stabling facilities for over 450 horses, which required hundreds of grooms and related workers.[31] The Megiddo fortress had seventeen well constructed stables, many with carved stone troughs. It also had two enclosed, smoothly paved courtyards for training, three sets of chambered gates, a massive granary (12,800-bushel capacity),

---

Jezebel," in *Israel in Transition: From Late Bronze II to Iron IIA (c. 1250–850)* (ed. L. L. Grabbe; LHBOTS 491; London: Continuum, 2008), 53–54.

27. Jennie Ebeling, Norma Franklin, and Ian Cipin, "Jezreel Revealed in Laser Scans: A Preliminary Report of the 2012 Survey Season," *NEA* 75 (2012): 232–39.

28. It has been suggested that Hosea's naming of his son "Jezreel" was a symbolic toponym based on Jezreel's universal recognition as an important military headquarters. See Shawn Z. Aster, "The Function of the City of Jezreel and the Symbolism of Jezreel in Hosea 1–2," *JNES* 71 (2012): 31–46.

29. Jezebel's fall from a second floor window—a drop of perhaps ten feet— would not have killed her, but the horses' hooves were certain to inflict immediate death.

30. Mario Liverani, "From Melid through Bastam to Megiddo: Stables and Horses in Iron Age II," in *Leggo! Studies Presented to Frederick Mario Fales* (ed. G. Lanfranchi, et al.; Wiesbaden: Harrassowitz, 2012), 443–59; John S. Holladay Jr., "The Stables of Ancient Israel," in *The Archaeology of Jordan and Other Studies Presented to Siegfried H. Horn* (ed. L. T. Geraty and L. G. Herr; Berrien Springs, Mich.: Andrews University Press, 1986), 103–66.

31. Deborah O. Cantrell, "Stable Issues," in *Megiddo IV* (ed. I. Finkelstein, D. Ussishkin, and B. Halpern; 2 vols.; Tel Aviv: Tel Aviv University Press, 2006), 2:630–42; Deborah O. Cantrell and Israel Finkelstein, "A Kingdom for a Horse: The Megiddo Stables and Eighth Century Israel," in ibid., 2:643–65.

and complex watering system. Megiddo was conquered by Assyrian king Tiglath-pileser III in 732 and converted into the regional headquarters for the use of the Assyrian army.[32]

In Judah, the major horse compound at Lachish, about thirty miles southwest of Jerusalem, also had stables, two sets of chambered gates, and enclosed training areas.[33] Assyrian king Sennacherib conquered Lachish in his campaign into Judah in 701 during Hezekiah's reign (715–686). Sennacherib was so pleased with his victory over the military headquarters at Lachish that he featured this conquest in a series of reliefs prominently positioned in the entrance hall of his palace in Nineveh, (currently in the British Museum).[34] During the siege of Jerusalem in 701, a commander of the Assyrian army taunted King Hezekiah and his advisers with the offer to provide two thousand horses, presumably to escape upon, if they would surrender the city (2 Kgs 18:23). This taunt was even more stinging, considering the recent capture of the warhorses and destruction wrought at Judah's military center at Lachish.

There were thousands of horses in Judah and Israel during the monarchic period. Their care and well-being was supported by a large number of the citizenry, as is reflected in the memory of the highly structured organization for feeding the royal horses attributed to the Solomonic period (1 Kgs 4:7, 26–27).[35] The infrastructure to support the horses required the involvement of many people, all of whom undoubtedly witnessed the power and superior force of the horse on a regular basis. Therefore, when the biblical prophets used the imagery of horses and chariotry symbolically, their audience had the real-world experience to relate with ease and clarity.

Many horses undoubtedly were bred in Israel, with its suitable topography in the areas near Jezreel and Megiddo,[36] and some horses reportedly were purchased from Que (Cilicia, modern-day Turkey; 1 Kgs 10:28)

---

32. David Ussishkin, *On Biblical Jerusalem, Megiddo, Jezreel and Lachish* (CKLS 8; Hong Kong: Chinese University, 2011), 60–69.

33. Ibid., 94–96.

34. David Ussishkin, *The Conquest of Lachish by Sennacherib* (Tel Aviv: Tel Aviv University, 1982), 59–126.

35. Cantrell, *Horsemen of Israel*, 53–56.

36. With as few as ten stallions and one hundred mares, near 1500 horses could be produced and trained for battle in twelve years. See Cantrell, *Horsemen of Israel*, table 3.1, p. 50.

and Beth Togarmah (modern-day Armenia; Ezek 27:16) by Israelite horse traders. However, it was the Egyptian horses that captured the imagination of the general public and held the greatest symbolic value. The large Egyptian warhorses were especially prized, and this memory is captured in several passages in the Hebrew Bible, some warning against making political overtures to Egypt for horses, while others acknowledge that Egyptian horses were purchased routinely for the royal stud (Deut 17:16; 1 Kgs 10:28; 2 Kgs 18:23–24).

In the eighth century, the Nubian/Kushite kings of Egypt's Twenty-Fifth Dynasty (approximately 750–650), especially King Piye (747–716), bred and trained the most desirable chariot horses.[37] The Kushite horses were exceptionally tall for the time, about sixteen hands, and especially favored by the Assyrian kings.[38] Sargon II received twelve large Kushite horses as tribute and recorded that they were superior to any that existed in Assyria.[39] In the late eighth century, Assyria established horse trading centers on the border with Egypt, which meant that Egyptian horses were a common sight passing north through Judah.[40] At El Kurru, the royal burial grounds for the Kushite kings, excavators uncovered a horse cemetery with twenty-four graves of grandly caparisoned horses buried standing up and identified as the royal chariot horses.[41] The luxurious funeral trappings found on these carefully buried horses are unsurpassed in the ancient world, and support the notion that the special Egyptian-bred horses of the Nubian kings were highly esteemed.

---

37. Robert G. Morkot, *The Black Pharaohs: Egypt's Nubian Rulers* (London: Rubicon, 2000), 187–94.

38. Lisa A. Heidorn, "The Horses of Kush," *JNES* 56 (1997): 105–14. The beautiful horses with excellent confirmation pictured on the Assyrian reliefs after the death of Sargon II (705) are probably Kushite horses, assuming typical royal preference for the best horses and faithful depiction by the artists. The difference in confirmation is easily apparent when compared to the smaller, leaner Assyrian horses depicted on the ninth-century Balawat Gate. See Yigael Yadin, *The Art of Warfare in Biblical Lands in Light of Archaeological Study* (trans. M. Pearlman; 2 vols.; New York: McGraw-Hill, 1963), 2:403, 432.

39. Andreas Fuchs, *Die Annalen des Jahres 711 v. Chr.: Nach Prismenfragmenten aus Ninive und Assur* (ed. R. M. Whiting; SAAS 8; Helsinki: Neo-Assyrian Text Corpus Project, 1998), lines 8–11.

40. Dalley, "Ancient Mesopotamian Military Organization," 418.

41. Dows Dunham, *The Royal Cemeteries of Kush* (5 vols.; Cambridge: Harvard University Press, 1950–63), 1:110, plates 28–29.

It is not an exaggeration to postulate that the Egyptian horses were "world famous" in the eighth century and that their celebrity status caused serious concern among the Hebrew prophets. During Sennacherib's invasion of Judah in 701, the Assyrian army fought a battle against the Egyptian chariotry forces on the plain of Eltekeh, about six miles northwest of Ekron and twenty-five miles north of Gaza.[42] The inscription on Sennacherib's prism describes how the rulers of Ekron banded together with the Kushite kings: "They called out for the kings of the land of Egypt, an army of bowman, charioteers, and horses of the king of the land of Cush, a host without number; they came to their aid."[43] The Assyrians claimed to have won this battle and secured control over the main highway leading up from the south into Judah.[44] However, the vast number of chariot horses available in Egypt meant that Judah also had a resource for mercenary troops in their defensive efforts against the Assyrian invaders in 701. Apparently King Hezekiah considered securing the assistance of Egyptian horses and chariots a viable option to protect Jerusalem, thereby provoking the Assyrian commander's taunt and disparagement of Egypt as a "splintered reed" that pierces and wounds those who lean on it (2 Kgs 18:21). It is against this political reality that Isaiah issued the rhetorical warning mentioned earlier: "Woe to those who go down to Egypt for help, who rely on horses, who trust in the multitude of their chariots and in the great strength of their horsemen, but do not look to the Holy One of Israel" (Isa 31:1).

Yet, symbolically, the image of the powerful Egyptian warhorses as a means of victory and rescue was so ingrained in the minds of the populace and rulers in Judah that Isaiah also had to remind his audience: "But the Egyptians are men and not God; their horses are flesh and not spirit" (Isa 31:3). Such was the grip of the emblematic imagery of the awe-inspiring power of the warhorse on the mindset of the ancient world.

Today, the memory of the horse as a killing machine has faded, and we are simply left with the elegant moves of a highly trained dressage horse in piaffe, passage, pirouette, and other battlefield-based maneuvers, all of which require a symbiotic relationship between the horse and rider and thereby recall the ancient rhetoric: "Some trust in horses...."

---

42. Rainey and Notley, *Sacred Bridge*, 240–41.

43. Ibid., 242.

44. Nadav Na'aman, "Sennacherib's 'Letter to God' on His Campaign to Judah," *BASOR* 214 (1974): 25–39.

Appendix: Notes on Various Scenes of Trampling by Warhorses as Portrayed in Ancient Near Eastern Iconography

Across time and diverse cultures, in the art of the ancient world, battle scenes of the enemy trapped under the hooves of the warhorses appear as a commonly repeated theme. From the Early Bronze Age (approximately 2600), the Sumerian Standard of Ur (British Museum) shows onagers pulling wagons over corpses. In Egyptian art beginning in the fifteenth century with Thuthmose IV (1411–1397) and afterward, streamlined chariots are depicted being pulled by extravagantly large warhorses plunging over enemies and crushing them underfoot. This artistic rendering of death in battle by trampling under horses' hooves is repeated by a long succession of pharaohs (for example. Seti I, Ramses II, Tutankhamun, and others), who showcase their rearing chariot horses on palace walls, temples, and in ceremonial halls at Karnak, Luxor, Abydos, Thebes, Abu Simbel, and other locations.[45]

From the thirteenth century, the ivory plaques found at Megiddo depict Canaanite chariots overrunning their enemies, with corpses underfoot (Museum of the Oriental Institute, Chicago).[46] In the tenth and ninth centuries, Neo-Hittite orthostats from Tel Halaf (National Museum, Aleppo, Syria) and Carchemish (Hittite Museum, Ankara) show warriors prostrate under the chariot horses.[47] And, from Assyria, in battle reliefs in the palace of Ashurnasirpal II (883–859) in Nimrud (British Museum), and on the bronze gates of Shalmaneser III (858–824) at Balawat (British Museum), enemy bodies are featured under the horse's hooves.[48] Also war reliefs from the palace of Sargon II (721–705) at Khorsabad (British Museum) and Sennacherib's (704–681) palace at Nineveh (capture of Lachish) (British Museum) depict mounted warriors using their horses to knock enemies to the ground and trample them, as they hold them with

---

45. For examples, see relief on north tower of the western wall of Rameseum, reproduced in Mark Healy, *The Warrior Pharaoh: Rameses II and the Battle of Qadesh* (Oxford: Osprey, 1993), 63; the battle relief of Rameses II at Abydos, reproduced in Robert B. Partridge, *Fighting Pharaohs: Weapons and Warfare in Ancient Egypt* (Manchester: Peartree, 2002), 114; and relief of the northern tower of the third pylon of Karnak, showing the wars of Seti I against the Shasu of Canaan, reproduced in Yadin, *Art of Warfare*, 1:230.

46. See Yadin, *Art of Warfare*, 1:243.

47. Ibid., 2:366.

48. See reproduction of Balawat gate scene in Kelle, *Ancient Israel at War*, 19.

their spears.[49] Assyrian iconography frequently depicts the fallen enemy dying under the horses' hooves in both chariot scenes and those illustrating mounted combat.

In classical Greece, long after the demise of chariot warfare, mounted warriors with long spears (*kamax*) continued to be shown artistically pinning enemies while horses trample them. An especially interesting scene on a fifth-century amphora (Louvre) shows an infantryman under the horse's hooves trying to defend himself by scaring the horse away with a leopard skin which he uses as a puppet to induce fear (horses are intrinsically afraid of lions and leopards).[50] The coin below, a tetradracma from Paeonia (approximately 335–313), features a horse trampling a fallen warrior who tries to defend himself with a shield.

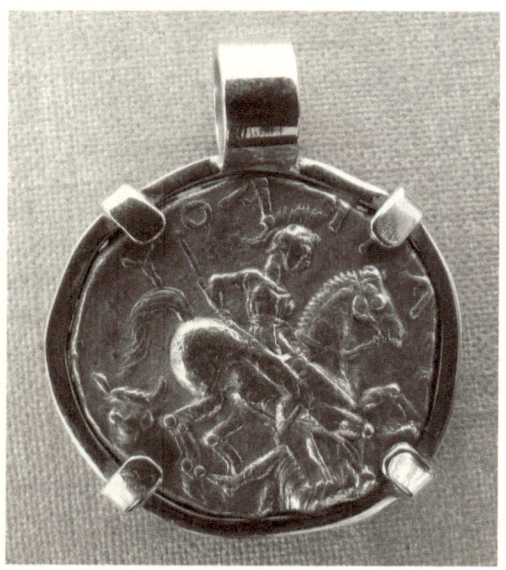

For more than a thousand years, from the Egyptians to the Greeks, artistic iconography emphasizing the power of the warhorse to destroy the enemy is displayed for public scrutiny. These battle scenes of enemies trampled by horses depict a frightful, almost instant death, commonly acknowledged in the ancient world.

Figure 1: Photo of coin from author's collection.

---

49. See reproduction of scenes in Norma Franklin, "A Room with a View: Images from Room V at Khorsabad, Samaria, Nubians, the Brook of Egypt and Ashdod," in *Studies in the Archaeology of the Iron Age in Israel and Jordan* (ed. A. Mazar; JSOTSup 331; Sheffield: Sheffield Academic Press, 2001), 257–77, Fig 10.4 at p. 268, and John M. Russell, *The Final Sack of Nineveh: The Discovery, Documentation, and Destruction of King Sennacherib's Throne Room at Nineveh, Iraq* (New Haven: Yale University Press, 1998), Plate 201, p. 198.

50. See "The Great Melos Amphora by the Suessula Painter" online at: http://www.louvre.fr/en/oeuvre-notices/attic-red-figure-neck-amphora; reproduced in detail in Nicholas Sekunda, *Warriors of Ancient Greece* (Oxford: Osprey, 1986), Plate C2, 16.

Bibliography

Aelian. *On the Characteristics of Animals III, XVI 25*. Translated by A. F. Scholfield. 3 vols. Loeb Classical Library. Cambridge: Harvard University Press, 1959.
Anthony, David W. *The Horse, The Wheel, and Language*. Princeton: Princeton University Press, 2007.
Aster, Shawn Z. "The Function of the City of Jezreel and the Symbolism of Jezreel in Hosea 1–2." *JNES* 71 (2012): 31–46.
Backer, Fabrice de. "Evolution of War Chariot Tactics in the Ancient Near East." *UF* 41 (2010): 29–46.
———. "Some Basic Tactics of Neo-Assyrian Warfare." *UF* 39 (2008): 69–116.
Becking, Bob. *The Fall of Samaria: A Historical and Archaeological Study*. Leiden: Brill, 1992.
Beek, Martinus A. "The Meaning of the Expression 'The Chariots and the Horsemen of Israel' (II Kings ii 12)." *OtSt* 17 (1972): 1–10.
Cantrell, Deborah O. *The Horsemen of Israel: Horses and Chariotry in Monarchic Israel (Ninth-Eighth Centuries b.c.e.)*. History, Archaeology, and Culture of the Levant 1. Winona Lake, Ind.: Eisenbrauns, 2011.
———. "Stable Issues." Pages 630–42 in volume 2 of *Megiddo IV*. Edited by I. Finkelstein, D. Ussishkin, and B. Halpern. 2 vols. Tel Aviv: Tel Aviv University Press, 2006.
Cantrell, Deborah O., and Israel Finkelstein. "A Kingdom for a Horse: The Megiddo Stables and Eighth Century Israel." Pages 643–65 in volume 2 of *Megiddo IV*. Edited by I. Finkelstein, D. Ussishkin, and B. Halpern. 2 vols. Tel Aviv: Tel Aviv University Press, 2006.
Dalley, Stephanie. "Ancient Mesopotamian Military Organization." Pages 413–22 in *Civilizations of the Ancient Near East*. Edited by Jack M. Sasson. New York: Simon & Schuster Macmillan, 1995.
———. "Foreign Chariotry and Cavalry in the Armies of Tiglath-pileser III and Sargon II." *Iraq* 47 (1985): 31–48.
Dalley, Stephanie, and John N. Postgate. *The Tablets from Fort Shalmaneser*. CTN 3. London: British School of Archaeology in Iraq, 1984.
Drews, Robert. *Early Riders: The Beginnings of Mounted Warfare in Asia and Europe*. New York: Routledge, 2004.
Dunham, Dows. *The Royal Cemeteries of Kush*. 5 vols. Cambridge: Harvard University Press, 1950–63.

Ebeling, Jennie, Norma Franklin, and Ian Cipin. "Jezreel Revealed in Laser Scans: A Preliminary Report of the 2012 Survey Season." *NEA* 75 (2012): 232–39.

Franklin, Norma. "Jezreel: Before and after Jezebel." Pages 53–54 in *Israel in Transition: From Late Bronze II to Iron IIA (c. 1250–850)*. Edited by Lester L. Grabbe. LHBOTS 491. London: Continuum, 2008.

———. "A Room with a View: Images from Room V at Khorsabad, Samaria, Nubians, the Brook of Egypt and Ashdod." Pages 257–77 in *Studies in the Archaeology of the Iron Age in Israel and Jordan*. Edited by A. Mazar. JSOTSup 331. Sheffield: Sheffield Academic Press, 2001.

Fuchs, Andreas. *Die Annalen des Jahres 711 v. Chr.: Nach Prismenfragmenten aus Ninive und Assur*. Edited by Robert M. Whiting. SAAS 8. Helsinki: Neo-Assyrian Text Corpus Project, 1998.

Gabriel, Richard A., and Karen S. Metz. *From Sumer to Rome: The Military Capabilities of Ancient Armies*. Contributions in Military Studies 108. Westport, Conn.: Greenwood, 1991.

Gottwald, Norman K. *The Politics of Ancient Israel*. Louisville: Westminster John Knox, 2001.

Gwynne, S. C. *Empire of the Summer Moon*. New York: Scribner, 2010.

Halpern, Baruch. "Centre and Sentry: Megiddo's Role in Transit, Administration and Trade." Pages 535–77 in volume 2 of *Megiddo III: The 1992–1996 Seasons*. Edited by I. Finkelstein, D. Ussishkin, and B. Halpern. 2 vols. Jerusalem: Tel Aviv University Press, 2000.

Healy, Mark. *The Warrior Pharaoh: Rameses II and the Battle of Qadesh*. Oxford: Osprey, 1993.

Heidorn, Lisa A. "The Horses of Kush." *JNES* 56 (1997): 105–14.

Holladay, John S., Jr. "The Stables of Ancient Israel." Pages 103–66 in *The Archaeology of Jordan and Other Studies presented to Siegfried H. Horn*. Edited by Lawrence T. Geraty and Larry G. Herr. Berrien Springs, Mich.: Andrews University Press, 1986.

Hyland, Ann. *The Horse in the Ancient World*. Westport, Conn.: Praeger, 2003.

Kelle, Brad E. *Ancient Israel at War 853–586 bc*. Essential Histories 67. Oxford: Osprey, 2007.

Knight, Douglas A. *Law, Power, and Justice in Ancient Israel*. Louisville: Westminster John Knox, 2011.

Lambert, Wilfred G. *Babylonian Wisdom Literature*. Oxford: Clarendon, 1960. Repr., Winona Lake: Eisenbrauns, 1996.

Lichtheim, Miriam. "The Kadesh Battle Inscriptions of Ramses II." Pages 57–72 in volume 2 of *Ancient Egyptian Literature: A Book of Readings*. 3 vols. Berkeley: University of California Press, 1973–1980.

Liverani, Mario. "From Melid through Bastam to Megiddo: Stables and Horses in Iron Age II." Pages 443–59 in *Leggo! Studies Presented to Frederick Mario Fales*. Edited by Giovanni B. Lanfranchi, Daniele Morandi Bonacossi, Cinzia Pappi, and Simonetta Ponchia. Wiesbaden: Harrassowitz, 2012.

Moore, Megan Bishop and Brad E. Kelle. *Biblical History and Israel's Past: The Changing Study of the Bible and History*. Grand Rapids: Eerdmans, 2011.

Morkot, Robert G. *The Black Pharaohs: Egypt's Nubian Rulers*. London: Rubicon, 2000.

Na'aman, Nadav. "Sennacherib's 'Letter to God' on His Campaign to Judah." *BASOR* 214 (1974): 25–39.

Odell, David. "Images of Violence in the Horse in Job 29:18–25." *Proof* 13 (1993): 163–73.

Partridge, Robert B. *Fighting Pharaohs: Weapons and Warfare in Ancient Egypt*. Manchester: Peartree, 2002.

Rainey, Anson F. and R. Steven Notley. *The Sacred Bridge*. Jerusalem: Carta, 2006.

Russell, John M. *The Final Sack of Nineveh: The Discovery, Documentation, and Destruction of King Sennacherib's Throne Room at Nineveh, Iraq*. New Haven: Yale University Press, 1998.

Schniedewind, William M. "Tel Dan Stela: New Light on Aramaic and Jehu's Revolt." *BASOR* 302 (1996): 75–90.

Sekunda, Nicholas. *Warriors of Ancient Greece*. Oxford: Osprey, 1986.

Tallis, Nigel. "Ancient Near Eastern Warfare." Page 47–66 in *The Ancient World at War*. Edited by Philip de Souza. New York: Thames & Hudson, Ltd., 2008.

Ussishkin, David. "Excavations at Tel Jezreel 1992–1993: Second Preliminary Report." *Levant* 26 (1994): 1–48.

———. *On Biblical Jerusalem, Megiddo, Jezreel and Lachish*. CKLS 8. Hong Kong: Chinese University, 2011.

———. *The Conquest of Lachish by Sennacherib*. Tel Aviv: Tel Aviv University, 1982.

Yadin, Yigael. *The Art of Warfare in Biblical Lands in Light of Archaeological Study*. Translated by M. Pearlman. 2 vols. New York: McGraw-Hill, 1963.

Yamada, Shigeo. *The Construction of the Assyrian Empire: A Historical Study of the Inscriptions of Shalmaneser III (859–824 B.C.) Relating to His Campaigns to the West.* CHANE 3. Boston: Brill, 2000.

War Rituals in the Old Testament: Prophets, Kings, and the Ritual Preparation for War

Rüdiger Schmitt

1. Introduction

No military action in the ancient Near East could be started without preceding ritual actions and omina. Accordingly, military actions in ancient Israel, as well as in Assyria and Babylonia, were accompanied by ritual actions and omina. War rituals and mantical consultations were an integral part of both preparations for war and postwar or postbattle activities in ancient times.[1] Rituals carried out in cases of war are acts with symbolic meaning and communicative functions directed to friend and foe. War rituals communicate military power, create solidarity within a nation and between military leaders and their troops, and stimulate confidence in victory. Ritual actions in the context of war not only have a communicative function for friends and foes, but they always involve a numinous or divine actor included or instrumentalized in the ritual process. This ritual communication with the divine was an indispensible part of human actions before and after war and battle in the ancient Near East.

Both the textual and iconographic evidence attests to a large number of ritual strategies to secure military success. These include execration rituals, ritual archery, and the smashing of pots and figurines (the *sd̠ dšrwt*

---

1. The following article is based on my book *Der 'Heilige Krieg' im Pentateuch und im deuteronomistischen Geschichtswerk* (AOAT 381; Münster: Ugarit-Verlag, 2011), esp. 137–43.

ritual) in Egypt,² ritual hunting in Egypt and Assyria,³ the military oaths of the Hittites,⁴ and posbattle rituals like the cleansing of the weapons in Assyria.⁵ Of utmost importance were oracle inquiries before a political decision was made or a military action started, which served to secure divine support and create confidence in victory.⁶

2. Ritual Preparations for War in the Old Testament

Actual ritual texts or prescriptions for war rituals do not appear in the Old Testament or extrabiblical sources. However, the historiographic texts of the Old Testament contain various references to war rituals and accounts of ritual actions performed before or during military actions.⁷ In most cases, the texts present short references to oracle inquiries to Yhwh, asking whether a campaign will be successful. These could be performed by a ritual or oracle specialist, a prophet or a "man of God" (Shemaiah in

---

2. For depictions of the Pharaoh as hunter and as archer, see Othmar Keel, "Der Bogen als Herrschaftssymbol: Einige unveröffentlichte Skarabäen aus Ägypten und Israel zum Thema 'Jagd und Krieg,'" in *Studien zu den Stempelsiegeln aus Palästina/ Israel III: Die frühe Eisenzeit: Ein Workshop* (ed. O. Keel, M. Shuval, and C. Uehlinger; OBO 100; Freiburg: Academic Press, 1990), 27–65. On the execration rituals, see G. Posener, "Ächtungstexte," *LÄ* 1:67–69; J. van Dijk, "Zerbrechen der roten Töpfe," *LÄ* 6:1389–96. For the texts, see *ANET*, 328–29; *COS*, 1:50–52; For execration figurines, see *ANEP*, 593. On the motif of slaying the enemy, see Sylvia Schoske, *Das Erschlagen der Feinde: Ikonographie und Stilistik der Feindvernichtung im alten Ägypten* (Heidelberg: Academic Press, 1982); Dietrich Wildung, "Erschlagen der Feinde" *LÄ* 2:14–17.

3. See Ursula Magen, *Assyrische Königsdarstellungen: Aspekte der Herrschaft* (Baghdader Forschungen 9; Mainz: von Zabern, 1986), 34–35.

4. See Johannes Friedrich, "Der Hethitische Soldateneid," *ZA* 35 (1924): 161–91; Norbert Oettinger, *Die militärischen Eide der Hethiter* (Wiesbaden: Harrassowitz, 1976).

5. See Walter Mayer, "Waffenreinigung im assyrischen Kriegsritual," in *Kult, Konflikt und Versöhnung: Beiträge zur kultischen Sühne in religiösen, sozialen und politischen Auseinandersetzungen des Antiken Mittelmeerraumes* (ed. R. Albertz; AOAT 285; Münster: Ugarit-Verlag, 2001), 123–33; Moshe Elat, "Mesopotamische Kriegsrituale," *BO* 39 (1982): 5–25; Magen, *Königsdarstellungen*, 82.

6. See Simo Parpola, *Assyrian Prophecies* (SAA 9; Helsinki: Helsinki University Press, 1997), xxxi; Ivan Starr, ed., *Queries to the Sungod: Divination and Politics in Sargonid Assyria* (SAA 4; Helsinki: Helsinki University Press, 1990), lvi; Steven W. Holloway, *Aššur is King! Aššur is King!: Religion in the Exercise of Power in the Neo-Assyrian Empire* (CHANE 10; Leiden: Brill, 2002), 78–79.

7. See Rüdiger Schmitt, *Magie im Alten Testament* (AOAT 313; Münster: Ugarit-Verlag, 2004), 274–82; Schmitt, *Der Heilige Krieg*, 137–42.

1 Kgs 12:22–24), by means of instrumental mantic techniques (the inquiry by David with an ephod, a ritual object of unclear character, sometimes described as a garment or a mask,[8] in 1 Sam 30:7–9), or by a direct inquiry of the king to Yhwh (the account of David's campaign against the Amalekites in 2 Sam 2:1–2). Accounts of war rituals that contain an execration ritual appear in the story of the ritual shooting and striking with arrows of King Joash with the support of Elisha in 2 Kgs 13:14–19 and in the performance with the horns made of iron by the prophet Zedekaiah in 1 Kgs 22:10–12. Psalm 2:9 also seems to refer to a war ritual performed by the king that is similar to the Egyptian execration ritual of smashing the red pots (the *sḏ dšrwt* ritual). Ritual destruction of pots is also attested in Mesopotamian ritual literature, in particular from *namburbis* and in other apotropaic rituals.[9] Actual war rituals depicting the smashing of pots by the king or religious functionaries, however, are not attested in Mesopotamian sources. Nevertheless, Assyrian rulers claimed in their royal inscriptions to have smashed the countries of the enemies like pots,[10] but this may be only a metaphorical expression.

The execration ritual performance with bow and arrows commanded by Elisha in 2 Kgs 13:14–19[11] provides a helpful example of the war rituals in the historiographic books. The context of the performance is the wars against the Arameans at the beginning of the eighth century b.c.e. Due to the Aramean threat, King Joash engages the famous old "man of God" (*'îš hā'ĕlōhîm*), Elisha, who is here called by his name of honor, "chariot of Israel and his rider" for having saved Israel in many situations of distress. The man of God of the northern state is not a prophet in the common sense, but a ritual specialist performing a great variety of rituals, in particular healing and other forms of magical intervention in situations of distress for the individual, family, or local community. Even so, the sources

---

8. See Rüdiger Schmitt, "Divination II: Hebrew Bible/Old Testament" in *Encyclopedia of the Bible and Its Reception* (eds. Hans-Josef Klauck et al.; Berlin: de Gruyter, 2009), 2:959–61.

9. See Stefan M. Maul, *Zukunftsbewältigung: Eine Untersuchung altorientalischen Denkens anhand der babylonisch-assyrischen Löserituale* (Baghdader Forschungen 18; Mainz: von Zabern, 1994), 82–84.

10. See Hayim Tadmor, *The Inscriptions of Tiglath-Pileser III King of Assyria: Critical Edition, with Introductions, Translations and Commentary* (Jerusalem: Israel Academy of Sciences and Humanities, 1994), 122–23, Z. 8 (Summay Inscription I); Maul, *Zukunftsbewältigung*, 83.

11. See also Schmitt, *Magie*, 275–80.

emphasize an often oppositional stance against the king and the elites as well as ritual specialists and ritual mediators in state affairs.[12]

The ritual commanded by Elisha contains two parts: (1) shooting with the bow in the direction of the enemy to the east, and (2) striking the ground with the arrows. During the first action, in which Joash has to shoot the arrow, Elisha as a ritual mediator guides his hands, thus assuring the support of the national god, Yhwh. The symbolic meaning of this ritual is a magical anticipation of victory. The ritual action is accompanied by the spell, "Yhwh's arrow of victory, the arrow of victory against Aram!" (v. 17). These words communicate a message of victory to the audience of political, military, and religious functionaries, as well as the troops, which are, however, not mentioned, but may be assumed to be present (as in Zedekiah's performance in 1 Kgs 22 and David's ritual performance of loyalty in 2 Sam 19:6–9). The second part of the ritual contains the striking on the ground with the arrows. The number of strikes symbolizes the number of victories granted by Yhwh. That the man of God criticizes the king for not having struck more times belongs to the tendency of the story to portray this king as a failure. Both ritual actions are without doubt acts of imitative magic. Like the arrow flying in the direction of Damascus, the Israelite troops will penetrate the heartland of the Arameans, and the victories will be achieved and granted by Yhwh, as often the king strikes the ground.

Previous scholarship has interpreted these rituals as a means by which the participants sought to coerce a deity to do human will. This interpretation does not fit the ancient perspectives.[13] No person in antiquity was so naïve as to believe that one could coerce a god to do his or her will. Rituals were likely performed with the conviction that a god will intervene as a savior, delivering the enemy into the hand of the king. But this conviction was based on the ritual authority of the man of God, rooted in his special relation to Yhwh (as the title "man of god" indicates), and the function of the king as *vicarius dei*. In particular, we have to assume that in the emic perception the man of God was believed to have a direct line to Yhwh and that Yhwh was bound to the word of his authorized mediators and thus made what his ritual mediators and *vicarii dei* were performing ritually happen in reality. Thus, the magic of these war rituals was not working automatically, *ex opere operato*, but worked according to the firm belief

---

12. Ibid., 294–98.
13. Ibid., 277.

that the deity intervenes in reaction to these faithful acts. The public performance of such rituals created strong emotions of confidence and trust in victory granted by the god.

Overall, these elements suggest that the first action of Elisha's laying on of hands in this context symbolizes that Yhwh, represented by his ritual mediator Elisha, leads the weapon of the king to its target. The second part of the ritual with the striking of the arrows works as a specification of the divine will and therefore has a stronger mantic character than the previous ritual action with the bow. Additionally, in the second part, the oracle replaces the conjuration formula. Thus, we can conclude that 2 Kgs 13:14–19 is a war ritual consisting of two performative acts accompanied by speech acts and includes an execration ritual, an anticipation of victory, and an oracle granting three victories over the enemy:

(1) Anticipation of Victory
    (1.1) command by the man of god
    (1.2) ritual action: shooting one arrow to the east by the king
    (1.3) conjuration by the man of god
(2) Specification
    (2.1) command by the man of god
    (2.2) ritual action: striking three times by the king
    (2.3) oracle proclaiming three victories

The background of this ritual is the symbolic significance of ritual shooting and royal bows in the ancient Near East. Ritual shooting is attested both in ancient Egypt[14] and Mesopotamia.[15] Moreover, the bow as a symbol for royal power and dominance over enemies has a longer local history in glyptic and other small art.[16] In Judean iconography of Iron Age II, the bow with arrows is, as attested by the seal of the śr hyr (fig. 1),[17] a symbol of

---

14. Cf. Othmar Keel, *Wirkmächtige Siegeszeichen im Alten Testament: Ikonographische Studien zu Jos 8,18–26; Ex 17,8–13; 2 Kön 13,14–19 und 1 Kön 22,11* (OBO 5; Fribourg: Universitätsverlag, 1974), 113; Keel, "Bogen," 172.

15. A survey is given in Keel, "Bogen," 278.

16. Ibid.

17. Nahman Avigad and Benjamin Sass, *Corpus of West Semitic Stamp Seals* (Jerusalem: Israel Academy of Sciences and Humanities, 1997), 402; Othmar Keel and Christoph Uehlinger, *Götter, Göttinnen und Gottessymbole: Neue Erkenntnisse zur Religionsgeschichte Kanaans und Israels aufgrund bisher unerschlossener ikonographischer Quellen* (QD 134; Freiburg: Herder, 1999), 346.

the authority and military power of the king. As the iconography of the seal shows, Judean royal representations of the Iron II period are strongly influenced by Assyrian models.[18] The impact of Egyptian iconography, reaching back to the late Bronze Age and still influential in the Iron Age, can also be demonstrated by the motif of the king slaying the enemy on the Egyptianizing ivories from Samaria (fig. 2).[19] The same motif appears on Iron Age seals and bullae both from Israel (figs. 3 and 4) and Philistine Ashdod (fig. 5).[20] The iconography of the seals and ivories relates to the aforementioned execration rituals, in particular with the smashing of the foes in Ps 2:9, which resembles the Egyptian *sḏ dšrwt* ritual. Another example of this type of execration ritual appears in Jer 19, where the prophet performs an execration ritual by smashing pots against his own city.

The mantic consultation of the prophet Zedekiah in 1 Kgs 22:10–12 provides a second helpful example of war rituals in the Old Testament historiographic books. The consultation takes place in front of the city gate of Samaria and belongs to a group of postdeuteronomistic war narrations including 1 Kgs 20:1–43; 22:1–38; 2 Kgs 3:4–27; and 6:24–7:20. The conflict between Zedekiah ben Chenaanah and Micaiah ben Imlah perhaps has its background in traditions about conflicts between prophets of salvation and prophets of doom in the late monarchic period, which may also be reflected in the story about Jeremiah and Hananiah in Jer 28.[21] In their present forms, however, both 1 Kgs 22 and Jer 28 are examples of the prophetical law in Deut 18,[22] and therefore do not readily permit historical facts to be extracted from them. Nevertheless, the

---

18. See Rüdiger Schmitt, *Bildhafte Herrschaftsrepräsentation im eisenzeitlichen Israel* (AOAT 283; Münster: Ugarit-Verlag, 2001), 197–98.

19. John W. Crowfoot and Grace M. Crowfoot, *Early Ivories from Samaria* (Samaria-Sebaste II; London: Palestine Exploration Fund, 1938), pl. XIV, 1.

20. See Avigad and Sass, *Corpus*, Nr. 400, 401, 1065; Benjamin Sass, "The Pre-exilic Hebrew Seals: Iconism Versus Aniconism," in *Studies in the Iconography of Northwest Semitic Inscribed Seals* (ed. Benjamin Sass and Christoph Uehlinger; OBO 125; Fribourg: Universitätsverlag, 1993), 145.

21. See Ernst Würthwein, *Die Bücher der Könige* (ATD 11.2; Göttingen: Vandenhoeck & Ruprecht, 1984), 262; Alexander Rofé, *The Prophetical Stories: The Narratives about the Prophets in the Hebrew Bible: Their Literary Types and History* (Jerusalem: Magnes, 1988), 262; Susanne Otto, *Jehu, Elia und Elisa: Die Erzählung von der Jehu-Revolution und die Komposition der Elia-Elisa-Erzählungen* (BWA(N)T 152; Stuttgart: Kohlhammer, 2001), 215.

22. See Schmitt, *Magie*, 281.

Figure 1. Seal depicting a bow with arrows. After Keel and Uehlinger, *Götter*, no. 346.

Figure 2. King slaying an enemy on an ivory from Samaria. After Keel and Uehlinger, *Götter*, no. 262b.

156　　　　　　　WARFARE, RITUAL, AND SYMBOL

Figures 3 and 4. Iron Age seals from Israel. (3) Drawing by the author. (4) After Sass, "Pre-exilic Hebrew Seals," 145.

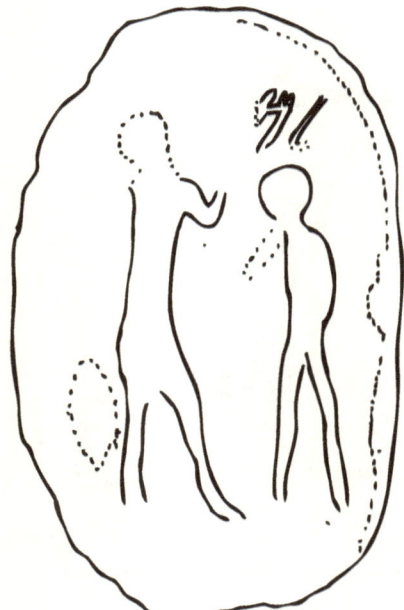

Figure 5. Iron Age seal from Philistine Ashdod. Drawing by the author.

ritual setting and the details of the ritual actions may be seen as typical for prophetical consultations in situations of national distress and ritual preparations for war. The public consultation of prophets in front of the gate of Samaria seems to belong to a whole complex of war related and royal rituals performed in or in front of the gate.[23] For example, in the context of Absalom's *coup d'état* in 2 Samuel, two ritual performances of David are reported. In 2 Sam 18:1–5, he reviews his troops before battle, and 2 Sam 19:6–9 contains a ritual confirmation of loyalty. War rituals and ritual confirmations of loyalty serve to establish or reestablish community and loyalty among the king, his generals and troops, and the population as a whole by public performance in front of the gate, the public place *per se* in ancient Israelite cities.[24]

The ritual action carried out by Zedekiah includes a performative act with the presentation of the iron horns and the oracle, "Thus speaks Yhwh, 'With these you shall gore the Arameans until they are destroyed.'" The symbolism of the horns is an expression of power owned by Yhwh, who is represented—like Baal/Hadad—by the bull, whose representations were erected in the royal sanctuaries of Dan and Beth-El (1 Kgs 12:26–33).[25] The function of the performative ritual actions is clear. The ritual consultation in public in front of the gate of the nation's capital makes the inquiry into a strategy to recreate and maintain the *communitas*[26] of the kings, the civil, military, and religious dignitaries, and the people. The kings of Israel and Judah, enthroned and arrayed in their full military equipment[27] are communicating military power. In addition to creating and confirming *communitas*, the ritual performance and the oracle underscore the military power and anticipate victory.

3. Conclusions

The rituals discussed above exemplify the importance of ritual strategies to secure military success, and they correspond to related rituals known

---

23. See Rüdiger Schmitt, "Der König sitzt im Tor: Überlegungen zum Stadttor als Ort herrschaftlicher Repräsentation im Alten Testament," *UF* 32 (2000): 475–85.
24. Ibid.
25. See Keel and Uehlinger, *Götter*, § 119.
26. See Victor W. Turner, *The Ritual Process: Structure and Anti-structure* (London: Routledge & Kegan Paul, 1969), 131–40.
27. With 1 Kgs 22:10 LXX: ἔνοπλοι.

from Egypt and Mesopotamia. However, in the context of 1 Kgs 22:1–38, the original meaning of the ritual is reversed into the opposite: Micaiah ben Imlah delegitimizes the positive oracle by his ritual act and the word of Yhwh which has come to him, and that act legitimizes him as a true prophet according to the prophetical law in Deut 18. Even so, this is not a critique of the ritual legitimation of war by prophets but comes from a later discourse about legitimate rule and prophetic authority. The miracle stories in 2 Kgs 3:4–27 (Elisha's water miracle in the context of the war against Moab), 2 Kgs 6:8–23 (the Aramean attack thwarted by Elisha), and the story about the critique of Ahab by an unnamed prophet during the Aramean war in 1 Kgs 20 reflect only a late, postdeuteronomistic stage of tradition. Due to their literary character, these narratives about interventions of men of god and prophets in military campaigns, in particular the miracle stories of Elisha, do not directly reflect ritual interventions by prophets that can be used to reconstruct war rituals. The insertion of 1 Kgs 20 into the Naboth narrative, for example, justifies the redemption of the Omride dynasty by Yhwh. These stories reflect a late stage of the picture of the prophet, who becomes a kind of "superhero" miracle worker.[28] First Kings 20 picks up traditional motifs, in particular the *ḥērem* as criterion for the obedience of the law. Thus, the story should not be interpreted as a historical account of a military campaign and cannot be used for the reconstruction of preexilic war ideologies and related ritual practices. Nevertheless, these later stories reflect in a more general sense the participation of prophets and men of god in cases of military campaigns.

With regard to the question of a specific preexilic Israelite ideology of Yhwh War, as assumed by Gerhard von Rad and other authors still to this day,[29] we have to conclude that the ritual practices of war preparation, in particular prophetical consultations and execration rituals, did not differ in ancient Israel, Egypt, and Mesopotamia, and that these practices should be understood in the context of the closely related concepts of kingship and divinely authorized war in the ancient Near East.[30]

---

28. Schmitt, *Magie*, 289.
29. For the history of research on this topic, see Schmitt, *Der Heilige Krieg*, 10–15.
30. See Manfred Weippert, "'Heiliger Krieg' in Israel und Assyrien: Kritische Anmerkungen zu Gerhard von Rads Konzept des 'Heiligen Krieges' im alten Israel," in *Jahwe und die anderen Götter: Studien zur Religionsgeschichte des antiken Israel in ihrem syrisch-palästinischen Kontext* (ed. Manfred Weippert; FAT 18; Tübingen: Mohr

BIBLIOGRAPHY

Avigad, Nahman, and Benjamin Sass. *Corpus of West Semitic Stamp Seals.* Jerusalem: Israel Academy of Sciences and Humanities, 1997.
Crowfoot, John W., and Grace M. Crowfoot. *Early Ivories from Samaria.* Samaria-Sebaste II. London: Palestine Exploration Fund, 1938.
Dijk, J. van. "Zerbrechen der roten Töpfe." Pages 1389–96 in volume 6 of the *Lexikon der Ägyptologie.* Edited by W. Helck. 7 vols. Wiesbaden: Harrassowitz, 1975.
Elat, Moshe. "Mesopotamische Kriegsrituale." *BO* 39 (1982): 5–25.
Friedrich, Johannes. "Der Hethitische Soldateneid." *ZA* 35 (1924): 161–91.
Holloway, Steven W. *Aššur is King! Aššur is King!: Religion in the Exercise of Power in the Neo-Assyrian Empire.* CHANE 10. Leiden: Brill, 2002.
Keel, Othmar. "Der Bogen als Herrschaftssymbol: Einige unveröffentlichte Skarabäen aus Ägypten und Israel zum Thema 'Jagd und Krieg.'" Pages 27–65 in *Studien zu den Stempelsiegeln aus Palästina/Israel III: Die frühe Eisenzeit: Ein Workshop.* Edited by O. Keel, M. Shuval, and C. Uehlinger. OBO 100. Freiburg: Academic Press, 1990.
———. *Wirkmächtige Siegeszeichen im Alten Testament: Ikonographische Studien zu Jos 8,18—26; Ex 17,8—13; 2 Kön 13,14—19 und 1 Kön 22,11.* OBO 5. Fribourg: Universitätsverlag, 1974.
Keel, Othmar, and Christoph Uehlinger. *Götter, Göttinnen und Gottessymbole: Neue Erkenntnisse zur Religionsgeschichte Kanaans und Israels aufgrund bisher unerschlossener ikonographischer Quellen.* QD 134. Freiburg: Herder, 1999.
Magen, Ursula. *Assyrische Königsdarstelllungen: Aspekte der Herrschaft.* Baghdader Forschungen 9. Mainz: von Zabern, 1986.
Mayer, Walter. "Waffenreingung im Assyrischen Kriegsritual." Pages 123–33 in *Kult, Konflikt und Versöhnung: Beiträge zur kultischen Sühne in religiösen, sozialen und politischen Auseinandersetzungen des Antiken Mittelmeerraumes.* Edited by R. Albertz. AOAT 285. Münster: Ugarit-Verlag, 2001.
Maul, Stefan M. *Zukunftsbewältigung: Eine Untersuchung altorientalischen Denkens anhand der babylonisch-assyrischen Löserituale.* Baghdader Forschungen 18. Mainz: von Zabern, 1994.

Siebeck, 1997), 71–97; Manfred Weippert, "Heiliger Krieg I: Alter Orient und Altes Testament," *RGG*[4] 3:1563; Schmitt, *Der Heilige Krieg*, 212–13.

Oettinger, Norbert. *Die militärischen Eide der Hethiter.* Wiesbaden: Harrassowitz, 1976.

Otto, Susanne. *Jehu, Elia und Elisa: Die Erzählung von der Jehu-Revolution und die Komposition der Elia-Elisa-Erzählungen.* BWA(N)T 152. Stuttgart: Kohlhammer, 2001.

Parpola, Simo. *Assyrian Prophecies.* SAA 9. Helsinki: Helsinki University Press, 1997.

Posener, G. "Ächtungstexte." Pages 67–69 in volume 1 of the *Lexikon der Ägyptologie.* Edited by W. Helck. 7 vols. Wiesbaden: Harrassowitz, 1975.

Rofé, Alexander. *The Prophetical Stories: The Narratives about the Prophets in the Hebrew Bible: Their Literary Types and History.* Jerusalem: Magnes, 1988.

Sass, Benjamin. "The Pre-exilic Hebrew Seals: Iconism Versus Aniconism." Pages 194–256 in *Studies in the Iconography of Northwest Semitic Inscribed Seals.* Edited by Benjamin Sass and Christoph Uehlinger. OBO 125. Fribourg: Universitätsverlag, 1993.

Schmitt, Rüdiger. *Bildhafte Herrschaftsrepräsentation im eisenzeitlichen Israel.* AOAT 283. Münster: Ugarit-Verlag 2001.

———. "Divination II: Hebrew Bible/Old Testament." Pages 959–61 in volume 2 of *The Encyclopedia of the Bible and Its Reception.* Edited by Hans-Josef Klauck, Bernard McGinn, Paul Mendes-Flohr, Choon-Leong Choow, Hermann Spieckermann, Barry Walfish, and Eric Ziolkowski. Berlin: de Gruyter, 2009.

———. *Der Heilige Krieg im Pentateuch und im deuteronomistischen Geschichtswerk.* AOAT 381. Münster: Ugarit-Verlag, 2011.

———. "Der König sitzt im Tor: Überlegungen zum Stadttor als Ort herrschaftlicher Repräsentation im Alten Testament." *UF* 32 (2000): 475–85.

———. *Magie im Alten Testament.* AOAT 313. Münster: Ugarit-Verlag, 2004.

Schoske, Sylvia. *Das Erschlagen der Feinde: Ikonographie und Stilistik der Feindvernichtung im alten Ägypten.* Heidelberg: Academic Press, 1982.

Starr, Ivan, ed. *Queries to the Sungod: Divination and Politics in Sargonid Assyria.* SAA 4. Helsinki: Helsinki University Press, 1990.

Tadmor, Hayim. *The Inscriptions of Tiglath-Pileser III King of Assyria: Critical Edition, with Introductions, Translations and Commentary.* Jerusalem: Israel Academy of Sciences and Humanities, 1994.

Turner, Victor W. *The Ritual Process: Structure and Anti-structure.* London: Routledge & Kegan Paul, 1969.
Weippert, Manfred. "Heiliger Krieg I: Alter Orient und Altes Testament." Pages 1562–63 in volume 3 of *Religion in Geschichte und Gegenwart.* 4th ed. Edited by H. D. Betz, Don S. Browning, Bernd Janowski, and Eberhard Jüngel. 9 vols. Tübingen: Mohr Siebeck, 1998–2007.
———. "'Heiliger Krieg' in Israel und Assyrien: Kritische Anmerkungen zu Gerhard von Rads Konzept des 'Heiligen Krieges' im alten Israel." Pages 71–97 in *Jahwe und die anderen Götter: Studien zur Religionsgeschichte des antiken Israel in ihrem syrisch-palästinischen Kontext.* Edited by M. Weippert. FAT 18. Tübingen: Mohr Siebeck, 1997.
Wildung, Dietrich. "Erschlagen der Feinde." Pages 14–17 in volume 2 of *Lexicon der Ägyptologie.* Edited by W. Helck, E. Otto, and W. Westendorf. 7 vols. Wiesbaden: Harrassowitz, 1975.
Würthwein, Ernst. *Die Bücher der Könige.* ATD 11.1–2. Göttingen: Vandenhoeck & Ruprecht, 1977–1984.

Part 3
Rituals and Symbols of Perpetuation, De-escalation, and Commemoration

Warfare Song as Warrior Ritual

Mark S. Smith

1. Introduction

Warrior poetry in the Bible has not been the subject of particular focus in biblical scholarship. What counts as warrior poetry, for example, Exod 15, Judg 5, and 2 Sam 1, has been subsumed under—or perhaps overwhelmed by—the twentieth century concern for so-called "old poetry." Appeals about "old poetry" as dating to the Iron I (approximately 1200–1000) and Iron IIA (approximately 1000–925), made in the 1950s and 1960s (e.g., by Frank Moore Cross and David Noel Freedman),[1] are rarely heard today in biblical scholarship. Such claims have come to be viewed as overconfident, in part because they were based on debatable criteria, as even Cross came to acknowledge.[2] Another objection involved the exaggerated claims made for old poetry as a source or series of sources for reconstructing early Israelite history, a problem on display in Johannes C. de Moor's detailed 1990 study, *The Rise of Yahwism*.[3] Research on the subject from David Noel Freedman[4] was likewise not immune from the temptation to reconstruct

---

1. Perhaps best exemplified by the joint 1950 dissertation of Frank Moore Cross Jr. and David Noel Freedman, most recently published as *Studies in Ancient Yahwistic Poetry* (2nd ed.; BRS; Grand Rapids: Eerdmans, 1997).

2. Cross, preface to ibid., viii.

3. Johannes C. de Moor, *The Rise of Yahwism: The Roots of Israelite Monotheism* (BETL 91; Leuven: Leuven University Press/Uitgeverij Peeters, 1990; rev. and enl. ed., 1997).

4. David Noel Freedman, "Early Israelite History in the Light of Early Hebrew Poetry," in *Unity and Diversity* (ed. Hans Goedicke and J. J. M. Roberts; Baltimore: Johns Hopkins University Press, 1975), 3–35, repr. in David Noel Freedman, *Pottery, Poetry and Prophecy: Collected Essays on Hebrew Poetry* (Winona Lake, Ind.: Eisenbrauns, 1980), 131–66; and David Noel Freedman, "Early Israelite Poetry and His-

early Israelite history based on old poetry. Between the problem of dating so-called old poetry and its being used as source material for reconstructing early Israelite history, "old poetry" came to be viewed as problematic.

Following this phase of discussion, in more recent years the debate over old poetry has issued in a general skepticism about being able to say anything about the premonarchic period when it comes to texts. One can see this in introductions to the Hebrew Bible. What Alexander Rofé calls "the epic poetry" receives only brief notices in his monumental book of 2009, *Introduction to the Literature of the Hebrew Bible*.[5] The early period is likewise the only phase of Israelite textual production not addressed by the detailed and otherwise comprehensive survey of David M. Carr, *The Formation of the Hebrew Bible: A New Reconstruction*.[6] Carr offers textual or literary "profiles"[7] for different periods in Israel's history, with the exception of the premonarchic period.[8] For Carr,[9] the early monarchic period is as far as he believes that scholars can go. The consideration of the earliest Israelite literature is also missing from Konrad Schmid's period-by-period survey of biblical literature, *The Old Testament: A Literary History*.[10] In these scholarly works, it is as if Israelite literature in this period never existed. At the moment, this is the state of the question; I would like to see it reopened.

It is part of my argument that poetry about war and warriors represents a significant component in the literary profile of early Israelite textual production beginning in the premonarchic period (Iron I). In a forthcoming book entitled *Poetic Heroes: The Literary Commemoration of Warriors and Warrior Culture in the Early Biblical World*,[11] I argue that

---

torical Reconstructions," in *Symposia Celebrating the Seventy-Fifth Anniversary of the Founding of the American Schools of Oriental Research (1900–1975)* (ed. Frank Moore Cross Jr.; Cambridge: American Schools of Oriental Research, 1979), 85–96; repr. in Freedman, *Pottery, Poetry and Prophecy*, 167-78.

5. Alexander Rofé, *Introduction to the Literature of the Hebrew Bible* (JBS 9; Jerusalem: Simor, 2009), 293, 413.

6. David McLain Carr, *The Formation of the Hebrew Bible: A New Reconstruction* (New York: Oxford University Press, 2011).

7. This is Carr's term in ibid., 8, 491.

8. See Carr's reflections in ibid., 8–9 and 488–90.

9. Ibid., 489.

10. For a specific statement, see Konrad Schmid, *The Old Testament: A Literary History* (trans. Linda M. Maloney; Minneapolis: Fortress, 2012), 51.

11. Mark S. Smith, *Poetic Heroes: The Literary Commemoration of Warriors and Warrior Culture in the Early Biblical World* (Grand Rapids: Eerdmans, forthcoming).

the traditions of the core of Judg 5, if not a good deal of the core itself in verses 14–29, can be dated to the premonarchic period. The present form of the poem, in particular much of its introduction (vv. 2–13), with the new emphasis on both Israel and Yhwh (entirely lacking in the poem's core, apart from the isolated piece of verse 23), essentially may be dated to the tenth century. Similarly, the core of 2 Sam 1:19–27, in particular the chiastically-arranged verses 19–25, fits well in the tenth century, and it is quite possible that what seems to be the secondary coda or reprise of verses 26–27 can be dated to the late tenth century as well. The tenth century would seem to be a fitting setting for the poem, by comparison with some later period, given the usage of "gazelle" in verse 19a as a leadership term, as well as the currency of the lament tradition over nature in verse 21a.[12] The syntax of the opening phrase in verse 19 is also a bit unusual. In short, the tenth century seems to be a viable setting for the poem, which draws on traditional warrior features going back to the Iron I period. Even if these two poems date somewhat later, they contain traditions of material that ostensibly predate their current form.

What has gone generally unnoticed is that poetry about war and warriors forms a particular topic within old poetry. So a point that I would like to emphasize is that textual production in early Israel seems to have included warfare and warriors in a significant way. To use Carr's notion of profiles for each period of Israelite literature,[13] warrior poetry is a distinctive part of the profile for early Israelite literature. Despite substantial limitations,[14] I attempt to hear once more the various—and largely anonymous—voices of early warrior life and culture embodied in these two poems.

What also seems to be lacking in the discussion is not just *that* warfare and warrior constitute an important topic of this poetry, but also *how* warfare forms one particular arena of activity that inspired the composition

---

12. These features would fit less well with a substantially later dating for the poem, even if one could find reasons for such a composition at a later period (whether it was composed later or simply received later). It is possible to argue that the reference to Philistines could have been made later based on knowledge from the prose sources, but it also fits the tenth-century era of the Philistines wars.

13. Carr, *Formation*.

14. Note generally the serious challenges to reconstructing the past via biblical sources, as outlined by Megan Bishop Moore and Brad E. Kelle, *Biblical History and Israel's Past: The Changing Study of the Bible and History* (Grand Rapids: Eerdmans, 2011).

of several of these relatively early poems. As a result, this has made me wonder what that might say about warfare as the setting for a significant portion of textual production in early Israel. Relatively little attention has been given to what these poems may say about the early culture of what we call Israel that gave rise to these texts. As scholars, we rightly spend a tremendous amount of time trying to discern the ritual elements from our texts, but the texts themselves as artifacts of ritual deserve our notice.

2. Postbattle Song as Commemoration in Warrior Poetry

The speech acts surrounding warriors and warfare that we see in the Bible (and here supplemented sometimes by some earlier and later material) occur over three phases surrounding battle: prebattle preparations; postbattle practices; and later commemoration. For the broad evidence that we have about warfare in West Semitic literature, for the phase of prebattle preparations, speech acts assume a number of different forms.

It is in the next phase, namely, in postbattle victory or defeat, where warrior poetry is arguably best known. In cases of defeat, lament following battle would ensue, performed either by other warriors (the lament over Saul and Jonathan in 2 Sam 1:19–25), by family members (the laments of El and Anat over Baal in KTU 1.5 VI 11–25 and KTU 1.5 VI 31–1.6 I 6–8), and by weeping women (for example, Anat over Aqhat in KTU 1.18 IV 39; 2 Sam 1:24; see also *Iliad* 19.287–300).[15] Thomas M. Greene emphasizes the community formed by the performance of epic lament: "In the common field of performance, … the grief of the poet merges with the performer's, and the character's, and the audience's."[16] Viewed in light of Green's observations, postbattle laments may be understood as a ritualized behavior that serves "to create a community of shared mourners."[17] Second Samuel 1 provides good material here. For example, 2 Sam 1:20 and 24 point to women's central role in this community-building activity. The poem as a whole serves to generate a communal identity for a post-Saulide "Israel" invoked in verse 19, even as it strives in verse 24 to deny such an identity-building opportunity to the Philistines.

---

15. C. H. Gordon, "Indo-European and Hebrew Epic," *ErIsr* 5 (1958): 12.

16. Thomas M. Greene, "The Natural Tears of Epic," in *Epic Traditions in the Contemporary World* (ed. Margaret Beissinger, Jane Tylus, and Susanne Wofford; Berkeley: University of California, 1999), 195.

17. Ibid., 189.

In cases of victory, women welcome men home from battle and celebrate their victory (1 Sam 18:6–7; 2 Sam 1:20; 2 Sam 6:20; see also Exod 15:20–21; Judg 9:34).[18] It is also their role to spread the good news of triumph (see Ps 68:12–13 [Eng. 11–12], and the image of Zion in Isa 40:9–10; compare 2 Sam 1:20).[19] A victory parade might ensue (see Ps 68:25–26 [Eng. 24–25]; compare *ANEP* figs. 305 and 332). The tradition of early heroic poetry is in no small way the domain of women, and it is arguable

---

18. See Eunice B. Poethig, "The Victory Song Tradition of the Women of Israel" (PhD diss., Union Theological Seminary, 1985); and Carol L. Meyers, "Mother to Muse: An Archaeomusicological Study of Women's Performance in Israel," in *Recycling Biblical Figures: Papers Read at a NOSTER Colloquium in Amsterdam, 12–13 May 1997* (ed. Athalya Brenner and Jan Willem van Henten; STAR 1; Leiden: Deo, 1999), 50–77. Both works are cited and discussed by Susan Ackerman, "Otherworldly Music and the Other Sex," in *The 'Other' in Second Temple Judaism: Essays in Honor of John J. Collins* (ed. Daniel C. Harlow, Karina Martin Hogan, Matthew Goff, and Joel S. Kaminsky; Grand Rapids: Eerdmans, 2011), 86–100, here 87–90. Note also the argument made for Prov 30:10–31 as a woman's "heroic poetry" by A. Wolters, "Proverbs XXXI 30–31 as Heroic Hymn: A Form-Critical Analysis," *VT* 38 (1988): 452–53; Richard J. Clifford, *Proverbs: A Commentary* (OTL; Louisville: Westminster John Knox, 1999), 273. In this reading, *ʿayil* in Prov 31:10 would echo its usage to denote a warrior (my thanks to Professor Clifford for drawing my attention to this reading).

19. See also the discussion over whether Miriam's song in Exod 15:21 reflects an older tradition of women's song in victory, rather than the song as Moses' as represented in Exod 15:1–18. See Frank Moore Cross Jr. and David Noel Freedman, "The Song of Miriam," *JNES* 14 (1955): 237–50; Rita J. Burns, *Has the Lord Spoken Only Through Moses? A Study of the Biblical Portrait of Miriam* (SBLDS 84; Atlanta: Scholars Press, 1987), 11–40; Phyllis Trible, "Bringing Miriam Out of the Shadows," *Bible Review* 5.1 (1989): 14–34; J. Gerald Janzen, "Song of Moses, Song of Miriam: Who is Seconding Whom?" *CBQ* 54 (1992): 211–20; Athalya Brenner and Fokkelien van Dijk-Hemmes, *On Gendering Texts: Female and Male Voices in the Hebrew Bible* (BInS 1; Leiden: Brill, 1996), 38–42; and Carol L. Meyers, "Miriam, Music, and Miracles," in *Mariam, the Magdalen, and the Mother* (ed. Deirdre Good; Bloomington: Indiana University Press: 2005), 27–48. For the further issue of musical instrumentation associated with women, see Carol L. Meyers, "Of Drums and Damsels: Women's Performance in Ancient Israel," *BA* 54 (1991): 16–27, esp. 24; Sarit Paz, *Drums, Women, and Goddesses: Drumming and Gender in Iron Age II Israel* (OBO 232; Fribourg: Academic Press; Göttingen: Vandenhoeck & Ruprecht, 2007); and Raz Kletter and Katri Saarelainen, "Judean Drummers," *ZDPV* 127 (2011): 11–28. I am grateful to Seth Chalmer for drawing my attention to this issue. As Chalmer suggests, the Ugaritic literary evidence (see KTU 1.3 III 4–8 and 1.101.15–18; 1.16 I 31–45 as well as 1.16 I 3–5, 17–19, II 40–42) points to a background for early biblical material such as Ps 68:26 (cf. Exod 15:20–21; Judg 11:34; 1 Sam 18:6).

that a good deal of heroic poetry in early Israel is to be situated in the context of women's oral song.[20] Perhaps the core of Ps 68 is a good example of postbattle victory celebration in early Israelite poetry. One a lament, the other a celebratory song, the poems of 2 Sam 1 and Ps 68 offer instances, to echo the title of this talk, of warfare song as ritual.

Postbattle warrior song may take the further form of later commemoration of warriors, for example, Judg 5 and the song of Achilles in *Iliad* 9. These texts largely consist of warriors singing on behalf of warriors after battle and away from the battlefield. This may also be the situation for song and lamentation of soldiers for leaders at their burials (see 2 Sam 3:32–34). A further form of postbattle commemoration involves postmortem recollection of great leaders (and the recollection of warriors—called Rephaim—seems to be a particular form of commemoration in both the Ugaritic texts and the Bible). As an example of commemoration in early Israelite poetry, scholars often discuss Judg 5, but it may also inform the last two verses of the lament over Saul and Jonathan in 2 Sam 1. It is arguable that verses 19–25 constitute a separate section and perhaps even a separate poem from verses 26–27. On one reading of 2 Sam 1:19–27, it is all one poem, with verses 19–25 being the public voice of the speaker and verses 26–27 a distinctive private voice. In another reading, verses 19–25 originated as an anonymous postbattle lament, re-recorded with the addition of verses 26–27 as a personal commemoration attributed to David. In this second reading, verses 19–25 would fall in the category of postbattle lament and verses 26–27 then would fall in the category of later postbattle commemoration.

---

20. See the probing discussion on this score by Brenner and van Dijk-Hemmes, *On Gendering Texts*, 1–42; and the discussion below for further suggestions in this vein. Such women poets may be analogous to what Jeremy M. Downes has called "the female Homer." See Jeremy M. Downes, *The Female Homer: An Exploration of Women's Epic Poetry* (Newark: University of Delaware Press, 2010). Note also his emphasis (102–19) on the production of oral epic by women; cf. the comparative study of Yiqun Zhou, *Festivals, Feasts, and Gender Relations in Ancient China and Greece* (New York: Cambridge University Press, 2010), 267–320 on "What Women Sang Of." Women singers later in Israel are also known. Second Chronicles 35:25 mentions Jeremiah's laments for Josiah and those of the male and female singers. Neo-Assyrian records include women singers sent from Judah by Hezekiah as part of his tribute. See Sherry Lou Macgregor, *Beyond Hearth and Home: Women in the Public Sphere in Neo-Assyrian Society* (SAAS 21; Publications of the Finnish Assyriological Research 5; Helsinki: Neo-Assyrian Text Corpus Project, 2012), 29–54, esp. 30.

3. Commemoration in Judges 5

The first-person lines in Judg 5 tend to be treated cursorily by some commentators, but given their number, they should be taken seriously. There are five first-person representations, in verses 3, 9a, 13b, 15, and 21b. This poem is hardly alone in having such first-person references (compare the first-person references in Gen 49:3, 6, 9, 18; Exod 15:1–2), but of all the so-called old poetry rendered in the third person (compare the first-person poems of Num 23–24), Judg 5 contains more than any other.

The first-person references in Judg 5 would appear to correspond thematically to its division-units, with each of the first-person references dramatizing the theme in each of these subunits. The poem's initial first-person reference in verse 3 declares the wish to sing to Yhwh, and verses 2–5 concern Yhwh's power. The wish expressed informs the whole poem, and it stresses Yhwh as the party ultimately responsible for the battle's positive outcomes. The next first-person reference, in verse 9a, states the first-person concern ("my heart"[21]) for the leaders of Israel, and verses 6–9 discuss human leadership. The third, in verse 13b, if not textually suspect, anticipates battle in the calls to song in verses 10–13. The fourth, in verse 15, shows the speaker referring to "my princes" (or "chiefs," so NJPS) as they go into battle. The fifth and final first-person reference in verse 21b, again if not textually suspect,[22] offers a command to the speaker's own self

---

21. For a defense of the MT against emendations, see Robert H. O'Connell, *The Rhetoric of the Book of Judges* (Leiden: Brill, 1996), 464.

22. Verse 21b is difficult. Christoph Levin ("Das Alter des Deboralieds," in *Fortschreibungen: Gesammelte Studien zum Alten Testament*, by Christoph Levin [BZAW 316; Berlin: Walter de Gruyter, 2003], 129 n. 30) regards it as "unverständlich" and emends the root of the verb from **drk* to **brk*. This would work with the two occurrences of **brk* in v. 24 especially if the composer builds his first-person expressions from the material that he then recounts. At the same time, such "building" might still work with **drk* if we may regard the proximity of the two roots as "sonant parallelism" (see the account by Adele Berlin, *The Dynamics of Biblical Parallelism* [Bloomington: Indiana University Press, 1985]). Moreover, there is no particular text-critical support for this emendation. The Greek versions favor "may you my strong soul trample" or the like. For the Greek versions, see Paul Harlé (with the collaboration of Thérèse Roqueplo), *La Bible d'Alexandrie: Les Juges* (Paris: Cerf, 1999), 126. It is the syntax of the final noun that may seem problematic, and it may be adverbial, a feature that the Greek versions might not represent. In either case, one may retain the root as is, and translate, "may you, my soul, march in strength" or the like. For this language of strength, perhaps compare Job 41:14a [E 22a]: "Strength (*'ōz*) dwells (*yālîn*) on his neck." For

to march imaginatively at the battle:[23] "My very self marches in power."[24] An emendation of verse 21b would eliminate what may be the point of the first-person reference.

This first-person voice fills out a picture of the singer voice announced first in verse 3. The poet moves on from this verse, purporting to be with the human leaders in verse 9, acknowledging their victory in verse 13, referring to the heads as "mine" in verse 15, and calling on the first-person self to participate in the battle victory in verse 21. This is a kind of participation in the narrated past. The first-person lines rhetorically foreground the represented singer's excitement for the past events, arguably designed to similarly move the audience. What the first-person references accomplish is to express the imaginative participation of the composer in the battle, and by implication, to induce the audience to do likewise.[25] The second-person addresses (in vv. 4, 7, 12, 14, and 16)[26] likewise contribute to this imagined relationship between the "singer-I" and the divine and human figures addressed in the poem. In view of the command to Deborah to sing in verse 12, the first-person "I-voice" was likely not hers originally, but belonged to an unnamed singer who sought to imitate what was thought to have been Deborah's role as a singer in battle as marked in this verse. The participation of the "I-voice" extends not only to being with the leaders and participating imaginatively in the events of battle, but also in imitating Deborah's role as singer.[27]

---

discussion of the verse, see Frank Moore Cross Jr., "Ugaritic DB'AT and Hebrew Cognates," *VT* 2 (1952): 162–63.

23. According to Peter C. Craigie, this line is a war cry. See Peter C. Craigie, "The Song of Deborah and the Epic of Tukulti-Ninurta," *JBL* 88 (1969): 257. The question is, in context, whose cry would this be?

24. This essentially follows Baruch A. Levine's translation (*Numbers 21–36: A New Translation with Introduction and Commentary* [AB; New York: Doubleday, 2000], 200): "My body marches powerfully." For ʿz in conflict, see Baal and Mot in KTU 1.6 VI 16–20.

25. Some of these usages as well as their representation as "spontaneous response to the victory" are noted by Yaira Amit, *The Book of Judges: The Art of Editing* (trans. J. Chipman; BInS 38; Leiden: Brill, 1999), 219.

26. Cf. the second-person addresses made in the *Iliad*, for example to Patroklos in 16.843, discussed by Deborah Beck, *Homeric Conversation* (Washington, D.C.: Center for Hellenic Studies, Trustees for Harvard University, 2005), 181–82.

27. For this notion, see the comments of Guy Debord, *The Society of Spectacle* (New York: Zone, 1994), no. 61, cited in Adam T. Smith, "Representational Aesthetics and Political Subjectivity: The Spectacular in Urartian Images of Performance," in

In this reading, the singer of the poem as presently constructed identifies her or his anonymous singing role in the persona of Deborah. In a sense, she is represented somewhat like the Muse of the *Odyssey*, characterized by Ralph Hexter as the "repository of the community's memory and the acknowledged source of the bard's song, the guarantee that *The Odyssey* draws on and transmits communal truth. The Muse represents sung tradition itself and guides the epic singer in the right paths as he chooses elements from the vast ocean of memory and song."[28] Deborah, too, is a model for the unnamed composer of Judg 5; she is the model of communal memory about this primordial, foundational conflict, and her example inspires the composer in his choice of the varied elements of Judg 5. Like Deborah in verse 7, the Muse is addressed in the second-person by an explicit first-person voice (*Odyssey* 1.1).[29]

The first-person voice in Judg 5 might be called the represented "singer 'I,'" as this singing is the stated intent of verse 3. Initially, in verse 3 this "I" sings or at least represents the self as a singer. This is the "I" of what Peter Machinist calls the "epic poet-reciter" of archaic Greek and ancient Near Eastern cultures, or what Susan Niditch calls "the epic-bardic voice."[30] What may be called the epic "I" voice of the *Iliad* (e.g., in 2.484–493, 761; 11.218; 12.176) noted by Gregory Nagy[31] is a comparable first-person voice in the poetic piece, in Judg 5:3, 9, 13 (if not to be emended), 15, and 21.[32]

Archaeology of Performance: Theaters of Power, Community, and Politics (ed. Takeski Inomata and Lawrence S. Coben; Lanham, Md.: AltaMira, 2006), 111. It is often assumed that Deborah is the singer of the song as a whole. Furthermore, it is viewed as an example of a woman's victory song, expressing a number of women's concerns and perspective. For this approach, see Fokkelien van Dijk-Hemmes in Brenner and van Dijk-Hemmes, *On Gendering Texts*, 32–34.

28. Ralph Hexter, *A Guide to the Odyssey: A Commentary on the English Translation of Robert Fitzgerald* (New York: Vintage Books, 1993), lxvii.

29. For this aspect of *Iliad* 1.1, see Gregory Nagy, "Ellipsis in Homer," in *Written Voices, Spoken Signs: Tradition, Performance and the Epic Text* (ed. Egbert Baker and Ahuvia Kahane; Cambridge: Harvard University Press, 1997), 188.

30. Peter Machinist, "The Voice of the Historian in the Ancient Near East and Mediterranean World," *Int* 57/2 (2003): 117–37, esp. 120–21, 126, and 131–36; and Susan Niditch, *Judges: A Commentary* (OTL; Louisville: Westminster John Knox, 2008), 9–10 and 77–78. Note also Susan Niditch, *War in the Hebrew Bible: A Study of the Ethics of Violence* (New York: Oxford University Press, 1993), 90–105.

31. Nagy, "Ellipsis in Homer," 186–89.

32. For this commonly overlooked "I"-voice in Judg 5, see Mark S. Smith, "What Is Prologue Is Past: Composing Israelite Identity in Judges 5," in *Thus Says the Lord:*

Similarly, second-person address appears in Judg 5:10, 12, 16, and in *Iliad* 4.127, 146; 7.104; 13.603; 17.679, 702; 23.600 (addressed to Menelaus), and in 16.20, 584, 692–693, 744, 754, 787, 812, 843 (addressed to Patroklos).[33] In addition, rhetorical questions (for example, Judg 5:8b, 16–17; *Iliad* 8.273-274) seem pertinent to the sort of voice in these texts. The general thrust of these observations may suggest that the poet-reciter as a represented voice is not entirely masking another identity, but "adding" one.

With this broad sense of the first-person voice in the older poetic tradition, we may turn to its attestations in Judg 5 and ask what the representations of the "I-voice" "sound like" in this poem. At its most expansive in verse, the "I-voice" relates specifically to an imagined royal audience:

Hear, O kings, Listen, O rulers,
I, to Yhwh, may I sing,
May I intone to Yhwh, the God of Israel.

This verse expresses a devotion to a vision of Yhwh as the national god of Israel addressed to the kings and rulers. As possibly suggested by this verse as well as other features of the poem, the "singer-I" is a representation by a tenth century composer-singer creatively participating in the Iron I events with reference to the recalled site of the battle. Such a creative voice is operating in a context where an address to king and rulers might make sense.

Yet in what way would one call this ritual or ritualistic? While perhaps not ritualistic in a traditional religious sense, it is arguably a sort of political ritual that uses pieces of the past for its audience to participate in and thus to be literally "in-formed". Again to return to Thomas Greene's comment on lament, even Judg 5 contains pieces of a heroic, but arguably insufficiently political, past to help to create a community of those who should see the need for king and country. In sum, some of the variegated material of the core of Judg 5:14–30 may go back to an old postbattle tradition, but this poem's introduction in verses 2–13 as well as some material

---

Essays on the Former and Latter Prophets in Honor of Robert R. Wilson (ed. John J. Ahn and Stephen L. Cook; LHBOTS 502; New York: T&T Clark, 2009), 43–58.

33. Noted by Seth Benardete and Ronna Burger, *Achilles and Hector: The Homeric Hero* (Southbend: St. Augustine's, 2005), 80, 108–109. Is second-person address showing a particular sympathy for the tragedy of these two figures?

within the core of the poem, such as the "I"-voice, seems to represent a commemorative act.

4. Song as Postbattle Ritual in 2 Samuel 1:19–27

For this phase of postbattle practices, song is a central act. It might be thought that David's lament in 2 Sam 1:19–27 is to be assigned to the phase of relatively immediate postbattle lament. While David's lament draws on the tradition of postbattle lament, I suggest the possibility that the poem reflects two parts: the first is the chiastically arranged verses 19–25, which may belong to the immediate postbattle phase; the second is a coda, or better, a reprise in verses 26–27, that is possibly to be seen as a later commemoration. Before beginning with this poem, I should note that it is not my view that "stable meanings and static models of performance"[34] are to be assumed across such celebrations and lamentation. I rather suggest that song or laments following battle would hold political ramifications and messages, and these would inform the content of such singing performance. With this as backdrop, I would like to make some remarks on the poem of 2 Sam 1.

The speaker seems to be represented as someone who is either a family member or not present at the battle. This particular lament is notable in a number of other respects. What stands out for many readers is verse 26, with its shift in voice and highly personal and charged expression. It does not offer an evocative description as in verses 19–25, and it is not addressed to a public audience. Rather, it is an invocation, a very personal one, addressed to one of the fallen, namely Jonathan. In context, it follows the public voice of verses 19–25, but it represents a private voice "overheard" (to echo Todd Linafelt).[35] This distinctive first-person voice comes to the fore only beginning in verse 26, using the phrase "to me" (*lî*) three times, along with the first-person suffix on "brother."[36] It is a personal lamenting voice (compare *ṣar lî* in 2 Sam 24:14 // 1 Chr 21:13;

---

34. Lawrence S. Coben and Takeski Inomata, "Behind the Scenes: Producing the Performance," in Inomata and Coben, *Archaeology of Performance*, 6.

35. Todd Linafelt, "Private Poetry and Public Eloquence in 2 Samuel 1:17–27: Hearing and Overhearing David's Lament for Jonathan and Saul," *JR* 88 (2008): 497–526.

36. Compare Prov 18:24: "there is a friend (lit., one who loves) who is closer (lit., clings more) than a brother." See Clifford, *Proverbs*, 169.

Pss 31:10, 59:17, 69:18; 102:3; Lam 1:20; see also Ps 66:14). It is reminiscent of Gilgamesh's first-person voice in his lament for Enkidu in SBV X.132–133//233–234 (compare SBV X.245–246): "my friend, whom I love so deeply, who with me went through every danger." The singular address to Jonathan is quite pronounced, with the second-person singular forms of various sorts used four times in this verse. This is a first-person singular voice locked in lament over a second-person singular intimate. Such singular devotion to Jonathan is what an audience might expect of David.

The personal voice of David in this poem also includes his famous gender marked line of verse 26: "O Jonathan, you were so lovely to me. / Wondrous (*npl'th*) was your love for me, / Greater than the love of women."[37] For this expression, I would note the analysis of Gilgamesh and Enkidu by Tikva Frymer-Kensky: "The gods' solution to Gilgamesh's arrogance indicates a cultural sense that the truest bonding possible is between two members of the same gender. The true equality that leads to great bonding is between male and male. The closeness of same-sex bonding holds true for females."[38] Susan Ackerman comments on the verse in similar terms: "I would interpret David's words in 2 Sam 1:26 to mean that David perceived Jonathan to have loved him in a way analogous to the sexual-emotional way in which a woman (Michal, say) would love a man and to imply that David returned that love, finding it to be something 'wonderful.'"[39]

---

37. For recent discussions, see Susan Ackerman, *When Heroes Love: The Ambiguity of Eros in the Stories of Gilgamesh and David* (New York: Columbia University Press, 2005); and the review of Jean-Fabrice Nardelli in *Bryn Mawr Classical Review* 2007.10.46; online: http:///ccat.sas.upenn.edu/bmcr/2007/2007-10-46.html. Nardelli has written his own book on the subject entitled *Homosexuality and Liminality in Gilgamesh and Samuel* (Amsterdam: Hakkert, 2007).

38. See Tikva Frymer-Kensky, *In the Wake of the Goddesses: Women, Culture, and the Biblical Transformation of Pagan Myth* (New York: Free, 1992), 30. As evidence of the latter, Frymer-Kensky also cites the figure of Saltu, a double of Ishtar, created to battle her and to curb her ferocity. For this text, see Benjamin R. Foster, "Ea and Saltu," in *Ancient Near Eastern Studies in Memory of J. J. Finkelstein* (ed. Maria de Jong Ellis; Hamden: Academy of Arts and Sciences, 1977), 79–84. For discussion, see Rivkah Harris, "Inanna-Ishtar as Paradox and Coincidence of Opposites," *HR* 30 (1991): 266–67.

39. Ackerman, *When Heroes Love*, 192. In the case of David and Jonathan, Ackerman goes on to suggest, "David and Jonathan were in fact imagined to be same-sex partners by the Samuel narratives" (p. 194). While this could be so, the broader question about the sexual relations among these male pairings lies largely beyond reach. Her characterization of this relationship as "sexual-emotional" is arguably enhanced

Somewhat like Achilles lamenting the dead Patroklos in *Iliad* 19 or Gilgamesh mourning Enkidu in SB tablet VIII, the represented David builds here on traditional formulary for his personal voice, vibrant with emotion for his fallen beloved.[40] This reuse may be seen in how the reprise with its "I-voice" in verses 26–27 echoes the lament of verses 19–25, with some rather brilliant turns. Perhaps most cleverly and certainly with powerful affective force, the term used for the comparison of "love," namely, "wonderful" (*npl'th*) brilliantly echoes the recurring expression of the heroes as "fallen" (**npl*). The roots **nʻm* and **'hb* in verse 26 echo their use in verse 23. The voice here personalizes what this lovely and beloved of verse 26 means personally to the speaker, "to me." This voice laments the one who has fallen as the most wonderful to the speaker. David's voice in verse 27 echoes the inclusion element, "how the mighty have fallen," in verses 19 and 25. Verse 27 closes the poem by recalling the perishing of the weapons that had been named in verses 21 and 22. The picture of the single man lamenting over Jonathan in verses 26–27 offers a rhetorical counterpart to the collective of women who would weep over Saul in verse 24. It also seems to offer a counterclaim to the representation of Saul and Jonathan in verses 19–25: whereas these verses represent the father and son as inseparable in life and death, verses 26–27 represent David as the figure no less—and arguably more—deeply tied to Jonathan.

These differences between verses 19–25 and verses 26–27 are striking. The most economical explanation for this shift is that verses 19–25 provide a more formal or public lament of David directed to the wider community, as suggested by the addressees in verses 20 and 24. With verse 26, the poetic David in a sense turns aside (compare Gen 42:24) and offers his own personal expression addressing the particular one of the two royals whom he loves. Thus the poem would represent both the public face of

---

by comparisons with Gilgamesh and Enkidu. Here Ackerman is drawing on Saul M. Olyan's article (in a prepublication version), "'Surpassing the Love of Women': Another Look at 2 Samuel 1:26 and the Relationship of David and Jonathan," in *Authorizing Marriage: Canon, Tradition, and Critique in the Blessing of Same-Sex Unions* (ed. Mark D. Jordan, Meghan T. Sweeney, and David M. Mellott; Princeton: Princeton University Press, 2006), 7–16.

40. See Ackerman, *When Heroes Love*, 189. Note also the acts of lamentation, including weeping, upon receiving the news, in 2 Sam 1:11–12. Cf. the figure of Odysseus weeping in *Odyssey* 8.499–534, as he hears the song of Demodocus recounting the story of the fall of Odysseus's comrades at Troy.

David along with his private moment of grief.[41] Both are voices that the figure permits, perhaps even desires, to have "heard" and "overheard."

There is another possibility that I would also like to consider. It is speculative, but it is one that I think deserves a hearing: it is only after an anonymous lament of verses 19–25 that David's represented voice begins.[42] Verse 26 shows a powerful shift in voice addressed to Jonathan alone, unlike the verses 19–25 devoted to both Saul and Jonathan. While this could represent a shift from a public voice to a private one, as I have entertained above, it is also possible that verses 26–27 may be the represented David's personal reprise[43] that was added to this poem (or was added by another poet in his voice or name) as received in the aftermath of the battle on the part of those who had fought in it, survived it, and sung it. Verses 19–25 may be a traditional lamentation pronounced earlier (compare the lament at the burial of fallen leaders in 2 Sam 3:32–34).[44] The additional reprise that I am entertaining for a represented David in verses 26–27 perhaps compares with Achilles' lament for Patroklos in *Iliad* 19.315–337.

---

41. This approach was suggested to me by Susan Niditch, in conjunction with other members of the Colloquium for Biblical Research, at the meeting held on August 15, 2010 at Princeton Theological Seminary. I am grateful to Professor Niditch.

42. Cf. Diana Vikander Edelman, "The Authenticity of 2 Sam 1, 26 in the Lament over Saul and Jonathan," *SJOT* 1 (1988): 73: "I would suggest that v. 26, and possibly also v. 27, represents a secondary expansion of the original lament over Saul and Jonathan that was quoted in the Book of Jashar." Edelman takes v. 26 as "probably to be a literary creation by the biblical writer responsible for shaping the Saulide narratives." At the same time, Edelman concedes: "it is not impossible that David could have written the lament himself." It is evident that the matter of authorship of v. 26, much less the entirety of vv. 19–27, remains rather speculative, but it does not eviscerate the literary observations that Edelman has noted.

43. This view is close to that of Hans J. Stoebe, *Das zweite Buch Samuelis* (Gütersloh: Gütersloher Verlagshaus, 1994), 96, discussed by Olyan, "Surpassing the Love of Women," 168 n. 15.

44. The voice of vv. 20 and 24 advises women in v. 20 that the news of vv. 21–23 is not be spread so that Philistine women not announce it for the pleasure of the Philistines. In v. 24 this voice counsels that Israel's daughters should weep for Saul, perhaps with these words. Had the poem not been attributed to David in the prose framework, one might hear in vv. 20 and 24 the voice of someone present at the battle, perhaps the voice of an unnamed lamenting warrior. The content of what is not to be told by women in v. 20, that is the object of the verbs of v. 20a, may be the content that follows in vv. 21–23; in v. 24, the verse corresponding to v. 20, the weeping of the daughters of Israel is perhaps to be accompanied by a repetition of the lament of vv. 21–23.

Achilles, like David, was not present when his comrade fell.[45] David was not there, while the voice of verses 19–25 sounds like someone who was.

This approach would solve a long-standing crux: the distribution of the so-called "refrain" in the poem.[46] As the poem stands, this "refrain" appears at verses 19, 25 and 27. Commentators have noted that refrains usually take place after sections, which are regularly rather well-balanced in length (e.g., Pss 42–43, with its refrain at 42:6, 12 and 43:5). While there is some variation in the use of refrains,[47] they exhibit "a highly developed sense of symmetry."[48] Such refrains show nothing that approaches the alleged "refrain" at the opening of the poem in verse 19, or with the difference of length involving what would be stanzas in verses 20–24 and in verse 26. With the so-called "refrain" appearing in the opening verse, and with the lack of balance in the units that the alleged "refrain" would govern, the line "how the warriors have fallen" seems to be no refrain. Instead, in the reading that I am entertaining here, the instances in verses 19 and 25 would not be a "refrain," but an envelope or inclusion around the older lament, while the further use of the line in verse 27 serves to tie the highly personal reprise to Jonathan in verses 26–27 to the earlier poem of verses 19–25. Diana Vikander Edelman puts the point about verse 27 in this way: "In its present placement, it serves as an *inclusio* framing the expansion introduced in verse 26."[49] In this reading, Jonathan is evoked in verse 25c in a manner parallel to Saul in verse 19, providing a transition for David's first-person invocation of Jonathan in the following verse 26.

To summarize, 2 Sam 1:19–25 may reflect a traditional feature of warrior culture, namely the circulation of songs for its fallen warriors, to which oral alterations or additions might have been made as the songs circulated. The reprise in verses 26–27 may have been David's represented response in receiving the news of the death of the heroes as expressed in

---

45. See Andrew Dalby, *Rediscovering Homer: Inside the Origins of the Epic* (New York: W. W. Norton, 2006), 12. See also Achilles' speeches in *Iliad* 23.19–23, 43–53. Note also the poignant *Iliad* 23.54–107. Cf. *Iliad* 23.391 for the idea of the victorious warriors singing their victories as they return from battle.

46. The problem was noted by Cross and Freedman, *Studies*, 15; and Freedman, *Pottery, Poetry, and Prophecy*, 263.

47. See Paul R. Raabe, *Psalm Structures: A Study of Psalms with Refrains* (JSOTSup 104; Sheffield: Sheffield Academic Press, 1990), 164–66.

48. Ibid., 165, commenting on the refrains found in Pss 39, 42–43, 46, 49, 56, 57, 59, 67, 80, and 80.

49. Edelman, "The Authenticity of 2 Sam 1, 26," 74.

2 Sam 1:19–25. His own represented voice is added, perhaps as a claim to both his poetic talent[50] and his great attachment to one of the fallen heroes, not to mention the implicit claim to their succession. This reading of the poem and its context could work with a theory of different stages in its production and transmission: the poem produced in the aftermath of battle by an anonymous elegist; the poem's circulation more broadly; and its reception and expansion in the represented voice of David, whether on David's own part or on the part of later Davidic propaganda.[51] I could entertain the possibility that this poem is David's political propaganda, one that could include some of his own feelings. The political heart is complex, and even calculating political intention may be freighted with deep emotion. However, it is also possible that the "historical David" had nothing to do with this poem and that he never had the level of relationship with Jonathan that is represented in this poem and in some of the prose passages in 1 Samuel. All of this could well be understood as largely the creation of monarchic political propaganda, whether during David's own reign or during the reigns of the immediately subsequent Davidic dynasts.

What this discussion suggests is a series of stages in the development of the poem. Poetic commemoration in the case of this poem shows the use of traditional tropes, along with a number of departures from such conventional material. In other words, the traditional components of the lament in verses 19–25 serve the poem's basic scheme, which also goes beyond the traditional in verses 26–27. The emotional expression directed to the memory of Jonathan, especially in verse 26, builds on the traditional elements otherwise seen in the poem. This mode of poetic commemoration also seems to constitute an effective means to reach the intended audience of the wider Israelite society. The poem begins with well-known elements that would have resonated for an Israelite audience and then moves into the internal emotional world of the heroic speaker. Poetic commemoration serves not only to recall the past event and to make the audience feel its emotionally laden force, but also brings the audience into a new way of understanding this past event; it offers a revelation of the heart of its great

---

50. I have been struck by male poetic competitions reported in later cultures. See the discussion of Heikki Palva, review of Nadia G. Yaqub, *Pens, Swords, and the Springs of Art*, ZDPV 160 (2010): 185–88.

51. Cf. "Let the first one hear and te[ll it] to the later ones!" in "The Hunter," in Benjamin R. Foster, *Before the Muses: An Anthology of Akkadian Literature* (3rd ed.; Bethesda: CDL, 2005), 337.

hero. Within the larger narrative, the poem's act of commemoration marks a watershed in the representation of David, transformed from a successful warrior into a military leader who knows and feels devastating loss for himself and for Israel.

Largely oral in medium and legendary in character, the battle story in song is a product preserved not by hard historical memory. That such a heroic poem as 2 Sam 1:19–27 sounds legendary is not a flaw of history, but a fact of cultural reality. It should not be taken as a sign of historical absence or lack, but as a signal of the societal setting of old textual production. This heroic song may detail battle, yet in this case it focuses on legends of the warriors' fall; the effect is to dramatize loss, not simply to report facts. The poem's commemorative purpose is not limited to evoking and invoking fallen heroes. It also points to some aspects of this commemoration's wider dissemination in Israel. One of its purposes seems to be to place David in the larger warrior tradition of early Israelite warrior poetry. David's lament in 2 Sam 1 provides him with his place—and we may say, the final and concluding place—in the lineage of early Israelite heroes. We might say that this lament speaks over and against an earlier poem such as Judg 5, with its collective polities, politics, and personalities. On the literary level, the "epic struggle" is waged in early Israel's poetic tradition over the reputations of differing groups, polities, and personalities. The lament tells Israel that David is not simply some sort of latecomer to this heroic tradition. Its implicit claim is that he is much more: its best exemplar as well as the founder of the royal "Davidic" age. The person of David as represented so personally in this poem is more a "person" than any other figure in early Israelite poetry, and he is the most important person to emerge from the early era of Israel. Just as the final form of Judg 5 prepares its audiences for royal governance across tribal lines, the poem of 2 Sam 1 summons up communal identity for a post-Saulide "Israel," specifically with David and his line as its head. "David's" lament is a ritual instrument of public speech that serves to constitute its audience(s) as political subjects,[52] in other words as Israel and specifically as David's Israel.

---

52. For performed texts as political vehicles of public spectacle, see Coben and Inomata, "Behind the Scenes," 5. To be sure, we have no archaeological evidence for this spectacle in David's case.

Bibliography

Ackerman, Susan. "Otherworldly Music and the Other Sex." Pages 86–100 in *The 'Other' in Second Temple Judaism: Essays in Honor of John J. Collins*. Edited by Daniel C. Harlow, Karina Martin Hogan, Matthew Goff, and Joel S. Kaminsky. Grand Rapids: Eerdmans, 2011.

———. *When Heroes Love: The Ambiguity of Eros in the Stories of Gilgamesh and David*. New York: Columbia University Press, 2005.

Amit, Yaira. *The Book of Judges: The Art of Editing*. Translated by J. Chipman. BInS 38. Leiden: Brill, 1999.

Beck, Deborah. *Homeric Conversation*. Washington, D.C.: Center For Hellenic Studies, Trustees for Harvard University, 2005.

Benardete, Seth, and Ronna Burger. *Achilles and Hector: The Homeric Hero*. South Bend: St. Augustine's, 2005.

Berlin, Adele. *The Dynamics of Biblical Parallelism*. Bloomington: Indiana University Press, 1985.

Brenner, Athalya, and Fokkelien van Dijk-Hemmes. *On Gendering Texts: Female and Male Voices in the Hebrew Bible*. BInS 1. Leiden: Brill, 1996.

Burns, Rita J. *Has the Lord Spoken Only Through Moses? A Study of the Biblical Portrait of Miriam*. SBLDS 84. Atlanta: Scholars Press, 1987.

Carr, David McLain. *The Formation of the Hebrew Bible: A New Reconstruction*. New York: Oxford University Press, 2011.

Clifford, Richard J. *Proverbs: A Commentary*. OTL. Louisville: Westminster John Knox, 1999.

Coben, Lawrence S., and Takeski Inomata. "Behind the Scenes: Producing the Performance." Pages 3–10 in *Archaeology of Performance: Theaters of Power, Community, and Politics*. Edited by Takeski Inomata and Lawrence S. Coben. Lanham, Md.: AltaMira, 2006.

Craigie, Peter C. "The Song of Deborah and the Epic of Tukulti-Ninurta." *JBL* 88 (1969): 253–65.

Cross, Frank Moore, Jr. Preface to *Studies in Ancient Yahwistic Poetry*. By Frank Moore Cross Jr. and David Noel Freedman. 2nd ed. BRS. Grand Rapids: Eerdmans, 1997.

———. "The Song of Miriam." *JNES* 14 (1955): 237–50.

———. "Ugaritic DB'AT and Hebrew Cognates." *VT* 2 (1952): 162–63.

Cross, Frank Moore, Jr., and David Noel Freedman. *Studies in Ancient Yahwistic Poetry*. 2nd ed. BRS. Grand Rapids: Eerdmans, 1997.

Dalby, Andrew. *Rediscovering Homer: Inside the Origins of the Epic*. New York: W. W. Norton, 2006.

Debord, Guy. *The Society of Spectacle*. New York: Zone, 1994.
Downes, Jeremy M. *The Female Homer: An Exploration of Women's Epic Poetry*. Newark: University of Delaware Press, 2010.
Edelman, Diana Vikander. "The Authenticity of 2 Sam 1, 26 in the Lament over Saul and Jonathan." *SJOT* 1 (1988): 66–75.
Foster, Benjamin R. *Before the Muses: An Anthology of Akkadian Literature*. 3rd ed. Bethesda: CDL, 2005.
———. "Ea and Saltu." Pages 79–84 in *Ancient Near Eastern Studies in Memory of J. J. Finkelstein*. Edited by Maria de Jong Ellis. Hamden: Academy of Arts and Sciences, 1977.
Freedman, David Noel. "Early Israelite History in the Light of Early Hebrew Poetry." Pages 3–35 in *Unity and Diversity: Essays in the History, Literature, and Religion of the Ancient Near East*. Edited by Hans Goedicke and J. J. M. Roberts. Baltimore: Johns Hopkins University Press, 1975.
———. "Early Israelite Poetry and Historical Reconstructions." Pages 85–96 in *Symposia Celebrating the Seventy-Fifth Anniversary of the Founding of the American Schools of Oriental Research (1900–1975)*. Edited by Frank Moore Cross Jr. Cambridge: American Schools of Oriental Research, 1979.
———. *Pottery, Poetry and Prophecy: Collected Essays on Hebrew Poetry*. Winona Lake, Ind.: Eisenbrauns, 1980.
Frymer-Kensky, Tikva. *In the Wake of the Goddesses: Women, Culture, and the Biblical Transformation of Pagan Myth*. New York: Free, 1992.
Gordon, C. H. "Indo-European and Hebrew Epic." *ErIsr* 5 (1958): 10–15.
Greene, Thomas M. "The Natural Tears of Epic." Pages 189–95 in *Epic Traditions in the Contemporary World*. Edited by Margaret Beissinger, Jane Tylus, and Susanne Wofford. Berkeley: University of California, 1999.
Harlé, Paul, with the collaboration of Thérèse Roqueplo. *La Bible d'Alexandrie: Les Juges*. Paris: Cerf, 1999.
Harris, Rivkah. "Inanna-Ishtar as Paradox and Coincidence of Opposites." *HR* 30 (1991): 261–78.
Hexter, Ralph. *A Guide to the Odyssey: A Commentary on the English Translation of Robert Fitzgerald*. New York: Vintage Books, 1993.
Janzen, J. Gerald. "Song of Moses, Song of Miriam: Who is Seconding Whom?" *CBQ* 54 (1992): 211–20.
Kletter, Raz and Katri Saarelainen. "Judean Drummers." *ZDPV* 127 (2011): 11–28.

Levine, Baruch A. *Numbers 21–36: A New Translation with Introduction and Commentary.* AB. New York: Doubleday, 2000.

Levin, Christoph. "Das Alter des Deboraliedes." Page 124–41 in *Fortschreibungen: Gesammelte Studien zum Alten Testament.* By Christoph Levin. BZAW 316. Berlin: de Gruyter, 2003.

Linafelt, Todd. "Private Poetry and Public Eloquence in 2 Samuel 1:17–27: Hearing and Overhearing David's Lament for Jonathan and Saul." *JR* 88 (2008): 497–526.

Macgregor, Sherry Lou. *Beyond Hearth and Home: Women in the Public Sphere in Neo-Assyrian Society.* SAAS 21. Publications of the Finnish Assyriological Research 5. Helsinki: Neo-Assyrian Text Corpus Project, 2012.

Machinist, Peter. "The Voice of the Historian in the Ancient Near East and Mediterranean World." *Int* 57 (2003): 117–37.

Meyers, Carol L. "Miriam, Music, and Miracles." Pages 27–48 in *Mariam, the Magdalen, and the Mother.* Edited by Deirdre Good. Bloomington: Indiana University Press, 2005.

———. "Mother to Muse: An Archaeomusicological Study of Women's Performance in Israel." Pages 50–77 in *Recycling Biblical Figures: Papers Read at a NOSTER Colloquium in Amsterdam, 12–13 May 1997.* Edited by Athalya Brenner and Jan Willem van Henten. STAR 1. Leiden: Deo, 1999.

———. "Of Drums and Damsels: Women's Performance in Ancient Israel." *BA* 54 (1991): 16–27.

Moor, Johannes C. de. *The Rise of Yahwism: The Roots of Israelite Monotheism.* BETL 91. Leuven: Leuven University Press/Uitgeverij Peeters, 1990; rev. and enl. ed., 1997.

Moore, Megan Bishop, and Brad E. Kelle. *Biblical History and Israel's Past: The Changing Study of the Bible and History.* Grand Rapids: Eerdmans, 2011.

Nagy, Gregory. "Ellipsis in Homer." Pages 167–89 in *Written Voices, Spoken Signs: Tradition, Performance and the Epic Text.* Edited by Egbert Baker and Ahuvia Kahane. Cambridge: Harvard University Press, 1997.

Nardelli, Jean-Fabrice. *Bryn Mawr Classical Review* 2007.10.46. Online: http:///ccat.sas.upenn.edu/bmcr/2007/2007-10-46.html.

———. *Homosexuality and Liminality in Gilgamesh and Samuel.* Amsterdam: Hakkert, 2007.

Niditch, Susan. *Judges: A Commentary.* OTL. Louisville: Westminster John Knox, 2008.

———. *War in the Hebrew Bible: A Study of the Ethics of Violence.* New York: Oxford University Press, 1993.

O'Connell, Robert H. *The Rhetoric of the Book of Judges.* Leiden: Brill, 1996.

Olyan, Saul M. "'Surpassing the Love of Women': Another Look at 2 Samuel 1:26 and the Relationship of David and Jonathan." Pages 7–17 in *Authorizing Marriage: Canon, Tradition, and Critique in the Blessing of Same-Sex Unions.* Edited by Mark D. Jordan, Meghan T. Sweeney, and David M. Mellott. Princeton: Princeton University Press, 2006.

Palva, Heikki. Review of Nadia G. Yaqub, *Pens, Swords, and the Springs of Art. ZDPV* 160 (2010): 185–88.

Paz, Sarit. *Drums, Women, and Goddesses: Drumming and Gender in Iron Age II Israel.* OBO 232. Fribourg: Academic Press; Göttingen: Vandenhoeck & Ruprecht, 2007.

Poethig, Eunice B. "The Victory Song Tradition of the Women of Israel." PhD diss., Union Theological Seminary, 1985.

Raabe, Paul R. *Psalm Structures: A Study of Psalms with Refrains.* JSOTSup 104. Sheffield: Sheffield Academic Press, 1990.

Rofé, Alexander. *Introduction to the Literature of the Hebrew Bible.* JBS 9. Jerusalem: Simor, 2009.

Schmid, Konrad. *The Old Testament: A Literary History.* Translated by Linda M. Maloney. Minneapolis: Fortress, 2012.

Smith, Adam T. "Representational Aesthetics and Political Subjectivity: The Spectacular in Urartian Images of Performance." Pages 103–34 in *Archaeology of Performance: Theaters of Power, Community, and Politics.* Edited by Takeski Inomata and Lawrence S. Coben. Lanham, Md.: AltaMira, 2006.

Smith, Mark S. "What Is Prologue Is Past: Composing Israelite Identity in Judges 5." Pages 43–58 in *Thus Says the Lord: Essays on the Former and Latter Prophets in Honor of Robert R. Wilson.* Edited by John J. Ahn and Stephen L. Cook. LHBOTS 502. New York: T&T Clark, 2009.

———. *Poetic Heroes: Literary Commemorations of Warriors and Warrior Culture in the Early Biblical World.* Grand Rapids: Eerdmans, forthcoming.

Stoebe, Hans J. *Das zweite Buch Samuelis.* Gütersloh: Gütersloher Verlagshaus, 1994.

Trible, Phyllis. "Bringing Miriam Out of the Shadows." *BRev* 5.1 (1989): 14–34.

Wolters, A. "Proverbs XXXI 30–31 as Heroic Hymn: A Form-Critical Analysis." *VT* 38 (1988): 446–57.

Zhou, Yiqun. *Festivals, Feasts, and Gender Relations in Ancient China and Greece*. New York: Cambridge University Press, 2010.

A Messy Business: Ritual Violence after the War

Susan Niditch

Juxtaposing classical texts with the experiences of Vietnam War veterans suffering from PTSD, Jonathan Shay points to the many ways in which the traumatic violence of war follows soldiers home, extending beyond the combat even once the battles have concluded and normal life is expected to resume.[1] A number of biblical texts informed by patterns of ritual and often by ritual violence point to the realization among ancient Israelites that return to normalcy after the war is no easy journey and that the transition from war to peace is not automatic.

Several of the texts dealing with events after the war point back to unresolved issues stemming from ritual actions that precede and frame the fighting: the sacrifice of Jephthah's daughter resulting from her father's war vow (Judg 11); the taking of women for Benjamin made necessary by another sort of vow that is said to have preceded the fighting (Judg 21); the killing of Achan and his family due to Achan's breaking of the ban (Josh 7), a war vow; and the slaying of Agag by Samuel (1 Sam 15:33), again relating to the prophet's understanding of the vow of the ban that precedes the battle (v. 3). In each of these texts, acts of controlled sacrificial violence mark the exit from a particular war. Another set of texts more overtly reflects an effort to transition from the violence of combat to the state of peace. This transition as well, however, is not achieved without violence. In this set of texts we include Num 31:1–24, describing the elimination of young males and adult females among enemy prisoners, the transition from the uncleanness of war death to the cleanness of quotidian normalcy on the part of Israelite fighters, and the cleansing of inanimate spoil and virgin conquests who are allowed to live. Deuteronomy 21:10–14

---

1. *Achilles in Vietnam: Combat Trauma and the Undoing of Character* (New York: Scribner, 1995).

also discusses the transformation of female captives from the otherness of the enemy to the possibility of becoming receptacles for the reproduction of Israelites, a transformation marked by ritual action which the woman herself would have no doubt have experienced as a continuation of the violence of war. Finally, we look at Saul's actions in 1 Sam 14:31, a scene in which the king takes control of the way in which food is obtained from cattle captured from the enemy. In heroic fashion, the king establishes an altar and turns a wild melée of slaughtering and eating blood that would offend the deity into a sanctioned sacrificial act. Saul's action allows for the proper preparation and consumption of animal protein, turning a messy business after the war into a ritual participation in normalcy.

1. Vows Gone Awry

Describing vows in terms of obligations, reciprocity, and relationships, clinical psychologist H. J. Schlesinger explores the deeply human and social dimensions of vows and relates vows to a variety of cultural and social expectations.[2] Schlesinger's understanding of the webs of meaning implicit in taking a vow are relevant to the tale of Jephthah's daughter. One needs to take account not only of the ritual and sacrificial implications of the warrior's vow, but also of the way in which its imagined violent fulfillment brings closure to violence on mythological, psychological, and symbolic levels. The story justifies an actual form of social fissure, passage, and redefinition in the life cycle of fathers and daughters and in the formation and evolution of social groups.

Jephthah's war vow to the deity promising sacrifice for success in battle is framed in formulaic language found also in Num 21:2–3: And [name of vower] vowed a vow to Yhwh: "If you will indeed give [enemy's name] into my hands, then I will [terminology for sacrifice]." A reciprocal relationship between warriors and the deity is marked by obligation on each side.

In Num 21:2–3 and other examples of the war ideology of the ban, including the Mesha Inscription in which the Moabite king has promised enemies as a sacrifice to Chemosh,[3] the sacrifice is the killing that takes place in the heat of battle itself. I have argued that the sacralization

---

2. H. J. Schlesinger, *Promises, Oaths, and Vows: On the Psychology of Promising* (New York: The Analytic Press, 2008).

3. See Andrew Dearman, ed., *Studies in the Mesha Inscription and Moab* (SBLABS 2; Atlanta: Scholars Press, 1989).

of killing in war, the very completeness of destruction enjoined, and the language of ritual sacrifice used to justify and frame the destruction are ways of making sense of all the killing, of reducing guilt and a sense of personal responsibility for the violent death of other human beings.[4] The ideology that considers the killing in war to be a devotion to destruction, vowed to the deity, makes the slaughter a necessity, for the dead are promised to a god. Soldiers need not choose whom to kill and whom to spare. How this ideology informed the actual prosecution of wars in ancient Israel is a complex and difficult-to-answer question. In the imaginings of biblical writers and the ways in which religious texts reveal, in Geertz's terms, "a cultural system,"[5] the vow to enact ritual violence is fulfilled in battle. Jephtah's vow, however, involves an action after the war: devoting to destruction the first thing he sees upon his victorious return, after his returning in "shalom," in peace and fullness. His daughter, his only child, greets him in joy with timbrels, as the audience expects because of traditional social and narrative patterns. The scene induces intense pathos precisely because the revelation that she is lost follows the warring violence, once the hero returns in shalom. The sacrifice, a consequence of the war vow, is a controlled, promised violent ritual act that ends the violence.

In narrating the fulfillment of Jephthah's war vow, this value-rich myth shapes cultural identity and symbolically encapsulates cultural anxieties. A variety of mediations hold in tandem critical oppositions that define both cosmology and social structure in ancient Israel: human and divine; male and female; peace and war; life and death. The classic study of Hubert and Mauss explores the ways in which anthropologists have approached sacrifice in terms of gift-giving that achieves mediation.[6] Various relationships are highlighted explicitly or implicitly in this process of exchange and mediation: that between Yhwh and Jephtah, that between fathers and daughters, and that between husbands and wives.

Marking the end of war, itself an enactment of ritual violence, with an additional act of ritual violence actually points, as Peggy L. Day has

---

4. Susan Niditch, *War in the Hebrew Bible: A Study in the Ethics of Violence* (New York: Oxford University Press, 1993), 28–55.

5. Clifford Geertz, *The Interpretation of Cultures: Selected Essays* (New York: Basic Books, 1973), 112.

6. Henri Hubert and Marcel Mauss, *Sacrifice: Its Nature and Function* (trans. W. D. Hall; Chicago: University of Chicago Press, 1968), 2–3, 97.

suggested,[7] to marriage, a form of social transformation that like combat itself is fraught with anxiety, fissure, and reconstitution. These nuances are made clear in the description of the yearly ritual for women, following Jephthah's realization that he has unwittingly promised his own daughter to the deity. Women are the ultimate sacrifices, mediating relationships between men. The activities undertaken by Jephthah's daughter and her cohort of young women effect a rite of passage from a state of unattached youth when the woman lives among her own immediate kin, the daughter of her father, to the marriage with a man from another family, in which she will undertake the life-threatening role of procreator. She links the two groups and creates social cohesion. The mourning of their virginity, their stint in the mountains away from the cultural contours of the village, and the shared condition and status of the young woman all point to a life passage. The break with the father is a kind of rupture, the giving of the woman a sacrificial gift on her father's part to another male. A new family and relationship is formed between the wife and husband that links social groups. The imagining of actual slaughter and the male recipient as the deity underscores symbolically the emotion and the pathos of the ordinary real-world trade in daughters.

As Gayle Rubin has noted, social relationships between men are mediated through the exchange of women.[8] Rubin explores and interprets social and economic theories of Marx and Engels, ideas concerning kinship developed by Claude Lévi-Strauss, and psychoanalytical models proposed by Freud to examine ways in which the exchange of women has been seen as fundamental to the origins and development of human society. In its mythological context in Judg 11, the exchange has sacrificial nuances, suggesting ways in which notions about the primeval transfer of women from one group of men or one male to another relates to the ideas of thinkers who see the origin of culture in other sorts of violence.[9]

---

7. Peggy L. Day, "From the Child Is Born the Woman," in *Gender and Difference in Ancient Israel* (ed. Peggy L. Day; Minneapolis: Fortress Press, 1989), 58–74.

8. Gayle Rubin, "The Traffic of Women: The Political Economy of Sex," in *Toward an Anthropology of Women* (ed. Rayna R. Reiter; New York: Monthly Review Press), 157–210.

9. See, for example, Walter Burkert's view on the role of violence in the formation of culture ("The Problem of Ritual Killing," in *Violent Origins: Walter Burkert, René Girard, and Jonathan Z. Smith on Ritual Killing and Culture Formation* [ed. Robert G. Hamerton-Kelly; Stanford, Calif.: Stanford University Press, 1987], 163); René Girard,

The exchange of women in actual societies hopefully makes for a peaceful relationship between participants, based upon an act of reciprocity, as is the case for participation in literal ritual sacrifice and the meal that often follows.[10] The tale of Jephthah's daughter is thus rich in nuances of sacred violence even though the woman's death is alluded to quite obliquely (Judg 11:39). This tale is not the only one in the Hebrew Bible in which a war vow relates to the violent taking of women. One begins to see that women and warring are integrally interrelated in men's imaginings of power, the balance of power, and the formation of societies. The treatment of women after the war frequently suggests patterns of ritual violence.

The taking of women, violence, and nuances of ritual sacrifice following the war are also exemplified by scenes in Judg 21. Here too a war vow has gone awry, and the relationship between men is mediated by the sacrifice of women. The immediate cause of the war is the rape and murder of a sojourning Levite's concubine by evildoers of the city of Gibeah in the tribe of Benjamin. The husband attempts to call up the Israelite league to exact vengeance upon the perpetrators by cutting the dead woman's corpse in pieces and sending them to the tribes. In a shocking way, the man appears to evoke a ritual act of calling allies to battle whereby an animal is sacrificed, divided, and sent, a process undertaken, for example, by the hero Saul in preparing to do battle with the threatening Ammonites (1 Sam 11:7). Benjaminites refuse to join the Israelites in rooting out the evil ones in their midst and instead protect their fellow tribesman (Judg 20:13). A vicious civil war ensues, a lengthy stalemate in which the advantage in battle goes back and forth until the Israelites finally win. The story that ends with the events narrated in Judg 21 is thus built of a series of violations and violent acts: the murder and rape of the woman; the sacrifice and distribution of her corpse; the deadly war itself; and the aftermath concerning the taking of women by irregular means.

After the war, we learn that the men of Israel had made a vow never again to give their daughters in marriage to the men of Benjamin (Judg 21:1). Given that women are the links between groups of men, this vow

---

Violence and the Sacred (trans. Patrick Gregory; Baltimore: Johns Hopkins University Press, 1977), 276.

10. On group cohesion and the sacrificial meal see Marcel Detienne, "Culinary Practices and the Spirit of Sacrifice," in *The Cuisine of Sacrifice among the Greeks* (ed. Marcel Detienne and Jean-Pierre Vernant; trans. Paula Wissing; Chicago: University of Chicago Press, 1989), 14.

promises an internal breach among Israelites, a permanent state of civil discord. The men of Israel regret their vow after the intense heat of battle has subsided, and seek to devise a way both to keep the vow and yet to recommence the giving of women in order to mend the fabric of Israelite society, one that includes Benjamin. The solution is found in the violent taking of women.

Both concluding tales about providing women for Benjamin after the war are framed by custom and obligation, again by vows, implicit or explicit. The men of Jabesh-Gilead are said to have broken an implicit vow to aid their fellow Israelites in war. The curse against Meroz in Judg 5 is a consequence of such a broken implicit promise in the context of war. Jabesh-Gilead thus becomes subject to the ban, group punishment, and revenge (21:8–12). As in Num 31 (to be discussed below), the virgin daughters are spared as women-gifts for Benjamin, and still, the number of women does not suffice. A second solution is to steal young women at the yearly festival of Shiloh when they come out to dance as is their custom, with the tacit but nonformalized permission of their male kin (21:16–23). In this way, the vow concerning Benjamin is not broken, and social healing can begin. The men's healing, of course, in both scenes involves acts of violence, the killing of the men, adult women, and male children of Jabesh-Gilead, the forcible taking of their virgin girls, and the kidnapping of young women who dance at the festival of Shiloh.

It is possible that Judg 21:19–23 reflects an ancient ritual for obtaining wives as 11:29–40 reflects an ancient ritual marking the giving of daughters in marriage. Vows, wars, violence, and the taking of women intermingle in complex webs of cultural meaning involving social continuities and discontinuities, and the fall and rise of social groups.

The tales of Judg 21 in the context of an epic war story point to the way in which war is mythologically associated with the making of a new order and how, after the war, the social world requires reconstitution. War always leaves loose ends: new enmities and resentments emerge due to the traumatic events of battle, the loss of fellow soldiers, and the collateral damage sustained by noncombatants dear to the fighters. There is also a need to make good on promises to those who helped in the war, divine or human. Reciprocity has its costs. The ultimate goal is reconciliation and finally leaving the war behind.

The sacrifice of the war-vowed daughter of Jephthah offers one such inclusio whereby a final act of violence ends the war. In Judg 21, the taking of virgin women from the extirpated men of Jabesh-Gilead and the stealing of the dancing young women at Shiloh provide means of dealing with issues in reciprocity and power relations, in reconciliation and vow-keeping. The enmity of the past is honored, but a new beginning in social relations is allowed. Nevertheless, this transformation and subsequent return to normalcy is made possible by acts of violence: the killing of all but the virgin girls of Jabesh-Gilead and the violent capture of women.

The killing of Achan and his family following the battle of Jericho (Josh 7:10–26) once again includes a war vow gone awry and a ritual process after the war leading to a final act of violence that can be understood in sacrificial terms. Achan has disobeyed terms of the ban, taking for himself some of the objects of Jericho devoted to destruction. As a result, the Israelites fail to succeed in their battle at Ai. A war vow has been broken and Achan, the miscreant, has been identified by divinatory means and confesses his guilt. A highly ritualized violence follows to rid the community of this now cancerous other. Not only Achan is viewed as infected but also his entire family and all that belongs to him. A kind of magic circle is formed by their consignment to the Valley of Achor where the people stone him with stones and burn them and stone them with stones. The language of the text as preserved in MT intensifies the violence with three references to killing and two verbs for stoning (7:25). The killing of Achan and his family might be seen both as scapegoating and as a form of purification. Defeat is blamed on the actions of an individual thereby explaining defeat, assuaging self-doubt, and avoiding inner tensions about the group's failure.[11] Achan's uncleanness, a result of stealing Yhwh's spoil, in turn attaches to those around him. All who are so tainted are to be eradicated in order to reset the relationship with the deity and end the crisis.

Agag's killing by Samuel is also framed by the war vow. Saul has been instructed by the prophet to impose the ban on Amalek, but keeps the best of the cattle for normal sacrificial purposes (1 Sam 15:15) and spares the enemy king Agag. Saul shows himself a pragmatist. Why not use captured animals for food protein and to enhance his own status, for power derives from the capacity to provide and distribute meat. Total burning offers no such practical benefits. A captured king allows for negotiation and ransom

---

11. Building on the work of Mary Douglas concerning pollution behaviors and the creation of "symbolic boundaries," sociologist of religion Meredith B. McGuire discusses socio-historical settings and cultural situations, perceived as threatening, insecure, and shifting, which are most conducive to scapegoating (*Lived Religion: Faith and Practice in Everyday Life* [New York: Oxford University Press, 2008], 41–43).

(as in 1 Kgs 20:32–34) or the status displayed in having a disabled enemy under your feet (for example, Judg 1:6–7). Samuel chastises Saul for ignoring the ban. The climax occurs when Samuel "cuts Agag in pieces before the Lord in Gilgal," an image which strongly suggests the ritual preparation of animals for sacrifice.[12]

Stories about the killing of Achan and Agag, in which an act of violence, ritually framed, occurs after the battle, point to the fraying of groups in the aftermath of war. When the war results in defeat as in the initial battle against Ai, there are recriminations. In the Achan episode, the accusation stems from notions about warring under the auspices of the war-vowed ban and is thereby sacralized and solemnized. The intragroup violence after the battle also points to the way in which fighting often leads to more violence inside the group after the battle. Initial unity often breaks down, and not only after defeat.

These ancient texts suggest that war corrupts and has the potential to corrode social groups, even in the midst of making and confirming the formation of new social realities. The acts of violence perhaps suggest efforts to impose, at least temporarily, a strict unity of purpose and worldview in order to prevent dissolution. While issues concerning the ban inform Samuel's treatment of Agag, at the background are ongoing political disputes: intergroup rivalry between Samuel and Saul and disagreements concerning forms of governance, the chieftaincy versus the monarchy. The argument about the disposition of Agag and his virtual sacrifice under the ban points to these heightened tensions, following the war.

2. The Passage from War: Violence in Peace

Acknowledging that war is a messy business and that the transition to peace is a rocky one, several biblical scenes describe ritual means of achieving this passage with emphases on rituals of purification and regularization of status. These rites of passage, however, are also characterized by violence.

Numbers 31:8 describes in brief the victorious battle waged against the kings of Midian who had hired Balaam to curse Israel in order to assure their defeat. Initially, the successful Israelites take as spoil all their enemies' women, children, animals, and wealth. The Israelites burn the towns in language reminiscent of the ban (31:10). Moses, however, tells

---

12. See Niditch, *War in the Hebrew Bible*, 62.

the people that their acts of destruction are not adequate to please the deity and to properly wreak vengeance on the Midianites. Instructions for acts of violence to follow the battle might be viewed as reflecting a postwar effort to define categories of "us" and "them," for the presence of prisoners presents a challenge in the aftermath of war, another messy situation that must be dealt with. How to integrate the enemy into a new order once peace has been declared is as problematical as the matter of reintegrating one's own soldiers into workaday roles, an issue that also will be addressed in Num 31:1–24.

A troubling aspect of violence following the war is Moses' order to kill all the male children and all women who have had sex with a man. The extensiveness of the killing suggests the war-view of the ban in which the enemy is to be destroyed in entirety, a promised sacrifice to the deity. In this case, however, the order to kill is a considered afterthought, apparently involving the extermination of prisoners rather than an act of bloodlust enjoined by the deity and an example of collective apoplexy during the war itself. We have described a variety of the ban that emphasizes the exacting of justice, from the perspective of the deity and the Deuteronomic-style writers who invoke his name.[13] The ban is thus not merely a vowed offering to the deity in recompense for victory as in the case of Jephthah discussed above, but a necessary act of purification, eradicating the evil in Israel's midst and the temptation to do evil. As the writer of Num 31:16 notes, Midianites, in particular Midianite women, were implicated in the apostasy at Baal Peor, tempting Israelite men to abandon their deity and break covenant (Num 25). And so, Midianite women who have "known a man" are to be killed, as are male children who presumably grow up to be warrior enemies. Neither young males nor adult women can somehow be integrated into the people Israel; they are marked, formed, and cursed by the identity of their elders or their mates, which in an embodied, physical sense seems to come from the existence of or sexual contact with males from the forbidden ethnic group. Virgin girls, however, are a clean slate and can become the mates of Israelite men, marked and bounded by their Israelite partner's identity. The young girls can become one of "us" as they are unstained by the male physical identity of "them." Thus, the imposition of the ban is peculiarly partial, the violence thoughtfully premeditated, the killing very much like Samuel's elimination of Agag, an act of sacred

---

13. Ibid., 56–77.

violence following the war. In the case of Num 31:1–24, the immediate social context involves doubts and tensions concerning group identity in the wake of conquest.

The completeness of ban ideologies, whether sacrificial or a matter of divine justice, allows the conquerors, at least in their imaginings of war, to deal with the disposition of defeated enemies in a way that does not compromise the identity of the winners. Absorption of the conquered or their continued existence may well lead not only to further physical threat but also to cultural threat, for the worldviews of conquerors and colonizers are always affected and altered by those of the colonized.[14] The authors of the banning threads in Hebrew Bible are acutely aware of threats to their own circumscribed sense of identity, and it is this tension that frames the violence following the battle with the Midianites. Complicating questions about identity and matters of authorship is the likelihood that Num 31 probably stems from those who are the military and political "losers" rather than "winners" in the background realities of actual ancient Near Eastern wars and conquests that are contemporary with the composition of Numbers. The text, probably no earlier than the Babylonian conquest, thus reflects a fear of losing cultural identity and independence that is probably rooted in subservience to ancient near Eastern superpowers. Nevertheless, the composers of this material can imagine the implications of being the conquering winners and explore what to do with their prisoners, a concern rooted in wish fulfillment and imposed on constructed memories of the national past. It is interesting that in the pericope that follows, the distribution of booty includes human spoil, and no distinction is made between men and women or between girls and adult women (31:40, 46; see also 31:11). The writer of verses 25–31 seems to be able to imagine the absorption of foreign conquests as useful commodities and does not seem to be concerned with the tainting and temptation that their presence implies.

Concerned with issues of purity and the unclean-rendering nature of death itself, the priestly writers of Num 31 also include instructions for the purification of soldiers after the war. This ritual transformation allows

---

14. On "syncretism" and "religious blending" see McGuire, *Lived Religion*, 188–90. On questions concerning the ability of a conquering group to absorb the conquered framed in terms of concrete ecological and physical criteria, see Andrew P. Vayda, "Primitive War," in *War: Studies from Psychology, Sociology, Anthropology* (eds. Leon Bramson and George W. Goethals; New York: Basic Books, 1968), 281–82.

for the transition to peace and, as is typical of Israelite rituals of purification, involves the sacrifice of animals, a form of controlled violence that in this case, after a war, marks the return to the everyday. The passage from unclean to clean, from death to everyday life, and from war to peace is achieved by the imposition of a time frame and a spatial separation; the soldiers are to stay outside the camp for seven days. All who have killed in battle or touch a corpse are to offer purification sacrifices on the prime-numbered third and seventh days. For the author, war itself is unclean-rendering because it involves contact with death. Not only must the fighters' persons be purified but objects taken in conquest also must be made pure by fire or water, depending upon their composition. In this way, soldiers can make a clear transition from a state of war to a state of peace and grapple ritually with the recognition that killing is not easy, that the death of enemies in battle is still a loss of human life, that many of one's own comrades will not return from the battle, and that a resumption of ordinary life after the war will not be easy. The emphasis at 31:50 on atonement via sacrificially offering to the deity valuable objects that have been taken as spoil is also an admission that war is an irregular, unclean-rendering activity that rips apart psyches and makes difficult the enjoyment of the simple daily pleasures of living.[15] Acts of atonement and purification by means of ritual offerings allow for a way back from war. The ancient texts thus admit of what we might call the trauma of war and offer a means of reparation and healing.

Another biblical instruction that grapples with issues of "us" versus "them" after the fighting and what to do with the human spoils of war is found in Deut 21:10–14. In contrast to Num 31:1–24, no explicit distinction is made between women at various life stages nor is the passage framed, even in part, by the ideology of the ban. War is treated as business as usual in the political life of groups, and in any such war, should a man see a woman prisoner of war who tempts him, he may take her as a wife. Women are thus the spoils of war, treated as one of the potential rewards of victory, valuable commodities over which wars are sometimes fought. Like Num 31:1–24, this passage points to postwar problems inherent in making the conquered "them" into members of "our" group, in this case the need to transition desirable captured woman from belonging to the

---

15. On the difficult passage from war to peace in classical Greek literature see David Konstan, "War and Reconciliation in Greek Literature," in *War and Peace in the Ancient World* (ed. Kurt A. Rauflaub; Oxford: Blackwell, 2007), 191–205.

defeated enemy to assuming roles as wives in the victorious group. Such transitions are fraught with anxiety, tension, and perhaps guilt. Ritual means are described to effect the necessary passage from them to us, and the symbolic actions that mark the alteration of the woman suggest fissure, violence, and sacrifice. The captors and the captives would no doubt experience this process of transition differently. For the men of Israel what occurs is a making whole whereas for the women it is a matter of separation and rupture.

The language and the acts imposed upon the captive woman are of shaving, paring, and removing—her hair, her nails, and her clothing. These ritual acts suggest transformation and separation, as Saul Olyan and I have both discussed in relation to the treatment of hair. Hair removal may serve as a sign of mourning, as part of the purification of the leper, or in the present case, a signal of shedding ethnicity to allow for social remaking in the eyes of her captors.[16] The person shaved is to make a new start, to achieve a change in status. The acts of cutting and removal imposed on the woman's body are signs not only of transformation, in some neutral or constructive sense, but from the captive's perspective acts of violence that ritually remove her identity. Joshua Berman has made similar observations about implications of Joseph's cosmetic preparations for his audience with Pharaoh.[17] Identity resides in the body, the hair, the nails, and the clothing. The woman is moreover expected to engage in ritual crying as she mourns for parents now deceased or physically and ethnically separated from her. As in the purification after battle in Num 31, locus and time length are also involved: she cries for lost mother and father for a month in her house. The circumscribed period of time and the physical sequester, like the severing of hair and nails and the removal of clothing, allows, from the captors' perspective, for her new persona as one of us versus one of them. That the Israelite authors are not entirely comfortable with the prescribed treatment of captive woman emerges both from the placement of this passage in context and from the final comment on the process.

---

16. Saul Olyan, "What Do Shaving Rites Accomplish and What Do They Signal in Biblical Ritual Contexts," *JBL* 117 (1998): 611–22; Susan Niditch, *"My Brother Esau Is a Hairy Man": Hair and Identity in Ancient Israel* (New York: Oxford University Press, 2008), 95–120.

17. Joshua Berman, "Identity Politics in the Burial of Jacob (Genesis 50:1–14)," *CBQ* 68 (2006): 14.

As anthropologists such as Mary Douglas and folklorists such as Barbara Kirshenblatt-Gimblett have emphasized in their work, all human beings try to make order out of the inherently chaotic nature of existence.[18] The authors of Deuteronomy have a particular orientation towards and a particular concept of order. Discussing holy war traditions in Deuteronomy, Norman Gottwald notes that they suit "a cultic conception" of Israel "as a single people sharply separated in religious practice from all the nations."[19] This emphasis on clear and strong self-definition, on putting a sacred circle around the true Israel, is reflected in exacting rules for clean versus unclean, in a theological emphasis on blessings and curses, in a clear demarcation between us versus them, and stems ultimately from a particular priestly orientation to life in the context of wars, threats of invasion, and conquest in the late eighth to sixth centuries B.C.E. Themes are about taking control, addressing pollution and ambiguity, and the wholeness of the covenant community. The complex of laws pertaining to the captured bride is found in a series of five seemingly unrelated sets of laws in Deut 21, but as noted by Calum Carmichael, these sets of laws in fact have much in common.[20]

All of the laws in Deut 21 deal with ambiguities that reflect or cause or result from social conflict, often conflict in the family itself. These messy situations are sources of individual and community guilt: the body found in the outback, an unsolved murder described in 21:1–9 which must be communally acknowledged, and the guilt arising from its presence must be openly expressed, although the perpetrator is unknown; the captured bride in 21:10–14 who is of the people but clearly not of the people, who is treated like a wife and yet, given the means of acquisition, clearly is not a typical wife; the situation in 21:15–17 in which preference for a second wife tempts the husband to ignore laws of primogeniture and show preference to the son of the preferred wife; the troubling case in 21:18–21 allowing for the slaying of one's own children; and in 21:22–23 the criminal execution of a human being whose body is nevertheless shown some respect after

---

18. Mary Douglas, *Purity and Danger: An Analysis of Concepts of Pollution and Taboo* (New York: Praeger, 1966), and Barbara Kirshenblatt-Gimblett, "Culture Shock and Narrative Creativity," in *Folklore in the Modern World* (ed. Richard M. Dorson; The Hague: Mouton, 1978), 109–22.

19. Norman Gottwald, "Holy War," *RevExp* 61 (1964): 303, 305.

20. Calum Carmichael, "A Common Element in Five Supposedly Disparate Laws," *VT* 29 (1979): 129–42.

death. These situations raise questions about fairness, justice, and the right thing to do when one's emotions may be in conflict with the legal tradition or when the law seems inadequate to resolve an issue or assuage guilt. Situations after a war produce just such conflicts and tensions, as noted in relations to various postwar situations discussed above. The ambivalence of Israelites in response to the issue of women captives of war emerges in the very language that concludes this little section of Deut 21.

If the woman does not please her captor/husband, he is free to end the arrangement, but he is instructed that he may not sell her into slavery because he has "abused her," the *piel* of the verb 'nh. The same terminology is applied to Sarah's treatment of Hagar (Gen 16:6), to the Egyptians' treatment of the Israelite slaves (Exod 1:11), to the rape of Dinah (Gen 34:2), and to Amnon's rape of Tamar (2 Sam 13:12, 14). Implicit are notions of oppression or, more specifically, forced sex. The very use of this language in Deut 21 suggests that all is not right with this means of obtaining a wife and again that after-wars are a messy business, requiring ritual action for cleanup and closure. The efforts to deal with such lose ends are fraught with moral ambiguities and never fully satisfying.

A final case study that points to the uneasy state of affairs after the war and the ways in which the transition to peace is achieved by controlled ritual violence is offered by 1 Sam 14, a story about Saul as epic hero. Once again a war vow is implicated in the aftermath of war in ancient Israel. Saul has taken an oath, pronouncing a curse upon any of his troops who eat before victory against the Philistines is achieved (1 Sam 14: 24, 28). Returning from their victorious battle, the famished soldiers fall upon the captured animal spoil, slaughter it hastily on the ground, and begin to eat "on the blood" or "with the blood." In other words, they do not adhere to proper slaughtering practices that release the blood, pouring it into the earth as ritually required to make the meat acceptable as food. Eating "with the blood" is expressly forbidden by the deity, for blood contains the life force and its consumption is the purview of Yhwh. As indicated by a range of biblical texts including Gen 9:3-4 a food prohibition set in the denouement of the flood myth, and a variety of priestly texts (Lev 17:10-14; 7:26-27; Deut 12:15-16; 23-24), meat is not to be consumed with the blood.[21] The ravenous soldiers of Saul thus risk angering the deity with a forbidden act of commensal apostasy.

---

21. For a full discussion of the blood prohibition with special reference to imag-

Upon hearing about the men's forbidden eating, Saul intervenes, obtains a large stone, and orders the men to slaughter the animals on the stone, presumably allowing the blood to run off in proper sacrificial fashion. He is said to build an altar there. The scene of wild uncontrolled consumption thus becomes one of proper sacrifice and eating; Saul himself becomes remembered for a heroic act, as an altar builder in the style of the ancient patriarchs.

Writing about the portrayal of Heracles by Euripides, David Konstan points out that the madness of war makes it impossible for the hero to turn off the violence: "Having tasted blood, it is difficult for him to calm down and be rational again."[22] On the one hand, the Israelites' behavior after the battle with the Philistines might be seen to be driven by hunger, but it also seems likely that the frenzy of war, the bloodletting, and the madness now evidences itself, after the battle is over, in their treatment of the animals captured, in a lust to consume meat with blood.

Stephen A. Geller's thoughtful observations on rules pertaining to the preparation of meat suggest that allowance to eat meat is a kind of "concession" in postflood contexts, an admission that human beings are in their very nature violent beings. He writes, "Perhaps there is a hint that by refraining from blood (= 'life') it is as if no life had been taken, a comforting fiction. Maybe there is an intimation that even through licit slaughter humanity incurs a degree of 'blood-guilt.'"[23] The portrayal of Saul's actions points to the border shared by various kinds of slaughter, in and out of war. Blood-spilling warriors become the uncontrolled eaters of blood after the war, and Saul's ritual actions help to bring them back to a form of bloodletting that allows for the consumption of meat and return to the ordinary. The bloodletting, however, need not have ended with the setting up of the altar. A subsequent episode 1 Sam 14, dealing further with loose ends stemming from Saul's oath of fasting before the war, grapples with tensions in worldview and points again to a messy business following the battle. This tale concerning Jonathan relates to various scenes discussed above concerning violence after the war and war vows gone awry, in particular, the tale of Achan.

---

ery in Zech 9, see Susan Niditch, "Good Blood, Bad Blood: Multivocality, Metonymy and Mediation in Zechariah 9," *VT* 61 (2011): 629–45.

22. Konstan, "War and Reconciliation," 193.

23. Stephen A. Geller, "Blood Cult: Toward a Literary Theology of the Priestly Work of the Pentateuch," *Proof* 12 (1992): 112–13.

The king's own son Jonathan has not heard (or paid attention to) his father's fasting battle oath, and eats a little honey before the victory, insisting that the energy allows him to succeed. When his father's inquiries to the deity concerning subsequent war plans are met with silence, the assumption is that some sin has been committed. As in the case of Achan, the perpetrator is located by divinatory means, but whereas Achan is dealt with by elimination—a scapegoat who is sacrificed with all his family—here the people protest and ransom Jonathan. Implicit are continuing tensions between the old war ways whereby war is often framed by ritual vows between men and between men and the deity versus a concept of war whose outcome still depends upon divine favor, but is also a more practical enterprise involving preparation and strategy.[24] Like the scene involving preparation of the animals for food, this scene, another unintended consequence of Saul's vow of fasting, offers a transition to peace that controls violence; indeed violence towards Jonathan is avoided altogether.

3. Conclusions

All the cases explored in this essay acknowledge and underline the difficulties of transitioning from war. In particular, war vows frequently lead to tensions after the battle, and resolution is made via various forms of controlled ritual violence: the sacrifice of Jephthah's daughter; the execution of Achan and Agag; the forcible taking of women for Benjamin. Numbers 21:1–24 and Deut 21 overtly grapple with the transition from the condition of war to a state of peace and achieve this transition through symbolically charged ritual means that include aspects of sacrifice, purification, and transformation. These passages deal not only with the transition of Israelite soldiers to peacetime but also, in particular, with captured objects and objectified human enemies, exploring how they are to be dealt with after the war, whether by elimination or absorption. Concerns with the reciprocity implicit in vows, group identity, and challenges to cultural self-definition inform the need to deal with these "loose ends" after the battle, but also point to guilt concerning the winners' success in war.

---

24. See Niditch, *War in the Hebrew Bible*, 123–32.

Bibliography

Berman, Joshua. "Identity Politics in the Burial of Jacob (Genesis 50:1–14)." *CBQ* 68 (2006): 11–31.
Burkert, Walter. "The Problem of Ritual Killing." Pages 149–76 in *Violent Origins: Walter Burkert, René Girard, and Jonathan Z. Smith on Ritual Killing and Culture Formation*. Edited by Robert G. Hamerton-Kelly. Stanford, Calif.: Stanford University Press, 1987.
Carmichael, Calum. "A Common Element in Five Supposedly Disparate Laws." *VT* 29 (1979): 129–42.
Day, Peggy L. "From the Child Is Born the Woman." Pages 58–74 in *Gender and Difference in Ancient Israel*. Edited by Peggy L. Day. Minneapolis: Fortress Press, 1989.
Dearman, Andrew, ed. *Studies in the Mesha Inscription and Moab*. SBLABS 2. Atlanta: Scholars Press, 1989.
Detienne, Marcel. "Culinary Practices and the Spirit of Sacrifice." Pages 3–22 in *The Cuisine of Sacrifice among the Greeks*. Edited by Marcel Detienne and Jean-Pierre Vernant. Translated by Paula Wissing. Chicago: University of Chicago Press, 1989.
Douglas, Mary. *Purity and Danger: An Analysis of Concepts of Pollution and Taboo*. New York: Praeger, 1966.
Geller, Stephen A. "Blood Cult: Toward a Literary Theology of the Priestly Work of the Pentateuch." *Proof* 12 (1992): 97–124.
Geertz, Clifford. *The Interpretation of Cultures: Selected Essays*. New York: Basic Books, 1973.
Girard, René. *Violence and the Sacred*. Translated by Patrick Gregory. Baltimore: Johns Hopkins University Press, 1977.
Gottwald, Norman. "Holy War." *RevExp* 61 (1964): 296–310.
Hubert, Henri, and Marcel Mauss. *Sacrifice: Its Nature and Function*. Translated by W. D. Hall. Chicago: University of Chicago Press, 1968.
Kirshenblatt-Gimblett, Barbara. "Culture Shock and Narrative Creativity." Pages 109–22 in *Folklore in the Modern World*. Edited by Richard M. Dorson. The Hague: Mouton, 1978.
Konstan, David. "War and Reconciliation in Greek Literature." Pages 191–205 in *War and Peace in the Ancient World*. Edited by Kurt A. Rauflaub. Oxford: Blackwell, 2007.
McGuire, Meredith B. *Lived Religion: Faith and Practice in Everyday Life*. New York: Oxford University Press, 2008.

Niditch, Susan. "Good Blood, Bad Blood: Multivocality, Metonymy and Mediation in Zechariah 9." *VT* 61 (2011): 629–45.

———. *"My Brother Esau Is a Hairy Man": Hair and Identity in Ancient Israel*. New York: Oxford University Press, 2008.

———. *War in the Hebrew Bible: A Study in the Ethics of Violence*. New York: Oxford University Press, 1993.

Olyan, Saul. "What Do Shaving Rites Accomplish and What Do They Signal in Biblical Ritual Contexts," *JBL* 117 (1998): 611–22.

Rubin, Gayle "The Traffic of Women: The Political Economy of Sex." Pages 157–210 in *Toward an Anthropology of Women*. Edited by Rayna R. Reiter. New York: Monthly Review Press.

Shay, Jonathan. *Achilles in Vietnam: Combat Trauma and the Undoing of Character*. New York: Scribner, 1995.

Schlesinger, H. J. *Promises, Oaths, and Vows. On the Psychology of Promising*. New York: The Analytic Press, 2008.

Vayda, Andrew P. "Primitive War," Pages 275–82 in *War: Studies from Psychology, Sociology, Anthropology*. Edited by Leon Bramson and George W. Goethals. New York: Basic Books, 1968.

Postwar Rituals of Return and Reintegration

Brad E. Kelle

"I wish I had been *untrained* afterward ... reintegrated and included. My regret is wasting the whole of my productive adult life as a lone wolf." — Jim Shelby, Vietnam veteran[1]

"There is a boot camp to prepare for war, but there is no boot camp to reintegrate veterans to civilian life. They were taught reflexive fire shooting, but not how to recover a shredded moral identity."[2]

1. Introduction

The effects of war upon returning soldiers have long been of interest, especially within modern, Western cultures. At one point during World War I, Sigmund Freud wrote: "[W]hen the frenzied conflict of this war shall have been decided, every one of the victorious will joyfully return to his home, his wife and his children, undelayed and undisturbed by any thought of the enemy he has slain either at close quarters or by distant weapons of destruction."[3] Freud was, of course, lamenting this potential outcome, expressing his fear that the civilized person's ethical sensitivity would be

---

1. Quoted in Jonathan Shay, *Odysseus in America: Combat Trauma and the Trials of Homecoming* (New York: Scribner, 2002), 1, emphasis original.

2. Rita Nakashima Brock and Gabriella Lettini, *Soul Repair: Recovering from Moral Injury after War* (Boston: Beacon, 2012), 42.

3. Sigmund Freud, "Thoughts for the Times on War and Death," quoted in Bernard J. Verkamp, *The Moral Treatment of Returning Warriors in Early Medieval and Modern Times* (2nd ed.; Scranton: University of Scranton Press, 2006), 143. In a similar vein, Immanuel Kant challenged the dignity of war by referencing an ancient Greek sentiment: "War is an evil inasmuch as it produces more wicked men than it takes away" (quoted in Zainab Bahrani, *Rituals of War: The Body and Violence in Mesopotamia* [New York: Zone Books, 2008], 131).

lost as a result of war's activities. In spite of the legacy of such expressions of concern, however, the academic study of warfare in the ancient world has not examined the aspect of postwar return and reintegration for warriors in any substantial way. Certain elements connected to the conclusion of military conflict, including rituals and symbolic practices, appear consistently throughout the historical sources.[4] Yet, the classic work by von Clausewitz, for instance, which set the agenda for much of the modern study of warfare, does not even mention the practices involved in the conclusion of hostilities.[5] Likewise, the classic study within biblical scholarship, Gerhard von Rad's *Holy War in Ancient Israel*, assumed that holy war arose out of a well-formed social/cultic community (the so-called amphictyony) to which warriors would have returned, but identified only rituals concerned with the preparation for and conduct of battle.[6]

The aim of this essay is to explore the possible indications of postwar rituals of return and reintegration within the Hebrew Bible. The goal is to offer something akin to a mapping survey. I seek to map the Hebrew Bible texts that likely present postwar rituals of return and reintegration and then to consider those texts against the backdrop of similar rituals from the ancient Near East and elsewhere. In a subsequent, but more tentative and suggestive move, I conclude with an interdisciplinary exploration of connections between these rituals and recent perspectives within contemporary warfare studies, psychology, and clinical literature that may illuminate the symbolic functions of the rituals. I will suggest that postwar rituals of return and reintegration in the Hebrew Bible and related contexts treat pragmatic issues but are not merely pragmatic: they construct a semiotics for the realities of war that serves particular symbolic functions related to what contemporary warfare studies describes as "moral injury."

---

4. E.g., Martin Van Creveld (*The Culture of War* [New York: Ballantine, 2008], 149) surveys the evidence for end of war practices from various historical periods and identifies four things that "must be done, though not necessarily in this order": (1) care for casualties; (2) distribute the spoils and prisoners; (3) celebrate victory with ceremonies to mark the transition from war to peace; and (4) reach a formal agreement to end hostilities.

5. Ibid., 149. See Carl von Clausewitz, *On War* (trans. O. J. Matthijs Jolles; The Modern Library of the World's Best Books; New York: The Modern Library, 1943).

6. See Gerhard von Rad, *Holy War in Ancient Israel* (trans. Marva J. Dawn; Eugene, Ore.: Wipf & Stock, 2000; orig. German 1951), 50–51.

2. Two Preliminary Considerations

There are two preliminary considerations for the inquiry undertaken in this essay. First, the task represents another attempt to broaden the scholarly study of warfare in ancient Israel and the Hebrew Bible beyond the category of so-called "holy war," "divine war," or "Yhwh war" that has so often dominated research.[7] While the precise definition of this category has been and remains the subject of ongoing debate,[8] at least since the work of von Rad, scholars have tried to identify an institution of "holy war" in ancient Israel that contained certain elements reflected in the biblical texts. Von Rad himself proposed that ancient Israelite warfare had a religious and cultic character, originating as a cultic institution of the amphictyony in the premonarchical period.[9] This initial formulation has, of course, undergone significant criticism and reformulations have moved toward broader definitions and different sociological and historical assumptions.[10]

---

7. For examples of recent general works on warfare and the Hebrew Bible that represent a variety of different approaches and perspectives, see T. R. Hobbs, *A Time for War: A Study of Warfare in the Old Testament* (Wilmington, Del.; Michael Glazier, 1989); Susan Niditch, *War in the Hebrew Bible: A Study in the Ethics of Violence* (New York: Oxford University Press, 1993); Tremper Longman III and Daniel G. Reid, *God Is a Warrior* (Studies in Old Testament Biblical Theology; Grand Rapids: Zondervan, 1995); Eckart Otto, *Krieg und Frieden in der Hebräischen Bibel und im Alten Orient: Aspekte für eine Friedensordnung in der Moderne* (Theologie und Frieden 18; Stuttgart: W. Kohlhammer, 1999); Cynthia R. Chapman, *The Gendered Language of Warfare in the Israelite-Assyrian Encounter* (HSM 62; Winona Lake, Ind.: Eisenbrauns, 2004); Brad E. Kelle and Frank Ritchel Ames, eds., *Writing and Reading War: Rhetoric, Gender, and Ethics in Biblical and Modern Contexts* (SBLSymS 42; Atlanta: Society of Biblical Literature, 2008); Bahrani, *Rituals of War*; Carly L. Crouch, *War and Ethics in the Ancient Near East: Military Violence in Light of Cosmology and History* (BZAW 407; Berlin: de Gruyter, 2009).

8. See the comprehensive discussion in Sa-Moon Kang, *Divine War in the Old Testament and the Ancient Near East* (BZAW 177; Berlin: de Gruyter, 1989).

9. Von Rad, *Holy War in Ancient Israel*, 23.

10. E.g., Rudolph Smend, *Yahweh War and Tribal Confederation: Reflections upon Israel's Earliest History* (trans. from 2nd ed. by Max Gray Rogers; Nashville: Abingdon, 1970); Peter C. Craigie, *The Problem of War in the Old Testament* (Grand Rapids: Eerdmans, 1978); Kang, *Divine War*; Niditch, *War in the Hebrew Bible*; John J. Collins, *Does the Bible Justify Violence?* (Facets; Minneapolis: Fortress, 2004).

What is of interest for the purposes of this essay is that the general notion of holy war/divine war has often functioned as a filter that focused the study of war in the Hebrew Bible on particular textual elements and sociological constructions and screened out certain aspects that might have otherwise been observed or emphasized. Although the concept of holy war connected warfare with religious and cultic dimensions and highlighted the importance of rituals in the practice of such war, there has been little, if any, interest in possible postbattle rituals and their significance. As noted above, von Rad assumed that holy war arose out of a well-formed social/cultic community (the amphictyony) to which warriors would have returned after battle, but he identified only rituals concerned with the preparation and conduct of the war. The militia was simply dismissed after the campaign had ended.[11] While some recent interpreters have included postbattle activities such as praise songs and the giving of plunder to Yhwh in the elements typically assigned to divine war in the Hebrew Bible,[12] the long-standing preoccupation with the concept of holy war has often led interpreters to cease the inquiry when the battle ends.[13]

A second preliminary consideration for the identification of postwar rituals of return and reintegration in the Hebrew Bible concerns the nature of the available sources. The biblical texts do not allow any comprehensive picture of postwar rituals within ancient Israel. The Hebrew Bible as a whole contains very few detailed accounts of military activity and even fewer explicit and reflective accounts of postwar rituals devoted to the subsequent status and actions of the warriors who fought in the conflict.[14] The texts that contain elements that are at least suggestive of rituals for return and reintegration appear in various books, with predictably high concentrations in the Pentateuch and Deuteronomistic History. They reflect different historical backgrounds, compositional histories, and

---

11. Von Rad identifies the main elements of holy war as the muster of the army, consecration, offering of sacrifices, proclamation and march, battle, utter annihilation of the enemy (חרם), and dismissal of the militia. See von Rad, *Holy War in Ancient Israel*, 50–51.

12. E.g., Longman and Reid, *God Is a Warrior*, 32–47.

13. See, for instance, the list of five common elements in the Hebrew Bible's Yhwh war stories enumerated by Peter Weimar ("Die Jahwekriegserzählungen in Exodus 14, Joshua 10, Richter 4 und 1 Samuel 7," *Bib* 57 [1976]: 38–73). These include no postwar rituals beyond the annihilation of the enemy. See discussion in Kang, *Divine War*, 4.

14. See Brad E. Kelle, *Ancient Israel at War 853–586 BC* (Essential Histories 67; Oxford: Osprey, 2007).

literary genres, with no explicit connections among them other than the shared subject of postbattle activities. As the following discussion will show, there is perhaps only one Hebrew Bible text that explicitly depicts ritual acts associated with the reintegration of warriors (Num 31:13–54). Even this text, however, does not provide any sustained reflection on the significance of the postbattle activities described or on what they might have meant to those who engaged in them. While the following analysis attempts to map the postwar rituals that appear in various biblical texts and consider them in their comparative social and cultural contexts, the nature of the available sources does not allow the formulation of a standard practice of postwar rituals, even for specifically defined time periods or traditions within ancient Israel and Judah.

3. Postwar Rituals of Return and Reintegration in the Hebrew Bible

Bearing the above considerations in mind, the following discussion seeks to identify and map postwar rituals of return and reintegration in the Hebrew Bible and invites reflection upon their significance from different interpretive perspectives. The presentation begs several questions regarding the precise definition of "ritual," including what counts as ritual behavior and how one identifies such behavior within Hebrew Bible texts. The effort to define ritual behavior remains vexed and different emic and etic formulations are possible.[15] We may assume that a number of routine activities such as the burial of the dead (e.g., 2 Sam 2:24–32; Ezek 39:11–12) occurred at the conclusion of battle, many of which likely go undescribed in biblical texts and may or may not have constituted ritual behavior. Nonetheless, the textual map given here will use the category of ritual in the most general sense—a set of prescribed or stylized actions performed for their symbolic function in certain contexts.

---

15. Saul M. Olyan, *Social Inequality in the World of the Text: The Significance of Ritual and Social Distinctions in the Hebrew Bible* (Journal of Ancient Judaism Supplements 4; Göttingen: Vandenhoeck & Ruprecht, 2011); Saul M. Olyan, *Rites and Rank: Hierarchy in Biblical Representations of Cult* (Princeton: Princeton University Press, 2000); James W. Watts, *Ritual and Rhetoric in Leviticus: From Sacrifice to Scripture* (Cambridge: Cambridge University Press, 2007); William K. Gilders, *Blood Ritual in the Hebrew Bible: Meaning and Power* (Baltimore: Johns Hopkins University Press, 2004).

The Hebrew Bible texts that are suggestive of postwar rituals of return and reintegration fall into five categories based on the actions that they describe, with some overlap among them:[16]

(1) Purification of Warriors, Captives, and Objects: Num 31:13–24

(2) Appropriation of Booty
  (2.1) Simple taking of booty: Deut 20:10–18; Josh 7:1; 8:24–29; 11:14; 1 Sam 14:31–35; 15:1–9; 23:1–5; 27:8–12; 2 Chr 28:8–15
  (2.2) Redistribution of booty among combatants, noncombatants, and sanctuaries: Gen 14:17–24; Num 31:25–47; Josh 6:24; 22:7–9; Judg 5:28–30; 1 Sam 5:1–8; 30:21–31; 2 Sam 8:9–12; 1 Chr 26:26–28; 2 Chr 15:11; Ps 68:11–14

(3) Construction of Memorials and Monuments: Exod 17:14–16; Num 31:48–54; Josh 6:24; 1 Sam 5:1–8; 31:8–10; 2 Sam 8:9–12; 1 Chr 18:7–8, 10–11; 26:26–28; Dan 1:1–2; 5:2–3

(4) Celebration or Procession: Exod 15:1–18, 20–21; 1 Sam 18:6–9; 2 Sam 19:1–8 (implied by opposite); 2 Chr 20:24–30; Esther 9:16–17; Ps 68:21–27; Isa 25:6

(5) Lament (usually corporate): 2 Sam 1:19–27; Pss 44; 60; 74; 79; 80; 89; Isa 14:3–20 (ironic); 15–16 (ironic); Jer 48 (ironic); Lam 5; Ezek 32:1–16 (ironic); Joel 1:2–2:17

The following discussion will highlight representative texts from each category to identify some of the central elements that appear across the depictions.

---

16. Two additional texts that relate to possibly recurring postbattle activities are Judg 9:45, which describes sowing the enemy's lands with salt, and Deut 7:1–11, which outlines the procedures for חרם. However, these texts do not deal directly with elements concerning the warriors themselves but focus on actions taken against the enemy or its territory.

3.1. Purification of Warriors, Captives, and Objects

The texts in the first category depict purification rites for returning warriors, captives, and objects. Numbers 31:13–24 is the only explicit example of this category within the Hebrew Bible. The larger unit of Num 31:13–54 is the most, and perhaps only, explicit depiction of postbattle rituals for returning warriors, and the unit as a whole devotes much more space to the postwar activities than to the battle itself, bringing together in unique ways several elements found individually elsewhere. The passage describes an encounter among Moses, Eleazar the priest, and Israelite warriors returning to the congregation at the camp in the plains of Moab after a victorious battle with the Midianites. Having slaughtered all the Midianite men, the returning warriors bring with them "the women of Midian and their little ones," as well as "their cattle, flocks, and all their goods as booty" (Num 31:9 NRSV). In this context, Moses's first instructions are to kill all the male children and nonvirgin women. In the following verses, the instructions turn to activities to be carried out by the warriors prior to their reintegration into the camp. The first section of these instructions (vv. 19–24) prescribes the ceremonial (and literal) purification (and washing) of the warriors, captives, and booty. Moses commands the returning warriors who killed a person or touched a corpse to remain outside the camp seven days, purify themselves and their captive virgin women on the third and seventh day, and purify the captured garments and articles. Eleazar then stipulates (vv. 21–24) that any nonflammable objects (gold, silver, bronze, iron, tin, lead)—presumably both booty and weapons—must be passed through the fire and perhaps also purified with water. Objects that cannot withstand fire are simply passed through the water. Additionally, the warriors must wash their clothes on the seventh day.

The actions depicted in Num 31:13–24 reflect the ideology and concerns of the Hebrew Bible's priestly tradition. The chapter has generated a large amount of commentary that tries to understand the postbattle prescriptions within the origin, development, and expressions of priestly notions of purity and impurity found in various pentateuchal texts.[17] The

---

17. E.g., George Buchanan Gray, *Numbers: A Critical and Exegetical Commentary* (ICC; Edinburgh: T&T Clark, 1903); Martin Noth, *Numbers* (OTL; Philadelphia: Westminster, 1968); Gordon J. Wenham, *Numbers* (TOTC 4; Downer's Grove, Ill.: InterVarsity Press, 1981); Philip J. Budd, *Numbers* (WBC 5; Waco, Tex.: Word, 1984);

traditional view since the time of Martin Noth, for instance, has been that the passage is one of the latest parts of the Pentateuch, perhaps even a later supplement to the Pentateuch as a whole.[18] Much more could be said about issues of compositional history, yet no other Hebrew Bible text contains this ritual prescription of postbattle purification or explicit examples of such purification taking place. Within the priestly tradition, the purification ritual here seems to depend most directly upon priestly laws concerning defilement caused by corpse contamination (especially Num 5:1–4 and 19:1–22).[19] The underlying conviction in these laws is that death defiles the person and the camp. Numbers 5 provides the initial statement that contact with a corpse defiles a person, and Num 19 stipulates the procedures for purification from corpse contamination with the red heifer ritual. In the latter, the priests involved in disposal of the red heifer must wash their clothes and bathe before returning to the camp (vv. 5–6), the one touching a human corpse is unclean for seven days and must wash on the third and seventh day (vv. 11–13), and one touching specifically a corpse that was "killed by a sword" in an open field is unclean for seven days (v. 16).[20] A possibly additional background text is the legislation con-

---

Timothy R. Ashley, *The Book of Numbers* (NICOT; Grand Rapids: Eerdmans, 1993); Thomas B. Dozeman, "Numbers," in *The New Interpreter's Bible* (12 vols.; Nashville: Abingdon, 1998), 2:1–268; W. H. Bellinger, Jr., *Leviticus, Numbers* (NIBCOT; Peabody: Hendrickson, 2001).

18. Noth, *Numbers*, 229; Gray, *Numbers*, 418–19. For other views, see Ashley, *The Book of Numbers*, 588.

19. See David P. Wright, "Purification from Corpse-Contamination in Numbers XXXI 19–24," *VT* 35 (1985): 213–23; David P. Wright, *The Disposal of Impurity: Elimination Rites in the Bible and in Hittite and Mesopotamian Literature* (SBLDS 101; Atlanta: Scholars Press, 1987), 169–72; Dozeman, "Numbers," 247. For other references to corpse defilement, see Num 6:6–12; 9:6–14; 31:13–24; Lev 10:4–5; 21:1–4, 10–12; 2 Kgs 23:16; Isa 65:4; Ezek 9:6; 39:11–16; 43:7–9; 44:25–27; Hag 2:10–19. Priestly laws concerning pollution through blood and bloodshed may also underlie the ritual in Num 31, although Hebrew Bible texts typically distinguish accidental killing and combat from the type of moral acts such as murder that constitute bloodshed. See Num 35:33; Ps 106:38–39; Isa 59:1–3; Jer 2:34; Lam 4:14.

20. Niditch (*War in the Hebrew Bible*, 87) observes that the corpse-contamination laws in Numbers differ from those found in Leviticus. Leviticus typically treats contact with a corpse or blood from a wound as ritually defiling only for priests (e.g., Lev 21:1–11). In Num 5:1–4, the priestly writer extends the defiling nature of corpse contact to all Israelites, and Num 19 develops the notion into a general principle that extends even to aliens in the community. For an analysis of the different biblical tra-

cerning the transition of a captive woman taken in battle in Deut 21:10–14. Before an Israelite can marry the woman, she must shave her head, cut her nails, change her clothing, and remain for a month in the man's house—all symbols of a new birth and transition into a new identity.

The ritual in Num 31 uniquely applies these background provisions to the practice of war and demands the purification of warriors who have killed someone, enemy captives, and even objects.[21] Perhaps the most noticeably unique aspect of the Numbers construction, however, is the way in which the priestly notion of warfare as a ritually defiling activity departs from the typical understandings within the Hebrew Bible's other war traditions. No other traditions make (at least explicitly) this connection between warfare and corpse contamination.[22] It seems likely that the underlying notion of death being the "utmost desacralization" is what leads to warfare being considered a defiling activity.[23] In the conceptions represented by biblical and extrabiblical texts, defilement most essentially represents estrangement from the divine presence and death constitutes the ultimate form of such separation.[24] Hence, often the determining factor of whether something causes defilement is whether it represents

---

ditions concerning corpse uncleanness, see Jacob Milgrom, "Studies in the Temple Scroll," *JBL* 97 (1978): 501–23.

21. With regard to the demand for the purification of the captive virgin women, Budd (*Numbers*, 334) proposes that the text is expanding the older law in Deut 21:10–14 concerning the transition of a captive woman from a distant city. Niditch's reading (*War in the Hebrew Bible*, 81–87) of Num 31 also focuses on the sparing of the virgin girls and compares the text with Deut 21:10–14. She claims that element reveals the priestly view of the world centered on biological purity of bloodlines.

22. For example, Niditch (*War in the Hebrew Bible*, 78–89) notes the particular contrast on this point between the priestly conception in Num 31 and the holy war or ban traditions in the Hebrew Bible. See also Roland de Vaux, *Ancient Israel* (McGraw-Hill Paperbacks; New York: McGraw-Hill, 1965), 461–62, which interprets the demand for purification in Num 31 as an indication that the warriors needed to desanctify themselves out of a state of holiness now that the battle was over.

23. Emanuel Feldman, *Biblical and Post-biblical Defilement and Mourning: Law as Theology* (New York: Yeshiva University Press, 1977), xix.

24. See E. N. Fallaize, "Purification, Introductory and Primitive," in volume 10 of *Encyclopedia of Religion and Ethics* (ed. James Hastings; 12 vols.; Edinburgh: T&T Clark, 1956), 455–66. Fallaize points out that the identification of death as the ultimate source of defilement is, at times, connected with the notion that postbattle purification rituals for warriors serve to protect the warrior from the ghosts or souls of those he killed (ibid., 457). For an older, general discussion of purification in the Hebrew Bible

death in some manner.[25] In the Priestly view of warfare represented by Num 31, war becomes defiling because it brings about direct contact with death by various means.[26]

3.2. Appropriation of Booty

The next section of the story in Num 31 (vv. 25–47) moves the narrative focus away from the purification of the warriors and onto the second category of postwar rituals listed above—the appropriation of booty after battle. Notwithstanding the uniqueness of the preceding purification ritual, several commentators have noted that the handling of the booty occupies the central place in the narrative as a whole.[27] In verses 25–47, the people are to divide the booty (presumably equally) between "the warriors who went out to battle" and "all the congregation" (v. 27 NRSV).

---

in the context of purification concepts and rituals in ancient cultures, see S. M. Cooke, "Purification (Hebrew)," in Hastings, *Encyclopedia of Religion and Ethics*, 10:489–90.

25. Feldman, *Biblical and Post-biblical Defilement and Mourning*, xix, 14. Feldman identifies defilement of the dead—caused by contact with corpses, carrion, or certain "creeping things"—as the first of three major categories of defilement within Hebrew Bible and rabbinical law (ibid., 31–32).

26. The text reflects the Priestly legislation as a whole, in which Israelites—even priests—are permitted to defile themselves via contact with a corpse on certain occasions after which specific restrictions are placed upon them (see Lev 21:1–6; Num 19:11–20). In addition to the stipulations to wash and remain outside the camp for seven days—which appear in rituals for nonwar corpse contact in the priestly texts (Num 5; 19)—the use of water as a purifying agent in the ritual in Num 31 appears widely in biblical and extrabiblical texts related to purification, although the use of fire in this text is unique. Wright ("Purification," 222) observes that Num 31 is the only place in the Hebrew Bible where fire is required for purification.

More recent interpreters (e.g., Niditch, *War in the Hebrew Bible*, 87–88) have turned their attention to possible ethical dimensions, proposing that the new elements found in Num 31 reveal a changed "ethical perception" in postmonarchic traditions that sees even killing in war as an abomination and expresses doubts about the practice of warfare itself. For Niditch, the purification part of the postwar ritual in Num 31:19–24 itself is enough to push readers toward "fascinating questions about the psychology and ethics of violence" similar to those explored in contemporary warfare studies (88). For a similar sentiment, Niditch cites Wenham, *Numbers*, 212.

27. E.g., Noth (*Numbers*, 231) calls the division of the booty in Num 31:25–47 an "essential element of the whole chapter" and Dozeman ("Numbers," 245) states, "Booty is the central concern underlying the rules and procedures for holy war in Numbers 31."

From the warriors' share, items are set aside as a levy to the priests and offering to Yhwh at the rate of one per five hundred, while from the congregation's share items are set aside for the Levites at the rate of one per fifty.[28] The background for the priestly legislation concerning booty is the general principle in Deut 20 that prohibits booty from cities within the land but allows women, children, and animals to be taken as plunder from distant cities. Similarly, Deut 21:10–14 allows for an Israelite to marry a woman taken as booty in war after she undergoes a makeover process signifying her transition to a new identity. Numbers 31 develops these principles by restricting the human booty to virgin women and including a levy for the priests.

Although the levy for the priests in Num 31 is unique in the Hebrew Bible, this practice of the redistribution of the spoils features prominently in various biblical and extrabiblical texts.[29] In fact, the postbattle activity of handling spoils dominates all others in Hebrew Bible texts. Many texts within this category simply report the taking of plunder by the victorious warriors and do not allude to any kind of ritual of return or reentry (e.g., Deut 20:14–15; Josh 8:24–29; 11:14; 1 Sam 14:31–35; 15:1–9; 23:1–5; 27:8–10; 2 Chr 28:8–15).[30] Other texts beyond Num 31, however, depict the postbattle practice of redistributing portions of the booty among the combatants and noncombatants upon the warriors' return.[31] First Samuel 30:21–25 provides the clearest example. Here, David redistributes the spoil from his victory against the Amalekites among the 400 men who went to battle and the 200 who stayed behind, specifically countering the objection that only the warriors should receive the spoil. He also sends other portions of the booty to his supporters among the elders of Judah. The deuteronomistic writer includes the claim that this practice became a "statute and an ordinance for Israel" that continued to the "present day" (v. 25

---

28. The booty described in this passage exceeds 800,000 animals and 16,750 shekels of gold (Dozeman, "Numbers," 245).

29. For priestly legislation concerning the priests' portion of offerings in nonwar contexts, see Num 7:1–89; 18:8–32; 28:1–31. For discussion of the levy given to the priests, see ibid., 247–48; Ashley, *The Book of Numbers*, 597; Budd, *Numbers*, 331.

30. Reports of the taking of plunder especially appear in the battle texts in Joshua and Judges. Perhaps because of the premonarchic literary setting of the stories, there are no significant rituals of warriors returning to their town, but the postbattle activities often involve booty.

31. See David Elgavish, "The Division of the Spoils of War in the Bible and in the Ancient Near East," *ZABR* 8 (2000): 242–73.

NRSV). Likewise, Gen 14:17–24 notes Abram's division of the remainder of the spoil after his gift to Melchizedek between the warriors and the king of Sodom. Joshua 22:7–9 instructs the tribal warriors from the Transjordan returning home after the conquest to share the booty with their kindred who had remained outside the land. Psalm 68:11–14 alludes to the women who remained home "among the sheepfolds" (v. 13) dividing the plunder captured from the defeated foe. In perhaps the most poetic depiction, the conclusion of Deborah's song in Judg 5:28–30 personifies Sisera's mother gazing out the window and imagining the victorious Canaanite warriors tarrying to divide their booty—human and otherwise.[32]

3.3. Construction of Memorials and Monuments

The third category of potentially postwar rituals of return and reintegration in the Hebrew Bible appears explicitly in the final portion of the story in Num 31 (vv. 48–54), with a few suggestive texts elsewhere—the practice of using a portion of the booty to construct memorials on the battlefield or in the sanctuary via dedication to Yhwh. In Num 31, the army's commanders voluntarily bring to Moses an "offering" to Yhwh consisting of various gold articles of booty and serving to "make atonement" (לכפר, v. 50) for themselves. Moses and Eleazar bring this gold into the tent of meeting and set it up as a "memorial" (זכרון, v. 54) before Yhwh. The atonement offering and subsequent memorial appear in this precise form only here, and debate continues over how to interpret the motivation of the warriors and the significance of the acts.[33]

---

32. In a recent study of textual representations of plunder in Second Temple Period and early Jewish texts, Kvasnica notes these Hebrew Bible examples of plunder with a "pious element" of redistribution to the temple or other people became fully developed in the Jewish exegetical tradition as plundering increasingly came to be seen as an unlawful activity according to the Torah. See Brian Kvasnica, "Shifts in Israelite War Ethics and Early Jewish Historiography of Plundering," in Kelle and Ames, *Writing and Reading War*, 175–96 (quotation on 176). Among these later texts, for instance, 2 Macc 8:21–29 reports that Judas redistributed the booty he claimed at the battle of Ammaus (165 B.C.E.), especially to those who had suffered or were widows and orphans among them (2 Macc 8:28).

33. Some commentators point to other Hebrew Bible texts in which the act of taking a census is sinful and demands atonement (e.g., Exod 30:11–16; 2 Sam 24:1–17). For this view, see Noth, *Numbers*, 232; Ashley, *The Book of Numbers*, 599. Alternatively, other explanations include the soldiers' disregard of the strict ban provision

In spite of the unique formulation in Num 31, however, comparable postwar actions occur elsewhere in the Hebrew Bible. Concerning the erecting of battlefield memorials, Exod 17:14–16 is merely suggestive, as it describes Moses's building of an altar with a militaristic name ("the LORD is my banner," v. 15 NRSV) in the aftermath of Israel's defeat of the Amalekites. Concerning the use of booty for memorials in sanctuaries, the ending of the Jericho story in Josh 6:24 reports that the Israelites took the material booty of precious metals and placed it into the "treasury of the house of the LORD" (NRSV). Similarly, 1 Chr 26:26–28 reports that the booty was dedicated for the maintenance of the temple (see also 2 Sam 8:9–12; 2 Chr 15:11).[34] Similar acts of temple dedication from the opposite perspective appear in the stories of Israel's defeat at the hands of the Philistines in 1 Samuel. In 1 Sam 5:1–8, the Philistines place the captured Ark of the Covenant into the temple of Dagon as a victory memorial. In 1 Sam 31:8–10, they place Saul's armor into the temple of Astarte and hang his body on the wall of Beth-shan. One might also note the reference in Dan 1:1–2 to Nebuchadnezzar's placement of vessels from Jerusalem's temple into the "treasury of his gods" (see also Dan 5:2–3). These depictions of the captured ark and temple vessels fit within the broader category of the taking of divine images as trophies in the ancient world (see below), but the Hebrew Bible preserves explicit depictions of this ritual only as it was done *to* Israel or Judah in defeat.[35]

---

and the sense of having received unmerited divine favor during the battle (see Budd, *Numbers*, 332; Gray, *Numbers*, 425). Norman H. Snaith (*Leviticus and Numbers* [The Century Bible; London: Thomas Nelson and Sons, 1967], 329) proposes that the warriors' motivation is gratitude that their lives have been spared. Hence, the root כפר here carries a denominative force meaning, "to give a ransom for our lives." Yet the context of ch. 31 suggests the need for atonement reflects the sense that participation in the battle was ritually defiling and the offering is part of the purification process (see Dozeman, "Numbers," 248; Wenham, *Numbers*, 212).

34. One might also consider in this category Gen 14:17–24, which depicts Abram giving part of his booty to the priest Melchizedek.

35. Perhaps the one-sided portrayal is due to the "ideological prohibition of images" in various Hebrew Bible traditions that resulted in commands to destroy rather than capture foreign gods and their images (e.g., Exod 34:13; Num 33:52; Deut 7:25) and possibly generated some textual emendations in which the MT obscures references to Israel's taking of divine images as trophies (Kathryn Frakes Kravitz, "Divine Trophies of War in Assyria and Ancient Israel" [Ph.D. diss., Brandeis University, 1999], 118). See the apparent MT emendation of 2 Sam 12:30 from the "crown of Milcom" to the "crown of their kings."

3.4. Celebration or Procession

The fourth category of Hebrew Bible texts contains several passages that portray the victorious returning army participating in rituals of celebration, procession, and thanksgiving.[36] The texts include celebratory praise songs (Exod 15:1–18), feasting (Esth 9:16–17; Isa 25:6), triumphal processions back to the city (Ps 68:21–27; 2 Chr 20:24–30), and women coming out to meet the returning warriors with music and dancing (Exod 15:20–21; 1 Sam 18:6–9).[37] Notable examples here include 1 Sam 18:6–9, which describes women coming out with singing, dancing, and instruments to meet Saul and David's forces returning from victory over the Philistines, and 2 Chr 20:24–30, which depicts Jehoshaphat leading "all the people of Judah and Jerusalem" into the capital and to the temple with "harps and lyres and trumpets" (vv. 27–28).[38] Psalm 68:21–27 also seems to place a possible allusion to a postbattle procession in the context of military victory and celebration, although the reference is opaque.[39] Perhaps as a part

---

36. For an overview listing, see Leland Ryken, James C. Wilhoit, and Tremper Longman III, eds. *Dictionary of Biblical Imagery* (Downer's Grove, Ill.: InterVarsity Press, 1998), 78–79.

37. The overall textual evidence in the Hebrew Bible suggests that postbattle songs were the particular domain of women in ancient Israel (especially the tradition of early heroic poetry). See Mark Smith's contribution to this volume ("Warfare Song as Warrior Ritual"). See also Athalya Brenner and Fokkelien van Dijk-Hemmes, *On Gendering Texts: Female and Male Voices in the Hebrew Bible* (BInS 1; Leiden: Brill, 1993), 1–42 and Sherry Lou Macgregor, *Beyond Hearth and Home: Women in the Public Sphere in Neo-Assyrian Society* (SAAS 21; Publications of the Foundation for Finnish Assyriological Research 5; Helsinki: Neo-Assyrian Text Corpus Project, 2012), 29–54. On the topic of women celebrating victory, see Eunice B. Poethig, "The Victory Song Tradition of the Women of Israel" (Ph.D. diss., Union Theological Seminary, 1985) and Carol Meyers, "Mother to Muse: An Archaeomusicological Study of Women's Performance in Israel," in *Recycling Biblical Figures: Papers Read at a NOSTER Colloquium in Amsterdam, 12–13 May 1997* (ed. Athalya Brenner and Jan Willem van Henten; Studies in Religion and Theology 1; Leiden: Deo, 1999), 50–77.

38. The story in 2 Sam 19:1–8 may represent the emotional distress caused by the failure to provide returning victorious warriors with these kinds of celebratory processionals. The text reports that David's troops, although victorious over Absalom's forces, "stole into the city that day as soldiers steal in who are ashamed when they flee in battle" (v. 3). The implication is that a celebratory processional was expected, and the king somewhat rectified the situation by gathering the troops before him (v. 8).

39. See Crouch, *War and Ethics in the Ancient Near East*, 76.

of this procession, defeated enemies are said to be brought to Jerusalem so that the victors may "bathe" their feet in blood (v. 23; see also Ps 58:10).[40] It is tempting to see this text as an allusion to a postbattle ritual of bathing the warriors' feet with the blood of the defeated and connect it with other evidence for the shame and mutilation of enemies.[41] Yet, it is unclear whether the language is literal or metaphorical and the action does not appear in any subsequent or developed form.

3.5. LAMENT (USUALLY CORPORATE)

The final category of Hebrew Bible texts contains several references to lamentations (typically communal in nature) offered in response to military failure or defeat in battle. These laments are a natural counterpart to the victory songs and celebrations that comprise the preceding category.[42] The major example in the historiographical books occurs in David's lamentation over the death of Saul and Jonathan in battle in 2 Sam 1:19–27. Although the passage as a whole is an individual lament by David,[43] verses 21–23 seem to envision a communal lament to be given by women (see verse 24). The highest concentration of such postbattle laments occurs in the psalms, which include several communal laments related to military failure. Psalm 44 is a national lament and communal plea for help that refers to the failure of Israel's army and the taking of spoil by the enemy (vv. 9–10). Psalms 60 and 79 offer communal laments after defeat that express the disastrous consequences that have come from Yhwh's refusal to grant victory to the army (see also Pss 74; 80), while Ps 89 has an individual form with a focus on the defeat and humiliation of the king and a plea for a reversal of royal fortune.[44]

---

40. The Hebrew term is "shatter" (מחץ), but most translators follow the Greek, Syriac, and Targum, which suggest "bathe" (רחץ) (see NRSV).

41. See T. M. Lemos, "Shame and Mutilation of Enemies in the Hebrew Bible," *JBL* 125 (2006): 225–41.

42. See William S. Morrow, *Protest against God: The Eclipse of a Biblical Tradition* (Hebrew Bible Monographs 4; Sheffield: Sheffield Phoenix, 2006) and F. W. Dobbs-Allsopp, *Weep, O Daughter of Zion: A Study of the City-Lament Genre in the Hebrew Bible* (BibOr 44; Rome: Biblical Pontifical Institute, 1993).

43. Note the presence of the expression, "How" (איך) known from other lament contexts (e.g., Jer 2:21; 9:18; Mic 2:4). For similar postbattle laments in 2 Samuel, see David's lament over Abner (3:33–44) and his mourning over Absalom (18:33).

44. Note the contrast with other royal psalms that reflect warfare contexts but

Outside of the Psalms, laments after defeat occur in other poetic contexts. The highest concentration appears in texts that fit the genre of Hebrew Bible city laments. These laments treat the common subject matter of the destruction of cities (usually due to enemy invasion) and feature elements such as divine abandonment of the city, assignment of responsibility for the destruction of the city, and somber expressions of grief. F. W. Dobbs-Allsopp demonstrates that while the book of Lamentations represents the fullest example of this genre in the Hebrew Bible, comparisons with extrabibiblical writings (see below) reveal that texts from this genre appear throughout the prophetic literature (especially the oracles against the nations) and in some psalms. He concludes that a native city lament genre existed in Israel at least between the eighth and sixth centuries B.C.E.[45] The poems in the book of Lamentations offer ceremonial and, in some cases, communal (especially ch. 5) laments in response to the Babylonian destruction of Jerusalem that reflect most of the features of the city lament genre known throughout the ancient Near East. These laments reflect on military defeat, express the suffering and violence that followed, and plead for relief. The relevant prophetic oracles at times employ ironic or sarcastic laments to condemn enemy kingdoms such as Babylon, Moab, and Egypt (e.g., Isa 14:3–20; 15–16; Jer 48; Ezek 32:1–16). Additionally, Joel 1:2–2:17 features a prophetic call for an extended communal lamentation intertwined with references (literal or metaphorical) to an invasion that has devastated the land (see 1:6–8).

4. Postwar Rituals of Return and Reintegration Outside the Hebrew Bible

The five kinds of practices represented by the categories discussed above—purification of warriors, captives, and objects, appropriation of booty, trophy/monument construction, celebration or procession, and communal lament—are the most suggestive postwar rituals of return and reintegration in the Hebrew Bible, with various levels of overlap among them.

---

offer thanksgiving for victory in battle (Ps 18) or prayer for the king prior to going to war (Ps 20). See also the likely royal prayer for safety and victory in war in Ps 144.

45. Dobbs-Allsopp, *Weep, O Daughter of Zion*, 156. Dobbs-Allsopp speculates that the city laments may reflect "partial transformations of funeral laments" and appear most prominently (outside of Lamentations) in the oracles against the nations in the prophetic books (160).

The next step in considering these texts and practices is to place them against the backdrop of comparable texts and practices from other sources in ancient and modern contexts. Prior to doing so, however, there are two lingering questions for the sources under consideration here that place ongoing limitations on the analysis. First, as noted above, all of the relevant biblical texts remain only suggestive, so we are left to ask whether and to what extent the depictions in these texts reflect actual practices or recurring rituals related to the reintegration of warriors in ancient Israel. The exact correspondence between these textual expressions and the actual practices of ancient Israel and Judah cannot be taken for granted. Second, it remains unclear whether one should (or could) distinguish among the practices described above those that are truly postwar rituals and those that are more immediate postbattle rituals. In other words, do some (most?) of these practices envision activities that took place to mark the homecoming at the completion of a campaign ("war") or simply the end of one particular battle. This question likely bears on the possible symbolic functions fulfilled by the acts themselves, but the available evidence suggests a high level of overlap among the different kinds of practices and permits few clear-cut distinctions. As the following discussion shows, these same two questions bear upon the evidence for postwar practices in sources outside the Hebrew Bible, as well.

The potential extrabiblical evidence for postwar rituals from the ancient Near East and other contexts is diverse and widespread, with significant source material coming from ancient Mesopotamia, Egypt, Greece, and Rome, as well as modern, especially tribal, cultures and early and medieval Christianity. What follows is a representative survey that does not claim comprehensiveness.[46] As with the Hebrew Bible, a lack of clear textual evidence for certain areas, most notably Syria-Palestine, makes it difficult to describe the various elements of warfare practice in any systematic or detailed manner. Additionally, Sa-Moon Kang observes that the overall framework for many of the ancient Near Eastern war texts, just as for the Hebrew Bible, is the notion of divine war, which includes both a divine command to execute the war and the belief that the gods

---

46. For a survey of practices and ideological formulations undergirding warfare in the ancient Near East and the Hebrew Bible more generally, see Otto, *Krieg und Frieden*. For an overall survey of rituals, art, monuments, especially related to the body in warfare, see Bahrani, *Rituals of War*.

fight alongside the armies (mainly through natural phenomena).⁴⁷ This larger framework shapes the ancient texts' descriptions of activities before, during, and after battle.⁴⁸ Even so, while the relevant practices can vary greatly in different cultures and societies, the efforts to handle booty, celebrate victory, and help warriors transition back to life in the community correspond in general terms to the categories found in the Hebrew Bible.

The first category of the ritual purification of warriors returning from battle, which appears explicitly in only one Hebrew Bible text (Num 31), is by contrast extensively attested in several comparative contexts.⁴⁹ Sources from Mesopotamia and the wider ancient Near East, including Hittite, Egyptian, Ugaritic, and Akkadian texts, refer to a variety of practices involving ceremonial purification after battle, especially through the washing of the body or the weapons used in battle. In some cases, the texts seem to imply that deities themselves became defiled through warfare or bloodshed and underwent ritual acts of purification following the conflict.⁵⁰ For the purposes of this study, however, one may note that postbattle purification rituals for human warriors appear in a number of Mesopotamian texts.⁵¹ An early representative example appears in an inscription

---

47. For a full treatment of this issue, including extended discussion of prebattle, battle, and postbattle practices within the framework of divine war in texts from Mesopotamia, Arabia, Syria–Palestine, and Egypt see Kang, *Divine War*.

48. Kang (ibid., 109) observes that in most texts, battle begins with "divine consultation" to discern the divine will and descriptions of the battle include claims that the gods participated in the conflict through natural phenomena, as well as the recounting of symbols that represent the divine presence.

49. Kang (ibid., 48) identifies the postbattle purification ritual as "one of the most important motifs of the divine war in the ancient Near East." In a broader context, already in 1903, Gray (*Numbers*, 243, 422) drew upon anthropological studies and claimed the purification of warriors and their weapons is a primitive custom evidenced among modern cultures such as the Basutos of South Africa. See also Snaith, *Leviticus and Numbers*, 324.

50. For full discussion, see Jason A. Riley's essay in this volume ("Does Yhwh Get His Hands Dirty? Reading Isaiah 63:1–6 in Light of Depictions of Divine Postbattle Purification"). Riley's particular focus is to consider whether this depiction that appears in some ancient Near Eastern texts is also present implicitly in the Hebrew Bible in relationship to Yhwh's defilement and subsequent ritual purification. See especially his discussion of Anat's purification following several acts of killing in the Baal Cycle.

51. These texts imply the seemingly shared view in ancient Near Eastern cultures that shedding blood in battle rendered one physically and ceremonially unclean. See

of Yahdum-Lim from Mari that reports that the king marched to the Mediterranean Sea and offered sacrifices while "his troops washed themselves in the Ocean."[52] Likewise, the Gilgamesh Epic features Gilgamesh washing himself and his equipment after battle.[53] The Assyrian royal inscriptions contain numerous similar examples of postbattle ritual washings, usually of the soldiers' weapons not bodies and typically featuring some form of the common expression that "I washed my weapon in the sea."[54] Inscriptions from Sargon, Ashurnasirpal II, Shalmaneser III, and Ashurbanipal, for instance, record washing their weapons in the Mediterranean Sea and offering sacrifices.[55] Admittedly, these rituals take place while the army is still abroad and whether they imply ritual impurity remains debated. Yet, the connection of the washings with offering sacrifice in the Mari and Assyrian texts suggests a cultic and ritual dimension.

Most historians of Greek warfare have concluded that the evidence for postwar purification rituals is limited at best.[56] There may be sporadic

---

Robert Parker, *Miasma: Pollution and Purification in Early Greek Religion* (Oxford: Clarendon, 1983), 104–43; Verkamp, *Moral Treatment*, 11.

52. *COS* 2:243; *ANET*, 556. See Abraham Malamat, "Campaigns to the Mediterranean by Iahdunlim and Other Early Mesopotamian Rulers," in *Studies in Honor of Benno Landsberger on His Seventy-Fifth Birthday* (eds. H. Güterbock and T. Jacobsen; The Oriental Institute of Chicago Assyriological Studies 16; Chicago: University of Chicago Press, 1965), 367 and Kang, *Divine War*, 48.

53. Tablet VI. *ANET*, 83–84.

54. See Jan van Dijk, "Un Rituel de Purification des Armes et de l'Armée: Essai de Traduction de YBC 4184," in *Symbolae Biblicae et Mesopotamicae* (ed. M. A. Beek; Studia Francisci Scholten Memoriae Dicata 4; Leiden: Brill, 1973), 107–17.

55. For Sargon, see *COS* 2:243; *ANET*, 267–68; for Ashurnasirpal II, *ANET*, 276; for Shalmaneser III, *ANET*, 277; and for Ashurbanipal, Malamat, "Campaigns to the Mediterranean," 367. Perhaps the origin of the ritual washing of the weapons lies in the fact that some Assyrian texts depict the weapons used in battle as having been provided by the gods and thus in need of ritual purification after the battle. See Bahrani, *Rituals of War*, 197; Bustenay Oded, *War, Peace, and Empire: Justifications for War in Assyrian Royal Inscriptions* (Wiesbaden: Ludwig Reichert, 1992), 15. Albrecht Goetze ("Warfare in Asia Minor," *Iraq* 25 [1963]: 124–30) argues that there is evidence of a purification ritual for the Hittite army between 1800 and 1200 B.C.E. The army marched through a makeshift symbolic gate made of wood and between the two halves of a sacrificed captive. The context appears to be specifically one where the army has suffered defeat and the ritual serves to remove the pollution that made the army unable to conquer the enemy (197 n. 139).

56. E.g., W. Kendrick Pritchett, *The Greek State at War Part III: Religion* (Berkeley: University of California Press, 1979), 202.

indications that a soldier required ceremonial atonement before participation in the temple, but only one seventh-century passage seems to suggest that soldiers had a formal postwar purification ritual.[57] The Greek texts that most explicitly indicate a purification ritual for the army occur under particular circumstances and do not seem to reflect a mandated ceremony upon return from battle.[58] Roman sources, however, provide more indication of ceremonies of purification for returning armies, largely revolving around lustrations to remove the blood from battle and other evil contagions.[59] The most famous Roman victory ritual, the "Triumph" (discussed below), includes a ritual of purification and thanksgiving for the army before it began a celebratory procession.[60] Other Roman practices are suggestive but their exact meaning remains uncertain. For instance, Roman soldiers from some eras were prohibited from wearing their red capes into the city or from marching past the Rubicon into the city of Rome. These prohibitions may connote a sense of defilement associated with combat.[61]

---

57. The text in question is from Aeschylus. See Parker, *Miasma*, 113. The Delphic Oracle, for instance, did not view killing in warfare as causing guilt or defilement. See Herbert W. Parke and Donald E. W. Wormell, *The Delphic Oracle* (Oxford: Blackwell, 1956), 383.

58. Pritchett, *The Greek States at War Part III: Religion*, 197–98. Pritchett examines four general statements in sources such as Plutarch, as well as seven incidents in various texts that refer to a purification rite for the Greek army, often having the army pass between halves of a corpse (ibid., 197–202). Based on the contexts, however, he concludes that such purification rituals in the Greek military occurred while the army was still in the field and as a response to some military disorder such as a mutiny. Van Creveld (*Culture of War*, 166) also notes that Greek postwar texts include some references to rituals related specifically to the defeat of the army. These often take the form of seeking to place blame, sometimes by putting losing generals on trial.

59. See Bahrani, *Rituals of War*, 197. W. Warde Fowler (*The Religious Experience of the Roman People* [New York: Cooper Square, 1971], 217, 297) cites the Roman "Calendar of Numa" as evidence that returning warriors had to perform purification rituals related to any possible "evil contagion" and the "taint of bloodshed."

60. Van Creveld, *Culture of War*, 164.

61. Additionally, the typical Roman practice did not reintegrate warriors into the life of the community. Rather, after thirty years of service in the legions, soldiers received a plot of land in a newly conquered territory. A. Kirk Grayson ("Assyrian Civilization," in *The Cambridge Ancient History Volume 3 Part 2: The Assyrian and Babylonian Empires and Other States of the Near East, from the Eighth to the Sixth Centuries B.C.* [Cambridge: Cambridge University Press, 1991], 218) notes that some Assyrian sources also indicate that veterans were settled in military colonies in newly conquered territories. The likely primary motivation for this practice was the desire to

Anthropological research into tribal societies from various periods, including modern peoples such as the African Zulus, Eskimos, and Native Americans, has also produced evidence of postbattle rituals for returning warriors that include the removal of bloodstained clothes and equipment, washing, and isolation.[62] Among the ancient practices of the ethnic Meru people of Kenya, for instance, return required the sacrifice of a ram and the placing of a portion of the sacrifice on the warrior's spear.[63] Similarly, the early Irish/Celtic literary epic, the *Táin*, describes a multistep purification process for the hero's return from combat that includes women baring their breasts to the warrior—likely a symbol of the nurture provided by children, family, and community—the warrior being placed into successive baths of water that symbolize a "cooling down," and the changing of the soldier's clothes.[64] These kinds of postwar rituals for returning warriors received their fullest and most explicit articulation in the formulations of the early and medieval Christian church. Writings from the church in this era frequently required soldiers to do various kinds of penance as a means of purification, expiation, and return to the community, even when the war itself was considered just.[65] The texts vary in their prescriptions but generally involve requirements such as abstaining from communion, church gatherings, or eating certain foods for a particular length of time. One of the earliest examples is a canon of Basil the Great that distinguished killing in war from homicide but stipulated that returning warriors should

---

secure control in the new territories, but one wonders if it also speaks of an uneasiness related to participation in warfare.

62. Van Creveld, *Culture of War*, 163–64.

63. Jeffrey A. Fadiman, *Meru of Mount Kenya: An Oral History of Tribal Warfare* (Athens: Ohio University Press, 1982), 118–19.

64. See Karl Marlantes, *What It Is Like to Go to War* (New York: Atlantic Monthly, 2011), 191–92; Robert Bly, *Iron John: A Book about Men* (New York: Vantage Books, 1992), 196–97.

65. See the major study by Verkamp, *Moral Treatment*. The assumption in these practices seems to be that returning warriors would feel guilty as a result of their killing in war and needed practices to offer resolution of those feelings. In this way, these writings resemble the distinction between war as ritually defiling but not sinful that some have suggested is at work in the prescriptions in Num 31. Some scholars have expressed caution about the assumption that such penances were a universal church practice in the early Middle Ages and concluded that they more likely reflect local and regional perspectives (see Raymund Kottje, *Die Tötung im Krieg: Ein moralisches und rechtliches Problem im frühen Mittelalter* [Barsbuettel: Institut für Theologie und Frieden, 1991], 3–10).

still "abstain from communion for three years."⁶⁶ A penitential ascribed to Theodore of Tarsus (Archbishop of Canterbury 668–690 C.E.) near the end of the seventh century declared that one who had killed in war even "at the command of his lord" must "keep away from the church for forty days."⁶⁷ Postwar penance within the church began to lose ground under the influence of Thomas Aquinas and others by the time of the high Middle Ages, but the practice would continue to appear in Christian writings through the centuries following the Reformation.⁶⁸

The second category observed in Hebrew Bible texts—the appropriation of booty—features prominently in postwar rituals found in texts from the ancient world, often being the most frequently described postbattle element.⁶⁹ Mesopotamian sources attest the postwar redistribution of booty among the king, military officers, and other persons in a manner not unlike the distribution between combatants and noncombatants in Num 31 and other Hebrew Bible texts. The practice appears in Mari and Hittite texts,⁷⁰ with clear examples in other Akkadian inscriptions. The Akkadian inscription of Idrimi includes the ruler's claim that he distributed captured booty to his servants, family, and friends,⁷¹ and Esarhaddon's inscriptions for his sixth campaign report, "From the booty of the lands ... I selected from among them, and added to my royal equipment. From the great spoil of enemy-(captives), I apportioned (men) like sheep to all of my camp, to my governors, and to the people of my (large) cities."⁷² Greek postwar texts

---

66. Quoted in Verkamp, *Moral Treatment*, 1.

67. Quoted in ibid., 2; for further examples, see 2–4.

68. E.g., as late as the sixteenth century, Carlo Borromeo, archbishop of Milan, published a penitential text that required anyone who had killed in combat to do penance on certain days during three Lenten seasons (ibid., 8).

69. K. Lawson Younger Jr. (*Ancient Conquest Accounts: A Study in Ancient Near Eastern and Biblical History Writing* [JSOTSup 98; Sheffield: JSOT Press, 1990], 75–76) concludes that the taking of booty "appears as an all but universal element in ancient Near Eastern accounts of war and conquest."

70. A letter from Mari contains a king's complaint that he has not received his share of the booty or the portion to be given to the gods from his officers (see Kang, *Divine War*, 47), and Hittite texts describe kings bringing spoil to their palace for the purpose of distribution (ibid., 71).

71. See Kvasnica, "Shifts in Israelite War Ethics," 176–77 n. 7; Edward L. Greenstein and David Marcus, "The Akkadian Inscription of *Idrimi*," *JANES* 8 (1976): 59–96; Elgavish, "The Division of the Spoils," 242–73.

72. Quoted in Kang, *Divine War*, 48.

focus on memorials in temples (see below) but also attest that the military commander was free to distribute booty or proceeds from its sale according to his discretion while the army remained in the field.[73]

The third category observed in the Hebrew Bible texts—the construction of memorials and monuments—also appears prominently among ancient postwar rituals in Hittite, Assyrian, Egyptian, and Greek sources. Many Mesopotamian texts feature the giving of some or all of the booty to the gods, presumably through dedication to the temple. The practice reminds biblical readers of the military officers' donation to the sanctuary in Num 31 and may derive from the ancient Near Eastern conviction that the battles were a form of divine war.[74] Ashurbanipal's inscriptions state, "The people and spoil of Elam, which at the command of Ashur, Sin, Shamash, Adad … I had carried off, the choicest I presented unto my gods."[75] Likewise, Nebuchadnezzar claims, "I had them brought into Esagila and Ezida before Marduk the great lord of the gods and before Nabu his beautiful son who loves my royalty."[76] Greek postwar texts frequently refer to the dedication of portions of booty to the gods, especially in the form of a "tithe" set aside from the spoils and given to the temple.[77] This *dekate* could consist of various items such as money, captured armor, land, and slaves, and could be offered by military leaders, as well as ordinary soldiers.[78]

A significant subdivision of this postbattle category is the practice of taking divine trophies from the defeated enemy.[79] Although trophies

---

73. Once the army returned home, the booty became property of the state treasury. See W. Kendrick Pritchett, *The Greek State at War Part I* (Berkeley: University of California Press, 1971), 85; Van Creveld, *Culture of War*, 159.

74. See Kang, *Divine War*, 46–48.

75. *ARAB* 2:308; quoted in ibid., 47.

76. Quoted in ibid.; Kang (ibid., 106) notes that some Egyptian texts also refer to the postbattle dedication of booty to the gods.

77. For Greek texts related to this aspect, see Pritchett, *The Greek State at War Part I*, 53–100. For the donation of the tenth, see also Walter Burkert, *Greek Religion* (trans. John Raffan; Cambridge: Harvard University Press, 1985), 267.

78. Pritchett, *The Greek State at War Part III: Religion*, 249, 277–80. Kvasnica ("Shifts in Israelite War Ethics," 180) notes that the practice appears in the earliest Greek texts (see Homer, *Iliad* 10.460) and became a mandatory practice in treaties "for the Athenian league after its victory in the Persian war."

79. For a major study, see Kravitz, "Divine Trophies." See also Bahrani's (*Rituals of War*, 159–81) discussion of the "assault and abduction of monuments in war."

taken at the conclusion of battle included statues of kings and other public monuments, the primary trophies were images of gods, which were subsequently exhibited in ceremonies for the public when the army returned home.[80] The practice appears most prominently in Assyrian royal inscriptions, primarily from the time of Tiglath-pileser I in the late Middle Assyrian period and the Sargonids in the eighth and seventh centuries B.C.E.[81] The precise function of this postwar practice remains debated and likely varied in different periods and areas,[82] probably serving primarily to legitimate the newly expanded kingship of the conqueror and reframe the soldiers' actions as part of the divine world and its orchestration of human, especially royal, affairs.[83]

In addition to the dedication of portions of booty for memorials in temples, the postwar rituals in this third category also take the form of erecting a monument or boundary stone (often on the battlefield) to commemorate the victory and offer praise to a deity.[84] The Zakkur Stela, for instance, mentions the king's establishment of a stela before the god Iluwer,[85] Esarhaddon's inscriptions refer to erecting a victory stela recording the praise of the god Ashur,[86] and Egyptian texts record Thutmose III's carving of a stela into a rock following a campaign to the Euphrates.[87] Although Greek sources highlight the giving of a tithe of the booty to temples, they also include the ritual of erecting a monument or trophy (τρόπαιον) on the battlefield as one of the primary postbattle rituals.[88]

---

80. As noted above, the Hebrew Bible preserves explicit depictions of this ritual only as it was done *to* Israel or Judah in defeat and a general prohibition against images perhaps obscures any such capture of foreign gods and their images by Israel (e.g., Exod 34:13; Num 33:52; Deut 7:25). This statement holds unless some texts have been later edited to obscure original realities. See Kravitz, "Divine Trophies," 118.

81. For a survey of the major Assyrian "trophy texts," see ibid., 29–117.

82. Ibid., 6–18.

83. For a survey of Assyrian texts related to ceremonies for the taking of divine trophies, see ibid., 19–28. For example, a sculpture from Tiglath-pileser III's palace depicts Assyrian soldiers "carrying the gods of a defeated enemy as part of the booty paraded before the king" (ibid., 27).

84. See Kang, *Divine War*, 48, 71.

85. See ibid., 80.

86. *ANET*, 293. For the construction of victory stelae and monuments by earlier Assyrian kings such as Ashurnasirpal II and Shalmaneser III, see Kravitz, "Divine Trophies," 29.

87. See Kang, *Divine War*, 107.

88. Pritchett (*The Greek State at War Part III: Religion*, 186) argues that the raising

These monuments often consisted of captured armor, shields, and weapons, among other items, which were placed around a pole or tree, often at the place where the battle turned.[89]

For the fourth category of postwar rituals observed in Hebrew Bible texts, numerous references exist to various kinds of victory celebrations that involve processions, music, sacrifice, and so on in many ancient and modern cultures. Egyptian texts refer to the celebratory homecoming of the king and army, sometimes including a divine speech by a god about the king and offerings of praise by the soldiers.[90] Greek texts associate various drink offerings and sacrifices with the end of battle.[91] Later Roman texts from the second century B.C.E. describe what is perhaps the most famous victory celebration ritual, the "Triumph" (*triumphus*).[92] This celebration featured a public ceremony honoring certain victorious military leaders and included an organized procession of the troops and spoils ending at the temple of Jupiter.

The final category observed in the Hebrew Bible texts—laments (communal and otherwise) following military failure—is also attested in different forms within various ancient Near Eastern writings. Some epic poetry and ritual texts envision defeat in battle being followed by laments offered by family members of the defeated warrior, often by weeping women figures. Note, for instance, the laments of El and Anat for Baal or Anat's lament for Aqhat.[93] The most explicit examples of postbattle laments, however, appear in the so-called Mesopotamian city laments.[94] These texts contain laments over destroyed cities and their sanctuaries (usually due to

---

of a battlefield trophy is as old as the time of Homer. The most detailed description appears in Virgil's *Aeneid* (11.4–11) (see Van Creveld, *Culture of War*, 160–61).

89. Burkert, *Greek Religion*, 267; Kravitz, "Divine Trophies," 9 n. 17.

90. See Kang, *Divine War*, 105–106. For example, one text records the gods extolling Ramses II upon his return in victory: "Welcome, our beloved son, King *Usermaresotpenre*, the Son of Re, Ramses, Beloved of Amun, given life!" (quoted in ibid., 106).

91. See Burkert, *Greek Religion*, 267. For a list of Greek texts referring to a postbattle sacrifice, see Pritchett, *The Greek State at War Part III: Religion*, 187–89.

92. See H. S. Versnel, *Triumphus: An Inquiry into the Origin, Development, and Meaning of the Roman Triumph* (Leiden: Brill, 1970); Kravitz, "Divine Trophies," 9 n. 17; Van Creveld, *Culture of War*, 164.

93. KTU 1.5 VI 11–25; 1.5 VI 31–1.6 I 6–8; 1.18 IV 39.

94. See Dobbs-Allsopp, *Weep, O Daughter of Zion*. The genre consists of distinct but related types and the label, "city lament" most often refers to literary laments related to the destruction of Sumer at the end of the Ur III period (13).

230   WARFARE, RITUAL, AND SYMBOL

enemy invasion) and some likely functioned as part of ceremonies accompanying refounding and restoration more so than the return after battle. They share common features related to subject, mood, divine abandonment, assignment of responsibility, destruction, and a weeping goddess.[95] As noted above, these Sumerian city laments show similarities to the book of Lamentations in which the patron deity of the city is said to have withdrawn from it and given it over to enemies.[96]

5. The Symbolic Functions of Postwar Rituals of Return and Reintegration

The preceding survey of the potential Hebrew Bible examples of postwar rituals and their extrabiblical parallels leads to two preliminary observations. First, the texts do not explicitly state that the practices mentioned were intended to fulfill certain functions for returning soldiers, and they certainly are not systematized in a coherent or comprehensive way. Second, the available texts only describe the practices and rarely, if ever, offer insight into what possible meanings the various postwar rituals may have had. Even so, the identification of these rituals begs the question of their function and meaning for those involved in the practices or the production of the writings that depict them. The function of ritual is often determined by a socio-historical context in which the inherent relationship between an act and its meaning was understood, even if, over time and distance, this connection became obscured and not always explicitly expressed.[97] Clearly, at the most initial level, the postwar rituals depicted in these texts deal with pragmatic issues. They are concerned with handling the material objects used in and gained from combat, compensating and sustaining those involved and affected, and bringing the soldiers back to their local and domestic responsibilities. Considered as a whole, however, the postwar rituals give the impression that they are not merely pragmatic but had larger symbolic functions unidentified in the available sources.

---

95. Ibid., 30–31.
96. Five compositions constitute the best representations of the genre: "Lamentation over the Destruction of Ur;" "Lamentation over the Destruction of Sumer and Ur;" "Nippur Lament;" "Eridu Lament;" "Uruk Lament" (see *ANET*, 455–63).
97. See Yitzhaq Feder, *Blood Expiation in Hittite and Biblical Ritual: Origins, Context, and Meaning* (SBLWAW Supplement Series 2; Atlanta: Society of Biblical Literature, 2011), 2, 151–55.

If this is the case, a concluding, albeit tentative and suggestive, interdisciplinary exploration of these rituals using contemporary warfare studies, psychology, and clinical literature may allow readers to recognize symbolic functions that remain unacknowledged (and, perhaps, unintended) by the sources themselves.[98] What follows is more of a suggestive outline for research than the research itself, and scholars should always bear in mind the problems and possibilities of interdisciplinary and comparative study. Yet, perspectives and proposals within contemporary warfare studies, psychology, and clinical literature concerning how soldiers need to conceive, experience, and respond to the realities of warfare and return point to some potential functions of the Hebrew Bible postwar rituals. This comparison recognizes that ancient warriors may not have experienced the emotional or physical trauma of war in the same way as moderns and the need for reintegration may have been different due to the nature of war and day-to-day life.[99] Still, taking a cue from Zainab Bahrani's study of rituals, art, and monuments related to war and the body, we might consider whether the postwar rituals under consideration here constitute a "semiotics" of war designed for the warriors themselves and, to a lesser extent, the community as a whole.[100] Perhaps the postwar rituals concerning purification, booty, memorials, celebration, and lamentation form a set of signs related to the representation of war that functions to reframe the

---

98. Perhaps the most apparent function is to provide a transitional or liminal space between the war space and the community space, with the rituals as practices that help warriors modulate out of the physical and existential battle space (see Bly, *Iron John*, 191–94).

99. Comparisons between ancient and contemporary experiences of warfare operate on the assumption that combat generated the same kinds of feelings, effects, and needs in ancient soldiers that it does in modern ones—an assumption articulated in many contemporary studies of warriors and the dynamics of postwar return and reintegration (see Verkamp, *Moral Treatment*, 49; Van Creveld, *Culture of War*, 163). The points of connection in interdisciplinary study are not intended as one-to-one correspondences, and the conversation continues about what methodological controls and constraints should be applied. The goal of comparison is to "raise new possibilities for the interpretation of ancient evidence ... by alerting the modern reader to a wider spectrum of possible models of social behaviours and responses" (Daniel L. Smith-Christopher, "Engendered Warfare and the Ammonites in Amos 1.13," in *Aspects of Amos: Exegesis and Interpretation* [ed. A. C. Hagedorn and A. Mein; LHBOTS 536; New York: T&T Clark, 2011], 33 n. 41).

100. Bahrani, *Rituals of War*, 16.

way warriors and communities conceive, experience, and respond to the realities of combat.

The topic of the return and reintegration of soldiers has been at the forefront of contemporary military studies in the United States since the 1980s in particular and much of the conversation has been generated by the experiences of veterans from the Vietnam War.[101] There has been an increasing awareness that the transition of soldiers back from war to home is a vital topic and that intentional practices can play a key role in that transition.[102] Throughout much of the contemporary conversation, the focus has been on the psychological needs of returning soldiers, with special attention to trauma and so-called Post–Traumatic Stress Disorder (PTSD).[103] Most importantly for our purposes here, however, newer work within contemporary warfare studies, psychology, and clinical literature has foregrounded a new category of effects upon returning soldiers referred to as "moral injury" or "soul injury."[104] Recent clinical literature defines this category as the deleterious effects of war on the soldier's moral and ethical conceptions—the wrecking of the soldier's fundamental assumptions about "what's right" and how things should work in the world.[105] The recent study by Rita Nakashima Brock and Gabriella

---

101. See Bly, *Iron John*, 196–97.

102. E.g., Van Creveld, *Culture of War*, 160.

103. For a recent, convenient summary of today's prominent theories of Post-Traumatic Stress Disorder, see Brett T. Litz et al., "Moral Injury and Moral Repair in War Veterans: A Preliminary Model and Intervention Strategy," *Clinical Psychology Review* 29 (2009): 698–99. Discussion of postwar practices of return has largely focused on how such practices might fulfill psychological functions such as restoring confidence, overcoming depression, and so on. The field of trauma studies has recently come into biblical scholarship, especially in studies of the exile and prophetic literature. See, for example, Daniel L. Smith-Christopher, *A Biblical Theology of Exile* (OBT; Minneapolis: Fortress, 2002); Brad E. Kelle, *Ezekiel* (New Beacon Bible Commentary; Kansas City: Beacon Hill Press, 2013); Kathleen M. O'Connor, *Jeremiah: Pain and Promise* (Minneapolis: Fortress, 2011).

104. See especially Brock and Lettini, *Soul Repair* and Edward Tick, *War and the Soul: Healing Our Nation's Veterans from Post–Traumatic Stress Disorder* (Wheaton, Ill.: Quest Books, 2005).

105. For a major recent study and clinical articulation of "moral injury," see Litz et al., "Moral Injury," 695–706. See additional articulations in Jonathan Shay, "Casualties," *Daedalus* 140 no. 3 (2011): 179–88; Jonathan Shay, *Achilles in Vietnam: Combat Trauma and the Undoing of Character* (New York: Atheneum, 1994); Shay, *Odysseus in America*; Verkamp, *Moral Treatment*.

Lettini distinguishes moral injury from PTSD in particular, noting that the former is a "violation of core moral beliefs" that does not necessarily include physical effects or psychological disorders.[106] Moral injury refers to "souls in anguish"—experiences of guilt, shame, and moral and ethical ambiguity that result from a sense of having "transgressed one's basic moral identity," abandoned one's ethical standing as a decent person, and lost any reliable, meaningful world in which to live.[107] Clinical literature identifies potentially morally injurious events as "perpetrating, failing to prevent, or bearing witness to acts that transgress deeply held moral beliefs and expectations,"[108] and some scholars identify a betrayal of what's right by those with legitimate authority in a "high stakes" situation as the most powerful cause of moral injury.[109]

The operative assumption in the contemporary study of moral injury is that although the clinical research on this category is recent, warriors' experiences of moral injury in war are ancient.[110] Moreover, some researchers insist that aspects of moral injury are best dealt with through various postwar practices that serve certain symbolic functions, and recent research increasingly looks to rituals and practices from traditional and ancient societies for models.[111] Perhaps the most important work along these lines has been done by Jonathan Shay, especially in his works, *Achilles in Vietnam* (1994) and *Odysseus in America* (2002).[112] Shay concludes that the primary function that needs to be fulfilled for the healthy reintegration

---

106. Brock and Lettini, *Soul Repair*, xiii. PTSD (unlike moral injury) results from physical effects on the brain due to prolonged or extreme trauma, and these effects disrupt normal responses to fear, emotions, and memory.

107. Ibid., 51.

108. Litz et al., "Moral Injury," 695.

109. Shay, "Casualties," 4. See also Shay, *Achilles in Vietnam*, 3 and Brock and Lettini, *Soul Repair*, xv.

110. See explicitly Brock and Lettini, *Soul Repair*, 4.

111. E.g., ibid., xviii; Verkamp, *Moral Treatment*, 95–108; Shay, *Odysseus in America*, 245; Marlantes, *What It Is Like to Go to War*, 205. Van Creveld (*Culture of War*, 149–68) offers a lengthy discussion of "Ending War" that focuses on historical examples of postwar rituals and their importance for modern settings.

112. See also Shay, "Casualties," and Jonathan Shay, "The Birth of Tragedy—Out of the Needs of Democracy," *Didaskalia: The Journal for Ancient Performance*, online: http://www.didaskalia.net/issues/vol2no2/shay.html. Besides Shay, see especially Tick, *War and the Soul*; Brock and Lettini, *Soul Repair*; and Dave Grossman, *On Killing: The Psychological Cost of Learning to Kill in War and Society* (New York: Back Bay Books, 1995).

of morally wounded warriors is the "communalization" of the warfare and the trauma associated with it. The warriors' reintegration depends upon their ability to reframe the warfare as a communally, rather than individually or personally, owned and executed affair.[113] Returning warriors are in need of practices that give a sense that the moral burden and responsibility are equally distributed among soldiers, leaders, and their community, even those who remained outside of the direct conflict.[114]

Perhaps this perspective within contemporary warfare studies points to a possible symbolic function for the extensive rituals related to the redistribution and sharing of booty within the biblical and extrabiblical rituals of return and reintegration. As noted above, this prominent practice usually involved dividing the booty not only among the warriors but even among parts of the community that remained at home during the conflict. Additionally, portions of the booty were given over to the sanctuary or temple that stood at the center of the community's religious and social life. Both actions would seemingly reframe the returning warriors' conception of the combat, resisting the sense that the warfare had been about selfish acquisition of plunder and closing the perceived gap between the soldiers and the community that stayed behind. The practice of corporate lament after defeat also potentially served as a mechanism to forge a sense of community and mutuality in the face of trauma.

A second function identified by contemporary study as necessary for return and reintegration is to help returning warriors reframe the local and specific encounters of combat within a larger perspective or plotline that gives them a broader and perhaps more meaningful significance. Such reframing allows the soldiers to "emplot" their local and limited actions within a larger framework that is shared by the community as a whole and, within many societies, by the deity whose wishes and actions the soldiers are thought to have carried out. Perhaps these symbolic functions are at work in the postwar rituals related to the establishment of memorials and

---

113. For Shay (*Achilles in Vietnam*, 4), this "communalization" of the trauma means "being able safely to tell the story to someone who is listening and who can be trusted to retell it truthfully to others in the community."

114. Brock and Lettini, *Soul Repair*, 65. Shay ("The Birth of Tragedy") identifies the Athenian theater in ancient Greece as a means to achieve these functions in that society. He argues that the theater was created and performed by veteran soldiers for an audience of veteran soldiers in order to rejoin them to the community, reframe their understanding of their experiences, and restore a shared sense of "what's right."

the performance of celebrations and processions observed in the biblical and extrabiblical texts. Given the religious character of these memorials and celebrations, they rearticulate the completed conflict into the realm of larger cosmologies, theologies, and divine action.[115] The conversion of portions of booty into memorial offerings in temples and the taking of divine images as trophies both imply that local conflicts are part of larger divine actions in the world.

Finally, and perhaps surprisingly, contemporary warfare studies, psychology, and clinical literature increasingly propose that some sense of undergoing purification after battle is a need that must be addressed by today's practices of return and reintegration.[116] Many contemporary works explicitly cite ancient ceremonial rituals like those found in Num 31 and other sources as models.[117] Without practices that can serve a function of symbolic purification, warriors may find themselves unable to shed not only any feelings of guilt or shame from killing but also social adaptations and behavioral norms that characterize warfare contexts. Perhaps this is a symbolic function of the ancient rituals of purification that seem ceremonial and pragmatic on their surface. They mark with clarity the boundary and transition from a combat context, with its norms and behaviors, to a noncombat context, with a different set of norms and behaviors. They also create time and space for self-reflection and honest disclosure of the actions, experiences, and human effects of participation in the battle.[118] Likewise, the practice of communal lament gives cathartic voice to the community's sense that their moral understanding of how the

---

115. E.g., Crouch (*War and Ethics in the Ancient Near East*) explores the ways that biblical and Assyrian texts place specific warfare practices into the larger cosmology and theology of the ancient Near East. A similar reframing function may be fulfilled by the various justifications for going to war that appear throughout the Assyrian royal inscriptions. See Oded, *War, Peace and Empire*.

116. For example, Marlantes (*What It Is Like to Go to War*, 185) relates the reflections of a modern era Vietnam veteran on his struggles with homecoming and reintegration who describes wishing someone would put him in a tub of water, wash him with soap, and "bring my body back from the dead."

117. E.g. ibid.; Shay, *Odysseus in America*, 245.

118. See Shay, "Casualties" and Marlantes, *What It Is Like to Go to War*, 1. The recognition of these possible social functions has led some recent military scholars and psychologists to advocate for the establishment of communal rituals with "religious force" for both returning soldiers and the sending community (e.g., Shay, *Odysseus in America*, 245). Marlantes (*What It Is Like to Go to War*, 205) suggests such reconnec-

world should work has been violated, providing a type of purification and a plea for reordering.[119]

6. Conclusion

The preceding discussion has identified five types of potential postwar rituals of return and reintegration in the Hebrew Bible—purification of warriors, captives, and objects, appropriation of booty, memorial/monument construction, celebration or procession, and communal lamentation—each of which has various parallels in ancient Near Eastern and other extrabiblical sources. In a subsequent, but more tentative and suggestive move, the final section offered an interdisciplinary exploration of some potential points of connection between these rituals and recent perspectives within contemporary warfare studies, psychology, and clinical literature that may illuminate the symbolic functions of the rituals that remain unexplained within the ancient texts. Seen in this way, the postwar rituals of return and reintegration in the Hebrew Bible and related contexts, which treat mainly pragmatic issues, are not merely pragmatic. They construct a semiotics for the realities of war and potentially serve particular symbolic functions related to what contemporary warfare studies describes as "moral injury."

Many questions remain concerning the function, significance, and virtue (or lack thereof) of such rituals in ancient and modern contexts. Whatever symbolic functions the rituals may have had in their ancient context, contemporary readers may worry that the rituals fail to raise critical questions about the moral appropriateness of war and its deeds, perhaps allowing the participants too easily to justify (or celebrate) their actions without dealing with the effects their acts have "inscribed on the bodies, cities, and soil of the conquered."[120] On the other hand, perhaps the same rituals help warriors take responsibility for the morality of their actions, creating space for reflection, contrition, and perhaps atonement. In any case, consideration of postwar rituals of return and reintegration pushes scholars of warfare toward a more fully orbed study that moves

---

tion could take the form of religious services and acts or nonreligious practices such as sharing poetry and stories.

119. Morrow (*Protest against God*) identifies lament and protest in the Hebrew Bible as a type of therapy that attempts to deal with the pathology of guilt.

120. Brock and Lettini, *Soul Repair*, 107.

beyond how war was done to how war was conceived, constructed, and experienced personally, socially, and culturally. In this way, the study of these rituals might be a contribution that scholarship on ancient Israelite warfare can make to the broader quest of understanding more fully what it means to be human, especially in war-related circumstances.

Bibliography

Ashley, Timothy R. *The Book of Numbers*. NICOT. Grand Rapids: Eerdmans, 1993.
Bahrani, Zainab. *Rituals of War: The Body and Violence in Mesopotamia*. New York: Zone Books, 2008.
Bellinger, W. H., Jr. *Leviticus, Numbers*. NIBCOT. Peabody, Mass.: Hendrickson, 2001.
Bly, Robert. *Iron John: A Book about Men*. New York: Vantage Books, 1992.
Brenner, Athalya, and Fokkelien van Dijk-Hemmes, *On Gendering Texts: Female and Male Voices in the Hebrew Bible*. BInS 1. Leiden: Brill, 1993.
Brock, Rita Nakashima, and Gabriella Lettini, *Soul Repair: Recovering from Moral Injury after War*. Boston: Beacon, 2012.
Budd, Philip J. *Numbers*. WBC 5. Waco: Word, 1984.
Burkert, Walter. *Greek Religion*. Translated by John Raffan. Cambridge: Harvard University Press, 1985.
Chapman, Cynthia R. *The Gendered Language of Warfare in the Israelite-Assyrian Encounter*. HSM 62. Winona Lake, Ind.: Eisenbrauns, 2004.
Clausewitz, Carl von. *On War*. Translated by O. J. Matthijs Jolles. The Modern Library of the World's Best Books. New York: The Modern Library, 1943.
Collins, John J. *Does the Bible Justify Violence?* Facets. Minneapolis: Fortress, 2004.
Cooke, S. M. "Purification (Hebrew)." Pages 489–90 in volume 10 of *Encyclopedia of Religion and Ethics*. Edited by James Hastings. 12 vols. Edinburgh: T&T Clark, 1956.
Craigie, Peter C. *The Problem of War in the Old Testament*. Grand Rapids: Eerdmans, 1978.
Crouch, Carly L. *War and Ethics in the Ancient Near East: Military Violence in Light of Cosmology and History*. BZAW 407. Berlin: de Gruyter, 2009.
Dijk, Jan van. "Un Rituel de Purification des Armes et de l'Armée: Essai de Traduction de YBC 4184." Pages 107–17 in *Symbolae Biblicae et Meso-*

potamicae. Edited by M. A. Beek. Studia Francisci Scholten Memoriae Dicata 4. Leiden: Brill, 1973.

Dobbs-Allsopp, F. W. *Weep, O Daughter of Zion: A Study of the City-Lament Genre in the Hebrew Bible*. BibOr 44. Rome: Biblical Pontifical Institute, 1993.

Dozeman, Thomas B. "Numbers." Pages 1–268 in volume 2 of *The New Interpreter's Bible*. 12 vols. Nashville: Abingdon, 1998.

Elgavish, David. "The Division of the Spoils of War in the Bible and in the Ancient Near East." *ZABR* 8 (2000): 242–73.

Fadiman, Jeffrey A. *Meru of Mount Kenya: An Oral History of Tribal Warfare*. Athens: Ohio University Press, 1982.

Fallaize, E. N. "Purification, Introductory and Primitive." Pages 456–66 in volume 10 of *Encyclopedia of Religion and Ethics*. Edited by James Hastings. 12 vols. Edinburgh: T&T Clark, 1956.

Feder, Yitzhaq. *Blood Expiation in Hittite and Biblical Ritual: Origins, Context, and Meaning*. SBLWAW Supplement Series 2. Atlanta: Society of Biblical Literature, 2011.

Feldman, Emanuel. *Biblical and Post-biblical Defilement and Mourning: Law as Theology*. New York: Yeshiva University Press, 1977.

Fowler, W. Warde. *The Religious Experience of the Roman People*. New York: Cooper Square, 1971.

Gilders, William K. *Blood Ritual in the Hebrew Bible: Meaning and Power*. Baltimore: Johns Hopkins University Press, 2004.

Gray, George Buchanan. *Numbers: A Critical and Exegetical Commentary*. ICC. Edinburgh: T&T Clark, 1903.

Grayson, A. Kirk. "Assyrian Civilization." Pages 194–228 in *The Cambridge Ancient History Volume 3 Part 2: The Assyrian and Babylonian Empires and Other States of the Near East, from the Eighth to the Sixth Centuries b.c.* Cambridge: Cambridge University Press, 1991.

Greenstein, Edward L. and David Marcus. "The Akkadian Inscription of Idrimi." *JANES* 8 (1976): 59–96.

Goetze, Albrecht. "Warfare in Asia Minor." *Iraq* 25 (1963): 124–30.

Grossman, Dave. *On Killing: The Psychological Cost of Learning to Kill in War and Society*. New York: Back Bay Books, 1995.

Hobbs, T. R. *A Time for War: A Study of Warfare in the Old Testament*. Wilmington, Del.; Michael Glazier, 1989.

Kang, Sa-Moon. *Divine War in the Old Testament and the Ancient Near East*. BZAW 177. Berlin: de Gruyter, 1989.

Kelle, Brad E. *Ancient Israel at War 853–586 BC.* Essential Histories 67. Oxford: Osprey, 2007.

———. *Ezekiel.* New Beacon Bible Commentary. Kansas City: Beacon Hill Press, 2013.

Kelle, Brad E., and Frank Ritchel Ames, eds. *Writing and Reading War: Rhetoric, Gender, and Ethics in Biblical and Modern Contexts.* SBLSymS 42. Atlanta: Society of Biblical Literature, 2008.

Kottje, Raymund. *Die Tötung im Krieg: Ein moralisches und rechtliches Problem im frühen Mittelalter.* Barsbuettel: Institut für Theologie und Frieden, 1991.

Kravitz, Kathryn Frakes. "Divine Trophies of War in Assyria and Ancient Israel." Ph.D. diss., Brandeis University, 1999.

Kvasnica, Brian. "Shifts in Israelite War Ethics and Early Jewish Historiography of Plundering." Pages 175–96 in *Writing and Reading War: Rhetoric, Gender, and Ethics in Biblical and Modern Contexts.* Edited by Brad E. Kelle and Frank Ritchel Ames. SBLSymS 42. Atlanta: Society of Biblical Literature, 2008.

Lemos, T. M. "Shame and Mutilation of Enemies in the Hebrew Bible." *JBL* 125 (2006): 225–41.

Litz, Brett T., Nathan Stein, Eileen Delaney, Leslie Lebowitz, William P. Nash, Caroline Silva, Shira Maguen. "Moral Injury and Moral Repair in War Veterans: A Preliminary Model and Intervention Strategy." *Clinical Psychology Review* 29 (2009): 698–99.

Longman, Tremper, III, and Daniel G. Reid. *God Is a Warrior.* Studies in Old Testament Biblical Theology. Grand Rapids: Zondervan, 1995.

Macgregor, Sherry Lou. *Beyond Hearth and Home: Women in the Public Sphere in Neo-Assyrian Society.* SAAS 21. Publications of the Foundation for Finnish Assyriological Research 5. Helsinki: Neo-Assyrian Text Corpus, 2012.

Malamat, Abraham. "Campaigns to the Mediterranean by Iahdunlim and Other Early Mesopotamian Rulers." Pages 365–75 in *Studies in Honor of Benno Landsberger on His Seventy-Fifth Birthday.* Edited by H. Güterbock and T. Jacobsen. The Oriental Institute of Chicago Assyriological Studies 16. Chicago: University of Chicago Press, 1965.

Marlantes, Karl. *What It Is Like to Go to War.* New York: Atlantic Monthly, 2011.

Meyers, Carol. "Mother to Muse: An Archaeomusicological Study of Women's Performance in Israel." Pages 50–77 in *Recycling Biblical Figures: Papers Read at a NOSTER Colloquium in Amsterdam, 12–13 May*

1997. Edited by Athalya Brenner and Jan Willem van Henten. Studies in Religion and Theology 1. Leiden: Deo, 1999.

Milgrom, Jacob. "Studies in the Temple Scroll." *JBL* 97 (1978): 501–23.

Morrow, William S. *Protest against God: The Eclipse of a Biblical Tradition*. Hebrew Bible Monographs 4. Sheffield: Sheffield Phoenix, 2006.

Niditch, Susan. *War in the Hebrew Bible: A Study in the Ethics of Violence*. New York: Oxford University Press, 1993.

Noth, Martin. *Numbers*. OTL. Philadelphia: Westminster, 1968.

O'Connor, Kathleen M. *Jeremiah: Pain and Promise*. Minneapolis: Fortress, 2011.

Oded, Bustenay. *War, Peace, and Empire: Justifications for War in Assyrian Royal Inscriptions*. Wiesbaden: Ludwig Reichert, 1992.

Olyan, Saul M. *Rites and Rank: Hierarchy in Biblical Representations of Cult*. Princeton: Princeton University Press, 2000.

———. *Social Inequality in the World of the Text: The Significance of Ritual and Social Distinctions in the Hebrew Bible*. Journal of Ancient Judaism Supplements 4. Göttingen: Vandenhoeck & Ruprecht, 2011.

Otto, Eckart. *Krieg und Frieden in der Hebräischen Bibel und im Alten Orient: Aspekte für eine Friedensordnung in der Moderne*. Theologie und Frieden 18. Stuttgart: W. Kohlhammer, 1999.

Parke, Herbert W., and Donald E. W. Wormell, *The Delphic Oracle*. Oxford: Blackwell, 1956.

Parker, Robert. *Miasma: Pollution and Purification in Early Greek Religion*. Oxford: Clarendon, 1983.

Poethig, Eunice B. "The Victory Song Tradition of the Women of Israel." Ph.D. diss., Union Theological Seminary, 1985.

Pritchett, W. Kendrick. *The Greek State at War Part I*. Berkeley: University of California Press, 1971.

———. *The Greek State at War Part III: Religion*. Berkeley: University of California Press, 1979.

Rad, Gerhard von. *Holy War in Ancient Israel*. Translated by Marva J. Dawn. Eugene, Ore.: Wipf and Stock, 2000.

Ryken, Leland, James C. Wilhoit, and Tremper Longman III, eds. *Dictionary of Biblical Imagery*. Downer's Grove, Ill.: InterVarsity Press, 1998.

Shay, Jonathan. *Achilles in Vietnam: Combat Trauma and the Undoing of Character*. New York: Atheneum, 1994.

———. "The Birth of Tragedy—Out of the Needs of Democracy." *Didaskalia: The Journal for Ancient Performance*. Online: http://www.didaskalia.net/issues/vol2no2/shay.html.

———. "Casualties." *Daedalus* 140 (2011): 179–88.
———. *Odysseus in America: Combat Trauma and the Trials of Homecoming*. New York: Scribner, 2002.
Smend, Rudolph. *Yahweh War and Tribal Confederation: Reflections upon Israel's Earliest History*. Translated from 2d ed. by Max Gray Rogers. Nashville: Abingdon, 1970.
Smith-Christopher, Daniel L. *A Biblical Theology of Exile*. OBT. Minneapolis: Fortress, 2002.
———. "Engendered Warfare and the Ammonites in Amos 1.13." Pages 15–40 in *Aspects of Amos: Exegesis and* Interpretation. Edited by A. C. Hagedorn and A. Mein. LHBOTS 536. New York: T&T Clark, 2011.
Snaith, Norman H. *Leviticus and Numbers*. The Century Bible. London: Thomas Nelson and Sons, 1967.
Tick, Edward. *War and the Soul: Healing Our Nation's Veterans from Posttraumatic Stress Disorder*. Wheaton, Ill.: Quest Books, 2005.
Van Creveld, Martin. *The Culture of War*. New York: Ballantine, 2008.
Vaux, Roland de. *Ancient Israel*. McGraw-Hill Paperbacks. New York: McGraw-Hill, 1965.
Verkamp, Bernard J. *The Moral Treatment of Returning Warriors in Early Medieval and Modern Times*. 2nd ed. Scranton: University of Scranton Press, 2006.
Versnel, H. S. *Triumphus: An Inquiry into the Origin, Development, and Meaning of the Roman Triumph*. Leiden: Brill, 1970.
Watts, James W. *Ritual and Rhetoric in Leviticus: From Sacrifice to Scripture*. Cambridge: Cambridge University Press, 2007.
Weimar, Peter. "Die Jahwekriegserzählungen in Exodus 14, Joshua 10, Richter 4 und 1 Samuel 7." *Bib* 57 (1976): 38–73.
Wenham, Gordon J. *Numbers*. TOTC 4. Downer's Grove, Ill.: InterVarsity Press, 1981.
Wright, David P. *The Disposal of Impurity: Elimination Rites in the Bible and in Hittite and Mesopotamian Literature*. SBLDS 101. Atlanta: Scholars Press, 1987.
———. "Purification from Corpse-Contamination in Numbers XXXI 19–24." *VT* 35 (1985): 213–23.
Younger, K. Lawson, Jr. *Ancient Conquest Accounts: A Study in Ancient Near Eastern and Biblical History Writing*. JSOTSup 98. Sheffield: JSOT Press, 1990.

Does Yhwh Get His Hands Dirty?
Reading Isaiah 63:1-6 in Light of Depictions of Divine Postbattle Purification*

Jason A. Riley

Does Yhwh "get his hands dirty"? That is, was Yhwh considered, as were other ancient Near Eastern deities, to have become defiled or unclean due to his acts of killing and/or contact with blood? Postbattle purification rituals for human warriors, including those intended to purify warriors from defilement caused by bloodshed, are commonly attested throughout the ancient Near East and beyond.[1] However, this article moves beyond the human aspect of postbattle rituals to investigate divine postbattle purifica-

---

* This essay benefited greatly from the comments of Christopher B. Hays, Andrew J. Riley, Daniel Rickett, and Alex Ramos. I am also thankful to the editors Brad E. Kelle, Frank Ritchel Ames, and Jacob L. Wright for the opportunity to present my research in the SBL Warfare in Ancient Israel Section at the 2012 Annual Meeting.

1. Israelite, Num 31:13–21 (purification from corpse/blood contamination); Hittite, *CTH* 426 (this ritual is for the entire army to purify them after a defeat; see "The Ritual Between the Pieces," translated by Billie Jean Collins [*COS* 1:160–61]; Olivier Masson, "A propos d'un rituel hittite pour la lustration d'une armée: le rite de purification par le passage entre les deux parties d'une victime," *Revue de l'historie des religions* 137 [1950]: 5–25; James C. Moyer, "The Concept of Ritual Purity among the Hittites" [Ph.D. diss., Brandeis University, 1969], 94–95); Assyrian (several royal inscriptions describing postbattle purification; Abraham Malamat, "Campaigns to the Mediterranean by Iahdunlim and Other Early Mesopotamian rulers," *AS* 16 [1965]: 365–74); Egyptian ("The Victory Stela of King Piye," translated by Miriam Lichtheim [*COS* 2:44]); Greek (Hektor admits that he must purify himself after battle in order to make an offering to Zeus [Homer, *Iliad* 6:263–68]). Relatively modern examples include North American Indians (Lewis R. Farnell, *The Evolution of Religion* [New York: G. P. Putnam's Sons, 1905], 94) and the Basutos of South Africa (E. Casalis, *The Basutos; Or, Twenty-three Years in South Africa* [London: Nisbet, 1861], 267).

tion. The method of this study is to establish a typology of divine postbattle purification in the ancient Near East, with which to evaluate the possible existence of a similar phenomenon within ancient Israel and associated with Yhwh. To anticipate the conclusion, the following analysis suggests that a common motif, or perhaps even literary form, existed throughout the ancient Near East in which gods who engaged in individual, bloody combat were thought to have become ritually impure and in need of purification, and the Divine Warrior hymn in Isa 63:1–6 supports the idea that Yhwh was considered in similar terms.

1. General Divine Defilement and Purification

Prior to discussing examples of defilement and purification of ancient Near Eastern deities after battle, it will be helpful to demonstrate more generally that deities could become impure and need to be purified. Several ancient Near Eastern texts depict gods as capable of becoming ritually defiled and needing purification.[2] Examples exist in Akkadian, Sumerian, Ugaritic, and Hittite literature.[3]

---

2. By this I mean literary depictions of gods and not the defilement and purification of statues and other physical representations of gods.

3. Ugaritic literature provides at least three references to Anat cleansing or purifying herself: *KTU*² 1.3 II.1–III.8 (discussed below; Manfried Dietrich, Oswald Loretz, and Joaquín Sanmartín, *The Cuneiform Alphabetic Texts from Ugarit, Ras Ibn Hani and Other Places* [*KTU*; 2nd ed.; ALASP 8; Münster: Ugarit-Verlag, 1995]); *KTU*² 1.101 (see Loren R. Fisher, "A New Ugaritic Calendar from Ugarit," *HTR* 63 [1970]: 495, n. 41; Johannes C. de Moor, "Studies in the New Alphabetic Texts from Ras Shamra I," *UF* 1 [1969]: 180–83); and possibly *KTU*² 1.96 (see Mark S. Smith, "Anat's Warfare Cannibalism and the West Semitic Ban," in *The Pitcher is Broken: Memorial Essays for Gösta W. Ahlström* [eds. Steven W. Holloway and Lowell K. Handy; JSOTSup 190; Sheffield: Sheffield Academic Press, 1995], 368–86). For Hittite literature, see Moyer, "Ritual Purity Among the Hittites," 38, 49. One example is the Myth of Telipinu, a "disappearing deity text" that describes the disappearance of the Storm God's son, Telipinu. At one point in the story, a bee is sent to find Telipinu, and upon locating him purifies (*parkunu*-) and sanctifies (*šuppiyaḫḫ*-) Telipinu from anger, evil, and sin before returning him to the divine assembly and his land. See "The Disappearance of Telipinu," §22 (A iii 28–34) (Harry A. Hoffner Jr., *Hittite Myths* [ed. Gary M. Beckman; SBLWAW 2; Atlanta: Scholars Press, 1990]). On the ritual meaning of the verbs *parkunu*- and *šuppiyaḫḫ*-, see Hans G. Güterbock and Harry A. Hoffner Jr., eds., *The Hittite Dictionary of the Oriental Institute of the University of Chicago, Vol. P* (Chicago: Oriental Institute, 1989–), 171. In a myth of Canaanite origin in Hittite translation, the

Akkadian literature offers a number of examples of divine defilement and purification.[4] In Atrahasis (Tablet 1, V: 204–209), Enki speaks of instituting a purification ritual for the gods to purify themselves after the slaughter of the god Wê-ila:[5]

^{d}enki piamšu īpušamma issaqar ana ilī^{meš} rabûti ina arḫi sebûti u šapatti
tēliltam lušaškin rimka ilam išten litbuḫū-ma litellilū ilū^{meš} ina ṭibi

---

god Baal must be purified from injuries done to him by Asherah (see Harry A. Hoffner Jr., "Hittite Mythological Texts: A Survey," in *Unity and Diversity: Essays in the History, Literature, and Religion of the Ancient Near East* [ed. Hans Goedicke and J. J. M. Roberts; Johns Hopkins University Near Eastern Studies; Baltimore: Johns Hopkins University Press, 1975], 141–42).

4. Only two examples are discussed here; however, others could be added. For example, in the Myth of Nergal and Ereshkigal, after Ereshkigal has intercourse with Erra, she says, "I am unclean, and I am not pure enough to perform the judging of the great gods" ("Nergal and Ereshkigal," translated by Stephanie Dalley [*COS* 1:387]). Due to her impurity she cannot perform her divine function (see E. Jan Wilson, *"Holiness" and "Purity" in Mesopotamia* [AOAT 237; Kevelaer: Butzon and Bercker, 1994], 74). In this same myth, when the divine messenger Namtar enters the divine assembly, an unknown god tells Ea, "Let Namtar, the messenger who has come to us, drink our water, wash, and anoint himself" (*COS* 1:388). The Descent of Ishtar also illustrates this phenomenon. After Dumuzi has died, his body is to be washed with pure water and anointed with sweet oil—common language of purification ("The Descent of Ishtar to the Underworld," translated by Stephanie Dalley [*COS* 1:383]). Sumerian literature offers a few examples of the defilement and purification of deities. In a Sumerian hymn to Inanna, prior to eating sacrifices offered to her, her worshipers "clean up a place" and "set up handwashing (things) for her." This hymn, and the immediate context, is full of language of purity. Several lines later, the hymn states that "the holy one eats in the pure places, the clean places," and further along the hymn refers to "pure libations." Her worshipers purify the bedding they put down for her, and Inanna herself bathes the loins of another god, Iddin-Dagan, with whom she subsequently sleeps and also bathes herself. It is unlikely that the imagery of washing refers simply to physical cleansing, but rather means some sort of ritual purification. See Thorkild Jacobsen, *Harps That Once...: Sumerian Poetry in Translation* (New Haven: Yale University Press, 1987), 121–23.

5. For the text, see W. G. Lambert and Alan R. Millard, *Atra-ḫasis: The Babylonian Story of the Flood* (Oxford: Clarendon Press, 1969), 57–59. See also William L. Moran, "The Creation of Man in Atrahasis I 192–248," *BASOR* 200 (1970): 50. For a brief discussion, see Pamela Barmash, *Homicide in the Biblical World* (Cambridge: Cambridge University Press, 2005), 111. Enki's purification bath parallels Aruru's hand-washing prior to creating Enkidu in the Gilgamesh Epic (see Jeffrey H. Tigay, *The Evolution of the Gilgamesh Epic* [Philadelphia: University of Pennsylvania Press, 1982], 192–97).

Enki opened his mouth and spoke to the great gods "On the first day, seventh day, and fifteenth day of the month let me institute a purification bath.[6] Let them slaughter one god, and then let the gods be purified by submersion."[7]

W. G. Lambert and Alan R. Millard read the last two lines to mean, "Let one god be slaughtered so that all the gods may be cleansed in a dipping,"[8] as if the god is slaughtered for the purpose of the other gods' purification. However, the overall structure of the passage shows that the god is killed in order for his blood to be mixed with clay to create humans (lines 210–13), not so that his blood may be used to purify the gods. As William Moran has argued, at no time in Mesopotamia was blood believed to have had magical cleansing powers.[9] The blood is what makes the gods impure. Although it is possible that this passage is an etiology for the institution of the ritual purification bath,[10] as Moran notes, the purification is presented as occurring after the god's slaughter.[11] The purpose of the cleansing then

---

6. Literally, "let me establish a purification, a bath," since the syntax seems to suggest that *rimka* is in apposition to *tēliltam*. See "Atra-ḫasis," translated by Benjamin R. Foster (*COS* 1:451).

7. All translations are the author's unless otherwise noted.

8. Lambert and Millard, *Atra-ḫasis*, 59.

9. Moran, "The Creation of Man," 51. See also A. Leo Oppenheim, *Ancient Mesopotamia: Portrait of a Dead Civilization* (Chicago: University of Chicago Press, 1964), 192. Even in the *Akītu* festival, the one who slaughters the sacrificial sheep became contaminated (see Julye Bidmead, *The Akītu Festival: Religious Continuity and Royal Legitimation in Mesopotamia* [Gorgias Dissertations, Near East Series 2; Piscataway: Gorgias Press, 2002], 74).

10. Moran, "The Creation of Man," 51, n. 9.

11. See "*balālu*," *CAD* 2:42: *ilam ištēn liṭbuḫuma lītellilu ilū ina ṭibi ina šērišu u damišu* DN *li-ba-li-il ṭidda ilumma u awīlum li-ib-ta-al-li-lu puḫur ina ṭiddi* "let them slaughter one of the gods, and the gods purify themselves through immersion (after this deed), let Nintu mix clay with his flesh and blood, let god and man (thus) become altogether of the same nature through the clay." Von Soden renders the equivalent lines in an Old Babylonian version of the myth as "Einen Gott soll man schlachten, dann mögen sich die Götter reinigen durch Untertauchen in seinem Fleisch und seinem Blut!" See Wolfram von Soden, "Zu einigin altbabylonischen Dichtungen," *Or* 26 (1957): 309. He takes the next line of Enki's speech, *ina širīšu u damišu*, as a part of the purification instructions. However, the syntax and structure require this line to be interpreted with the following line; that is, the flesh and blood are what Nintu is going to mix with the clay in order to make humans.

was to purify the gods from both blood-contamination and responsibility for the god's death.[12]

2. Divine Purification Related to Battle

A specific context in which ancient Near Eastern deities become defiled and undergo some type of purification ritual is after battle. In the Sumerian mythic poem *Lugal-e*, the god Ninurta battles Azag, a figure which appears to be a personified mountain (but which has also been interpreted as a dragon, volcano, pine tree, or other type of monster).[13] Prior to Ninurta's first encounter with Azag, Ninurta is instructed to purify his weapons after battle (lines 126–27): "Ninurta, after gathering the enemy in a battle-net, after erecting a great reed-altar, lord, heavenly serpent, purify (*a tu$_5$-bi$_2$-ib$_2$*) your pickaxe and your mace!"[14] Ninurta later attacks, kills, and subsequently dismembers Azag. Ninurta then follows his victory by washing his belt and weapon (lines 302–303): "The lord ... his belt and mace in water, he washed the blood from his clothes, the hero wiped his brow, he made a victory-chant over the dead body."[15] Thorkild Jacobsen understands the broken text to refer to washing: "The lord rinsed belt and weapon in water, rinsed the *mittu*-mace in water."[16] In another mythical text, "The Return

---

12. Moran, "The Creation of Man," 51.
13. See Fumi Karahashi, "Fighting the Mountain: Some Observations on the Sumerian Myths of Inanna and Ninurta," *JNES* 63 (2004): 114–15.
14. For transliteration, see Jeremy A. Black, et al., *The Electronic Text Corpus of Sumerian Literature* (*ETCSL*) (Oxford 1998–2006), online: http://etcsl.orinst.ox.ac.uk/cgi-bin/etcsl.cgi?text=c.1.6.2& display =Crit&charenc=j&lineid=c162. 122#c162.122. For translation, see http://etcsl.orinst.ox.ac.uk/cgi-bin/etcsl .cgi?text=t.1.6.2&display =Crit&charenc =j&lineid=t162.p9#t162.p9. Jacobsen renders these lines as "do, Ninurta, after you have made the netlike enclosure and have put down the (cultic) reed hut rinse, (O) adder of heaven, arrow and weapon with water!" (Jacobsen, *Harps That Once*, 242–43). Van Dijk, in his critical edition of this myth, also interprets the verbal phrase here as referring to purification: "aprés les avoir ramassés comme dans un filet de guerre, après avoir érigé un autel de purification; Seigneur, Constrictor céleste, purifie ton pic et ta massue" (J. J. A. van Dijk, *Lugal ud me-lám-bi nir-Ğál: Le récit épique et didactique des Travaux de Ninurta, de Déluge et de la Nouvelle Création*, vol. 1 [Leiden: Brill, 1983], 68).
15. Black et al., *ETCSL*, http://etcsl.orinst.ox.ac.uk/cgi-bin/etcsl.cgi?text=t.1.6.2 &display=Crit&charenc =j&lineid=t162.p22#t162.p22. Again, van Dijk interprets the act here as purification. See van Dijk, *Lugal ud me-lám-bi nir-Ğál*, 89.
16. See, Jacobsen, *Harps That Once*, 250.

of Ninurta to Nipru," Ninurta requests that his weapons be purified (lines 152–54): "Let my father therefore bring in my battle trophies and weapons for me. Let Enlil bathe (*a he₂-em-tu₅-tu₅-[de₃]*) my heroic arms. Let him pour holy water on the fierce arms which bore my weapons."[17] The phrase used in both of these contexts, "to wash, to purify" (*a tu₅*), is the equivalent of the Akkadian verb *ramāku* ("to bathe, to wash")[18] and similar to the Akkadian *rimku* (purification bath). Thus, the Sumerian phrase *a-tu₅-* seems to refer to a ritual washing ceremony.[19] The verbal phrase *a tu₅* is also used in cultic contexts. For instance, the verb is used in a tablet providing instructions for cultic chores to be done in the sixth month of the year by the highest official of the Inanna Temple.[20] On day fifteen, the official is to bathe (*a tu₅*) the goddess—this has been called the "main rite of the deity."[21]

This Ninurta versus Azag episode is particularly instructive since it parallels the postbattle purification rituals referred to in the Mesopotamian royal inscriptions. In fact, in reference to Ninurta washing his weapons, Jacobsen makes this very identification in a footnote to his translation: "Rinsing the weapons in water was done after the battle or campaign was over."[22] This demonstrates that postbattle purification was a common practice, and the language of "washing one's weapons" was a common idiom symbolic of purification. A typical example of these statements

---

17. Black et al., *ETCSL*, http://etcsl.orinst.ox.ac.uk/cgi-bin/etcsl.cgi?text=t.1.6.1&display=Crit&charenc= gcirc&lineid=t161. p31#t161.p31. For transliteration see, http://etcsl.orinst.ox.ac.uk/cgi-bin/etcsl.cgi?text=c.1.6.1& display=Crit& charenc=gcirc&lineid=c161.152#c161.152.

18. See "*a tu*" in *The Electronic Pennsylvania Sumerian Dictionary*, online at: http:// psd.museum.upenn.edu/epsd/nepsd-frame.html. See also *ramāku* in *CAD* 14:111–14.

19. See Albrecht Goetze, "A Drehem Tablet Dealing with Leather Objects," *JCS* 9 (1955): 21.

20. See further Miguel Civil, "Daily Chores in Nippur," *JCS* 32 (1990): 229–32; Richard L. Zettler and Walther Sallaberger, "Inana's Festival at Nippur under the Third Dynasty of Ur," *Zeitschrift für Assyriologie und vorderasiatische Archäologie* 101 (2011): 25.

21. Zettler and Sallaberger, "Inana's Festival," 25. They also note, "The 'daily chores' date the 'bathing' of Inana to the fifteenth day, a rite which symbolized the ritual renewal of the divine statue in the annual main festival of a deity" (24).

22. Jacobsen, *Harps That Once*, 243 n. 13.

appears in Sargon of Akkad's (2334–2279 B.C.E.)²³ inscription detailing the defeat of Uruk and the South (lines 44–58):²⁴

é-nin-mar.KI SAG.GIŠ.RA *ù* BÀD-*śu* ⌈Ì.GUL.GUL⌉ ⌈*ù*⌉ KALAM. MA.KI-*śu ù lagaš* (LA.BUR.ŠIR.RI).KI *a-dì-ma ti-a-am-tim* SAG.GIŠ. RA *kakkīsu* [GIŠ.TUKUL] *in tiāmtim imsi* [Ì.LUḪ]

He conquered Eninmar, destroyed its walls, and conquered its district and Lagaš as far as the sea. He washed his weapons in the sea (*kakkīsu* [GIŠ.TUKUL] *in tiāmtim imsi*).

Similar statements are found in inscriptions by Naram-Sin (2260–2213 B.C.E.),²⁵ Yaḫdun-lim (Mari, approximately nineteenth to eighteenth centuries B.C.E.),²⁶ Aššurnasirpal II (Assyria, 883–859 B.C.E.),²⁷ Shalmaneser

---

23. See Douglas Frayne, *Sargonic and Gutian Periods (2334–2113 BC)* (RIMA Early Periods 2; Toronto: University of Toronto Press, 1993), 7. See also Malamat, "Campaigns to the Mediterranean," 365. For translations, see "Inscription of Sargon," translated by Burkhart Kienast (*COS* 2:243); "Sargon of Agade," translated by A. Leo Oppenheim (*ANET*, 267–68).

24. Frayne, *Sargonic and Gutian Periods*, 11.

25. *kakkīsu* [GIŠ.TUKUL-*kí-śu₄*] *i*[*n*] *tiāmtim sapiltim imsi* "and washed his weapons in the Lower Sea" (Frayne, *Sargonic and Gutian Periods*, 97). For the dates, see Piotr Bienkowski and Alan Millard, eds., *Dictionary of the Ancient Near East* (Pennsylvania: University of Pennsylvania Press, 2000), 330.

26. *ina lē'ûtim u gāmirūtim ana kišad tiāmtim illik-ma ana ayyabba nīqî šarrūtišu rabiam iqqi u ṣabušu ina qereb ayyabba mê irmuk* "by means of his strength and overpowering might went to the shore of the sea, and made a great offering (befitting) his kingship to the Sea. His troops bathed themselves in the Sea" (Douglas Frayne, *Old Babylonian Period (2003–1595 BC)* [RIMA Early Periods 4; Toronto: University of Toronto Press, 1990], 605–606). See also Malamat, "Campaigns to the Mediterranean," 367. This inscription is particularly interesting because of the deified nature of the Sea (see Abraham Malamat, "The Divine Nature of the Mediterranean Sea in the Foundation Inscription of Yaḫdunlim," in *Mari in Retrospect: Fifty Years of Mari and Mari Studies* [ed. Gordon D. Young; Winona Lake: Eisenbrauns, 1992], 211–15; and Sa-Moon Kang, *Divine War in the Old Testament and in the Ancient Near East* [BZAW 177; New York: Walter de Gruyter, 1989], 48).

27. *ina tâmti rabīti* [GAL-*te*] *kakkīy*[*a* (GIŠ.TUKUL.MEŠ-ia) *lū ullil niqê* "[I washed] my weapons in the Great Sea" (A. Kirk Grayson, *Assyrian Rulers of the Early First Millennium BC I (1114–859 BC)* [RIMA Assyrian Periods 2; Toronto: University of Toronto Press, 1991], 298). See also Malamat, "Campaigns to the Mediterranean," 369.

III (Assyria, 858–824 B.C.E.),[28] as well as the postbattle cleansing of Gilgamesh after his battle with Humbaba (Standard Babylonian, Tablet VI, lines 1–30):[29]

> *imsi mališu ubbib tillīšu / unassis*[30] *qimmatsu elu ṣerišu / iddi maršutišu ittalbiša zakutišu*[31]

> He washed his filthy hair, then cleansed his battle equipment / he tossed his hair over his back / He threw down his soiled *garments* and put on clean *ones*.

The line common in the royal inscriptions is: "He/I washed (that is, purified) his/my weapon in the sea."[32] These statements in the royal inscrip-

---

28. *kakkīya* [GIŠ.TULUL.MEŠ-*ia*] *ina tâmti ullil niqî* [UDU.SISKUR.MEŠ] *ana ilīya* [DINGIR.MEŠ-*ia*] *inqi* [BAL-*qî*] "I washed my weapons in the sea [and] made sacrifices to my gods" (A. Kirk Grayson, *Assyrian Rulers of the Early First Millennium BC II (858–745 BC)* [RIMA Assyrian Periods 3; Toronto: University of Toronto Press, 1996], 15). For other similar statements by Shalmaneser, see ibid., 9, 21, 25, 29, 34, 39, 48, 51, 65, 74, 75, 103, 104. See also, Malamat, "Campaigns to the Mediterranean," 369. Shalmaneser's inscriptions use the phrase "to wash my weapon" numerous times. Occasionally, the phrase changes forms: "washed my weapons," "washed the fierce weapons of Aššur," "washed the weapon(s) of Aššur." As the discussion in *CAD* under *kakku* indicates, it is not always easy to determine meaning of the word *kakku* in royal inscriptions. It could mean a weapon in general, a ceremonial weapon or object, or the Assyrian army. The phrase "weapon of Aššur" may also designate some type of battle standard with a divine symbol (see "*kakku*," *CAD* 8:55–57).

29. Postbattle purification in individual combat is attested in Akkadian and Sumerian legends of Gilgamesh. In tablet VI of the Gilgamesh epic, Gilgamesh kills the monster Huwawa, cuts off his head, washes himself and his equipment and takes his throne. See "The Epic of Gilgamesh," translated by E. A. Speiser (*ANET*, 83–84). Malamat provides a brief discussion concerning the typological and geographical parallels between Gilgamesh's expedition and the expeditions of Mesopotamian rulers. Postbattle purification could also be added to the parallels he draws. See Malamat, "Campaigns to the Mediterranean," 372–73.

30. According to George, the form *unassis* "defies interpretation" but is the only reasonable reading of the tablet (see Andrew R. George, *The Babylonian Gilgamesh Epic* [Oxford: Oxford University Press, 2003], 2:829).

31. Akkadian text taken from Simo Parpola, *The Standard Babylonian Epic of Gilgamesh* (SAA Cuneiform Texts 1; Helsinki: Neo-Assyrian Text Corpus Project, 1997), 91. See also, George, *The Babylonian Gilgamesh Epic*, 1:618.

32. *kakkēja ina tâmti ú-lil*. The verb here is *elēlu*, which in these contexts means to purify in a ritual sense. See "*elēlu*," *CAD* 4:81. See also "*kakku*," *CAD* 8:51.

tions are not merely metaphor[33] but rather refer to a form of ritual cleansing, particularly since several of the inscriptions also mentions sacrifice in the same context.[34]

Finally, a possible example appears in *Enuma Eliš* (Tablet V, lines 90–93) and refers to Marduk after he has defeated and slaughtered Tiamat:[35]

[…] ⌜x⌝ *ubbuḫu turbuʾ šašmi* / [… m]*êʾ-ma taḫu qu* ⌜LIŠ?⌝[36] /*ḫašurru* x [
…] *zumuršu ušalbak* / *ūteddiq tēdīq rubûti*[*šu*]

… surrounded by the dust of combat, (water?) … he conditioned his body with oil, he clothed himself with royal attire.

At this point in the narrative Marduk returns from battle with Tiamat and is covered in dust. After a difficult line (line 91) in which the word "water" may be read, the text says that Marduk covered his body with oil and put on royal garb. In light of the affinities with the depiction of Gilgamesh's washing and changing clothes described above, the reference to Marduk anointing himself with oil and the possible reading of "water" in line 91 suggest that the difficult line would have referred to Marduk washing himself.[37]

Overall, the Sumerian and Assyrian mythological examples parallel the acts of ritual purification described in the royal inscriptions.[38] In this

---

33. See J. J. A. van Dijk, "Un Rituel de Purification des Armes et de l'Armée: Essai de Traduction de YBC 4184," in *Symbolae Biblicae et Mesopotamicae* (ed. M. A. Beek et al.; Studia Francisci Scholten Memoriae Dicata 4; Leiden: Brill, 1973), 107.

34. See Malamat, "Campaigns to the Mediterranean," 367.

35. For the text, see Philippe Talon, *The Standard Babylonian Creation Myth: Enūma Eliš* (SAACuneiform Texts 4; Helsinki: Neo-Assyrian Text Corpus Project, 2005), 20, 59.

36. Based on Talon's transcription, the first half of line 91 is damaged, and the second half makes little, if any, sense. In fact, Talon does not even attempt to render the line other than the possible reading of the word "water" (see ibid., 97).

37. Foster provides a brief summarizing preface to this section in his translation which supports this analysis: "Marduk cleans himself and dons his insignia." See Bejamin R. Foster, *Before the Muses: An Anthology of Akkadian Literature* (3rd ed.; Bethesda: CDL, 2005), 466.

38. This would not be the only instance of a portion of the Gilgamesh epic with parallels to Mesopotamian royal inscriptions. For instance, the section of the Gilgamesh hymn in the late version of the epic which describes Gilgamesh's creation in terms of being destined by the gods parallels parts of several royal inscriptions that

case, art seems to imitate life—or rather, myth seems to imitate ritual—and the mythological and inscriptional acts should be considered as describing the same phenomenon—ritual purification after battle.[39] One critique which may be raised regarding the connection made between these various examples is that there is an inconsistent use of terms to refer to washing: Sumerian A TU₅ ("to wash") // Akk *ramāku*), LUḪ ("to clean, wash" // Akk *mesû*), Akkadian *ramāku* ("to bathe"), *mesû* ("to wash"), *ubbubu* ("to cleanse, ritually purify"), and *ullulu* ("to purify"). Even so, each of these verbs may connote ritual purification and are all used in ritual texts describing purification.[40] The distinction between the verbs is mainly in the manner of the purification. The verbs *ubbubu* and *ullulu* are overarching terms which may mean "to purify" but do not specify the means. The verb *ramāku* refers to purification through bathing, while *mesû* refers to purification through washing of an object (for example, hands, feet, a weapon, and so on), and its purificatory connotations are most explicit in its uses in reference to *mīs pî* and *mīs qātē* rituals. Thus, although various terms are used, they each refer to ritual cleansing in these texts.

Ugarit provides one explicit example of a deity purifying herself after bloody battle. This occurs in *KTU*² 1.3 II.1–III.8, part of the Baal Cycle, in which Anat slaughters a number of human warriors, feasts on her victims, and then ritually cleanses herself from the bloodshed. Only the most relevant section is presented here (II: 23–41):[41]

(23) *maʾda timtaḫiṣuna*[42]*wa-taʿānu*
(24) *tiḫtaṣibu wa-taḥdiyu ʿanatu*
(25) *tigdadu kabiduhi bi-ṣaḥaqi*

---

describe the gods calling the king's name for kingship either before birth or during the king's childhood. Additionally, Ishtar's marriage proposal to Gilgamesh has been compared to a sacred marriage ritual. See Tigay, *The Evolution of the Gilgamesh Epic*, 153–58, 174–76.

39. See also Moyer, "Ritual Purity Among the Hittites," 95.

40. Wolfram von Soden, *The Ancient Orient: An Introduction to the Study of the Ancient Near East* (trans. Donald G. Schley; Grand Rapids: Eerdmans, 1994), 197.

41. See also Mark S. Smith, "The Baal Cycle," in *Ugaritic Narrative Poetry* (ed. Simon B. Parker; SBLWAW 9; Atlanta: Scholars Press, 1997), 107–109. For a lengthy discussion of the passage, including text critical notes, see Mark S. Smith and Wayne T. Pitard, *The Ugaritic Baal Cycle, Vol. 2: Introduction with Text, Translation and Commentary of KTU/CAT 1.3–1.4* (Leiden: Brill, 2009), 186–94.

42. This is a Gt 3fs imperfect + enclitic *–na*.

yamluʾu (26) *libbuhi bi-šimḫati*
kabidu ʿanati (27) *tūšiyati*
ki-birkêma tagʿallilu bi-dami (28) *ḏamīri*
hilqīma bi-mimaʿi mahîrīma
(29) *ʿadê tišbaʿu timtaḫiṣu bi-bêti*
(30) *tiḫtaṣibu bêna ṯulḫanīma*
yamḫû. (31) *bi-bêti dama ḏamīri*
yûṣaqū šamna (32) *šalimu bi-ṣaʿi*
tirḥaṣu yadêhi batū (33) *[l]atu ʿanatu*
ʾuṣbātihi yabamatu liʾmīma
(34) *[t]irḥaṣu yadêhi bi-dami ḏamīri*
(35) *[ʾu]ṣbātihi bi-mimaʿi mahîrīma*
(36) *[ṯa]ʿāru kissiʾāti li-kissiʾāti*
ṯulḫanāti (37) *li- ṯulḫanā<ti>*
hadumīma tiṯʿaru li- hadumīma
(38) *taḫsupīna mêhi wa-tirḥaṣu*
(39) *ṭalla šamīma šamna arṣi*
rabība (40) *[rā]kibi ʿurpati*
ṭalla šamūma tissakūhi
(41) *[ra]bība nasakūhi kabkabūma*

She kills abundantly and looks *around,*
Anat fights and observes.
Her innards swell with laughter,
Her heart fills with joy,
the innards of Anat with victory.
For she plunges *her* knees into warrior blood,
her limbs into the innards of the combatants.
Until she is sated, she kills in *her* house,
She fights between the tables.
They clean the warrior blood from *her* house,
they pour out the oil of peace from a bowl.
The virgin Anat washes her hands,
her fingers, the sister-in-law of the people.
She washes her hands in warrior blood,[43]

---

43. Contra Smith and Pitard, who understand this line as meaning Anat washed her hands *of,* i.e., *from,* the blood, rather than *in* the blood. See Smith and Pitard, *Ugaritic Baal Cycle,* 136, 189–90. Dennis Pardee left the question open of whether *rḥṣ b* means "wash in" or "wash from" due to lack of evidence (see Dennis Pardee, "The Preposition in Ugaritic," *UF* 8 [1976]: 266–67). There is no way to decisively determine which meaning is correct. However, it seems overly redundant to state that Anat

> her fingers in the innards of the combatants.
> Arranging chairs to chairs,
> tables to tables,
> footstools she arranges to footstools.
> She draws water and she bathes.
> Dew of the heavens, oil of the earth,
> drizzle of the Cloudrider.
> Dew, the heavens pour on her,
> drizzle, the stars pour on her.

After the slaughter, the blood is wiped from Anat's house, she washes her hands *in* warrior blood, and then finally water is drawn and she washes again.[44] Similar to *KTU*[2] 1.101, Anat washes her hands and fingers and purifies herself. In this passage, the contaminating element is clearly blood.

The clear reference to oil and washing denotes some type of ritual purification. These actions parallel numerous references in Ugaritic and other ancient Near Eastern depictions of deities and humans being ritually purified using oil,[45] and Pardee understands these acts as purificatory rites used to prepare one for a change in status.[46] The oil referred to here may refer to either a libation or an element in the purification ritual. Purification baths are known at Ugarit particularly in the enthronement and atonement rituals in which the king ritually bathed and purified himself on specific days and in which the "oil of peace" was used as a libation.[47] However, oil was also used as a purifying agent or to anoint an individual during a purification rite.[48] Regardless of the intended purpose of the oil,

---

washes again (line 38) if she had previously washed herself from the blood and guts in lines 34–35. Logically, it makes more sense to understand the imagery as progressing from Anat washing in the blood of her opponents (lines 34–35) to then washing the blood from her (line 38). Furthermore, the imagery of washing in the blood of one's opponents is also found in biblical texts (1 Kgs 22:38; Ps 58:11; 68:24).

44. See Smith, "The Baal Cycle," 108–109; Smith and Pitard, *The Ugaritic Baal Cycle*, 186–94.

45. For a discussion of the various elements in purification rituals and an example in an Ugaritic letter, see Dennis Pardee, "A New Ugaritic Letter," *BO* 34 (1977): 14–17.

46. Ibid., 17.

47. See Gregorio del Olmo Lete, *Canaanite Religion According to the Liturgical Texts of Ugarit* (trans. W. G. E. Watson; Bethesda: CDL, 1999), 141, 144.

48. See Pardee, "A New Ugaritic Letter," 14–18.

the example in *KTU*² 1.3 is important because the washing and purification occur after battle and bloodshed.⁴⁹

What these examples demonstrate is that ancient Near Eastern deities were not considered to be impervious to impurity.⁵⁰ They could become defiled or polluted and required cleansing and purification, particularly after battle. These examples are obviously limited, and certainly not every ancient deity is depicted in such a manner.⁵¹ From the above examples, however, it is possible to determine a number of elements which exhibit a certain literary form: mythological setting, individual combat between a deity and another individual (or other individuals), blood (only explicit

---

49. As Smith and Pitard conclude, the ritual exhibited here represents "Anat's purificatory transition from battle" (Smith and Pitard, *Ugaritic Baal Cycle*, 188).

50. In his study on holiness and purity in Mesopotamia, Wilson notes, "One might think that the gods, at least, would always be considered pure, but this is not the case. Mesopotamian gods could fall from their own grace, as it were. In other words, there were certain rules that had to be followed by the celestial inhabitants … in order for them to be permitted to function in the roles of gods" (*"Holiness" and "Purity" in Mesopotamia*, 74). Other non–Near Eastern examples could be added to this. The Hindu goddess Kali, who mirrors Anat's bloody, warrior figure, remains continually in an impure state (see Smith and Pitard, *The Ugaritic Baal Cycle*, 193). In Tacitus' *Germania*, he records a Teutonic ritual in which the goddess Nerthus, after passing through and inspecting the villages, "solemnly washed in the waters of a sacred lake, as if the holy divinity had been polluted by her intercourse with men" (Farnell, *The Evolution of Religion*, 107–108).

51. This is probably due to a number of factors. First, the majority of examples of deities becoming impure and undergoing purification occur in mythological literature, and only a comparatively small number of deities are depicted to any extent in a mythological text. For instance, Ugaritic literature attests to approximately 240 names and epithets for various deities, although the total number of individual deities is less than that (see del Olmo Lete, *Canaanite Religion*, 78). Of these, only eight primary gods play any significant role in the major mythological texts (ibid., 46). Second, the genre and content of a text may not provide a context for the description of either the purity or impurity of a god, or any type of purification of a god. Furthermore, the rhetorical context may not necessitate a depiction of impurity or purification. Third, a text might simply be silent regarding a god's purification—following a context in which the god has clearly become defiled in some way—because necessary purification was assumed or because of a lacuna in the text. Fourth, the extant literature does not reflect consistent and comprehensive theologies or perspectives, and perspectives concerning the gods certainly evolved and changed over time. The idea that gods could become impure and require purification may have been a concept that is reflected in one text but not another—even two texts in which the same god is the subject.

in the Anat example) and dismemberment of the dead opponent, the deity becoming physical filthy and ritually defiled, and a description of washing/cleansing which signifies ritual purification. Based on the above examples, it is reasonable to assume that in cases in which a deity is depicted in individual, bloody combat, that deity would have been considered physically and ritually contaminated due to bloodshed and in need of cleansing and purification.

3. Defilement and Purification of Yhwh in the Hebrew Bible

In light of the depictions of other ancient Near Eastern deities becoming defiled and undergoing some type of purification, and particularly in light of the postbattle purification of gods such as Ninurta and Anat, it is appropriate to ask whether any depictions exist of Yhwh becoming unclean through battle and needing to purify or cleanse himself. Although some studies assume that Yhwh cannot become defiled,[52] there is no *a priori* reason to think that Yhwh would not have become polluted from contact with the dead and blood, or that he would not need to undergo some type of purification.

There can be no doubt that, in one sense, Yhwh did "get his hands dirty," so to speak. He is depicted in the Hebrew Bible as directly and actively involved in violent acts and battle. Terence Fretheim's words regarding this aspect of the Hebrew Bible are poignant: "The most basic theological problem with the Bible's violence is that it is often associated with the activity of God; with remarkable frequency, God is the subject of violent verbs."[53] Likewise, Cheryl A. Kirk-Duggan claims that there are around one thousand passages of divine violence in the Hebrew Bible.[54] One of Yhwh's most significant characteristics is that of divine warrior (for

---

52. For example, Mary Douglas writes, "The biblical idea of purity is simple and coherent. The nature of the living God is in opposition to dead bodies. Total incompatibility holds between God's presence and bodily corruption" (see Mary Douglas, *In the Wilderness: The Doctrine of Defilement in the Book of Numbers* [JSOTSup 158; Sheffield: Sheffield Academic Press, 1993], 24). Similarly, in his Old Testament theology, Ben Ollenburger states, "It would not be conceivable that Yahweh could be defiled" (see Ben C. Ollenburger, *Old Testament Theology: Flowering and Future* [SBTS 1; Winona Lake: Eisenbrauns, 2004], 235).

53. Terence E. Fretheim, "God and Violence in the Old Testament," *WW* 24 (2004): 21.

54. Cheryl A. Kirk-Duggan, "Violence," in *Eerdmans Dictionary of the Bible* (ed.

example, Exod 15:3, "Yhwh is a man of war, Yhwh is his name.").[55] Yhwh is depicted both as fighting on the side of Israel in historical accounts and as fighting various opponents in more mythological terms. As Patrick D. Miller Jr. argues, the idea of Yhwh as warrior is a very early part of Israel's understanding of the deity.[56]

One passage which may shed light on the question of Yhwh and defilement is Isa 63:1–6. This text may provide an explicit context within which to posit an earlier tradition that Yhwh could, in fact, become physically defiled from battle. Although a late passage, Isa 63:1–6 preserves imagery which is similar to the type of visual descriptions of Anat's bloody warfare (*KTU*² 1.3 II 3–30). Isa 63:1–6 reads as follows:

מִי־זֶה בָּא מֵאֱדוֹם
חֲמוּץ בְּגָדִים מִבָּצְרָה
זֶה הָדוּר בִּלְבוּשׁוֹ
צֹעֶה בְּרֹב כֹּחוֹ
אֲנִי מְדַבֵּר בִּצְדָקָה
רַב לְהוֹשִׁיעַ׃
מַדּוּעַ אָדֹם לִלְבוּשֶׁךָ
וּבְגָדֶיךָ כְּדֹרֵךְ בְּגַת׃
פּוּרָה דָּרַכְתִּי לְבַדִּי
וּמֵעַמִּים אֵין־אִישׁ אִתִּי
וְאֶדְרְכֵם בְּאַפִּי
וְאֶרְמְסֵם בַּחֲמָתִי
וְיֵז נִצְחָם עַל־בְּגָדַי
וְכָל־מַלְבּוּשַׁי אֶגְאָלְתִּי׃
כִּי יוֹם נָקָם בְּלִבִּי
וּשְׁנַת גְּאוּלַי בָּאָה׃
וְאַבִּיט וְאֵין עֹזֵר
וְאֶשְׁתּוֹמֵם וְאֵין סוֹמֵךְ
וַתּוֹשַׁע לִי זְרֹעִי

David Noel Freedman, Allen C. Myers, and Astrid B. Beck; Grand Rapids: Eerdmans, 2000), 1358.

55. The relationship between Yhwh and other war gods has been discussed at length in other places and need not be taken up here. See Patrick D. Miller Jr., *The Divine Warrior in Early Israel* (HSM 5; Cambridge: Harvard University Press, 1973); Frank Moore Cross, *Canaanite Myth and Hebrew Epic* (Cambridge: Harvard University Press, 1973), 91–111; and Mark S. Smith, *The Early History of God* (2nd ed.; Grand Rapids: Eerdmans, 2002), 101–107.

56. Miller, *The Divine Warrior*, 171.

וַחֲמָתִי הִיא סְמָכָתְנִי:
וְאָבוּס עַמִּים בְּאַפִּי
וַאֲשַׁכְּרֵם בַּחֲמָתִי
וְאוֹרִיד לָאָרֶץ נִצְחָם:

¹ "Who is this coming from Edom,
    crimson of clothes from Bozra?
Who is this honored by his garments,
    Striding in the fullness of his strength?"
"It is I, speaking of deeds of justice,
    Powerful to save."
² "Why are your garments red,
    And your clothes like one who treads in the winepress?"
³ "I have trodden the trough alone,
    And from the peoples there was not anyone with me;
and I trod them in my anger,
    and I trampled them in my rage,
and the juice spattered upon my clothes,
    and all of my garments I have defiled.
⁴ For a day of vengeance I had in mind,
    And the year of my revenge had come.
⁵ And I looked, but there was no helper,
    And I looked on amazed, but there was no supporter.
⁶ So my own arm assisted me,
    And my rage, it supported me.
And I trod down peoples in my anger,
    And I made them drunk in my rage,
        And I poured out their juice to the ground."

Verse 1 depicts a watchman's challenge to an approaching stranger—apparently a warrior as indicated by his blood-stained clothes.[57] The stranger responds with a statement which establishes his identity, based

---

57. See Claus Westermann, *Isaiah 40–66* (OTL; Philadelphia: Westminster Press, 1969), 380–81. A similar type of interaction is depicted in a prism inscription of Aššurbanipal: "his [mes]senger wi[th a present] approached to ask my health to the border of my land. The people of my country looked at him and said to him, 'Who are you, stranger, whose mounted messenger hitherto has never blazed a trail to the marches?'" (see Arthur C. Piepkorn, *Historical Prism Inscriptions of Ashurbanipal I* [The Oriental Institute of the University of Chicago Assyriological Studies 5; Chicago: University of Chicago Press, 1933], 17). These types of challenges are not much different than the standard modern military challenge, "Halt! Who goes there?"

on deeds of justice and ability to save. In verse 2, the watchman asks why this individual's clothes are stained red, and in verse 3 the warrior answers that he has just trampled his opponents in his anger, with the result that the juice (that is, blood) spattered on his garments and stained or defiled (אֶגְאָלְתִּי) his clothes.[58] The passage relies on the backdrop of mythological combat—Yhwh's individual and bloody battle with his opponents. Claus Westermann has compared the imagery here with that of Marduk's battle with Tiamat.[59] Other imagery of Yhwh treading the winepress (Lam 1:15; Jer 48:33) and Yhwh's sword devouring the enemy and drinking their blood (Jer 46:10) may further support presuming an earlier mythological tradition in which Yhwh battles his foes in the language of a bloody massacre. Isaiah 63:1–6 closely parallels the form of the passages from Ugarit and Mesopotamia described above: a mythological backdrop, a single deity's combat with opponents, and a bloody massacre. Clearly there is no description of ritual purification, but does the passage suggest that Yhwh became ritually impure?

The last line in verse 3 is the crux to interpreting this passage with regard to whether or not Yhwh is depicted as becoming defiled. The two words necessary to understand in order to decipher the imagery in this passage are the verbs נזה and גאל. The verb נזה occurs in the first colon of the line: וְיֵז נִצְחָם עַל־בְּגָדַי "and the juice spattered upon my clothes." The verb נזה occurs a total of twenty-four times in the Hebrew Bible, but only four times in the *qal* as it does here.[60] Although the meaning of the verb נזה in the *hiphil* would have obvious connotations of purification,[61] the same cannot be said of the verb used in the *qal* stem. Based on the very

---

58. The use of this verb also attests to the lateness of this passage (see *HALOT*, 169). The verb only appears ten times in the Hebrew Bible (Lam 4:4; Isa 59:3; 63:3; Zeph 3:1; Mal 1:7, 12; Ezra 2:62; Neh 7:64; Dan 1:8 [2x]), while the noun גֹּאָל, "defilement," appears once in Neh 13:9. However, the verb's appearance in Lamentations, an exilic text, warrants cautious acceptance of *HALOT*'s note regarding the lateness of the term.

59. Westermann, *Isaiah 40–66*, 382. He writes, "In the past, as I see it, comment on Isa 63:1–6 has paid too little attention to what is the really characteristic feature here, the change made in the description of the divine judgment on the nations so that it becomes a battle engaged in by a single person, a description which, strictly speaking and in respect of its origin, only suits a battle between two parties, a battle such as that of Marduk against Tiamat and those who came to her aid in *Enuma Elish*."

60. Jacob Milgrom, David P. Wright, "*nāzâ*," *TDOT*, 9:300.

61. Except for Isa 52:15, in which the use of the verb is unclear, the *hiphil* of נזה is

limited use of the verb in the *qal* stem, Jacob Milgrom and David Wright state, "the verb denotes unintentional, accidental spattering."[62] Apart from Isa 63:3, the *qal* form occurs in 2 Kgs 9:33 referring to Jezebel's blood spattering the wall and horses upon hitting the ground after she was thrown from an upper-level window. The verb also occurs twice in the *qal* in Lev 6:20 (Eng. 27), where it refers to the blood of the purification offering spattering the priests clothes.[63] In this case, the priest is instructed to wash (כבס, *piel*) in a holy place. The verb כבס in the *piel* most often refers to cleansing clothes from various types of uncleanness, often in ritual contexts and in addition to the purification of the individual (Lev 11:25; Num 8:7; 19:19).[64] In Lev 6:20 (Eng. 27) the blood from the purification offering imparts impurity and the priest's garment becomes unclean; thus, he must wash the blood spots from the garment.[65] Any contention that the imagery used in this passage actually reflects Yhwh being purified by the blood of his victims should be ruled out. First, the *qal* rather than the *hiphil* of נזה is used, and if there is an allusion in verse 3 to Lev 16:20 (Eng. 27), then it should be noted that the purification offering never purifies the one offering it.[66] With this in mind, it would appear that Isa 63:3 at the very least simply denotes the accidental spattering of blood on Yhwh's garments, and possibly (as in the case of Lev 6:20 [Eng. 27]) implies that Yhwh's clothes have become defiled by the blood, which the next colon appears to make explicit.

Most modern translations (for example, NRSV, NIV, ESV, JPS) render the verb אֶגְאָלְתִּי as "stained," without any implication of defilement.[67] In form, the verb (גאל II) appears to be a *hiphil/aphel* combination. However, in accordance with 1QIsa[a], 1QIsa[b], and other witnesses (Symmachus,

---

always used in ritual contexts and refers to the sprinkling of water or blood to consecrate or purify and object, person, or sanctuary (see ibid., 300–303).

62. Ibid., 300.

63. Most translations render חַטָּאת as "sin offering;" however, Milgrom has argued that a better rendering is "purification offering." See Jacob Milgrom, "Sin-offering or Purification-offering?" *VT* 21 (1971): 237–39; Jacob Milgrom, *Leviticus 1–16* (AB 3; New York: Doubleday, 1991), 253–54.

64. G. André, "*kābas*," *TDOT*, 7:40. The metaphorical uses of כבס referring to cleansing a person from sin may allude to purification ceremonies (ibid., 41).

65. Milgrom, *Leviticus 1–16*, 403–4.

66. Ibid., 254.

67. Even *HALOT*, 169 provides the gloss "to stain" for the *hiphil*.

Theodotion, the Syrohexeplar, Syriac, and Vulgate),⁶⁸ several scholars and lexicographers have proposed reading the verb as a *piel* stem (גֵּאַלְתִּי), "to pollute, to desecrate."⁶⁹ In regard to meaning, all other stems (*niphal, piel, pual,* and *hithpael*) carry the connotation of defiling in a ritual sense, whether passively, actively, or reflexively. Regardless of whether the verb is meant to be a *piel* or *hiphil/aphel*, there does not seem to be any reason to subdue the meaning of the term from "defile" to "stain," although staining is a natural consequence of being covered in blood.⁷⁰ The *hiphil/aphel* form of the verb גאל here would then function causatively⁷¹ and would best be rendered, "I made my garments defiled."⁷² In fact, in Isa 59:3, the prophet proclaims to his audience that their hands are defiled (נְגֹאֲלוּ) with blood. In Lam 4:14, the Jerusalemites are described as blindly wandering the streets so defiled (נְגֹאֲלוּ) with blood that no one could touch their garments. The blood-soaked Jerusalemites are then called "unclean" (verse 15, טָמֵא). This imagery is reminiscent of the depiction already discussed of Anat covered in blood and seemingly defiled.⁷³ Taken together, this

---

68. See *BHS*. Both 1QIsaᵃ and 1QIsaᵇ read גאלתי; see Eugene Charles Ulrich, Peter W. Flint, and Martin G. Abegg, *Qumran Cave 1. II: The Isaiah Scrolls* (DJD 32; Oxford: Clarendon Press, 2010), 100, 148.

69. See *HALOT*, 169; *BDB*, 145; *GKC*, §53p, n. 1.

70. Even so, certainly the visual imagery of the juice/blood staining Yhwh's clothes is part of the idea.

71. Paul Joüon and T. Muraoka, *A Grammar of Biblical Hebrew* (SubBi 27; Rome: Pontifical Biblical Institute, 2006), 150.

72. Cyrus Gordon and Edward Young render the *hiphil/aphel* form as "to defile" (see Cyrus H. Gordon and Edward J. Young, "אגאלתי (Isaiah 63:3)," *WTJ* 14 [1951]: 54).

73. The Greek translation of Isaiah may provide testimony to the offensive nature of this imagery. LXX-Isaiah translates around this particular imagery, in an otherwise fairly literal rendering of the larger context: Τίς οὗτος ὁ παραγινόμενος ἐξ Εδωμ, ἐρύθημα ἱματίων ἐκ Βοσορ, οὕτως ὡραῖος ἐν στολῇ βίᾳ μετὰ ἰσχύος; ἐγὼ διαλέγομαι δικαιοσύνην καὶ κρίσιν σωτηρίου. διὰ τί σου ἐρυθρὰ τὰ ἱμάτια καὶ τὰ ἐνδύματά σου ὡς ἀπὸ πατητοῦ ληνοῦ; πλήρης καταπεπατημένης, καὶ τῶν ἐθνῶν οὐκ ἔστιν ἀνὴρ μετ' ἐμοῦ, καὶ κατεπάτησα αὐτοὺς ἐν θυμῷ καὶ κατέθλασα αὐτοὺς ὡς γῆν καὶ κατήγαγον τὸ αἷμα αὐτῶν εἰς γῆν (Joseph Ziegler, *Jeremias, Baruch, Threni, Epistula Jeremiae* [Septuaginta 15; Göttingen: Vandenhoeck & Ruprecht, 1976], 353–54). I, however, accept Rahlf's punctuation in v. 3: "Who is this that comes from Edom, redness of robes from Bosor, so beautiful in flowing robe, in strength with power?" "It is I, I am discussing justice and judgment of salvation." "Why are your garments red and your clothes as if from a trodden winepress?" "Full of those having been trampled, and no man was with me

evidence suggests that Isa 63:3 depicts Yhwh as having been defiled by the blood of his victims; however, no purification is depicted.

Isaiah 63:1–6, then, exhibits all of the elements of the identified literary form except for purification. This may suggest a deliberate attempt by the author to depict Yhwh with the same militaristic imagery as other ancient Near Eastern deities without conceding that Yhwh needed to be purified. Other passages in the Hebrew Bible also depict a close association between Yhwh and the blood of his opponents without depicting Yhwh in direct contact with the blood. In Deut 32:42, Yhwh's arrows and sword, rather than Yhwh himself, are said to consume the blood and flesh of his enemies; thus, distancing Yhwh from a cannibalistic act: "I will make my arrows drunk from blood, and my sword will consume flesh; from the blood of the slain and captives, from the head of the leaders of the enemy." The imagery in Isa 34:5–6 is similar: "When my sword has drunk its fill in the heavens, behold, upon Edom it will descend, and upon the people of my destruction, for judgment. The sword of Yhwh is filled with blood, it drips with fat, from the blood of rams and goats, from the fat of the kidneys of rams, because Yhwh has a sacrifice in Bozra, and a great slaughter in the land of Edom." Jeremiah 46:10 also depicts Yhwh's sword as drinking the blood of his victims. This imagery parallels depictions of Anat and the Egyptian goddess Hathor devouring their enemies,[74] although Yhwh is distanced from the cannibalistic imagery. Mark Smith and Wayne Pitard propose that the difference between Yhwh, who is not directly depicted as eating the enemy, and Anat and Hathor may have developed due to a discomfort with the notion that Yhwh needs to eat, or because of a progressive deanthropomorphization of Yhwh.[75] Nevertheless, the use of most of the elements of the divine postbattle purification motif in Isa 63:1–6 confirms that it was well-known throughout the ancient Near East.

---

from the nations, and I trampled them in anger and I crushed them as earth, and I brought down their blood to the earth."

74. For Hathor's blood thirstiness, see "The Destruction of Mankind" (Miriam Lichtheim, *Ancient Egyptian Literature* [Berkeley: University of California Press, 1976], 2:197–99). Another connection between the warfare of Yhwh and that of Anat is the idea of wading or treading in the enemy's blood. However, in the Hebrew Bible, it is not Yhwh who wades in the enemy's blood but Israel (see Ps 68:22–23).

75. Mark S. Smith and Wayne T. Pitard, *The Ugaritic Baal Cycle, Vol. 2: Introduction with Text, Translation and Commentary of KTU/CAT 1.3–1.4* (VTSup 114; Leiden: Brill, 2009), 182–83.

4. Conclusions

The above argument may be summarized by the following points. First, ancient Near Eastern deities were not impervious to impurity and were often depicted as having become defiled and being purified, particularly after battle. Second, a literary form existed which depicted a deity in bloody combat, who was then defiled, and who undertook some type of purification ritual. In the case of the Mesopotamian examples, the divine purification seems to have been modeled after the human postbattle purification rituals displayed in royal inscriptions. The Divine Warrior Hymn in Isa 63:1–6 confirms the existence of this literary form and demonstrates that it was broadly known and used, both geographically and in time, throughout the ancient Near East. The author of Isa 63:1–6 was able to draw on several motifs to depict Yhwh's bloody battle in Bozra—motifs which were commonly used with regard to other ancient Near Eastern deities. Third, Isa 63:1–6 suggests that Yhwh was once considered able to be defiled from bloody battle as were other ancient Near Eastern deities. However, by the time of Third Isaiah, Yhwh had been disassociated from the full implications of defilement. Further investigation may reveal additional examples linking Yhwh to the broader ancient Near Eastern phenomenon of divine defilement and purification. Yet, this study already sheds light on war rituals as reflected in accounts of divine battle, and points to Israel's evolving understanding and depiction of Yhwh.

Bibliography

Barmash, Pamela. *Homicide in the Biblical World*. Cambridge: Cambridge University Press, 2005.

Bidmead, Julye. *The Akītu Festival: Religious Continuity and Royal Legitimation in Mesopotamia*. Gorgias Dissertations, Near East 2. Piscataway: Gorgias Press, 2002.

Bienkowski, Piotr, and Alan Millard, eds. *Dictionary of the Ancient Near East*. Pennsylvania: University of Pennsylvania Press, 2000.

Black, Jeremy A., Graham Cunningham, Jarie Ebeling, Esther Flückiger-Hawker, Eleanor Robson, Jon Taylor, and Gábor Zólyomi. *The Electronic Text Corpus of Sumerian Literature*. Oxford 1998–2006. Online: http://etcsl.orinst.ox.ac.uk/.

Botterweck, G. Johannes, Helmer Ringgren, and Heinz-Josef Fabry. *Theo-

logical Dictionary of the Old Testament. Translated by David E. Green. 15 vols. Grand Rapids: Eerdmans, 1974–2006.

Casalis, E. *The Basutos; Or, Twenty-three Years in South Africa.* London: Nisbet, 1861.

Civil, Miguel. "Daily Chores in Nippur." *JCS* 32 (1990): 229–32.

Cross, Frank Moore. *Canaanite Myth and Hebrew Epic.* Cambridge: Harvard University Press, 1973.

Dietrich, Manfried, Oswald Loretz and Joaquín Sanmartín. *The Cuneiform Alphabetic Texts from Ugarit, Ras Ibn Hani and Other Places (KTU: second, enlarged edition).* ALASP 8. Münster: Ugarit-Verlag, 1995.

Dijk, J. A. A. van. *Lugal ud me-lám-bi nir-Ǧál: Le récit épique et didactique des Travaux de Ninurta, de Déluge et de la Nouvelle Création. Vol. 1.* Leiden: Brill, 1983.

———. "Un Rituel de Purification des Armes et de l'Armée: Essai de Traduction de YBC 4184." Pages 107–17 in *Symbolae Biblicae et Mesopotamicae.* Edited by M. A. Beek, et. al. Studia Francisci Scholten Memoriae Dicata 4. Leiden: Brill, 1973.

Douglas, Mary. *In the Wilderness: The Doctrine of Defilement in the Book of Numbers.* JSOTSup 158. Sheffield: Sheffield Academic Press, 1993.

The Electronic Pennsylvania Sumerian Dictionary. Online: http:// psd.museum.upenn.edu/epsd/nepsd-frame.html.

Farnell, Lewis R. *The Evolution of Religion.* New York: G. P. Putnam's Sons, 1905.

Fisher, Loren R. "A New Ugaritic Calendar from Ugarit." *HTR* 63 (1970): 485–501.

Foster, Benjamin R. *Before the Muses: An Anthology of Akkadian Literature.* 3d ed. Bethesda: CDL, 2005.

Frayne, Douglas. *Old Babylonian Period (2003–1595 BC).* RIMA Early Periods 4. Toronto: University of Toronto Press, 1990.

———. *Sargonic and Gutian Periods (2334–2113 BC).* RIMA Early Periods 2. Toronto: University of Toronto Press, 1993.

Fretheim, Terence E. "God and Violence in the Old Testament." *WW* 24 (2004): 18–28.

George, Andrew R. *The Babylonian Gilgamesh Epic.* Oxford: Oxford University Press, 2003.

Goetze, Albrecht. "A Drehem Tablet Dealing with Leather Objects." *JCS* 9 (1955): 19–21.

Gordon, Cyrus H., and Edward J. Young. "אגאלתי (Isaiah 63:3)." *WTJ* 14 (1951): 54.

Grayson, A. Kirk. *Assyrian Rulers of the Early First Millennium BC I (1114–859 BC)*. RIMA Assyrian Periods 2. Toronto: University of Toronto Press, 1991.

———. *Assyrian Rulers of the Early First Millennium BC II (858–745 BC)*. RIMA Assyrian Periods 3. Toronto: University of Toronto Press, 1996.

Güterbock, Hans G., and Harry A. Hoffner Jr., eds. *The Hittite Dictionary of the Oriental Institute of the University of Chicago*. Chicago: Oriental Institute, 1989–.

Hoffner, Harry A., Jr. "Hittite Mythological Texts: A Survey." Pages 136–45 in *Unity and Diversity: Essays in the History, Literature, and Religion of the Ancient Near East*. Edited by Hans Goedicke and J. J. M. Roberts. Johns Hopkins University Near Eastern Studies. Baltimore: Johns Hopkins University Press, 1975.

———. *Hittite Myths*. Edited by Gary M. Beckman. SBLWAW 2. Atlanta: Scholars Press, 1990.

Homer. *Iliad*. Translated by A. T. Murray. Revised by William F. Wyatt. 2 vols. Loeb Classical Library. Cambridge: Harvard University Press, 1999.

Jacobsen, Thorkild. *Harps That Once...: Sumerian Poetry in Translation*. New Haven: Yale University Press, 1987.

Joüon, Paul, and T. Muraoka. *A Grammar of Biblical Hebrew*. SubBi 27. Rome: Pontifical Biblical Institute, 2006.

Kang, Sa-Moon. *Divine War in the Old Testament and in the Ancient Near East*. BZAW 177. New York: de Gruyter, 1989.

Karahashi, Fumi. "Fighting the Mountain: Some Observations on the Sumerian Myths of Inanna and Ninurta." *JNES* 63 (2004): 111–18.

Kirk-Duggan, Cheryl A. "Violence." Pages 1357–58 in *Eerdmans Dictionary of the Bible*. Edited by David Noel Freedman, Allen C. Myers, and Astrid B. Beck. Grand Rapids: Eermans, 2000.

Lambert, W. G., and Alan R. Millard. *Atra-ḫasīs: The Babylonian Story of the Flood*. Oxford: The Clarendon Press, 1969.

Lichtheim, Miriam. *Ancient Egyptian Literature Vol. 2*. Berkeley: University of California Press, 1976.

Malamat, Abraham. "Campaigns to the Mediterranean by Iahdunlim and Other Early Mesopotamian Rulers." *AS* 16 (1965): 365–74.

———. "The Divine Nature of the Mediterranean Sea in the Foundation Inscription of Yaḫdunlim." Pages 211–15 in *Mari in Retrospect: Fifty Years of Mari and Mari Studies*. Edited by Gordon D. Young. Winona Lake: Eisenbrauns, 1992.

Masson, Olivier. "A propos d'un rituel hittite pour la lustration d'une armée: Le rite de purification par le passage entre les deux parties d'une victime." *RHR* 137 (1950): 5–25.

Milgrom, Jacob. *Leviticus 1–16*. AB. New York: Doubleday, 1991.

———. "Sin-offering or Purification-offering?" *VT* 21 (1971): 237–39.

Miller, Patrick D., Jr. *The Divine Warrior in Early Israel*. HSM 5. Cambridge: Harvard University Press, 1973.

Moor, Johannes C. de. "Studies in the New Alphabetic Texts from Ras Shamra I." *UF* 1 (1969): 167–88.

Moran, William L. "The Creation of Man in Atrahasis I 192–248." *BASOR* 200 (1970): 48–56.

Moyer, James C. "The Concept of Ritual Purity among the Hittites." Ph.D. diss., Brandeis University, 1969.

Ollenburger, Ben C. *Old Testament Theology: Flowering and Future*. SBTS 1. Winona Lake, Ind.: Eisenbrauns, 2004.

Olmo Lete, Gregorio del. *Canaanite Religion according to the Liturgical Texts of Ugarit*. Translated by W. G. E. Watson. Bethesda: CDL, 1999.

Oppenheim, A. Leo. *Ancient Mesopotamia: Portrait of a Dead Civilization*. Chicago: University of Chicago Press, 1964.

Pardee, Dennis. "A New Ugaritic Letter." *BO* 34 (1977): 3–20.

———. "The Preposition in Ugaritic." *UF* 8 (1976): 215–93.

Parker, Simon B., ed. *Ugaritic Narrative Poetry*. SBLWAW 9. Atlanta: Scholars Press, 1997.

Parpola, Simo. *The Standard Babylonian Epic of Gilgamesh*. SAA Cuneiform Texts 1. Helsinki: Neo-Assyrian Text Corpus Project, 1997.

Piepkorn, Arthur C. *Historical Prism Inscriptions of Ashurbanipal I*. The Oriental Institute of the University of Chicago Assyriological Studies 5. Chicago: University of Chicago Press, 1933.

Smith, Mark S. "Anat's Warfare Cannibalism and the West Semitic Ban." Pages 268–86 in *The Pitcher is Broken: Memorial Essays for Gösta W. Ahlström*. Edited by Steven W. Holloway and Lowel K. Handy. JSOTSup 190. Sheffield: Sheffield Academic Press, 1995.

———. *The Early History of God*. 2nd ed. Grand Rapids: Eerdmans, 2002.

Smith, Mark S. and Wayne T. Pitard. *The Ugaritic Baal Cycle, Vol. 2: Introduction with Text, Translation and Commentary of KTU/CAT 1.3–1.4*. VTSup 114. Leiden: Bril, 2009.

Soden, Wolfram von. *The Ancient Orient: An Introduction to the Study of the Ancient Near East*. Translated by Donald G. Schley. Grand Rapids: Eerdmans, 1994.

———. "Zu einigin altbabylonischen Dichtungen." *Or* 26 (1957): 306–20.
Talon, Philippe. *The Standard Babylonian Creation Myth: Enūma Eliš*. SAA Cuneiform Texts 4. Helsinki: Neo-Assyrian Text Corpus Project, 2005.
Tigay, Jeffrey H. *The Evolution of the Gilgamesh Epic*. Philadelphia: University of Pennsylvania Press, 1982.
Tischler, Johann. *Hethitisches Handwörterbuch*. Innsbruck: Institut für Sprachen und Literaturen der Univ, 2001.
Ulrich, Eugene C., Peter W. Flint, and Martin G. Abegg. *Qumran Cave 1. II: The Isaiah Scrolls*. DJD 32. Oxford: Clarendon, 2010.
Westermann, Claus. *Isaiah 40–66*. OTL. Philadelphia: Westminster, 1969.
Wilson, E. Jan. *"Holiness" and "Purity" in Mesopotamia*. AOAT 237. Kevelaer: Butzon & Bercker, 1994.
Zettler, Richard L., and Walther Sallaberger. "Inana's Festival at Nippur under the Third Dynasty of Ur." *Zeitschrift für Assyriologie und vorderasiatische Archäologie* 101 (2011): 1–71.
Ziegler, Joseph. *Jeremias, Baruch, Threni, Epistula Jeremiae*. Septuaginta 15. Göttingen: Vandenhoeck & Ruprecht, 1976.

Response

Forging a Twenty-First-Century Approach to the Study of Israelite Warfare

T. M. Lemos

The twentieth century saw several important studies of Israelite warfare. Gerhard von Rad's *Holy War in Ancient Israel* and Susan Niditch's *War in the Hebrew Bible: A Study in the Ethics of Violence* stand as the two landmark examples, but works by Norbert Lohfink, Sa-Moon Kang, Philip D. Stern, and Manfred Weippert are also noteworthy.[1] As Charles Trimm's recent review of scholarship on warfare in the Hebrew Bible makes clear, biblical scholars have continued to produce many works on biblical warfare and violence in recent years.[2] At the same time, the study of Israelite ritual has flourished in the last two decades, with works by Saul M. Olyan, William K. Gilders, James W. Watts, and Gerald A. Klingbeil joining previous research by Frank H. Gorman Jr. and Philip P. Jenson in examining rituals described in the Hebrew Bible in a manner informed by research from anthropology and other disciplines.[3] With the contin-

---

1. See Gerhard von Rad, *Holy War in Ancient Israel* (trans. M. J. Dawn; Grand Rapids: Eerdmans, 1991) (German orig. *Der Heilige Krieg im alten Israel* [Göttingen: Vandenhoeck & Ruprecht, 1951]); Susan Niditch, *War in the Hebrew Bible: A Study in the Ethics of Violence* (New York: Oxford University Press, 1993); Norbert Lohfink, *Krieg und Staat im alten Israel* (Beiträge für Friedensethik 14; Barsbüttel: Institut für Theologie und Frieden, 1992); Sa-Moon Kang, *Divine War in the Old Testament and in the Ancient Near East* (BZAW 177; Berlin: de Gruyter, 1989); Philip D. Stern, *The Biblical Ḥerem: A Window on Israel's Religious Experience* (BJS 211; Atlanta: Scholars Press, 1991); and Manfred Weippert, "Heiliger Krieg in Israel und Assyrien: Kritische Anmerkungen zu Gerhard von Rads Konzept des 'Heiligen Krieges im alten Israel,'" *ZAW* 84 (1972): 460–93.

2. Charles Trimm, "Recent Research on Warfare in the Old Testament," *CBR* 10 (2012): 171–216.

3. Frank H. Gorman, *The Ideology of Ritual: Space, Time, and Status in the Priestly*

ued interest in biblical warfare and the surge of interest in biblical ritual, it is no surprise that eventually these two areas of interest would converge in a volume like this one. This volume presents an important step—not a first step exactly, but one no doubt early in the journey—toward understanding better the rituals and symbols of violence described in quite a large number of biblical texts. My response essay will reflect upon the approaches found in this volume, relate them to biblical studies as a whole, and present thoughts and suggestions for where the study of biblical violence should go from here.

Perhaps unsurprisingly, the essays in this volume reflect many of the most salient tendencies of biblical studies. For example, one sees in several essays a continued interest in redactional criticism and the dating of (layers of) texts, as well as an effort to situate biblical rites of war in their ancient Near Eastern environment. These are, of course, very longstanding trends in the field and, while each of these trends can at times present methodological problems, each is arguably indispensable for the field. Comparison with other ancient societies is particularly important when examining Israelite violence. Considering that the Israelites fought with other ancient groups and were often conquered by them, it would be truly nonsensical to cordon off the study of Israelite warfare from the study of ancient Mesopotamian warfare, ancient Egyptian warfare, or ancient Levantine warfare.

But what are we studying, really—biblical warfare or Israelite warfare? Or are the two equivalent? The essays in this volume represent different tendencies and approaches to this issue, which relates to the larger and quite thorny question of how closely biblical texts mirror Israelite realities of life.[4] While an extreme pessimism or skepticism regarding whether we

---

Theology (JSOTSup 91; Sheffield: Sheffield Academic Press, 1990); Philip P. Jenson, *Graded Holiness: A Key to the Priestly Conception of the World* (JSOTSup 106; Sheffield: Sheffield Academic Press, 1992); Saul M. Olyan, *Rites and Rank: Hierarchy in Biblical Representations of Cult* (Princeton: Princeton University Press, 2000); William K. Gilders, *Blood Ritual in the Hebrew Bible: Meaning and Power* (Baltimore: The Johns Hopkins University Press, 2004); James W. Watts, *Ritual and Rhetoric in Leviticus: From Sacrifice to Scripture* (Cambridge: Cambridge University Press, 2007); and Gerald A. Klingbeil, *Bridging the Gap: Ritual and Ritual Texts in the Bible* (Bulletin for Biblical Research Supplements 1; Winona Lake, Ind.: Eisenbrauns, 2007).

4. On this issue, see, for example, Megan Bishop Moore and Brad E. Kelle, *Biblical History and Israel's Past: The Changing Study of the Bible and History* (Grand Rapids: Eerdmans, 2011), 1–42.

can answer this question has grown in some quarters of the field, such pessimism is in my view unwarranted, considering that one can use archaeological evidence and other ancient Near Eastern texts to corroborate the evidence found in biblical sources, at least where many issues are concerned. As is well known, many biblical narratives do not find corroboration in the archaeological record and are not historical as the Hebrew Bible presents them, but even these sometimes reflect the realities of war from the times in which they were actually composed. To provide just one example: the Israelite conquest of Canaan may not have occurred, but the practice of *ḥērem* is not an invention of biblical authors, as the Mesha stele demonstrates. Despite our ability, however partial, to corroborate biblical sources and thus the lack of cogency in arguing that biblical texts cannot be trusted as sources for reconstructing Israelite history, there is still, it seems, a bit of a slippage in biblical scholarship between what is biblical and what is Israelite. The title of this volume is a case in point, referring as it does to "biblical and modern contexts." If our concern is with biblical texts as literary documents, that is, with "biblical contexts," it would be methodologically incongruous perhaps to compare war in biblical contexts to war in modern contexts unless what one is comparing is modern literary contexts. It seems to me that such a comparison between biblical and modern *social* contexts is warranted more by an interest in *Israelite* contexts, that is, Israelite social and historical realities, attested as they are by biblical, archaeological, and other sources. A lack of clarity on what is really our main area of focus as biblical scholars and what is really at stake in what we are doing is arguably one of the main problems facing biblical studies today as a field.[5]

Another problem in the field is the isolation of biblical scholars from other areas of the academy. This isolation is arguably evinced in some, though certainly not all, of the essays in this volume. The topics of warfare, ritual, and symbolism have been widely studied in various disciplines of the academy. For example, there is a decades-long, very rich, and very fruitful discussion concerning the nature of rituals—how to define ritual, what ritual does—that has gone on in anthropology and religious studies and is exemplified by such figures as Mary Douglas, Victor Turner, Clifford Geertz, Jack

---

5. See also my discussion of method in T. M. Lemos, "'They Have Become Women': Judean Diaspora and Postcolonial Theories of Gender and Migration," in *Social Theory and the Study of Israelite Religion: Essays in Retrospect and Prospect* (ed. Saul M. Olyan; SBLRBS 71; Atlanta: Society of Biblical Literature, 2012), 81–109.

Goody, Pierre Bourdieu, Catherine Bell, and others.[6] An engagement with the work of these scholars and familiarity with the larger trends of ritual studies, as well as with anthropological or sociological studies of violence, has lent depth to some of the works contained here (for example, the essays of Niditch, Olyan, Kelle, and Levtow). Still, more of the essays would benefit from the use of evidence, approaches, or theories from these disciplines, and such interaction is a desideratum for future research on the war-related rituals of the Israelites.

These issues aside, there is much to learn from this collection, and the collection as a whole should convince one of the fruitfulness of examining not just warfare on its own, or rituals and symbols on their own, but rituals and symbols as they are utilized in wartime contexts. Various essays here do not merely shed light on their designated area of focus but provide jumping off points for examining other rituals and symbols of war, often by use of an interdisciplinary method. For example, Brad E. Kelle's essay presents an entry point into research on moral injury that many biblical scholars, particularly those interested in trauma and/or exilic literature, might find useful for their own work. Frank Ritchel Ames's essay similarly presents interdisciplinary research on symbolism and bodily communication that biblical scholars could make use of to understand many different biblical texts or cultural phenomena. Saul M. Olyan's essay on circumstantially dependent rites encourages one to move away from overly wooden interpretation of ritual that sees ritual as functioning in the same way in all contexts. Olyan's more nuanced and supple approach, too, could be applied to the study of many different rituals, both those occurring in wartime contexts and those occurring outside of them. Nathaniel Levtow's article also presents a very nuanced approach to examining Israelite rituals in which textualization and ritualization come together in interesting ways. His essay draws upon the work of Catherine Bell in particular, a theorist whose writings present many avenues of research for biblical scholars.[7]

---

6. Bell summarizes and critiques research on ritual studies through the early '90's in Catherine Bell, *Ritual Theory, Ritual Practice* (New York: Oxford University Press, 1992). See also Catherine Bell, *Ritual: Perspectives and Dimensions* (Oxford: Oxford University Press, 1997; a revised ed. was published posthumously in 2009), and William S. Sax, Johannes Quack, and Jan Weinhold, eds., *The Problem of Ritual Efficacy* (Oxford: Oxford University Press, 2010), which discusses Bell's work and other more recent research.

7. In fact, some biblicists, e.g., Olyan, Gilders, and Klingbeil, have already drawn on her work in their own research. See above.

The essays by Kelle and Niditch address a topic that has been mulled over for centuries and is still the source of much consternation today— whether those who have committed violence in war can be reintegrated into regular social life, and if so, by what ritual or social mechanisms and facilitated by which psychological processes. Niditch's essay also addresses a subject important to the study of warfare or violence more generally—how social groups are constituted, reconstituted, or fragmented by violence. Her essay demonstrates that a neat division between warfare and other types of violence is neither possible nor beneficial. Political violence of the type we term warfare not only intersects with other types of violence (for example, gender violence or familial violence), but is arguably the product of the same or at least similar social processes. Without being simplistic, it seems fair to ask whether the socialization or subjectivity that allows one to kill on the battlefield is different from the one that allows one to kill or rape in other contexts. If they are different, what separates one socio-psychological phenomenon from the other? The evidence examined by Niditch seems to present wartime violence as seeping into other contexts, raising the question of whether there is as much of a break between military killing and other violence as many in our society would like to think.

Niditch's essay presents a useful segue into discussing future avenues of research on warfare in biblical studies, or, where we go from here as scholars. Naturally, there is much work left to be done in our field not only on Israelite warfare, but also on the rituals and symbols associated with it. Niditch's essay provides a good point of transition because, as I have already stated, for the study of Israelite warfare to develop to the fullest extent possible, examinations of Israelite warfare must be connected to examinations of other types of violence. Warfare is merely a subset of a wider category of violence, and the violence of warfare bleeds—if you will excuse the garish pun—into other types of aggression and force, just as aggression that happens at the lower levels of social organization can lead or contribute to the political violence of warfare.

In my view, it would also behoove scholars to be clearer about what their intentions are in studying biblical texts that speak of warfare. As a biblical scholar who sees herself as primarily a social and cultural historian, my primary interest is in *Israelites* and *Israelite history and contexts*, rather than in understanding biblical texts for their own sake. As a historian, biblical texts are for me data among other relevant data. Of course, for many the Bible is sacred scripture, and so an interest in understanding biblical texts over and above the historical contexts and social communities that produced these texts is often rooted in confessional theologies.[8] It is part and parcel of our postmodernist (post-postmodernist?) academic climate that one is expected to be aware of and upfront about one's own social location and biases. At times, biblical scholars are not explicit about what their ultimate goals are as scholars—what is at stake for them—and so slippages occur between what is "biblical" and what is "Israelite" and between literary, theological, and historical approaches.

With these initial observations in mind, I present suggestions for future research on Israelite warfare that are aimed at biblical scholars who are historians—and social historians, in particular—rather than biblical scholars who are literary critics or theologians.[9] First, to forge a twenty-first century approach to violence in ancient Israel, one must be in conversation with approaches current in the twenty-first century. As I have written elsewhere, in the late nineteenth and early twentieth centuries, biblical studies and the nascent social sciences had a mutually beneficial relationship that was the result of a conversation going in both directions.[10] One sees this in the work of W. Robertson Smith, James Frazer, Marcel Mauss, and Julius Wellhausen. In the past half century, however, biblical scholars have at times drawn on the social sciences and other areas of the humanities, but have rarely if ever contributed to wider discussions in other areas of academia. To add to the problem, biblical scholars are generally decades

---

8. This is not at all to say that all scholars who see the Bible as scripture approach their scholarship in the same way or are "cryptotheologians," to borrow a word from Russell McCutcheon (see, e.g., Russell McCutcheon, *Manufacturing Religion: The Discourse on Sui Generis Religion and the Politics of Nostalgia* [Oxford: Oxford University Press, 1997], 16, 93). I myself am a practicing Episcopalian who teaches in an Anglican seminary. I nonetheless consider myself to be a historian rather than a theologian or text critic, and my personal theological convictions in no way require me to interpret biblical texts in particular ways or force my scholarship to move in certain directions.

9. Until the early 1990s, much of the research on warfare in the Bible was dominated by theological concerns. Examples may be found in Peter C. Craigie, *The Problem of War in the Old Testament* (Grand Rapids: Eerdmans, 1978); Millard C. Lind, *Yahweh Is a Warrior: The Theology of Warfare in Ancient Israel* (Scottdale, Penn.: Herald, 1980); T. R. Hobbs, *A Time for War: A Study of Warfare in the Old Testament* (Wilmington: Michael Glazier, 1989); and even to a certain extent in von Rad, *Holy War*. Theological work on biblical warfare certainly continues, but in the past two to three decades there has been a greater variety of approaches to examining this topic.

10. See T. M. Lemos, "Cultural Anthropology: Hebrew Bible," in *Oxford Encyclopedia of Biblical Interpretation* (ed. Steven L. McKenzie; Oxford: Oxford University Press, 2013), 1:157–65.

out of date in making use of research from outside of their field. This is, I would argue, a result of the narrow training that biblical scholars receive at the doctoral level, training focused on philology, acquisition of multiple languages, and textual issues to the exclusion of method or engagement with other fields.[11] For the study of violence in ancient Israel to be truly contemporary and be something other than merely parasitic of other fields' ideas, biblical scholars—both those who consider themselves to be historians and those who do not—will in many cases have to read widely in order to overcome the possible lacunae in their doctoral training.

What areas would be particularly fruitful for the study of either Israelite violence in general or Israelite rituals of violence in particular? Already in the late 1990s, the anthropologists Michael Lambek and Andrew Strathern wrote of a neomaterialism "concerned with the domain of lived experience and the effects of the social realm on the human body."[12] They were referring to the increase in interest in embodiment and how people's physical experiences of the world are shaped by social and cultural forces. As Catherine Bell has noted, an interest in the body has unsurprisingly given rise to a renewed interest in ritual.[13] A focus on embodiment and lived experience also corresponds well with the study of violence, and recent works on violence have been informed by discussions of embodiment.[14] While some biblical scholars have been influenced by these dis-

---

11. While it is no doubt necessary for biblical scholars to have a firm grounding in biblical languages, the argument could be made that more training in method and interdisciplinary approaches could fruitfully replace training in cognate languages for many scholars, and that biblical scholars and specialists in other areas of ancient Near Eastern language, history, and culture should engage more frequently in research collaborations of the type that are very common in the sciences and social sciences. There is no need to be a jack-of-all-ancient-Near-Eastern-Studies-trades when one can be a master of one's own trade and collaborate fruitfully with masters of other trades. While one might counter that the same could be said for interdisciplinary methodological approaches, there is, in fact, no research without method. All academic study is undergirded by particular assumptions and methodologies, and so I would argue that more thorough discussion of and training in these areas should not be seen as optional.

12. Andrew Strathern and Michael Lambek, "Introduction: Embodying Sociality: Africanist-Melanesianist Comparisons," in *Bodies and Persons: Comparative Perspectives from Africa and Melanesia* (ed. Michael Lambek and Andrew Strathern; Cambridge: Cambridge University Press, 1998), 5.

13. Bell, *Ritual Theory*, 96.

14. See, for example, Veena Das et al., eds., *Violence and Subjectivity* (Berkeley:

cussions, there is much work left to be done by historians of Israel interested in warfare and violence.

Interest in embodiment and lived experience continues in the humanities and social sciences, and the neomaterialist approach that underlies these interests has led to a related flourishing of work in cognitive science approaches to the humanities. The recent work of Thomas Kazen on Israelite impurity texts has utilized cognitive science research to very good effect,[15] and it was exciting to see Frank Ritchel Ames's essay in this volume expand the use of this approach in biblical studies. A neomaterialist perspective can also be seen in academia in recent interest in environmental approaches to the humanities and perhaps even in disability studies or food studies. Certainly, the study of Israelite violence could benefit from work in these areas, as well, and these research trends are current enough that biblicists could contribute to the wider discussions on these topics before scholars in other fields turn their attention elsewhere.[16]

A focus on lived experience is evident in research on trauma, which is an area of study in which biblicists have shown a great deal of interest recently. In the past few years, there has been an explosion of work in this area, and the engagement of scholars with research on trauma from

---

University of California Press, 2000); Arturo J. Aldama, ed., *Violence and the Body: Race, Gender, and the State* (Bloomington: Indiana University Press, 2003); many of the essays in Nancy Scheper-Hughes and Philippe Bourgois, *Violence in War and Peace: An Anthology* (Malden, Mass.: Blackwell, 2004); and Veena Das, *Life and Words: Violence and the Descent into the Ordinary* (Berkeley: University of California Press, 2007). A work on ancient violence that deals with not only the body but ritual is Zainab Bahrani, *Rituals of War: The Body and Violence in Mesopotamia* (New York: Zone Books, 2008), an interesting book that in some ways models the approach to studying violence that I am advocating in this essay.

15. See especially Thomas Kazen, *Emotions in Biblical Law: A Cognitive Science Approach* (Hebrew Bible Monographs 36; Sheffield: Sheffield Phoenix Press, 2011).

16. In fact, various scholars have already performed research on disability in ancient Israel or in biblical literature. See, e.g., various works authored or edited by Jeremy Schipper, such as Hector Avalos, Sarah J. Melcher, and Jeremy Schipper, eds., *This Abled Body: Rethinking Disabilities in Biblical Studies* (SemeiaSt 55; Atlanta: Society of Biblical Literature, 2007); Jeremy Schipper, *Disability and Isaiah's Suffering Servant* (Biblical Refigurations; Oxford: Oxford University Press, 2011); and Candida R. Moss and Jeremy Schipper, eds., *Disability Studies and Biblical Literature* (New York: Palgrave Macmillan, 2011). See also Saul M. Olyan, *Disability in the Hebrew Bible: Interpreting Mental and Physical Differences* (New York: Cambridge University Press, 2008).

outside the field has already been very fruitful. For the most part, however, biblical scholars have drawn upon psychological or psychologically informed literary studies of trauma from the 1990s, making much less use of relevant anthropological literature on trauma and "social suffering." In the past twenty years, such scholars as Pierre Bourdieu, Arthur Kleinman, and Veena Das have pioneered research on social suffering, which deals with the social nature of suffering, as well as the social forces that affect human experiences.[17] Social suffering as an area of research intersects with and encompasses such topics as political and other forms of violence, trauma, illness, poverty, and depression. As Kleinman, Das, and Margaret Lock write: "Social suffering results from what political, economic, and institutional power does to people, and, reciprocally, from how these forms of power themselves influence responses to social problems. Included under the category of social suffering are conditions that simultaneously involve health, welfare, legal, moral, and religious issues. They destabilize established categories."[18] It is, I think, clear that social suffering as a concept could be applied to Israelite violence and Israelite experiences of warfare and violence in fruitful ways. Further, examining the intersections between Israelite violence, social suffering, and ritualization could present a fascinating new area of research.

Drawing upon Bell's research on ritual and ritualization that was cited above, one could examine different Israelite social settings as ritualized environments and explore the roles of violence and coercion in such environments. These examinations would do well to engage with Foucault's ideas concerning power relations and cultural discourses, as well as critiques of Foucault's "totalizing" view of social systems and writings on resistance that have often presented a more agentive view of social relations. In examining the nature of social relations in ancient Israel and the

---

17. See Pierre Bourdieu et al., *The Weight of the World: Social Suffering in Contemporary Society* (trans. Priscilla Parkhurst Ferguson; Stanford: Stanford University Press, 1993); Arthur Kleinman, Veena Das, and Margaret Lock, eds., *Social Suffering* (Berkeley: University of California Press, 1997), particularly ix, where the concept of social suffering is explained; Veena Das et al., eds., *Remaking a World: Violence, Social Suffering, and Recovery* (Berkeley: University of California Press, 2001); and Iain Wilkinson, "Social Suffering and the New Politics of Sentimentality," in *Routledge International Handbook of Contemporary Social and Political Theory* (ed. Gerard Delanty and Stephen P. Turner; New York: Routledge, 2011), 460–70, which provides a critical appraisal of the concept.

18. Kleinman, Das, and Lock, *Social Suffering*, ix.

influence of violence on these relations, historically minded biblical scholars could contribute to long-standing debates in the humanities and social sciences over the nature of subjectivity and how totalizing social systems are in determining the choices of individuals. Certainly, these debates directly relate to studies of resistance—in what ways do people resist and how is it possible for them to resist? That is, what about their subjectivity or the social or cultural setting allows them to resist? Related questions might center on why violence arose or was utilized in certain circumstances in ancient Israel as opposed to more indirect ways of controlling behavior. Historians could also make use of theories of "structural violence" in describing how ancient Israel's society was organized and, again, why physical violence was used or threatened in various situations as opposed to discursive practices that shape behavior or to structural forms of violence that privilege some and make the lives of others inherently more precarious.[19] Such examinations could incorporate ideas of ritualization and embodiment and newer materialist approaches that attempt to bridge the gap between older conceptions of materialism and the excessive constructivism of postmodernists, which leaves no room for the influence of physical needs and physiological tendencies.[20] Awareness of these contemporary approaches is necessary for biblical scholars to converse with scholars in other fields rather than merely adopting others' ideas, sometimes decades after they have lost currency in other quarters of academia.[21]

---

19. On "structural violence," see, e.g., Johan Galtung, "Violence, Peace, and Peace Research," *Journal of Peace Research* 6 (1969): 167–91, who coined the term; Nancy Scheper-Hughes, *Death Without Weeping: The Violence of Everyday Life in Brazil* (Berkeley: University of California Press, 1992); Paul Farmer, *Partner to the Poor: A Paul Farmer Reader* (ed. Haun Saussy; Berkeley: University of California, 2010); and Peter Iadicola and Anson Shupe, *Violence, Inequality, and Human Freedom* (3rd ed.; Lanham, Md.: Rowman & Littlefield, 2013), 379–450.

20. On these issues, see Edward Slingerland, *What Science Offers the Humanities: Integrating Body and Culture* (New York: Cambridge University Press, 2008).

21. My point here is not that biblical scholars are poor at keeping up with intellectual fads. The problem is not in applying ideas or methods that have become unfashionable in other fields, but rather in not being aware of how these ideas or methods have been critiqued or refined. Continuous refinement and critique are necessary parts of the progress of ideas in academia. Biblical scholars and historians of Israel cannot participate in interdisciplinary conversations if the conversation has already moved forward without them. Further, they sometimes make use of the ideas of other fields in naïve ways by not being aware of what is being said in those fields currently.

My final suggestion for historians of Israel hoping to forge a twenty-first century approach to studying Israelite violence in ritualized and other forms relates to the topic of cultural comparison. Biblical scholars, it could be argued, might be bolder in contributing to understandings of contemporary violence.[22] Violence, after all, is not merely an "academic" topic of inquiry in the prejorative sense of that term. Violence occurs in this world not merely every day, but every hour, every moment. Attempts at understanding today's very real and very destructive violence often falter when they do not look back far enough. This is why, for example, scholars of genocide have looked to ancient examples of mass violence not only to understand modern ethnic violence better but to challenge arguments about genocidal violence that were too centered upon conceptions of modernity.[23] Yet, these genocide scholars, not being specialists in ancient contexts, sometimes oversimplify or misunderstand ancient cultures and history. Naturally, scholars of the modern world cannot specialize in both past and present contexts any more than scholars of the ancient world can possess a complete understanding of areas in which *they* do not specialize. It is only through scholarly interaction, engagement, and collaboration that a fuller view of human life in all of its positive and negative dimensions becomes possible. We scholars of antiquity have no less to say about

---

22. There have been some works by biblicists comparing biblical and contemporary violence, e.g., Jeremy Young, *The Violence of God and the War on Terror* (New York: Church Publishing, 2008) and Richard S. Hess and Elmer A. Martens, eds., *War in the Bible and Terrorism in the Twenty-First Century* (Bulletin for Biblical Research Supplements 2; Winona Lake, Ind.: Eisenbrauns, 2008), but these have often been theological in focus and centered on interpretation of biblical texts rather than Israelite violence, presenting the incongruity in method discussed above. In my view, much more comparative work could be done by historically minded biblicists, with Bruce Lincoln perhaps offering a model in *Religion, Empire, and Torture: The Case of Achaemenian Persia, with a Postscript on Abu Ghraib* (Chicago: University of Chicago Press, 2007).

23. See T. M. Lemos, "Dispossessing Nations: Population Growth, Scarcity, and Genocide in Ancient Israel and Twentieth-Century Rwanda," (paper presented at Judaic Studies Moskow Symposium: Theorizing Ritual Violence in the Hebrew Bible; Brown University; Providence, R.I., May 5–6, 2013); Frank Chalk and Kurt Jonassohn, *The History and Sociology of Genocide: Analyses and Case Studies* (New Haven: Yale University Press, 1990), 58–93; Ben Kiernan, "The First Genocide: Carthage, 146 BCE," *Diogenes* 203 (2004): 27–39; and idem, *Blood and Soil: A World History of Genocide and Extermination from Sparta to Darfur* (New Haven: Yale University Press, 2007); Adam Jones, *Genocide: A Comprehensive Introduction* (New York: Routledge, 2006), xxi, 3–6.

the present than the scholars of the modern world whose ideas we so often apply to our own work have to say about the past. If anything, our view is longer. We historians of Israel and other scholars of the ancient world have a great deal to contribute to discussions about violence in our own time and about the human condition more broadly, adding in our own way to the effort to understand human life in a way that is nuanced and accounts for particularity, but also acknowledges commonality where it is found. We have something to say, and it is time that we say it.

Bibliography

Aldama, Arturo J., ed. *Violence and the Body: Race, Gender, and the State.* Bloomington: Indiana University Press, 2003.

Avalos, Hector, Sarah J. Melcher, and Jeremy Schipper, eds. *This Abled Body: Rethinking Disabilities in Biblical Studies.* SemeiaSt 55. Atlanta: Society of Biblical Literature, 2007.

Bahrani, Zainab. *Rituals of War: The Body and Violence in Mesopotamia.* New York: Zone Books, 2008.

Bell, Catherine. *Ritual: Perspectives and Dimensions.* Oxford: Oxford University Press, 1997.

———. *Ritual Theory, Ritual Practice.* New York: Oxford University Press, 1992.

Bourdieu, Pierre, et al. *The Weight of the World: Social Suffering in Contemporary Society.* Translated by Priscilla Parkhurst Ferguson. Stanford: Stanford University Press, 1993.

Chalk, Frank, and Kurt Jonassohn. *The History and Sociology of Genocide: Analyses and Case Studies.* New Haven: Yale University Press, 1990.

Craigie, Peter C. *The Problem of War in the Old Testament.* Grand Rapids: Eerdmans, 1978.

Das, Veena. *Life and Words: Violence and the Descent into the Ordinary.* Berkeley: University of California Press, 2007.

Das, Veena, Arthur Kleinman, Margaret Lock, Mamphela Ramphele, and Pamela Reynolds, eds. *Remaking a World: Violence, Social Suffering, and Recovery.* Berkeley: University of California Press, 2001.

Das, Veena, Arthur Kleinman, Mamphela Ramphele, and Pamela Reynolds, eds. *Violence and Subjectivity.* Berkeley: University of California Press, 2000.

Farmer, Paul. *Partner to the Poor: A Paul Farmer Reader.* Edited by Haun Saussy. Berkeley: University of California, 2010.

Galtung, Johan. "Violence, Peace, and Peace Research." *Journal of Peace Research* 6 (1969): 167–91.

Gilders, William K. *Blood Ritual in the Hebrew Bible: Meaning and Power.* Baltimore: The Johns Hopkins University Press, 2004.

Gorman, Frank H. *The Ideology of Ritual: Space, Time, and Status in the Priestly Theology.* JSOTSup 91. Sheffield: Sheffield Academic Press, 1990.

Hess, Richard S., and Elmer A. Martens, eds. *War in the Bible and Terrorism in the Twenty-First Century.* Bulletin for Biblical Research Supplements 2. Winona Lake, Ind.: Eisenbrauns, 2008.

Hobbs, T. R. *A Time for War: A Study of Warfare in the Old Testament.* Wilmington: Michael Glazier, 1989.

Iadicola, Peter and Anson Shupe. *Violence, Inequality, and Human Freedom.* 3rd ed. Lanham, Md.: Rowman & Littlefield, 2013.

Jenson, Philip P. *Graded Holiness: A Key to the Priestly Conception of the World.* JSOTSup 106. Sheffield: Sheffield Academic Press, 1992.

Jones, Adam. *Genocide: A Comprehensive Introduction.* New York: Routledge, 2006.

Kang, Sa-Moon. *Divine War in the Old Testament and in the Ancient Near East.* BZAW 177. Berlin: de Gruyter, 1989.

Kazen, Thomas. *Emotions in Biblical Law: A Cognitive Science Approach.* Hebrew Bible Monographs 36. Sheffield: Sheffield Phoenix Press, 2011.

Kierman, Ben. *Blood and Soil: A World History of Genocide and Extermination from Sparta to Darfur.* New Haven: Yale University Press, 2007.

Kiernan, Ben. "The First Genocide: Carthage, BCE." *Diogenes* 203 (2004): 27–39.

Kleinman, Arthur, Veena Das, and Margaret Lock, eds. *Social Suffering.* Berkeley: University of California Press, 1997.

Klingbeil, Gerald A. *Bridging the Gap: Ritual and Ritual Texts in the Bible.* Bulletin for Biblical Research Supplements 1. Winona Lake: Eisenbrauns, 2007.

Lemos, T. M. "Cultural Anthropology: Hebrew Bible." Pages 157–65 in volume 1 of *Oxford Encyclopedia of Biblical Interpretation.* Edited by Steven L. McKenzie. Oxford: Oxford University Press, 2013.

———. "Dispossessing Nations: Population Growth, Scarcity, and Genocide in Ancient Israel and Twentieth-Century Rwanda." Paper presented at Judaic Studies Moskow Symposium: Theorizing Ritual Violence in the Hebrew Bible. Brown University. Providence, R.I., May 5–6, 2013.

———. "'They Have Become Women': Judean Diaspora and Postcolonial Theories of Gender and Migration." Pages 81–109 in *Social Theory and the Study of Israelite Religion: Essays in Retrospect and Prospect*. Edited by Saul M. Olyan. SBLRBS 71. Atlanta: Society of Biblical Literature, 2012.

Lincoln, Bruce. *Religion, Empire, and Torture: The Case of Achaemenian Persia, with a Postscript on Abu Ghraib*. Chicago: University of Chicago Press, 2007.

Lind, Millard C. *Yahweh Is a Warrior: The Theology of Warfare in Ancient Israel*. Scottdale, Penn.: Herald, 1980.

Lohfink, Norbert. *Krieg und Staat im alten Israel*. Beiträge für Friedensethik 14. Barsbüttel: Institut für Theologie und Frieden, 1992.

McCutcheon, Russell. *Manufacturing Religion: The Discourse on Sui Generis Religion and the Politics of Nostalgia*. Oxford: Oxford University Press, 1997.

Moore, Megan Bishop, and Brad E. Kelle. *Biblical History and Israel's Past: The Changing Study of the Bible and History*. Grand Rapids: Eerdmans, 2011.

Moss, Candida R., and Jeremy Schipper, eds. *Disability Studies and Biblical Literature*. New York: Palgrave Macmillan, 2011.

Niditch, Susan. *War in the Hebrew Bible: A Study in the Ethics of Violence*. New York: Oxford University Press, 1993.

Olyan, Saul M. *Disability in the Hebrew Bible: Interpreting Mental and Physical Differences*. New York: Cambridge University Press, 2008.

———. *Rites and Rank: Hierarchy in Biblical Representations of Cult*. Princeton: Princeton University Press, 2000.

Sax, William S., Johannes Quack, and Jan Weinhold, eds. *The Problem of Ritual Efficacy*. Oxford: Oxford University Press, 2010.

Scheper-Hughes, Nancy. *Death Without Weeping: The Violence of Everyday Life in Brazil*. Berkeley: University of California Press, 1992.

Scheper-Hughes, Nancy, and Philippe Bourgois. *Violence in War and Peace: An Anthology*. Malden, Mass.: Blackwell, 2004.

Schipper, Jeremy. *Disability and Isaiah's Suffering Servant*. Biblical Refigurations. Oxford: Oxford University Press, 2011.

Slingerland, Edward. *What Science Offers the Humanities: Integrating Body and Culture*. New York: Cambridge University Press, 2008.

Stern, Philip D. *The Biblical Ḥerem: A Window on Israel's Religious Experience*. BJS 211. Atlanta: Scholars Press, 1991.

Strathern, Andrew, and Michael Lambek. "Introduction: Embodying Sociality: Africanist-Melanesianist Comparisons." Pages 1–28 in *Bodies and Persons: Comparative Perspectives from Africa and Melanesia*. Edited by Michael Lambek and Andrew Strathern. Cambridge: Cambridge University Press, 1998.

Trimm, Charles. "Recent Research on Warfare in the Old Testament." *CBR* 10 (2012): 171–216.

Rad, Gerhard von. *Holy War in Ancient Israel*. Translated by M. J. Dawn. Grand Rapids: Eerdmans, 1991. German orig. *Der Heilige Krieg im alten Israel*. Göttingen: Vandenhoeck & Ruprecht, 1951.

Watts, James W. *Ritual and Rhetoric in Leviticus: From Sacrifice to Scripture*. Cambridge: Cambridge University Press, 2007.

Weippert, Manfred. "Heiliger Krieg in Israel und Assyrien: Kritische Anmerkungen zu Gerhard von Rads Konzept des 'Heiligen Krieges im alten Israel.'" *ZAW* 84 (1972): 460–93.

Wilkinson, Iain. "Social Suffering and the New Politics of Sentimentality." Pages 460–70 in *Routledge International Handbook of Contemporary Social and Political Theory*. Edited by Gerard Delanty and Stephen P. Turner. New York: Routledge, 2011.

Young, Jeremy. *The Violence of God and the War on Terror*. New York: Church Publishing, 2008.

List of Contributors

Frank Ritchel Ames
Rocky Vista University College of Medicine

Deborah O'Daniel Cantrell
Vanderbilt University

Brad E. Kelle
Point Loma Nazarene University

David T. Lamb
Biblical Theological Seminary

T. M. Lemos
Huron University College at the University of Western Ontario

Nathaniel B. Levtow
University of Montana

Kelly J. Murphy
Central Michigan University

Susan Niditch
Amherst College

Saul M. Olyan
Brown University

Jason A. Riley
Fuller Theological Seminary

Thomas Römer
Université de Lausanne

Rüdiger Schmitt
University of Münster

Mark S. Smith
New York University

Jacob L. Wright
Emory University

Index of Ancient Sources

Hebrew Bible/Old Testament		
Genesis		
9:3–4	200	
9:23	17 n. 5	
14:7–24	210, 216, 217 n. 34	
16:6	200	
17	21	
24:14	74	
25:25	85	
28:18–22	38 n. 34	
33:20	38 n. 34	
34:2	200	
34:14	21	
42:24	177	
49:3	171	
49:6	171	
49:9	171	
49:18	171	

Exodus	
1:11	200
3	53
3:2–4	56
3:5	53
4:24–26	53–54, 104
12:1–28	53
12:7	104
12:43–50	53
12:48	21
14	53
15	165
15:1–2	171
15:1–18	169 n. 19, 210, 218
15:3	257
15:9	118
15:20	210
15:20–21	169, 169 n. 19, 218
15:21	169 n. 19, 210
17:14–16	210, 217
19:3–6	25
19:16	70
23:20	54
23:27	71 n. 20
24:8–11	104
30:11–16	217
32:20	40 n. 40
34:13	217 n. 35, 228 nn. 80–83, 86

Leviticus	
6:20	212 n. 20, 260
7:26–27	200
10:4–5	212 n. 19
11:25	260
14:8	18, 22, 23 n. 16
14:9	18, 22–23, 23 n. 16
17:10–14	200
21:1–4	212 n. 19
21:1–6	214 n. 26
21:1–11	212 n. 20
21:10–12	212 n. 19

Numbers	
5	54, 196, 212 n. 20, 213, 212, 214 n. 26
5:1–4	212, 212 n. 20
6:6–12	212 n. 19
6:18	19
7:1–89	215 n. 30
8:7	19, 260
9:6–14	212 n. 19

Numbers (cont.)
13–14	54
14:9	118
18:8–32	215 n. 30
19	212, 212 n. 20, 214 n. 26
19:1–22	212
19:11–20	214 n. 26
19:19	260
21:1–24	202
21:2–3	188
22:23	54
22:31	54
23–24	171
24:8–9	118
25	195
28:1–31	215 n. 30
31	192, 196, 198, 212 n. 19, 213–17, 213 nn. 21–22, 214 nn. 26–27, 217 n. 33, 222, 225 n. 65, 226–27, 235
31:1–24	9, 187, 195–97
31:8	194
31:9	211
31:10	194
31:13–21	243 n. 1
31:13–24	210–11, 212 n. 19
31:13–54	209, 211
31:16	195
31:19–24	211, 214 n. 26
31:25–47	210, 214 n. 27
31:48–54	210
31:50	197
33:52	217 n. 35, 228 nn. 80–83, 228 n. 86
35:33	212 n. 19

Deuteronomy 4, 199
5:17	95 n. 35
6:20–25	25
7:1–11	210 n. 16
7:23	71 n. 20
7:25	217 n. 35, 228 nn. 80–83, 86
10:16	21
11:29–32	26, 34
12:1–5	36
12:15–16	200
12:23	104
18	154, 158
19:1–22:8	95 n. 35
20	215
20:1–18	95 n. 35
20:10–18	210
20:11–12	55
21	199–200, 202
21:10–14	9, 187, 197, 213, 213 n. 21, 215
21:12	18
21:12–13	18
21:22–23	17
22:5	95 n. 35
23–24	200
26:5–10	25
27:1–8	26, 34
28:28–29	16–17
32:20	74 n. 34
32:42	262

Joshua 4–5, 50–51, 60, 73, 215 n. 30
1:3–6	50
2	55 n. 18
3–4	53
3:1–5:1	52
5	52–53, 56
5:2–3	54
5:2–9	52–54
5:4	54
5:9	21
5:10–12	52–53
5:13	54
5:13–14	54, 56
5:13–15	5, 52–55, 57, 60–61, 60 n. 31, 79
5:14	55
5:15	53, 55, 60
6	38, 40, 52
6:1	55, 73 n. 30
6:2	55, 60
6:2–3	73
6:4–5	73
6:4–20	70 n. 19
6:5	76 n. 42

6:24	210, 217	3:16	65
7	8, 187	3:21	71 n. 21
7:1	210	3:21–22	65
7:10–26	193	3:27	70
7:25	193	3:28	71 n. 21
8	60	3:30	71 n. 21
8:18	60	4:2	71 n. 21
8:18–26	79	4:7	71 n. 21
8:24–29	210, 215	4:9	71 n. 21
8:26	60	4:14	71 n. 21
8:29	17	4:15	71 n. 20
8:30–35	26, 34	4:16	65
10:8	50	4:21	71 n. 21
10:10	71 n. 20	4:24	71 n. 21
10:10–11	50	5	8, 117 n. 19, 165, 167, 170–71, 173–74, 173 n. 32, 181, 192
10:11	51, 71 n. 20		
10:24	17	5:2–5	171
10:27	17, 60	5:2–13	167, 174
10:28	60	5:3	171–73
10:32	60	5:4	172
10:39	60	5:6–9	171
11:6	50	5:7	172–73
11:10	60	5:8b	174
11:12	60	5:9	172–73
11:14	210, 215	5:9a	171
22:7–9	210, 216	5:10	174
24:2–13	25	5:10–13	171
24:7	71 n. 20	5:12	172, 174
24:25–27	26	5:13	172–73
		5:13b	171
Judges	5–6, 65, 67 n. 6, 69, 71, 73 n. 30, 112, 118, 215 n. 30	5:14	172
		5:14–29	167
1:2	71 n. 21	5:14–30	174
1:4	71 n. 21	5:15	171–73
1:6–7	71 n. 21, 194	5:16	172, 174
1:8	65	5:16–17	174
1:35	71 n. 21	5:21	172–73
2:14–16	71 n. 21	5:21b	171–72, 171 n. 22
2:18	71 n. 21	5:23	167
2:23	71 n. 21	5:24	171 n. 22
3:4	71 n. 21	5:26	71 n. 21
3:4–27	154	5:28–30	210, 216
3:8	71 n. 21	6	66
3:10	71 n. 21	6–7	77
3:15	71 n. 21	6–8	65–67, 80

Judges (cont.)

6:1–2	71 n. 21
6:1–6	66 n. 2
6:1–7:15	5
6:5	66
6:9	71 n. 21
6:11–24	66, 66 n. 3
6:12	67
6:12–14	56
6:14	66
6:15	77
6:16	77, 80
6:21	71 n. 21
6:24–7:20	154
6:25–32	66, 66 n. 3
6:33	70 n. 17
6:33–35	66, 70 n. 17
6:34	70, 77
6:34–35	70 n. 17
6:36–37	71 n. 21
6:36–40	66, 66 n. 3, 80
7	5, 66, 70, 74, 79
7:1–8	66, 66 n. 3, 70, 80
7:2	70, 71 n. 21
7:3	70
7:4	70
7:6–9	71 n. 21
7:7	70–71
7:9	71, 77
7:9–15	66, 66 n. 3, 76 n. 45, 77, 78, 80
7:10	77
7:11	71 n. 21
7:13	78
7:14	65, 76, 78–79
7:14–15	71
7:14–16	71 n. 21
7:15	77
7:15b	80
7:16	66, 68, 72–75
17:16b	75
7:16–21	66 n. 2, 67, 69, 78
7:16–22	65–66, 66 n. 1, 67 n. 5, 68–69, 71–72, 75–76, 79 n. 59, 80
7:16–23	73 n. 30
7:17–18	68, 73, 75
7:18	73–74, 76
7:18b	76
7:18–22	75 n. 37
7:19	68, 73–74
17:19b	75
7:19–20	71 n. 21
7:20	65, 68, 72–76, 75 n. 39, 78–80
7:20a	75
7:20b	76
7:21	68–69, 78
7:22	65, 68–69, 72–73, 73 n. 30, 76, 78–80, 79 n. 59
8	70 n. 17
8:3	71 n. 21
8:4	67 n. 5
8:4–21	66 n. 2, 67, 67 n. 5, 69, 70 n. 17
8:6–7	71 n. 21
8:7	118
8:7b	67 n. 5
8:10–12	67 n. 5
8:15	71 n. 21
8:16	118
8:18bR*	67 n. 5
8:20	65
8:22	71 n. 21
8:22–35	66 n. 3, 70 n. 17
8:34	71 n. 21
9	69
9:16–17	71 n. 21
9:24	71 n. 21
9:29	71 n. 21
9:33	71 n. 21
9:34	169
9:43	69
9:45	210 n. 16
9:48	71 n. 21
9:54	65, 91 n. 20
10:7	71 n. 21
10:12	71 n. 21
11	8, 187, 190
11:21	71 n. 21
11:26	71 n. 21
11:29–30	192

11:30	71 n. 21	11:11	70
11:32	71 n. 21	13:3	70 n. 19
11:34	169 n. 19	13:9–14	40
11:39	191	13:17–18	70
12:2–3	71 n. 21	14	200–201
13:1	71 n. 21	14:1	91 n. 20
13:5	71 n. 21	14:6	124
13:14–19	151, 153	14:15	71 n. 20
13:17	152	14:20	71 n. 20
13:23	71 n. 21	14:24	200
14:3	124	14:28	200
14:6	71 n. 21	14:31	188
15:12–15	71 n. 21	14:31–35	210, 215
15:16	118	15	8
15:17–18	71 n. 21	15:1–9	210, 215
15:18	124	15:3	187
16:18	71 n. 21	15:15	193
16:23–24	71 n. 21	15:33	187
16:26	71 n. 21	16–17	83, 89, 90 n. 16, 122 n. 31
17:3	71 n. 21	16:1–13	124 n. 42
17:5	71 n. 21	16:10–13b	89
17:12	71 n. 21	16:18b	89
18:10	71 n. 21	17	121–22
18:19	71 n. 21	17:1–58	89
19:27	71 n. 21	17:4	122
20:13	191	17:7	125
20:16	71 n. 21	17:10	122, 126
20:28	71 n. 21	17:11	122–24, 126
21	65, 187, 191–92	17:12–31	122 n. 31
21:1	191	17:16	122–23, 126
21:8–12	192	17:20	76 n. 42
21:10	65	17:23	122, 124, 126
21:16–23	192	17:24	124, 126
21:19–23	192	17:25–26	123
		17:26	122, 123 n. 39, 124, 126
1 Samuel	69, 118, 176 n. 39, 180, 217	17:28	124, 126
2:12–17	40	17:33	125–26
3	38	17:34–36	126
4:1–7:2	38, 41 n. 42	17:34–37	125
5:1–8	210, 217	17:36	123–24, 123 n. 39
5:11	71 n. 20	17:38–40	90
7:10	71 n. 20	17:41–47	112
10:10–12	23 n. 15	17:42	90, 94
11:2	16	17:42–43	99, 125
11:7	191	17:42–47	126

1 Samuel (cont.)

17:43	90, 125
17:44	125
17:45	123, 123 n. 39
17:46	16, 125
17:48–49	126
17:49	122 n. 31
17:51–54	126
17:52	76 n. 42
17:54	39
17:55–18:5	122 n. 31
18:6	169 n. 19
18:6–7	169
18:6–9	210, 218
18:27	21
19:24	23 n. 15
21:3–5	91 n. 20
21:9	39
23:1–5	210, 215
25:22	120 n. 27
27:8–10	215
27:8–12	210
30	22
30:7–9	151
30:21–31	210
30:21–25	215
31:4	124
31:8–10	16, 210, 217
31:12	20
31:13	20
31:16	39

2 Samuel	69, 118, 157, 176 n. 39
1	7, 17 n. 4, 165, 169–70, 175, 181
1:11–12	17, 177 n. 40
1:19	167, 169
1:19a	167
1:19–25	167, 169–70, 175, 177–80
1:19–27	167, 170, 175, 178 n. 42, 181, 210, 219
1:20	124, 169, 177, 178 n. 44
1:20–24	179
1:21	87, 177
1:21a	167
1:21–23	178 n. 44
1:22	177
1:23	177
1:24	169, 177, 178 n. 44
1:25c	179
1:26	175–77, 178 n. 42
1:26–27	167, 170, 175, 177–80
1:27	178 n. 42, 179
2:1–2	151
2:5	20
2:5–6	17
2:22	118
2:24–32	209
2:28	70 n. 19
3:14	21 n. 13
3:32–34	170, 177
3:33–34	219 n. 43
4:12	17
5:6	118
6:2	38, 38 n. 34
6:16	23
6:20	23, 23 n. 15, 169
8:9–12	210, 217
9–20	90
10	23
10:1–5	18
10:3	17
10:4–5	23
12:30	217 n. 35
13:12	200
13:14	200
18	23
18:1–5	157
18:2	70
18:33	219 n. 43
19:1–8	218 n. 38
19:1–18	210
19:3	218 n. 38
19:4	16 n. 2, 17
19:6–9	152, 157
19:8	218 n. 38
20:8	95 n. 35
21:12–14	19
21:21	118
24:1–17	217
24:14	175

INDEX OF ANCIENT SOURCES 295

1 Kings	118	9:15	134
1–2	90	9:15–16	139
2	83	9:22	120
2:5	9	9:24	134
2:5b	90	9:27	134
2:5–6	90, 99	9:31	120
4:7	140	9:33	134, 260
4:26–27	140	9:33–37	121
7:2	38 n. 34	14:8–10	119
8:6–9	37	14:10	16 n. 2
10:28	140–41	17	40
12:22–24	151	18–20	49
12:26–33	157	18:4	121
16:15	120, 120 n. 29	18:16	121
17:12	74	18:21	121, 142
18:27	120	18:23	140
18:34	74	18:23–24	121, 141
19:1–2	120	18:27	121
19:3	120	18:28–35	49
20	158	19:14–16	38
20:1–43	154	19:22–23	121
20:10–11	118	12:28	121
20:20	132	19:35–37	121
20:32–34	194	23:16	20, 212 n. 19
21:19	122 n. 31	23:18	20
21:19–24	120	24	40
22	152, 154	25:7	16
22:1–38	154, 158		
22:6	51	Isaiah	261 n. 73
22:10	157 n. 27	2:7	138
22:10–12	151, 154	5:28	136
22:19–25	119	7:3–4	119 n. 24
22:34–35	134	7:4	119
22:38	254 n. 43	9:1–7	85 n. 5
		9:5	86 n. 5
2 Kings	118	13:18	91 n. 20
2:23–24	119	14:3–20	210, 220
3:4–27	158	14:3–23	117
3:22–23	99	14:19	134
3:27	40	15–16	210, 220
6:8–23	158	20:3–4	16
6:17	132	21:5	87
7:6–7	114 n. 13	22:7	138
8:28	139	25:6	210, 218
9:10	120	30:15	137

Isaiah (cont.)		17:16	141
31:1	133, 142	18:7	17
31:3	142	18:16	17
34:5–6	262	23	83
40–56	59	23:6	132
40:9–10	169	23:11–27	88
47:3	16 n. 3	23:12	88
52:1	21	23:14	88
52:15	260 n. 61	23:14–15	88
58:7	17	26:11	134
59:1–3	212 n. 19	27:16	141
59:3	259 n. 58, 261	30	59
62:6	83	30:20–21	59
63	83	30:20–26	59
63:1	83, 85	30:22–26	59
63:1–3	99	32:1–16	210, 220
63:1–6	10, 83–85, 87, 94–95, 244, 257–59, 259 n. 59, 262–63	39:11–12	209
		39:11–16	212 n. 19
63:2	85	43:7–9	212 n. 19
63:2–3	85	44:7	21
63:3	85, 259 n. 58, 260, 262	44:9	21
63:3–6	85	44:25–27	212 n. 19
63:5	85		
63:6	85, 99	Hosea	
65:4	212 n. 19	14:3	137
Jeremiah		Joel	
2:21	219 n. 43	1:2–2:17	210, 220
2:34	212 n. 19	1:6–8	220
4:4	21		
4:19	70 n. 19	Amos	
8:1–2	19	2:2	70 n. 19
9:18	16 n. 2, 17, 219 n. 43	3:6	70 n. 19
19	154	4:10	137
22:14	88 n. 12		
22:19	17	Micah	
27:17–20	51	2:4	144
28	154	5:10	137
46:10	259, 262		
48	210, 220	Nahum	
48:33	259	2	83
		2:3b	87
Ezekiel		2:3–4	86, 99
7:18	16 n. 2, 17	3:1	99
9:6	212 n. 19	3:2–3	136

INDEX OF ANCIENT SOURCES

Habakkuk		68:21–27	210, 218
1:8	136–37	68:22–23	90, 262 n. 74
		68:23	219
Zephaniah		68:24	254 n. 43
1:16	70 n. 19	68:25–26	169
3:1	259 n. 58	69:18	176
		6:26	169 n. 19
Haggai		18	219–20 n. 44
2:10–19	212 n. 19	20	219–20 n. 44
		74	210, 219
Zechariah		76:6	133
1:8	86 n. 8	79	210, 219
6:2	86 n. 8	80	179 n. 48, 210, 219
9	83, 201–202 n. 21	89	210, 219
9:15	86, 86 n. 6	91:7	74 n. 34
12:4	133	102:3	176
		106:38–39	212 n. 19
Malachi		108:8–9	117
1:7	259 n. 58	144	219–20 n. 44
1:12	259 n. 58		
		Job	132
Psalms	117, 220	22:6	17
2:9	151, 154	39	132 n. 3
20:7	133	39:21–22	132
31:10	176	41:14a	171 n. 22
33:17	133		
39	179 n. 48	Proverbs	
42–43	179, 179 n. 48	18:24	175 n. 36
44	210, 219	30:10–31	169 n. 18
45	94	31:10	169 n. 18
46	179 n. 48		
49	179 n. 48	Song of Songs	88
53:6	16 n. 2, 17	1:9	88
56	179 n. 48	3:4	89 n. 15
57	179 n. 48	3:6–11	94
58:10	90, 219	3:7–8	88–89
58:11	254 n. 43	3:8	89 n. 15
59	177 n. 48	4:4	88
59:17	176	5	83
60	210, 219	5:10	88–89, 94
66:14	176	6:4	88, 89 n. 15
67	179 n. 48	6:10	89 n. 15
68	170	6:13	89 n. 15
68:11–14	210, 216	7:8	89 n. 15
68:12–13	169	8:8–11	89 n. 15

Song of Songs (cont.)
8:11	89 n. 15
Lamentations	220, 220 n. 45, 230, 259 n. 58
1:8	16, 16 n. 3
1:15	259
1:20	176
4	83, 90 n. 16
4:4	259 n. 58
4:7–9	90–91
4:14	212 n. 19, 261
4:15	261
5	210, 220

Esther
9:16–17	210, 218

Daniel
1:1–2	210. 217
1:8	259 n. 58
5:2–3	210, 217

Ezra
2:62	259 n. 58

Nehemiah
3:35	119
3:36	119
4:10	91 n. 20
7:64	259 n. 58
13:9	259 n. 58

1 Chronicles
18:7–8	210
18:10–11	210
20:5	122 n. 31
21:13	175
21:16	54
26:26–28	210, 217

2 Chronicles
13:12	70 n. 19
13:14	70 n. 19
13:15	75 n. 37
15:11	210, 217
20:21–22	76 n. 42
20:21–23	75 n. 37
20:24–30	210, 218
20:27–28	218
28:8–15	210, 215
35:23–24	135
35:25	170 n. 20

Ancient Near Eastern Texts

Amarna Letter 72	124 n. 43
Aqhatu Legend	83, 92–95, 92 n. 24, 103
Ashurbanipal	5, 56–57, 223, 223 n. 55, 227, 227 n. 75, 258 n. 57
Ashurnasirpal II	32, 32 n. 17, 37–38 n. 33, 39, 223, 223 n. 55, 228 n. 86, 249, 249 n. 27
Assyrian Horse Lists	133 n. 7
Assyrian Royal Inscriptions	223, 228, 235 n. 115, 243 n. 1
Atrahasis	245–46, 245 n. 5, 246 n. 6
Azatiwada	37 n. 33
Baal Cycle	74 n. 34, 222 n. 50, 252–54, 252 n. 41, 253–54 n. 43, 254 n. 44
Balawat Gate	141 n. 38, 143 n. 48
Beth-Shean Stele	57, 115
Broken Obelisk	58
Calendar of Numa	224 n. 59
Dadusha Stele	33 n. 21
The Descent of Ishtar	245 n. 4
Enuma Elish	114, 251, 251 nn. 35–36, 259 n. 59
Eridu Lament	230 n. 96
Esarhaddon	37, 40 n. 40, 50, 116, 226, 226 n. 72, 228
First Soldiers' Oath	83, 91–92, 91 n. 21, 92 nn. 22–23, 94, 99
Gilgamesh Epic	176–77, 223, 250, 250 n. 29, 250 n. 31, 251–52 n. 38, 245 n. 5
Great Melos Amphora	144 n. 50
Hymn to Inanna	245
Idrimi	226, 226 n. 71
Israel Stele	57
Karnak Inscription	57

INDEX OF ANCIENT SOURCES

Karnak Relief 143 n. 45
Kilamuwa Stela 37 n. 33
Kirta Epic 83, 93–94, 93 n. 30, 94 nn. 31–32
Lament of Anat over Aqhat 169, 229
Laments of El and Anat over Baal 169, 229
Lamentation over the Destruction of Sumer and Ur 230 n. 96
Lamentation over the Destruction of Ur 230 n. 96
Lugal-e 247, 247 n. 14
Mari Letter 226 n. 70
Mesha 37 n. 33, 188, 273
Mesopotamian City Laments 229
Myth of Nergal and Ereshkigal 245 n. 4
Myth of Telipinu 244 n. 3
Naram-Sin 249, 249 n. 25
Nimrud Prism 132
Nippur Lament 230 n. 96
"The Ox and the Horse" 132 n. 4
Ramses II 115, 131 n. 1, 143 n. 45
Ramses III 136 n. 19
Rameseum Relief 143 n. 45
The Return of Ninurta to Nipru 247–48
The Ritual Between the Pieces 243 n. 1
Sargon II 50, 114, 114 n. 13, 132, 223, 223 n. 55, 249, 249 n. 23
Sefire Treaty Stelae 37, 37 n. 32
Sennacherib 20, 114–15, 142
Shalmaneser III 223, 223 n. 55, 228 n. 86, 249–50, 250 n. 28
Sinuhe Narrative 114
Stele of Adad-nirari III 32
Stele of the Vultures 28–30, 30 nn. 10–11, 32, 39, 41 n. 42
Sumerian Standard of Ur 143
Tel Dan Inscription 4, 32 n. 18, 36–37, 36 n. 30, 134 n. 12, 138
Tell al Rimah Stele 32 n. 19
Terqa Letter 58
Thutmose 114
Tiglath-pileser I 33, 34 n. 22
Uruk Lament 230 n. 96
Victory Monument of Tiglath-pileser III 33
Victory Stele of King Piye 115, 243 n. 1
Yahdun-Lim 58, 223, 249, 249 n. 26, 249 n. 26
Zakkur Stela 37 n. 33, 228

Deuterocanonical Books

1 Maccabees
6:39 87

2 Maccabees
8:21–29 216 n. 32
15:15 79

Dead Sea Scrolls

1QIsa^a 260, 261 n. 68
1QIsa^b 260, 261 n. 68

Greek and Latin Authors

Aelian, *On Animals*
16.25 136 n. 19

Homer, *Iliad* 122
1.1 173 n. 29
2.484–493 173
2.761 173
4.127 174
4.146 174
6.263–268 243 n. 1
7.104 174
8.273–274 174
9 170
10.460 227 n. 78
11.218 173
12.176 173
13.603 174
16.20 174
16.584 174
16.692–693 174
16.744 174

Homer, Iliad (cont.)
16.754	174
16.787	174
16.812	174
16.843	172 n. 26, 174
17.679	174
17.702	174
19	177
19.315–337	178
22.249–272	116
22.416	116
23.19–23	179 n. 45
23.43–53	179 n. 45
23.54–107	179 n. 45
23.391	179 n. 45
23.600	174

Homer, Odyssey
1.1	173
8.499–534	177 n. 40

Tacitus, *Germania*	255 n. 50

Virgil, *Aeneid*
11.4–11	228–29 n. 88

RABBINIC AND MEDIEVAL JEWISH TEXTS

b. *Nazir* 59a	95 n. 35
Tg. Onkelos	95 n. 35

OTHER ANCIENT LITERATURE

Canon of Basil the Great	225, 226 n. 66
Penitential of Carlo Borromeo	226 n. 68
Penitential of Theodore of Tarsus	226, 226 n. 67
Táin	225

INDEX OF MODERN AUTHORS

Abegg, Martin G.   261 n. 68
Ackerman, Susan   8, 169 n. 18, 176, 176 n. 37, 176–77 n. 39, 177 n. 40
Aldama, Arturo J.   278 n. 14
Alter, Robert   123–24, 123 nn. 39–40, 124 nn. 44–45
Ames, Frank Ritchel   1 n. 1, 5–6, 84 n. 2, 92 n. 25, 95 n. 35, 207 n. 7, 216 n. 32, 274, 278
Amit, Yairah   71, 71 n. 22, 172 n. 25
Anderson, Gary A.   17 n. 4
Anderson, Jeff S.   117 n. 18
André, G.   260 n. 64
Anthony, David W.   136–36 n. 16
Arnold, Philip P.   98, 98 n. 48
Ashley, Timothy R.   212 nn. 17–18, 215 n. 29, 216 n. 33
Aster, Shawn Z.   139 n. 28
Avalos, Hector   278 n. 16
Avigad, Nahman   153 n. 17, 154 n. 20
Avramescu, S.   102 n. 61
Backer, Fabrice de   135 n. 15
Bahrani, Zainab   29 n. 9, 205 n. 3, 207 n. 7, 221 n. 46, 223 n. 55, 224 n. 59, 227 n. 79, 231, 231 n. 100, 278 n. 14
Baldwin, Joyce G.   123, 123 n. 40
Barmash, Pamela   245 n. 5
Barthélemy, Dominique   122 n. 31
Barton, Robert A.   102 n. 61
Beck, Deborah   172 n. 26
Becker, Uwe   74 nn. 35–36, 75, 75 n.. 38–41, 79 n. 59
Becking, Bob   133 n. 7
Beek, Martinus A.   132 n. 5
Bell, Catherine   27 n. 3, 41 n. 41, 274, 274 nn. 6–7, 277, 277 n. 13, 279
Bellinger, W. H., Jr.   212 n. 17
Benardete, Seth   174 n. 33
Ben-Dov, Rachel   36 n. 31
Bergmann, Claudia   115, 115 n. 14
Berlin, Adele   171 n. 22
Berlin, Brent   83 n. 1
Berman, Joshua   198, 198 n. 17
Bidmead, Julye   246 n. 9
Bieberstein, Klaus   52 n. 7, 53 n. 12
Bienkowski, Piotr   249 n. 25
Biran, Avraham   36 nn. 30–31
Black, Jeremy A.   247 nn. 14–15, 248 n. 17
Block, Daniel Isaac   69 n. 12, 69 n. 14, 69 n. 16, 74 n. 32, 77 n. 46, 78 n. 50, 79 n. 53
Blum, Erhard   51 n. 6, 54 n. 14
Bly, Robert   225 n. 64, 231 n. 98, 232 n. 101
Boivin, Nicole   101 n. 53
Borger, Rykle   19 n. 9
Bourdieu, Pierre   274, 279, 279 n. 17
Bourgois, Philippe   278 n. 14
Breasted, James Henry   57 n. 21
Bremmer, Jan N.   113, 113 n. 6
Brenner, Athalya   83 n. 1, 169 n. 19, 170 n. 20, 173 n. 27, 218 n. 37
Brettler, Marc Z.   54 n. 13
Briend, Jacques   55 n. 17
Brock, Rita Nakashima   205 n. 2, 232, 232 n. 104, 233 nn. 106–107, 233 n. 109–12, 234 n. 14, 237 n. 120

Budd, Philip J.   212 n. 17, 213 n. 21, 215 n. 29, 216–17 n. 33
Burger, Ronna   174 n. 33
Burkert, Walter   190 n. 9, 227 n. 77, 229 n. 89, 229 n. 91
Burns, Rita J.   169 n. 19
Cage, John   83 n. 1
Calefato, Patrizia   95 n. 34
Cameracanna, Emanuela   98 n. 45
Cantrell, Deborah O'Daniel   6, 132 n. 2, 134 n. 10, 135 n. 15, 138 nn. 24–25, 139 n. 31, 140 nn. 35–36
Carmichael, Calum   199, 199 n. 20
Carr, David McLain   166–67, 166 nn. 6–9, 167 n. 13
Casalis, E.   243 n. 1
Cathcart, Kevin J.   87 n. 10
Černý, J.   57 n. 22
Chalk, Frank   281 n. 23
Chalmer, Seth   169 n. 19
Chapman, Cynthia R.   88 n. 13, 207 n. 7
Charles, J. Daryl   86 n. 7
Chomsky, Noam   96 n. 40
Cipin, Ian   139 n. 27
Civil, Miguel   248 n. 20
Clausewitz, Carl von   30 n. 9, 206, 206 n. 5
Clifford, Richard J.   169 n. 18, 175 n. 36
Coats, George W.   124 n. 43
Coben, Lawrence S.   175 n. 34, 181 n. 52
Cohen, Abner   96 n. 36
Collins, Billie Jean   91 n. 21, 92 nn. 22–23, 243 n. 1
Collins, John J.   207 n. 10
Cooke, S. M.   213–14 n. 24
Cooper, Jerrold S.   28 n. 4, 29 n. 6
Craigie, Peter C.   172 n. 23, 207 n. 10, 276 n. 9
Croft, William   96 n. 40
Cross, Frank Moore   25 n. 1, 165, 165 nn. 1–2, 169 n. 19, 172 n. 22, 179 n. 46, 257 n. 55
Crouch, Carly L.   207 n. 7, 218 n. 39, 235 n. 115
Crowfoot, Grace M.   154 n. 19
Crowfoot, John W.   154 n. 19
Cruse, D. Alan   96 n. 40
Dalby, Andrew   179 n. 45
Dalley, Stephanie   132–33 n. 7, 137 n. 20, 141 n. 40, 245 n. 4
Das, Veena   277–78 n. 14, 279, 279 nn. 17–18
Davis, Fred   103 n. 63
Day, Peggy L.   189, 190 n. 7
De Vries, Simon J.   122, 122 n. 32
Dearman, Andrew   188 n. 3
Debord, Guy   172–73 n. 27
Dedrick, Don   83 n. 1
Detienne, Marcel   191 n. 10
Dietrich, Manfried   244 n. 3
Dijk, Jan van   150 n. 2, 223 n. 54, 251 n. 33
Dijk-Hemmes, Fokkelien van   169 n. 19, 170 n. 20, 173 n. 27, 218 n. 37, 247 nn. 14–15
Dijkstra, Meindert   93 n. 29
Dixon, Nicholas   113, 113 n. 11, 127
Dobbs-Allsopp, F. W.   219 n. 42, 220, 220 n. 45, 229 n. 94, 230 n. 95
Dotham, Trude   32 n. 18
Douglas, Mary   193 n. 11, 199, 199 n. 18, 256 n. 52, 273
Downes, Jeremy M.   170 n. 20
Dozeman, Thomas B.   212 n. 17, 212 n. 19, 214 n. 27, 215 nn. 28–29, 217 n. 33
Drews, Robert   135 n. 15
Driel, Govert van   26 n. 2
Drinkard, Joel   26 n. 2
Dunham, Dows   141 n. 41
Durand, Jean-Marie   58, 58 nn. 24–26
Eaton, Margaret R.   112, 112 n. 4, 114, 114 n. 12, 116 n. 15
Ebeling, Jennie   139 n. 27
Edelman, Diana Vikander   178 n. 42, 179, 179 n. 49
Elat, Moshe   150 n. 5
Elgavish, David   215 n. 31, 226 n. 71
Elliot, Andrew J.   101, 101 n. 58, 102 nn. 59–60

Emmorey, Karen	97 n. 41	Gilders, William K.	104 n. 65, 209 n. 15, 271, 272 n. 3, 274 n. 7
Evans, Vyvyan	97 n. 42		
Fadiman, Jeffrey A.	225 n. 63	Girard, René	190–91 n. 9
Fallaize, E. N.	213 n. 24	Gitin, Seymour	32 n. 18
Farmer, Paul	280 n. 19	Goetze, Albrecht	223 n. 55, 248 n. 19
Farnell, Lewis R.	243 n. 1, 255 n. 50	Gooding, David W.	122 n. 31
Feder, Yitzhaq	230 n. 97	Goody, Jack	273–74
Feldman, Emmanuel	213 n. 23, 214 n. 25	Gordon, Cyrus H.	95 n. 35, 169 n. 15, 261 n. 72
Feliu, Lluís	58 n. 27	Gordon, Robert P.	123, 123 n. 40
Fewell, Danna Nolan	121 n. 30	Görg, Manfred	73 n. 31
Finkelstein, Israel	139 n. 31	Gorman, Frank H., Jr.	271, 271–72 n. 3
Firth, David G.	122, 123 n. 36, 125–26 n. 46	Gottwald, Norman K.	133 n. 9, 199, 199 nn. 18–19
Firth, Raymond	104 n. 67	Gray, George Buchanan	212 nn. 17–18, 216–17 n. 33, 222 n. 49
Fischer, Robert S.	102 n. 60		
Fisher, Loren R.	244 n. 3	Grayson, A. Kirk	20 n. 12, 224 n. 61, 249 n. 27, 250 n. 28
Flanagan, James W.	90 n. 17		
Flint, Peter W.	261 n. 68	Greene, Thomas M.	169, 169 nn. 16–17, 174
Foster, Benjamin R.	176 n. 38, 180 n. 51, 246 n. 6, 251 n. 37		
		Greenstein, Edward L.	93 n. 30, 94 nn. 31–32, 226 n. 71
Foucalt, Michel	279		
Fowler, W. Warde	224 n. 59	Gries, Stefan Thomas	96 n. 40
Franke, John R.	72 n. 27	Groß, Walter	66 n. 2, 67 n. 5, 69 n. 16, 74 n. 33, 76 n. 45, 78 n. 50
Franklin, Norma	138 n. 26, 139 n. 27, 144 n. 49		
		Grossman, Dave	233 n. 112
Frayne, Douglas	249 nn. 23–26	Grossfeld, B.	95 n. 35
Frazer, James	276	Güterbock, Hans G.	244 n. 3
Freedman, David Noel	165, 165 n. 1, 165–66 n. 4, 169 n. 19, 179 n. 46	Gwynne, S. C.	136 n. 18
		Hagemann, Norbert	102 n. 61
Fretheim, Terence	256, 256 n. 53	Hahlen, Mark Allen	87 n. 9
Freud, Sigmund	205, 205 n. 3	Hallo, William W.	26 n. 2
Friedrich, Jannes	150 n. 4	Halpern, Baruch	137–38 n. 21
Fritz, Volkmar	55 n. 15	Harlé, Paul	171 n. 22
Frye, Northrop	95–96	Harris, Rivkah	176 n. 38
Frymer-Kensky, Tikva	176, 176 n. 38	Hastings, James	213–14 n. 24
Fuchs, Andreas	141 n. 39	Healy, Mark	143 n. 45
Gabriel, Richard A.	135 n. 13	Heidorn, Lisa A.	141 n. 38
Galtung, Johan	280 n. 19	Herr, Larry G.	119, 119 n. 22
Geertz, Clifford	189, 189 n. 5, 273	Hertzberg, Hans Wilhelm	123, 123 n. 37, 123 n. 40
Geller, Stephen A.	201, 201 n. 23		
Geyer, John B.	94 n. 33	Hess, Richard S.	281 n. 22
George, Andrew R.	250 nn. 30–31	Hexter, Ralph	173, 173 n. 28
George, Mark K.	123, 123 nn. 38–39	Hill, Russell A.	102 n. 61

Hinton, Timothy J.   135 n. 14
Hobbs, T. R.   207 n. 7, 276 n. 9
Hoffner, Harry A., Jr.   244 n. 3, 245–46 n. 3
Holladay, John S., Jr.   139 n. 30
Holloway, Steven W.   150 n. 6
Hubert, Henri   189, 189 n. 6
Hundley, Michael   35 n. 25
Hurrowitz, Victor A.   35 n. 25, 37, 37 n. 33
Hyland, Ann   136 n. 17
Iadicola, Peter   280 n. 19
Ilie, Andrei   102, 102 n. 62
Inomata, Takeski   175 n. 34, 181 n. 52
Ioan, S.   102 n. 61
Jacob, Edmond   55 n. 17
Jacobsen, Thorkild   245 n. 4, 247–48, 247 n. 14, 247 n. 16, 248 n. 22
Janzen, J. Gerald   169 n. 19
Jenson, Philip P.   271, 272 n. 3
Jonassohn, Kurt   281 n. 23
Jones, Adam   281 n. 23
Joüon, Paul   261 n. 71
Kang, Sa-Moon   71 n. 20, 77 nn. 48–49, 207 n. 8, 207 n. 10, 208 n. 13, 221, 222 nn. 47–49, 223 n. 52, 226 n. 70, 226 n. 72, 227 nn. 74–76, 228 nn. 84–85, 228 n. 87, 229 n. 90, 249 n. 26, 271, 271 n. 1
Kant, Immanuel   205 n. 3
Karahashi, Fumi   247 n. 13
Kaufman, Stephen A.   95 n. 35
Kay, Paul   83 n. 1
Kazen, Thomas   278, 278 n. 15
Keel, Othmar   57, 57 n. 20, 60 n. 31, 79, 79 nn. 54–57, 150 n. 2, 153 nn. 14–17, 156, 157 n. 25
Kelle, Brad E.   1 n. 1, 9, 134 nn. 11–12, 143 n. 48, 167 n. 14, 207 n. 7, 208 n. 14, 216 n. 32, 232 n. 103, 272 n. 4, 274–75
Kelso, James   74–75, 74 n. 34
Kertzer, David I.   96, 96 nn. 38–39
Kienast, Burkhart   249 n. 23
Kiernan, Ben   281 n. 23

Kirk-Duggan, Cheryl A.   256, 256 n. 54
Kirshenblatt-Gimblett, Barbara   199
Kitchen, Kenneth A.   57 n. 23
Klein, Ralph W.   122–23, 122–23 n. 36, 123 n. 41
Kleinman, Arthur   279, 279 nn. 17–18
Kletter, Raz   169 n. 19
Klingbeil, Gerald A.   271, 272 n. 3, 274 n. 7
Knight, Douglas A.   133 n. 8
Konstan, David   197 n. 15, 201, 201 n. 22
Kottje, Raymund   225 n. 65
Kotzé, Gideon R.   91 n. 20
Kravitz, Kathryn Frakes   217 n. 35, 227 n. 79, 228 nn. 80–83, 228 n. 86, 229 n. 89, 229 n. 92
Kubáč, Vladimír   90 n. 19
Kvasnica, Brian   216 n. 32, 226 n. 71, 227 n. 78
Laffin, John   67, 67 nn. 8–9
Lakoff, George   96 n. 40
Lamb, David T.   6, 118 n. 20, 119 n. 23, 120 n. 25
Lambek, Michael   277, 277 n. 12
Lambert, Wilfred G.   132 n. 4, 245 n. 5, 246, 246 n. 8
Leach, Edmund   100, 100 n. 52
Leißing, Jan   102 n. 61
Lemos, T. M.   10, 219 n. 41, 273 n. 5, 276 n. 10, 281 n. 23
Lettini, Gabriella   205 n. 2, 232–33, 232 n. 104, 233 nn. 106–107, 233 nn. 109–12, 234 n. 14, 237 n. 120
Levin, Christoph   171 n. 22
Levine, Baruch A.   172 n. 24
Levinson, Bernard M.   37 n. 32
Levtow, Nathaniel B.   4, 31 n. 15, 32 n. 18, 36 n. 27, 36 n. 29, 37 n. 32, 39 n. 39, 42 n. 43, 274
Lichtheim, Miriam   131 n. 1, 243 n. 1, 262 n. 74
Linafelt, Todd   175, 175 n. 35
Lincoln, Bruce   281 n. 22
Lind, Millard C.   276 n. 9

Litz, Brett T.   232 n. 103, 232 n. 105, 233 n. 108
Liverani, Mario   139 n. 30
Lock, Margaret   279, 279 nn. 17–18
LoConto, Daivd G.   112 n. 3, 113 n. 9, 120, 120 n. 28
Lohfink, Norbert   271, 271 n. 1
Longman, Tremper, III   207 n. 7, 208 n. 12, 218 n. 36
Loretz, Oswald   244 n. 3
Lynch, Matthew J.   85 n. 4
Macgregor, Sherry Lou   170 n. 20, 218 n. 37
Magen, Ursula   150 n. 3
Machinist, Peter   173, 173 n. 30
Maier, Markus A.   101, 101 n. 58, 102 n. 59
Malamat, Abraham   67, 67 n. 7, 223 n. 52, 223 n. 55, 243 n. 1, 244 n. 23, 249 nn. 26–27, 250 nn. 28–29, 251 n. 34
Marcus, David   226 n. 71
Marlantes, Karl   225 n. 64, 233 n. 111, 235 nn. 116–17, 235–36 n. 118
Martens, Elmer A.   281 n. 22
Marti, Lionel   50 n. 2
Masliyah, Sadok   113, 113 n. 7
Masson, Olivier   243 n. 1
Matthews, Victor H.   66, 66 n. 4, 74 n. 32, 78 n. 50, 79 n. 58
Maul, Stefan M.   151 nn. 9–10
Mauss, Marcel   189, 189 n. 6, 276
Mayer, Walter   150 n. 5
McCarter, P. Kyle, Jr.   21 n. 13, 23 n. 15, 38 n. 34, 122–23, 122 n. 36, 123 n. 40
McCarthy, Dennis J.   104 n. 65
McCutcheon, Russell   276 n. 8
McGuire, Meredith B.   193 n. 11, 196 n. 14
Meier, Brian P.   102 n. 60
Melcher, Sarah J.   278 n. 16
Merrell, Floyd   98 n. 44
Merton, Robert K.   96 n. 37
Metz, Karen S.   135 n. 13
Meyers, Carol L.   8, 38 n. 34, 88, 88 n. 14, 169 nn. 18–19, 218 n. 37

Milgrom, Jacob   212–13 n. 20, 259 n. 60, 260, 260 nn. 61–62, 260 n. 63, 260 nn. 65–66
Millard, Alan R.   26 n. 2, 245 n. 5, 246, 246 n. 8, 249 n. 25
Miller, Geoffrey David   6, 112, 112 n. 5
Miller, Patrick D., Jr.   257, 257 nn. 55–56
Mobley, Gregory   67 n. 6, 69 n. 15, 70 nn. 17–18, 75 n. 41
Moor, Johannes C. de   93 nn. 28–29, 165, 165 n. 3 , 244 n. 3
Moore, George F.   72, 72 n. 26, 73 n. 30, 76, 76 n. 44
Moore, Megan Bishop   134 n. 12, 167 n. 14, 272 n. 4
Moran, William L.   245 n. 5, 246, 246 nn. 9–10, 247 n. 12
Morgenstern, Julian   84 n. 3
Morkot, Robert G.   141 n. 37
Morrow, William S.   219 n. 42, 236 n. 119
Moss, Candida R.   278 n. 16
Moyer, James C.   243 n. 1, 244 n. 3, 252 n. 39
Muraoka, T.   261 n. 71
Murphy, Kelly   5
Na'aman, Nadav   51 n. 6, 142 n. 44
Nagy, Gregory   173, 173 n. 29, 173 n. 31
Nardelli, Jean-Fabrice   176 n. 37
Naveh, Joseph   32 n. 18, 36 nn. 30–31
Neitz, Jay   100 n. 51
Neitz, Maureen   100 n. 51
Nelson, Richard D.   55, 55 n. 16
Niditch, Susan   8–9, 66 n. 2, 73 n. 31, 86 n. 6, 173, 173 n. 30, 178 n. 41, 189 n. 4, 194 n. 12, 195 n. 13, 198 n. 16, 207 n. 7, 207 n. 10, 212 n. 20, 213 nn. 21–22, 214 n. 26, 271, 271 n. 1, 274–75
Niehr, H.   16 n. 3
Nissinen, Martti   50 n. 4, 56 n. 19
Noth, Martin   53 n. 11, 212, 212 nn. 17–18, 214 n. 27, 216 n. 33
Notley, R. Steven   138 n. 22, 142 nn. 42–43

Novotny, Jamie 20 n. 12
O'Connell, Robert H. 171 n. 21
O'Conner, Kathleen M. 232 n. 103
Oded, Bustenay 223 n. 55, 235 n. 115
Odell, David 132 n. 3
Oden, Thomas C. 72 n. 27
Ollenburger, Ben C. 256 n. 52
Olmo Lete, Gregorio del 254 n. 47, 255 n. 51
Olson, Dennis 77, 77 n. 47
Olyan, Saul M. 3–4, 15 n. 1, 17 n. 4, 18 n. 6, 20 nn. 10–11, 22 n. 14, 177 n. 39, 178 n. 43, 198, 198 n. 16, 201–202 n. 21, 202 n. 24, 209 n. 15, 271, 272 n. 4, 274, 274 n. 7, 278 n. 16
Openheim, A. Leo 246 n. 9, 244 n. 23
Ornan, Tallay 59 n. 28
Otto, Eckhart 53 n. 13, 207 n. 7, 221 n. 46
Otto, Susanne 154 n. 21
Page, Stephanie 32 n. 19
Palva, Heikki 180 n. 50
Pardee, Dennis 93 n. 28, 253 n. 43, 254, 254 nn. 44–46, 254 n. 48, 255 nn. 49–50
Parke, Herbert W. 224 n. 57
Parker, Robert 222–23 n. 51, 224 n. 57
Parker, Simon B. 92 n. 24, 92 nn. 26–27, 93 n. 30, 94 nn. 31–32
Parpola, Simo 150 n. 6
Partridge, Robert P. 143 n. 45
Payen, Vincent 102 n. 60
Paz, Sarit 8, 169 n. 19
Peirce, Charles S. 98–99, 99 n. 49
Perniss, Pamela 98 n. 45
Petersen, David L. 86–87 n. 8
Piepkorn, Arthur C. 258 n. 57
Pitard, Wayne T. 252 n. 41, 253 n. 43, 262, 262 n. 75
Poethig, Eunice B. 8, 169 n. 18, 218 n. 37
Posener, G. 150 n. 2
Postgate, John N. 133 n. 7
Pritchett, W. Kendrick 223 n. 56, 224 n. 58, 227 n. 73, 227 nn. 77–78, 228–29 n. 88, 229 n. 91
Quack, Johannes 274 n. 6
Raabe, Paul R. 179 nn. 47–48
Rad, Gerhard von 76, 76 n. 42, 158, 206–208, 206 n. 6, 207 n. 9, 208 n. 11, 271, 271 n. 1, 276 n. 9
Rahlfs, Alfred 261–62 n. 73
Rainey, Anson F. 138 n. 22, 142 nn. 42–43
Reid, Daniel G. 207 n. 7, 208 n. 12
Rendsburg, Gary A. 120, 120 n. 26
Richter, Sandra L. 26 n. 2, 33 n. 20, 34–35, 34 nn. 23–24, 35 nn. 25–26, 36, 36 nn. 28–29, 37, 41, 41 n. 41
Riley, Jason A. 9–10, 222 n. 50
Roebroeks, Wil 101 n. 56
Rofé, Alexander 154 n. 21, 166, 166 n. 5
Römer, Thomas C. 5, 54 n. 13
Rookes, Paul 100 n. 50
Roqueplo, Thérèse 171 n. 22
Roth, Tori J. 112 n. 3, 113 n. 9, 120, 120 n. 28
Roux, Jean-Paul 104 n. 64
Rubin, Gayle 190, 190 n. 8
Russell, John M. 144 n. 49
Ryken, Leland 218 n. 36
Saarelainen, Katri 169 n. 19
Sadowski, Piotr 101 n. 54
Sallaberger, Walther 248 nn. 20–21
Sanders, Seth L. 33 n. 21, 38, 38 n. 35, 39 n. 36
Sandulache, M. 102 n. 61
Sanmartín, Joaquín 244 n. 3
Sass, Benjamin 153 n. 17, 154 n. 20, 156
Sax, William S. 274 n. 6
Scheper-Hughes, Nancy 278 n. 14, 280 n. 19
Schipper, Jeremy 278 n. 16
Schlesinger, H. J. 188, 188 n. 2
Schmid, Konrad 166, 166 n. 10
Schmitt, Rüdiger 7, 149 n. 1, 150 n. 7, 151 n. 8, 151 n. 11, 152 nn. 12–13, 154 n. 18, 154 n. 22, 157 nn. 23–24, 158 nn. 28–29, 159 n. 30
Schneider, Tammi 77, 77 n. 46
Schniedewind, William M. 138 n. 23

INDEX OF MODERN AUTHORS 307

Schoske, Sylvia 150 n. 2
Scurlock, JoAnn 37 n. 32
Sekunda, Nicholas 144 n. 50
Setchell, J. M. 102 n. 59
Shay, Jonathan 8, 8 n. 2, 187 n. 1, 205 n. 1, 232 n. 105, 233, 233 n. 109, 233 nn. 111–12, 234 nn. 113–14, 235 nn. 117–18
Shupe, Anson 280 n. 19
Simons, Herbert D. 113, 113 n. 10
Simpson, Cuthbert A. 55 n. 15
Ska, Jean Louis 65–66 n. 1
Slanski, Kathryn E. 30 n. 10
Slingerland, Edward 280 n. 20
Smend, Rudolph 207 n. 10
Smith, Adam T. 173–73 n. 27
Smith, Contra 253 n. 43, 254 n. 44, 255 nn. 49–50
Smith, Mark S. 7–8, 39, 39 n. 37, 40 n. 40, 74 n. 34, 166, 166 n. 11, 173–74 n. 32, 218 n. 37, 244 n. 3, 252 n. 41, 257 n. 55, 262, 262 n. 75
Smith, W. Robertson 276
Smith-Christopher, Daniel L. 231 n. 99, 232 n. 103
Snaith, Normon H. 217 n. 33, 222 n. 49
Soden, Wolfram von 246 n. 11, 252 n. 40
Soggin, Alberto 66 n. 2, 69 n. 13, 69 n. 16, 70 n. 17, 72, 72 n. 29, 73 nn. 30–31, 75 n. 39, 76 n. 43, 78 n. 51
Speiser, E. A. 250 n. 29
Sperling, S. David 104 n. 66
Stansell, Gary 122, 122 n. 33
Starr, Ivan 150 n. 6
Stern, Philip D. 271, 271 n. 1
Stoebe, Hans J. 178 n. 43
Strathern, Andrew 277, 277 n. 12
Strauss, Bernd 102 n. 61
Štrba, Blažej 52 n. 7
Sweeney, Marvin A. 87, 87 n. 11
Taçon, Paul S. C. 101 n. 53
Tadmor, Hayim 33 n. 21, 151 n. 10
Tallis, Nigel 132 n. 6
Talon, Philippe 251 nn. 35–36

Taub, Sarah F. 96–98, 97 n. 41, 98 nn. 45–47
Thomas, D. Winter 113, 113 n. 8
Thompson, Robin L. 98 n. 45
Tick, Edward 232 n. 104, 233 n. 112
Tigay, Jeffrey H. 245 n. 5, 252 n. 38
Trible, Phyllis 169 n. 19
Trimm, Charles 271, 271 n. 2
Turner, Victor W. 95–96 n. 36, 97–98 n. 43, 157 n. 26, 273
Uehlinger, Christoph 153 n. 17, 156, 157 n. 25
Ulrich, Eugene Charles 261 n. 68
Ussishkin, David 138 n. 26, 140 nn. 32–34
Van Creveld, Martin 206 nn. 4–5, 224 n. 58, 224 n. 60, 225 n. 62, 227 n. 73, 228–29 n. 88, 229 n. 92, 231 n, 99, 232 n. 102, 233 n. 111
Van Seters, John 50, 50 n. 3
Vaux, Roland de 116 nn. 15–16, 213 n. 22
Vayda, Andrew P. 196 n. 14
Verkamp, Bernard J. 205 n. 3, 222–23 n. 51, 225 n. 65, 226 nn. 66–68, 231 n. 100, 233 n. 111
Versnel, H. S. 229 n. 92
Vigliocco, Gabriella 98 n. 45
Watts, James W. 42–43 n. 44, 209 n. 15, 271, 272 n. 3
Webb, Barry G. 74 n. 32, 78 n. 50
Weimar, Peter 208 n. 13
Weinhold, Jan 274 n. 6
Weippert, Manfred 158–59 n. 30, 271, 271 n. 1
Weisman, Ze'ev 117 n. 18
Wellhausen, Julius 72, 72 n. 28, 78, 78 n. 52, 276
Wenham, Gordon J. 212 n. 17, 214 n. 26, 217 n. 33
Westenholz, Joan Goodnick 31, 31 nn. 13–14
Westermann, Claus 258 n. 57, 259, 259 n. 59
Wickings, E. J. 102 n. 59

Wildung, Dietrich 150 n. 2
Wilhoit, James C. 218 n. 36
Wilkinson, Iain 279 n. 17
Willson, Jane 100 n. 50
Wilson, E. Jan 245 n. 4, 255 n. 50
Wilson, J. A. 136 n. 19
Winter, Irene J. 28 nn. 4–5, 29, 29 n. 8, 30 nn. 10–11, 31 n. 14, 35 n. 25, 41, 41 n. 41, 42 n. 43
Wiseman, Donald J. 119 n. 21
Wolters, A. 169 n. 18
Wong, Gregory T. K. 122, 122 n. 35
Woods, Christopher 29 nn. 6–7, 31 n. 12, 35 n. 25
Wormell, Donald E. W. 224 n. 57
Wreschner, Ernst E. 101, 101 nn. 55–57
Wright, David P. 212 n. 19, 214 n. 26, 259 n. 60, 260, 260 nn. 61–62
Wright, Jacob L. 1 n. 1, 36 n. 29, 70 n. 18, 74 n. 33, 74–75 n. 37
Würthwein, Ernst 154 n. 21
Yadin, Azzan 116, 116 n. 15, 116 n. 17, 122, 122 n. 34
Yadin, Yigael 50 n. 1, 141 n. 38, 143 nn. 45–47
Yamada, Shigeo 33 n. 21, 138 n. 22
Yaqub, Nadia G. 180 n. 50
Young, Edward J. 261 n. 72
Young, Jeremy 281 n. 22
Younger, K. Lawson, Jr. 26 n. 2, 50, 50 n. 3, 51 n. 5, 226 n. 69
Zanjani, Sally 90 n. 18
Zettler, Richard L. 248 nn. 20–21
Zhou, Yiqun 170 n. 20
Ziegler, Joseph 261 n. 73
Zimmerli, Walter 59 n. 29

www.ingramcontent.com/pod-product-compliance
Lightning Source LLC
Chambersburg PA
CBHW020056020526
44112CB00031B/195